Art Through The Ages

With the aid of almost 400 illustrations, Erwin O. Christensen traces the evolution of Western painting, sculpture, architecture, decorative arts and crafts from the cave painters to the abstractionists.

This lively and comprehensive history of art discusses the distinctive style and creative inspiration of each major artist and places each major work in its own historical setting.

All the great periods in art are covered— Egyptian, Greek, Etruscan, Gothic and Renaissance—down to nineteenth-century Impressionism and the most modern experiments of today. In each period, Mr. Christensen shows how the restless striving for change produced new problems and new solutions that gave Western art its drive, and makes its discovery and contemplation an exciting adventure.

Erwin O. Christensen is Curator of Decorative Arts and The Index of American Design at The National Gallery of Art in Washington, D.C. He is the author of *Early American Wood Carving, The Index of American Design, Primitive Art,* and *Popular Art in the United States.*

Ill. 1

Erwin O. Christensen # THE

HISTORY OF

WESTERN

ART

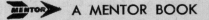 A MENTOR BOOK

Published by The New American Library, New York and Toronto
The New English Library Limited, London

The author is indebted to many museums and to several collectors and publishers for having granted permission to reproduce from their photographs, or to quote from their books, and herewith expresses his thanks. Specific acknowledgments appear with the captions. I am grateful to Dr. Fern Rusk Shapley, Assistant Chief Curator of the National Gallery of Art, and Mr. Jerome Rothlein, for having read the manuscript and for having made valuable suggestions that improved the accuracy on specific works of art. Mr. Henry Beville is responsible for the photographs of works in the National Gallery of Art. As always, my wife, Edna Florance Christensen, has contributed much by her constructive criticism.

Color Plate: (Front Cover) Titian: *Venus with a Mirror*. Courtesy National Gallery of Art, Mellon Collection, 1937.

Color Plate: (Back Cover) Matisse: *Odalisque with Raised Arms*. Courtesy National Gallery of Art, Chester Dale Collection.

EIGHTH PRINTING

Library of Congress Catalog Card No. 59-14350

MENTOR TRADEMARK REG. U.S. PAT. OFF. AND FOREIGN COUNTRIES
REGISTERED TRADEMARK—MARCA REGISTRADA
HECHO EN CHICAGO, U.S.A.

MENTOR BOOKS are published *in the United States* by
The New American Library, Inc.,
1301 Avenue of the Americas, New York, New York 10019,
in Canada by The New American Library of Canada Limited,
295 King Street East, Toronto 2, Ontario,
in the United Kingdom by The New English Library Limited,
Barnard's Inn, Holborn, London, E.C. 1, England

PRINTED IN THE UNITED STATES OF AMERICA

CONTENTS

a Source of Inspiration. Patrons. The Social Status of the Artist. Humanistic Learning. An Economic Interpretation of Renaissance Art. Individualism. Italian Painting of the Early Renaissance; the Grammar of Art. Character of Style in Painting. Venetian Painting before Titian. The Sentimental Trend in Florentine Painting. Italian Painting of the High Renaissance. Mannerism in Painting. Renaissance Sculpture in Italy. Painting in France, Spain, the Netherlands and Germany, 1400–1600: France. The School of Fontainebleau. Spain. The Netherlands. Hieronymus Bosch, c. 1450–1511. Pieter Brueghel the Elder, b. before 1530–1569. Germany. Renaissance Architecture: Italy. Renaissance Architecture and Sculpture Outside of Italy. France. Spain. England. The Netherlands and Germany. Decorative Art. Conclusion.

Cultural Background. Characteristics of the Baroque Style. The Baroque in Italy: Architecture and Sculpture. Academic and Baroque Painting. Venetian Painting. The Baroque in Germany. The Baroque in Spain. Flemish Painting in the Seventeenth Century: Rubens and Van Dyck. The Dutch School of Painting. Art in England after the Renaissance: Painting. Architecture. The Baroque Period in France. Economic Background. Architecture and Sculpture. Painting. Decorative Arts. Conclusion.

Cultural Background. General Survey: Architecture. Painting. Neo-Classicism. Romanticism. Painting Outside of France. Realism. Impressionism. Post-Impressionism. Neo-Impressionism. Abstract Traditions. Cubism. Guernica. Non-Objective Painting. Expressionism. Matisse and the "Fauves." Various Trends: Cubistic, Futuristic, Primitive, Fantastic. Dada and Surrealism. Sculpture. Modern Architecture. Conclusion.

Introduction. The Colonial Style. The National Period. Modern Trends. The "Group of Eight." Stieglitz, Marin, Demuth, O'Keeffe, Sheeler, Hopper, and Burchfield. American Scene Painters. Federal Art Projects. Social Realism. Abstraction. Contemporary Painting. Professional Primitivism. Graphic Art. Sculpture, Architecture, and Industrial Art. Conclusion.

PREFACE

Writing a history of Western art is possible only because the research of many scholars has laid a foundation. The specialized literature, old and new, is considerable, and is being added to constantly. Newly discovered facts correct old errors, expand our horizon and give us new insight. The kind of research that rounds out and fills in the lesser areas has no effect on the total development, which is the topic of this book. But even in this broad account of major periods and leading artists, more recent sources of information have been favored. The names of specialists identified with particular points of view have been indicated in the text; essential publications are listed in the bibliography. The author has tried to see the art of the past in the light of its own objectives and to present it in an unbiased manner. For the most part, this has not been difficult, as much of what is here said reflects an informed consensus. Lack of space made it necessary to select a few among many masterpieces and to pass over minor periods and minor artists. To have emphasized faults within the limitations of a highly condensed text would have indicated a lack of sympathy. Instead it has been a pleasure to record achievements, and it is our hope that the reader will gain both in understanding and enjoyment of Western art.

INTRODUCTION

History of art includes the description and interpretation of the development of painting, sculpture, and architecture and allied branches of decorative and graphic art. Western art includes the art of Europe, the post-Columbian art of the Western Hemisphere and Australia. The arts of ancient Egypt, Crete, Mesopotamia and Persia—the modern Iraq and Iran—are also presented. This is but a part of world art; Asia, Africa, and the Pacific islands, which developed styles of their own, are usually dealt with separately. Though to an extent the influence of Western art has been world-wide in our own day, we can take no account of this expansion here.

Art is rightly claimed as man's prerogative, not shared by his nearest relatives among the primates, but made possible by his intellectual endowment. However, there can be no sharp division between human and animal art. The conical structures of African termites surpass in height and interior elaboration the round man-made huts of the same regions. The artfully constructed nests of the Indian weaver birds resemble finely woven baskets; they are compact and waterproof. These animal structures are utilitarian, and, though they too must have originated in simpler forms, one cannot speak of them as showing any stylistic development as this term is used in art history.

In the rhythmic design of a spider's web, utility and beauty are inseparable, though a more ordinary web will also catch flies. But what shall we say to nature's artistic creations in leaves and flowers, or in the inorganic world in mineral and snow crystals? Here nature has shown man the way to develop a geometric ornament of his own after her models. The art of man is a part of nature's total creation, different from nature's art, but not more perfect. Whereas insects, birds, and animals, like the beaver with his lodge, are said to create by instinct, the artist works on a conscious level, his creativity impelled by forces that are derived from his unconscious and are aimed at nonutilitarian, aesthetic purposes.

The art of nature seems timeless. The development we stress in man-made art may well be a reflection of man's consciousness of his mortality, which is foreign to animals. The ever-changing variety shown by human art in contrast to animal art need not be considered basically human; it is rather due to culture and is of a comparatively recent date. Immortality was virtually assured to the ancient Egyptians during their long history of three millennia, and style changes are often absent or of minor importance in their art. This restless striving for change, so characteristic of Western art, appears first in Greek sculpture, the greatest expression of man's pride in himself the world has ever witnessed.

Animals build mostly for their families or for their species; man, more self-centered, creates for his own convenience and also for purposes of self-glorification. He directs his art to other men or to supernatural powers of his own creation. Utility is important in all periods, but aesthetic aims play an ever greater part as art develops.

In this discussion of art history we give special emphasis to three basic factors: first, the background—the religious, social, and economic conditions that make art possible in any period; second, the foreground—the work of art itself, its style and its variation from other styles; third, the contribution of the individual artist, revealing his inspirations and the extent of his gift. If we were to pay undue attention to environmental reflections, art history in its own right would be slighted. Any work of art may reflect its period regardless of artistic merit, but what is peculiarly artistic in any period must be our chief concern.

There are two fallacies we must guard against. First, art history is not a development from primitive beginnings in the past to final perfection in our own period. Styles change but artistic quality is more constant; superior works of art occur in many periods. Second, often one style of art is the characteristic expression of any one period. It is useless to attempt any evaluation between styles that have little in common. We should compare a work of art only with other work of the same period, as we must recognize that each period posed its own problems and arrived at its own unique solutions. The fact that succeeding generations have sought new problems and new solutions gives Western art its drive and makes its study an exciting adventure.

CHAPTER I

Prehistoric Art in Europe

Origins. Drawing may have originated accidentally when a prehistoric hunter scribbled playfully on the walls of some cave or rock shelter. Natural markings on the rock surface might have suggested an animal to which he added lines of his own to increase the resemblance. Contours of oxen (Ill. 2) have been found finger-drawn on the clay surface as well as interlaced lines made by hand or tool. This does suggest that we are here close to man's first attempts at drawing. It is this

Ill. 2   Contours of oxen. *After Breuil*

period after man began to draw and before he began to write that constitutes the period of prehistoric art.

Hand Silhouettes. (Ill. 3) Hand silhouettes in groups or rows appear on cave walls. One cave (Gargas) shows 150 well-preserved hand silhouettes. They are mostly of the left hand; tne right hand apparently was used to blow or spatter the red and black liquid coloring matter. They may represent the earliest cave paintings, if we can speak of them as paintings, and belong to the so-called Aurignacian period.

Periods. Pigments were used for bodily ornamentation during the Mousterian period, but the earliest as well as more

11

developed cave paintings belong to the Aurignacian period which followed, from 60,000 B.C. to 40,000 B.C., and to the Magdalenian period, dated 30,000 B.C. to 10,000 B.C.[1] These three periods together at the very end of the Old Stone or Ice Age are known as the late or upper Paleolithic period. The whole Paleolithic period was of much longer duration and has been dated back by some scholars to 1,000,000 B.C. Homo sapiens, Cro-Magnon, or modern man made his appearance during this late Paleolithic period. The term Ice Age, as here used, was but the last of four glaciations during which northern Europe, the mountains across Europe, and parts of Asia and North America were covered with ice. Around 10,000 B.C. the glaciers retreated to the north, and our present era began.

Ill. 3 Hand silhouettes and bison, cave at Castillo, Spain. *After Breuil*

The Old Stone Age with its evenly chipped stone axes was followed by the New Stone Age, or Neolithic period, with its ground and polished stone tools, and then by the Bronze period. Each of these periods had an art style of its own.

Man lived upon the bounty of nature; his was the roving life of a hunter of reindeer, mammoths, woolly rhinoceroses, bison, oxen, and other animals. Man seems to have become an artist even before he built permanent dwellings. He may have had tents or wattle huts as well as caves and rock shelters, but he engraved and painted the walls of particular caves, mainly with pictures of the animals he hunted.

Caves and Rock Shelters. These caves and rock shelters are located in southwestern France and in the Cantabrian Mountains of northern Spain. Altamira, the most celebrated cave, was discovered by accident in 1879. The French caves are on the small Vézere River, a tributary of the Dordogne River. Lascaux, now a rival to Altamira and the best-known cave in France, was discovered, also by chance, as recently as 1940. Other important sites of the Dordogne region include Laussel, Cap Blanc, La Grèze, Les Combarelles, La Madeleine, Font-de-Gaume, Le Moustier, and Cro-Magnon. We get the name Mousterian period from Le Moustier, and from Cro-Magnon, Cro-Magnon man. Farther south in the French Pyrenees are Les Trois Frères, Gargas, Maz d'Azil, Niaux and Aurignac; the term Aurignacian period is derived

from the name of the latter cave. European caves and rock shelters, some seventy in all, vary in size and in the number of engravings and paintings they contain. Font-de-Gaume has over 200 pictures of all periods; Les Trois Frères, over 500. Natural earth colors were used, red ocher or hematite red, yellow ocher, and lampblack made from animal fat burned in lamps. A hollow bone used as a tube for red ocher was found in a cave of the Aurignacian period. No blue nor green seems to have been used; landscape was not represented.

Ill. 4 Bison in profile, La Grèze (Dordogne), France

Aurignacian Art. The earliest engravings from the Aurignacian period represent animals in simple outline. At La Grèze (Ill. 4) a standing bison is engraved on the rock surface as a flat silhouette showing only one front and one hind leg. This early style is hard and rigid, the contour is continuous, and there is no interior modeling; but the animal is correctly drawn in profile and the resemblance is unmistakable. Details are observed, but the horns are in front view rather than in a visually correct side view. This representation of front view horns is characteristic of the early Aurignacian style. In the later Aurignacian period, as at Lascaux (Ill. 5), this detail appears more nearly in correct perspective. There are thousands of animal paintings and engravings in the Franco-Cantabrian caves, but only a small number have been studied. There are only a few examples of human figures; these are believed to represent sorcerers, as they are masked and disguised by animal pelts.

Lascaux. In this important cave bulls and galloping wild horses, some up to eighteen feet long, appear in friezes on the pure-white rock surface. The paintings are in excellent condition. Contours are fluent and the surface is broadly painted in flat tints. There is no interior modeling yet, but all four legs are represented. The technique is soft, as if dry powder had been applied with a blowgun, perhaps a hollow bone, though the painter also used brushes. Styles differ between caves, but also within the same cave. Lascaux is particularly noteworthy for monumentality of style. Cave paintings are often superimposed, later paintings over earlier ones, but this is not the case at Lascaux.

One scene of a wounded bison with a lance across his hindquarters and a man standing by represents an incident otherwise rare in Paleolithic art. This painting has given rise to a theory (Horst Kirchner, quoted by Herbert Kühn) that a shamanic incantation is depicted, the killing of the animal having taken place while the shaman, or sorcerer, was in a trance. A bird on a post beside the bison would point to the spirit migration of the shaman in his trance. As a hunting incident, this painting with a human figure could represent a link between the Paleolithic Franco-Cantabrian style and the later Neolithic East Spanish style.

The horse is the animal most frequently painted at

Ill. 5 Horse with flying arrows, Lascaux cave. *Archives Photographiques*

Lascaux; there are about sixty. In addition, there are twenty oxen, several bison, a few wounded deer and others, but all are animals of a temperate climate. Other caves emphasize other animals; Font-de-Gaume has bison and mammoths. Many caves have engravings and paintings of several periods existing side by side.

Magdalenian Art: Altamira. The great showplace of cave painting, Altamira, illustrates Magdalenian art at its best (Ill.

Ill. 6 The Altamira Ceiling (*After Breuil*), discovered in the late nineteenth century, extends over 40 feet in length, and is closely packed with some twenty-five animals, chiefly bison. The pigments are applied thickly in liquid form and in dry patches of natural earth colors. The painting could have been done more or less in one operation, modeling and color at the same time. The figures are slightly less than life-size. A suggestion of spontaneity which seemed so astonishing at first is perhaps due as much to the technique as to the action of the animals; most of them are really standing still. One bison with raised head is bellowing; the heads of others are lowered or the tails raised. There is a sensitive delineation of horns, nostrils, joints of legs, and tufts of hair. The small heads almost disappear under the weight of flesh (Ill. 7). Red is used for body color and black, for interior modeling and outlines.

6). The discovery of this cave revealed to the world the existence of prehistoric painting. When other painted caves were discovered soon after, the study of Paleolithic art began in earnest, pioneered by Abbé Henri Breuil. Other scholars followed, in our own day Leo Frobenius, Hugo Obermaier and Herbert Kühn, and the search was extended to Africa. At first the prehistoric dating of these paintings was questioned, but it became clear that they could not be recent, as in some cases they were covered with encrusted, transparent mineral layers.

At Altamira the profile style of La Grèze and the broadly painted style of Lascaux are replaced with full modeling (Ill. 7). The realism is extraordinary considering the simple tools

Ill. 7 Resting bison, Altamira. *After Breuil*

available to the painter. Bony structure is differentiated from soft fur and flesh, and massive bulk and correct anatomy are convincingly portrayed. The animals are turned in various directions and seem to conform to no apparent composition. The Altamira ceiling is rough and uneven, and the animals are adjusted to this natural relief. Projections are drawn into the painted animals not only at Altamira, but in other caves as well. The artists do not seem to have sought smooth surfaces.

Magic. Several explanations have been advanced as to why prehistoric man painted the animals he hunted and on which he depended for food. The theory that "the impulse behind art was bound to the development of magic," first advanced by Solomon Reinach, has been accepted with reservations by other scholars. This theory is supported by the fact that by 1930, thirty-four pictures of masked dancers had been demonstrated by Obermaier and Kühn. At Les Trois Frères such a masked sorcerer in stag's pelt and horse's tail in the midst of animals may be casting a spell or participating in a ritual for the multiplication of animals or the propitiation of dead animals. In various caves javelins, spearheads, and boomerangs are painted on the animals; on a bear at Les Trois Frères, lines are drawn from mouth and nostrils, presumably to suggest blood, and holes to indicate wounds appear on a carved bear at Montespan. It has been suggested that this points to ceremonial exercise before the hunt. At the Niaux cave a bison is painted seated on his hind legs before objects that are believed to represent votive offerings (Max Raphael). On the basis of this evidence, we may differentiate three kinds of magic: (1) fertility magic—to create new animals, sorcerers cast spells; (2) death magic—to assist the hunter's aim, weapons are painted on the animals and holes appear on carved animals; (3) propitiation magic—to appease dead animals, a bison appears propped up before votive offerings. Sympathetic magic is the belief that in nature there is an attraction between things that resemble each other; thus painted animals attract live animals. Presumably, the greater the resemblance, the more powerful the magic. Thus paintings that not only look like animals but also suggest their bulk, as those painted on the boulders of the Altamira ceiling, may have been conceived as being most effective.

Sanctuaries and Studios. For this reason certain caves appear to have had a magic or religious significance, and these were painted over many times, whereas most caves were not painted at all. Painted caves were known before the nineteenth century rediscovered them, and were believed to harbor demonic powers; at some early date Christian monks painted crosses over the paintings of a cave in the Lake Onega region between the Baltic and the White Sea (U.S.S.R.). Before the caves were opened to tourists and illuminated, they had an eerie atmosphere. Probably intentionally, the paintings were in places that a̶͟ ̶̶̶ ̶̶̶̶ ̶̶̶̶̶ ̶̶̶̶̶̶ caves show no paint̶ significance as sym̶

There is also so̶ Small slabs incis̶ some of them̶ done b̶

week's lapse. On the other hand, the evidence of a slow stylistic development of painting suggests that eidetic imagery did not function simply as an automatic transfer from animal to retina.

Scandinavian Rock Pictures. When the ice retreated from southern Europe, the hunters moved north in pursuit of the herds. The Franco-Cantabrian Ice Age style did not disappear suddenly. A late Magdalenian style lingered on in Scandinavia, where animals were engraved on horizontal glacier-worn rocks. These engravings of reindeer, fish, signs, and human beings are dated from a period after the melting of the ice, from about 8000 (or 6000) B.C. to the beginning of the Bronze Age, at 1000 B.C. (It should be noted that different authorities uphold different dates.) These still-realistic hunting-age rock engravings at Bardal, Norway (Ill. 8), are beneath later Bronze Age engravings.

Ill. 8   Rock engravings near Bardal, Norway. *After Hoernes* (1925)

Sculpture. There were also carvings of human and animal figures in relief and in the round in stone and clay. An Aurignacian female figure from Laussel about a foot and a half high holds a horn. Small stone and ivory statuettes of women have been found in various parts of Europe, like the 4½- inch *Willendorf* (Ill. 9). ...nse of beauty, is ...vell represented in ...'homme in Paris. ...er 7 feet long, ...elief carv-

...re difficult to get to, as more accessible
...ngs. Caves may have acquired a magical
...ools of the womb.

...he evidence that caves were used as studios.
...ed with animals were discovered at Limuel,
...more skillfully engraved than others, as if
...y master and pupil. Though grease lamps were used
for illumination, the artists may also have been aided by
eidetic, meaning identical, imagery. Even today persons so en-
dowed can reactivate retinal impressions after as much as a

have been found in various places in
inch statuette, the so-called *Venus of*
This obese type, so foreign to our se
paralleled by an elongated abstract type,
a figure from Lespugue in the Musée de
Four horses of the Magdalenian period, ov
form a frieze about 40 feet long. There are other re
ings, but they do not compare in quantity with engraving
and paintings. Prehistoric man also carved bone, as in the
well-known pieces engraved to represent a grazing reindeer,

galloping stags, or a charging mammoth. A dart-thrower carved in the shape of two reindeer (Saint-Germain Museum, and a small horse carved from ivory (Lourdes) are among the smaller pieces that show a close observation of the living animal and compare favorably with the cave paintings. Engraved, perforated pieces may have been used for personal ornaments as necklaces and bracelets. On a Paleolithic bracelet from Grimaldo (Italy), fish vertebrae, nassa shells, and deer teeth were found arranged in a regular pattern, indicating that order was appreciated. Paleolithic man must have been sensitive to aesthetic values and used principles of art as well as magic. We do not know at what stage in the development magic entered into art, or whether even the most primitive kind of art had a magical significance.

The East Spanish Style. In 1903 another style of prehistoric painting was discovered in open rock shelters in the mountains of eastern Spain. These paintings represent groups of men and animals 2½ to 6 inches high in silhouette with no interior details. They are usually reddish-brown, black, or occasionally white. Several types of figures can be distinguished, some thin-lined, others with wedge-shaped torsos and heavy thighs. The East Spanish style is of the Neolithic period; it developed

Ill. 9 Venus of Willendorf. *After photograph, Naturhistorisches Museum, Vienna*

into an abstract, schematic style during the Bronze Age. The Cueva Saltadora in the Valtorta Gorge (Castellón) yielded figures about 9 inches high. This site is as important for the East Spanish style as Altamira is for the Franco-Cantabrian. A painting of three walking figures (Ill. 1), discovered and published by Herbert Kühn, is a masterpiece in its sensitive, rhythmic movement. The painting is fresh and spontaneous, done by an artist who was working in a well-established style. A deer hunt (Ill. 10) of the same Valtorta Gorge shows group composition, lively movement, and close observation of postures and anatomical details. The figures are schematic, but the suggestion of action is emphatic. A bowman (Ill. 11) from the same site shows forward movement in an abstract style. The total effect is expressive and the painting is attractive as a pattern, though visually incorrect in details. Only a small number of paintings have been photographed and studied, but they reveal a worldly spirit, not exclusively devoted to m a g i c. There are also various group pictures that seem to tell a story, as well as battle scenes. Man appears in his own right and is no longer disguised as a sorcerer.

Ill. 10 Deer hunt, Valtorta Gorge. *After Mellado*

Transition to Agriculture. In the Neolithic period man developed p o l i s h e d stone implements, invented pottery, wove textiles, created monumental structures of roughly hewn stone, and took the first steps toward figure sculpture. Hunting persisted, but animals were also domesticated and a settled life began. As the handicrafts developed, ideas became important. The primitive magic of Paleolithic man emerged into religious beliefs centered around the sun and the heavens or the earth and its fertility. As man became dependent on the weather for sowing and harvesting, as he learned to make baskets and shape pottery, repetition of the same tasks led to a more orderly kind of life. The change from the painters of Altamira to the stone setters took place in the course of millennia, but we find no works of art comparable to Ice Age cave painting.

Ill. 11 Archer, Cueva Saltadora. *Courtesy Frobenius Institute*

Neolithic Art. Megalithic Structures. The most monumental
Neolithic works are the stone obelisks, or menhirs (long
stones); stone circles, or cromlechs; and piled-up boulders,
or dolmens (stone tables). They are in northern and western
Europe, particularly in Brittany. Stonehenge, near Salisbury,
England, dated around 2000 B.C., is the outstanding example
of megalithic architecture. Unconfirmed legends attribute it
variously to the Phoenicians, Druids, Romans, and Sumerians.
The Druids could not have been connected with the builders
of Stonehenge, as this Celtic priesthood did not appear in
history until the first century B.C., perhaps 1800 years after
Stonehenge. Excavations at Phoenician sites in Sicily fail to
show any links between Stonehenge and the Phoenicians.
Like other stone circles, Stonehenge was probably a religious
center connected with the worship of the sun and the
heavens. Certain stones outside the circle have been linked
to the sun, which rises over the so-called Hele (sun) stone on
Midsummer Day.

An outer circle, an inner circle, and an inner horseshoe
consist of upright stones (Ill. 12): 16 of the original 30 stones

Ill. 12 Stonehenge, restoration. *After the* Stonehenge Guide
Book. *By Permission of the Controller of Her Britannic Majesty's
Stationery Office*

of the outer circle are still standing, and 6 of the horseshoe.
In the outer circle, the uprights were connected by stone
lintels secured to uprights by mortises and tenons and joined
to one another with toggle joints. Stones of the inner circle
(bluestones) were transported to Stonehenge over a distance

of 180 miles, from a region where other stone circles were built. Five detached trilithons—two upright stones with a connecting stone lintel—are 22 feet high. The inner surfaces of the stones are dressed to correspond to the circumference of the circle. This refinement, which required skill, makes Stonehenge unique, although it is not the largest stone circle of Europe. This so-called megalithic, or "large stone," culture reached England and Wales about 2500 B.C. (Frank Stevens). At Stonehenge, beaker-shaped drinking cups were excavated, suggesting that Stonehenge may owe something to the influence of the so-called beaker folk, who introduced bronze into Britain from the Continent.

Dolmens. Dolmens were constructed of unhewn boulders or shaped slabs, which rest without the use of mortar on others set on end. They are the simplest type of post-and-lintel structures, less finished than Stonehenge, but true monuments intended for eternity. Originally they were earth-covered mounds that functioned as tombs, like the huge megalithic tomb at New Grange, Ireland. A still larger one at Antequera, Spain, is over 75 feet long and more than 15 feet wide.

Menhirs. Menhirs are neither architecture nor sculpture, but combine elements of both. They are single upright stone blocks, and are found, among other places, in Brittany, off Moriban Bay. Here, near Carnac, are rows of menhirs, some as high as 16 feet. One group has 1169 in 11 rows; another, 902 in 10 rows; a third, 579 in 13 rows. Such evidence of tremendous physical labor is awe-inspiring.

Ill. 13 (*upper left*) Menhir, Les Maurels. *After Hoernes* (1925)
Ill. 14 (*upper right*) Menhir, Saint-Sernin. *After Hoernes* (1925)

They were probably memorials or sanctuaries dedicated to religious observances. Similar stone monuments occur throughout Europe, around the Mediterranean, and in countries to the east. They are not found inland, but in regions close to the sea. It was once thought that they marked paths of human migration. It is also possible that the style of megaliths is characteristic of a period that covered many widely separated countries.

Menhirs from Italy (Gulf of Genoa) 3 to 6 feet high roughly suggest the human figure (Ill. 13). They are carved in low relief, with attributes like weapons and eyes and nose. A menhir from Saint-Sernin, France, one of thirty found interred, is elaborately carved, front and back (Ill. 14). Arms are indicated and legs depend like folds or parts of the mantle. Other details are recognizable, a fork (or slingshot), breasts, strands of a necklace, and horizontal lines of tattooing or painting. The carving is executed in a loose sketchy manner, realistic in intent, but with little skill. As isolated finds, they fit no tradition, but suggest that at one stage Neolithic man started on a basis of primitive realism.

Dwellings. Neolithic dwellings, partly subterranean pits with roofs resting on short posts, were neither permanent nor distinguished artistically. The earliest circular types developed into rectangular plans; square and oval types are intermediate stages (Oskar Montelius). Switzerland and the Danube region particularly are associated with lake dwellings on piles, connected to the land by a narrow gangway. Here such dwellings, as safe as hill fortresses, continued in use until after the Bronze Age.

Pottery. Many of the basic shapes known today were developed during this period. Neolithic pottery, made before the pottery wheel was known, shows a profusion of excellent shapes, decorated with geometric ornament of borders, chevrons, zigzags, and spirals (Ill. 15). Some decorations were

GROSSGARTACH   AULEBEN   HALLE

Ill. 15 Neolithic pottery. *After Hoernes* (1925)

made on the soft clay by finger, others by strings which may have held the pot together before firing. The string technique developed borders interspersed with linear motifs; in another type lines broaden into ribbon motifs. Archaeologists differ as to how types of pottery may be related in time and origin.

Painted pottery is rare in central Europe, but occurs in southeastern Europe, in Hungary, and in southern Rumania. Clay figurines with all-over spiral patterns have also been found in Cucuteni, Rumania; these need not be interpreted as indications of body painting or tattooing. Such decorations were used in pottery and, according to Moritz Hoernes, potters applied the style to figurines.

Bronze Age Art. Tin and copper combine to produce the alloy bronze, and copper alone seems to have been cast in primitive implements. The terms Stone Age, Bronze Age, and Iron Age represent stages of human culture, not divisions of time. They can be dated only loosely, as one merges into the other at different times in different countries. Not all parts of the world went through these stages; Africa had no Bronze Age except in Egypt, where it dates back to around 3000 B.C. Commerce and immigration rather than warfare were responsible for the introduction of bronze. Amber from the Baltic was bartered for objects of bronze from Italy. New inventions were looked upon with superstition; for ceremonial purposes the earlier materials were preferred. Stone knives continued in use after bronze was known, and bronze was used after iron had become the metal most commonly used.

Bronze Age Rock Engraving. The Scandinavian Bronze Age rock engravings represent a monumental kind of drawing (Ill. 8) which reflects the culture in a more varied manner. Ships are represented which seem large enough to have transported huge blocks such as those used to build Stonehenge. Other engravings include sleds, wagons, men on horseback, shields and spears, peasants plowing, grazing animals, and battle scenes. Circles, spirals, axes, and hammers may refer to the sun god. To what extent religion is involved, or how it may be separated from what is legend or purely secular, is not clear. These engravings were intended as communications, perhaps to the gods, but probably they were not considered art. In the language of art they are like the babble of children in contrast to the Paleolithic paintings, which are mature masterpieces. Whatever their meaning, to overcome the physical handicaps of engraving hard rock with primitive tools the artists must have been strongly motivated. Originally related to death and fertility cults, the engravings became memorials later. The figures are represented by a rectangle or an hourglass shape for a torso, a circle for the head, and two straight lines for legs. Animals too are given a geometric shape. Though the style remained largely unchanged, some figures vary from animated, freely placed silhouettes to rows of parallel strokes, uniform in shape.

Bronze Weapons and Utensils. Objects of bronze have been

found in tombs, in cinerary urns, and in caches. They are
preserved in many museums. Those of Scandinavian origin
have been attributed to six successive periods, from 1800 B.C.
to 550 B.C. (Oskar Montelius), though other scholars have suggested different dates (Sophus Müller). Purely ornamental
forms of a higher order appeared during the Bronze Age, and
sword hilts reflect an artistic development. Early hilts still had
wood covers; spiral-topped hilts, probably originating in Mediterranean countries, are characteristic of the Bronze Age.
Though highly developed in Scandinavia, circles, waves, and
spirals may have been derived from Mycenaean art. Bronze
was hammered and was also cast in solid and in hollow
forms; sand or clay cores were used for the latter. Knives
had cast heads in the shape of horses and human figures; the
blades were ornamented with ships and dragons. A remarkable example in the Copenhagen Museum is an engraved
bronze sundial mounted on two wheels and drawn by a
horse on four wheels (Ill. 16). The disk, six inches in diam-

Ill. 16 Sun disk on specimen carriage. *Courtesy British Museum,*
Bronze Age Catalogue *(1920)*

eter, is covered with gold foil and is dated before 1000 B.C.
(Sophus Müller). It is believed to have been deposited in the
moss in Trundholm (Denmark) as a votive offering. Before it
was deposited, disk and carriage were intentionally damaged,
a custom followed in other primitive cultures too.

The Bronze Age developed pottery that suggests the figure

or head. The reason for humanizing the pot may have been to give a suggestion of life to a cinerary urn, though not all face urns need be explained as monuments to the deceased. No historical relationship need be assumed between regions where they were made—Troy, central Italy, and northern Germany. Face pottery is not unique to Western art, but occurs outside of Europe.

The early Iron Age (1000 B.C.–100 B.C.) that followed the Bronze Age may be left for a later discussion (Chapter VII, p. 138), as well as Neolithic and Bronze Age sculpture. So far we have only touched upon Neolithic figure carving in connection with the rudely carved menhirs, more stone blocks than carved figures. Beyond this primitive stage, figure sculpture in the round had a development of its own that can be traced back to the Neolithic period.

It is noteworthy that prehistoric Europe developed early stages for all major arts, but only Paleolithic cave painting originated a kind of realism that was carried further during the historic period. Ornaments originating in braiding and weaving were continued in other materials as they became available; metal introduced ornamental motifs of its own. Though techniques contributed to the development of ornament, the technical explanation has been overemphasized (Gottfried Semper) and rightly criticized (Alois Riegl). Forms found in nature could also have been used in ornament. Motifs like zigzags also occur in nature, as on the backs of snakes. Plants show geometric patterns that could have enriched man's repertory of motifs used in art.

What strikes us as surprising is the fact that architecture is the least developed of prehistoric arts. Even Stonehenge is an open-air monument; it encloses no space. Early man put a roof over his head to keep out the weather, but left his temples open, not wanting to shut out the heavens.

CHAPTER II

Egyptian Art

Civilization. Egyptian civilization is as old as Mesopotamian and its monuments are more spectacular and better known. Both countries developed impressive art styles, one along the Nile and the other along the twin rivers, the Tigris and the Euphrates. Western art is essentially European art and, after the dawn of history, its early achievements were in Greece. Though this development was largely independent of Egypt, the two Mediterranean countries were in touch with each other. Even in antiquity, Manetho, an Egyptian priest of the Ptolemaic period, used the Greek language to transmit Egyptian history through his list of kings. More recently, the discovery in 1799 of the famous *Rosetta Stone* made it possible to interpret Egyptian hieroglyphics. This tablet bore an inscription in hieroglyphics, a translation into Coptic, the latest form of the ancient Egyptian language, and another translation into Greek. Ancient Egyptian was found to be Coptic written in hieroglyphics, that is to say, only the consonants were inscribed and all vowels omitted.

The existence in the Nile Valley of monumental ruins unparalleled in quantity and preservation attracted the archaeologists of the nineteenth century. Much lay buried beneath the sand, but what was above ground was accessible. Neglected tombs and temples had been ransacked for treasure and used as quarries for building material. With the beginning of scientific explorations, Egyptian art came into its own as an important part of the heritage of mankind. If we keep in mind that Europe for many centuries was very much a part of the Mediterranean world to which Egypt belonged, it seems clear that ancient Egypt can hardly be left out of a history of Western art. Where Egyptian art was most distinguished—in sculpture, painting, and the crafts—it has not been surpassed.

Environment. Egypt, more than any other country, shows
how art was influenced by geography, geology, and climate.
Located in the northeast corner of Africa, Upper Egypt is
a narrow strip of land on either side of the Nile. The river
flows north and branches out into the so-called Delta (Lower
Egypt), where it empties into the Mediterranean Sea. Here, at
Giza, near the modern capital of Cairo and the ancient city of
Memphis, are the Pyramids; over 350 miles to the south, lie
the temple ruins of Luxor, Karnak and the tombs of the
Valley of the Kings, the great rock-cut temples of Deir el-
Bahri and, on the upper Nile, Abu-Simbel.

Inundations of the river, before the days of irrigation, left
behind a layer of fertile soil. In a country without rain this
made agriculture possible and furnished material for sun-
dried bricks for building purposes. Papyrus stalks from the
river's banks, bound together, and palm trunks made posts.
Reeds covered with mud were formed into mats for roofs.
Sandstone, limestone and granite in unlimited quantity came
from the high cliffs through which the Nile had cut its course.

Bounded by deserts and with no powerful neighbors near
by, Egypt enjoyed long periods of peace, during which a
highly indigenous style developed. Egyptian art succumbed
but little to foreign influences; even the Romans, who carried
their art to all conquered countries, in Egypt built in the
Egyptian style.

The dry climate preserved what lay concealed in tombs;
only what was made of Nile mud disintegrated. The mud
walls, lacking in strength, were by necessity thick at the base,
though they tapered as they rose, creating a sloping line
known architecturally as batter. This batter, carried over into
stone, contributes to the massive character of Egyptian architecture. The cavetto cornice, a hollowed-out projection, rose
above the level of the roof, terminating the stone walls (Ill.
17). This construction had its origin in the reed-constructed
primitive house.[2] The flat unbroken surface character of
Egyptian architecture resulted from the structural weakness of
adobe brick and from the small openings for illumination
that sufficed in that land of brilliant sunshine. Plaster-
covered walls were painted in bright colors for elaborate
decoration, but hieroglyphics were carved into the stone.

The Predynastic Period, before 4000 B.C. (?).[3] During the
European Ice Age, North Africa had a damp climate and
lush vegetation. As the glacial period came to an end, rainfall
decreased and North Africa gradually turned into a desert.
Hunters became herdsmen and eventually sought the depend-
able water supply of the Nile Valley. As various tribes con-
verged on the Nile, the river itself provided the conditions

Ill. 17 Pylon, Temple of Edfu, showing cavetto cornice. *After Lübke*

for producing a uniform race, language, and culture. The earliest stage of this Nile culture is represented in the Delta at the village of Merimde by primitive stone implements and rough pottery vessels. These gave way in the early predynastic period to finely chipped flint implements and well-shaped pottery, polished and incised with zigzag lines filled in with white and burned on the inside to a shiny black. The middle predynastic period produced a finer buff-colored pottery with designs of sacred boats. It also produced small figures in the round, made of mud, terra cotta, and ivory. These show raised arms, broad hips, birdlike heads, and undifferentiated torsos; the technique is primitive. Flat paint palettes carved of hard slate are in the shapes of turtles, elephants, hippopotamuses, or fish in simple outline (Boston Museum of Fine Arts). Before the end of the predynastic period, flint implements declined and the invention of the stone borer produced fine stone vessels. Eventually, copper saws were used with sand and emery as the cutting materials.

Historical Periods: 3200 B.C.–*640* A.D. According to Manetho's list of rulers, Egyptian dynastic history was divided into thirty-one dynasties, which began with the archaic period, the Thinite period, named after the capital of This or Thinis, and ended with Persian domination in the fourth century B.C. The Ptolemaic or Greek period began with Alexander the Great (332–323 B.C.) and ended in 30 B.C. It was followed by the Roman (30 B.C.–324 A.D.) and the Byzantine or Coptic (Christian) periods (324–640 A.D.). Moslem rule (640 A.D.) marks the end of ancient Egypt and the beginning of the Middle Ages.

Little is known of the archaic period of the first two or three dynasties. They are well represented by the fine slate palette of King Narmer (Cairo), who is believed to be the legendary Menes who united, temporarily, the north, the Delta region of Egypt, with the south, extending beyond Memphis. For the most part, dynastic history before the Persian conquest is divided into the periods of the Old, Middle, and New Kingdoms (or Empires), and the late Saite period. The following periods were artistically the most productive. The IV Dynasty of the Old Kingdom, around 2600 B.C., was the age of the great pyramids, of fine painting, and the best sculpture. Memphis was the capital of a united Egypt. The XI and XII dynasties of the Middle Kingdom (around 2000 B.C. to 1700 B.C.) produced the royal statues of the Senusrets (Sesostris); Amenemhets, jewelry (pectorals), and much building activity, obliterated through later enlargements. The XVIII and XIX dynasties (between 1500 B.C. and 1200 B.C.) include the period of Queen Hatshepsut (Deir el-Bahri), of Ikhnaton (Akhenaton) or Amenhotep IV and his city Amarna, and the period of Tutankhamen. It is the period of empire and expansion (Palestine), the golden age of Ramesses II, the most celebrated of Egyptian rulers, of temples and tombs (Abu-Simbel, Karnak, Luxor, the Ramesseum, Abydos, and Thebes). In the late Saite period, art returned to the style of the Old Kingdom, and in spite of foreign domination, art continued to be productive. Compared to the duration and continuity of Egyptian art, the few centuries of art since the Renaissance seem contemporary. The Great Pyramid of about 2600 B.C. is about as far removed in time from Ramesses II of the XIX Dynasty around 1250 B.C. as the birth of Christ is from the High Gothic. Moreover, Egyptian art began perhaps 600 years before the Great Pyramid and continued for another 1000 years after the death of Ramesses.

Beliefs. The ancient Egyptian may well have imagined that he had solved for all time the problem of life and death. To

understand how art was related to religion, we must turn to
his beliefs and note how they affected his life. Religion was
important to the extent that the ancient Egyptian believed in
a life after death. Religion was the dominant influence in
art. Though not all art was dedicated to religion, the art
we know comes from tombs or temples. This does not mean
that the Egyptians thought only of the hereafter and had no
interest in the affairs of this life. There was an art connected
with the house, but it has not been preserved. However, the
sculpture and painting and the furniture, stoneware, pottery,
glass, and jewelry of tomb and temple reflect contemporary
life.

The Egyptian who could afford it took pains to have his
body preserved after death in a secure tomb with the walls
painted or even carved in low relief and painted to duplicate
pictorially tables loaded with food (Ill. 18). In the tomb

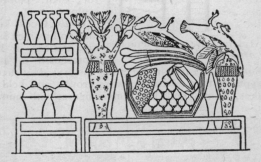

Ill. 18 Painted tables with jugs and food. *After Schäfer* (*1932*)

chapel, prayers to Anubis, a god of the dead, would bring
about a magic transformation of the paintings to assure a
continued supply of the necessities of life required by the ka,
the guardian spirit of the deceased in the hereafter (Ill. 19).
The Egyptian also had a soul (ba), conceived of as a bird and
later as a bird with a human head (Ill. 20). As souls could
move about freely, they could be symbolized by a bird. We
recall that in a painting at Lascaux a bird on a post has been
interpreted as a symbol for the soul. Paintings also represented activities to provide food, agriculture (Ill. 21), hunting, and the raising of cattle. Painted scenes of feasting, singing, and dancing would magically assure pleasant entertain-
ment. If destroyed, substitutes in the form of statues of the
dead man would replace the mummy. To ease his labors in
the future world, small statues (*ushebtis*) were placed in the

tombs to act as helpers. Magic formulas written on them would bring them to life. How magic was believed to operate is illustrated in one of the paintings of the Theban tomb of Menena, a scribe under Thutmose IV (XVIII Dynasty). In the otherwise well-preserved tomb, the face and the right hand in Menena's portrait have been damaged by some enemy who bore him a grudge and sought revenge. It was the general belief that damaging a person's image in his tomb would directly affect the person himself in his future existence.

These beliefs of the early Egyptians were responsible for their painting and sculpture.

Ill. 19 Taking leave of the mummy. *After Schäfer (1932)*

Gods. Gods, kings, and men and women from various stations in life were represented in art. Gods were humanized early in Egyptian history; they dressed like the Egyptians themselves and wore crowns and held scepters like rulers. Animal gods had human figures with animal heads

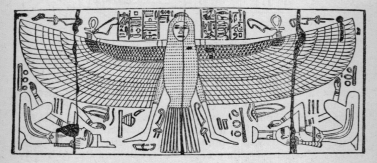

Ill. 20 Soul bird from coffin lid. *After Schäfer (1932)*

or masks. Sobek had a crocodile's head. Thoth, an ibis's head (Ill. 22), and Hathor, goddess of love and the heavens, had a human head with cow's horns. Like human beings, gods had wives and sons, such as Osiris, his wife Isis and their son Horus. Gods could also take on plant form; Heferten was worshiped in the form of a lotus flower. Animals could furnish abodes to

Ill. 21 Workers in the field. *After Schäfer (1932)*

the gods, falcons to the god Horus (Ill. 22), cats to Bubastis, the ibis to Thoth, and the crocodile to Sobek. Originally each town had its own "town god." Osiris was worshiped at Busiris in the Delta; Atum (Aten), at Heliopolis, Hathor at Dendera, Ptah, patron of artists, metalworkers and smiths, at Memphis. There were also universal gods worshiped everywhere, among them the sun god Ra (Re), who was given human form. Local gods of a city advanced in prestige and

Ill. 22 Ramesses between Thoth and Horus. *After Lübke*

became identified with the sun god as the rulers of the city advanced to power. When Thebes became the capital of the New Kingdom, Amen (Amon) became the national god, rival of his predecessor Horus. With Ikhnaton (Akhenaton or Amenhotep IV) the sun itself became the one and only god; Thebes as capital was given up and a new capital founded at Tell el-Amarna. This brought on a short-lived revolution in art, which for a time aimed at naturalism. After Ikhnaton's death, Osiris and Isis, gods of the underworld, and Anubis were reinstated as national gods, with Abydos as chief cult center.

Myths. Some oft-repeated emblems in Egyptian art are based on myths. Hathor, as goddess of the heavens, held the sun disk between the horns of a cow, and is so represented in art. The kings of Egypt wore in their crowns the uraeus serpent as an ornament, because the serpent was the symbol of the sun god Ra. According to myth, the serpent reared itself on the forehead of the sun god, breathing fire against his enemies. By day the sun god Ra sailed in a boat on the waters of the sky, and at night, in another boat through the underworld. When the two boats meet, the sun disk is represented as being handed over from one to the other (Heinrich Schäfer). Osiris was drowned in the Nile and later his body was cut to pieces by his wicked brother Seth. Avenged by his son Horus, Osiris was resurrected by Isis and ruled over the dead in the land to the west.

Architecture: Pyramids. The Egyptian name for public monuments, "firm things," is well illustrated in the pyramids, royal tombs. No other architectural style is so uncompromising in its emphasis on stability and strength. There are perhaps thirty pyramids in Egypt worthy of note, but the three pyramids at Giza on the edge of the desert are the most imposing. They are the *Great Pyramid of Khufu* (Cheops) (Ill. 23), the *Second (Middle) Pyramid of Khafre* (Chephren), and the smallest, the *Third Pyramid*, erected by Menkure (Mycerinus); these kings belonged to the IV Dynasty. The *Great Pyramid*, of yellowish limestone, is solid except for the burial chamber of the king, the *Great Hall* sloping toward it —actually a tall ramped corridor—shafts intended for ventilation or some as yet unknown religious purpose, and two smaller chambers. The outer facing of Tura limestone and the apex no longer exist, except for minor fragments. The long, empty, and mutilated granite sarcophagus occupies the burial or king's chamber, probably set in place while the chamber was being built. Fine-grained polished limestones lining the lower walls of the Great Hall (153 feet long) are laid with great accuracy. According to an oft-quoted statement of an Arab historian, "not even a pin or a feather could be inserted between the joints." The Great Pyramid is noted for its size; the building covers thirteen acres. The pyramid was

480 feet high (now 450 feet) and one side of its base, now measuring somewhat less than its original 750 feet, is over twice as long as the greatest width of the United States Capitol. Sir W. M. Flinders Petrie estimated that the Great Pyramid required 2,300,000 separate blocks of stone, each weighing about two and a half tons. The Greek historian Herodotus, who visited Egypt about 450 B.C., states that it took ten years to construct a road over which to transport the stones from

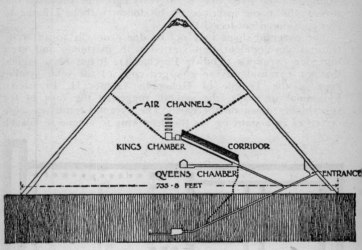

Ill. 23 Pyramid of Khufu. *After Simpson,* A History of Architectural Development *(1929)*

the banks of the Nile to the building site, and that it took twenty years to build the pyramid, using 100,000 men for three months of the year. Khufu, who ruled for twenty-three years, started his pyramid when he ascended the throne. Pyramids were usually begun on a small scale, allowing for successive enlargements, so that the pyramid would be completed during the king's lifetime. In spite of all precautions taken to protect the king's tomb, the pyramids were entered and robbed during antiquity as well as in later periods. The pyramids, placed to face north, east, south, and west, had chapels attached for offerings and ceremonies. They were connected by a covered causeway with the "valley temples." In the Second Pyramid the "valley temple" has polished red granite monolithic supports and lintels, well proportioned but without decoration. It provided a dignified place for

seated statues intended to take the place of the deceased king
should his body be destroyed. Rows of smaller tombs of
nobles, low and rectangular in plan, suggesting a truncated
pyramid and called mastabas (benches), adjoin the Great
Pyramid. Such a mastaba of the V Dynasty is set up stone for
stone in the Metropolitan Museum of Art in New York
City. It was the *tomb of Perneb,* an Egyptian dignitary of
Memphis, who lived over 4000 years ago. The deceased had
to have his name inscribed on his tomb; without a name he
was considered not to exist.

The pyramid shape may not be due primarily to an architectural development that started with mastabas and grew
into step pyramids (Ludwig Borchardt). It has been argued
that the pyramid was an enlarged copy of the solar symbol
kept in the Temple of Heliopolis (James H. Breasted).
Pyramidal in shape, the symbol suggested the rays of the
sun shining down on the earth. The pyramid tomb was conceived of as a staircase for the dead king to ascend to heaven

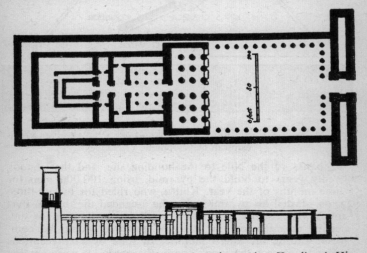

Ill. 24 Temple of Edfu, plan and section. *After Hamlin,* A History of Architecture (*1909*)

(I.E.S. Edwards). This concept, proposed and documented by
Edwards, is wholly in keeping with the magical thinking of
early religions, for which Egypt offers an abundance of archaeological evidence.

Next to the pyramids themselves, *the Sphinx,* a symbol of
royal power, is the best known monument of this vast burial

ground, the largest in the world. It was hewn out of the natural rock and, with the addition of stone blocks, was molded
into a recumbent human-headed lion. The head cloth with the
serpent indicated a king, the carving of the face was to resemble Khafre, whose valley temple is close by. Though
mutilated, the Sphinx is still an impressive monument. It has
been excavated repeatedly in the course of history, but the
shifting sands of the desert have as often obliterated the
work. A paved open temple was discovered between the
paws.

Temples. The temple, constructed on the post-and-lintel
system, was conceived as a lasting monument for a god, not
a place for a congregation. Only the priests and kings were
permitted to enter the sanctuary, a small dark chamber at
the far end of the entrance. The small Ptolemaic *temple of
Edfu* (Ill. 24) on the Nile above Thebes is basically like the
Great Temple of Amon at Karnak. Both their plans contain
the same four elements: a pylon, or entrance gate, flanked
by massive sloping towers with flagpoles (Ill. 17); an open, or
peristyle, court; a hypostyle hall (Ill. 26) with, at Karnak,
a central double row of columns higher than the others (Fig.
1), and the sanctuary itself (Ill. 24). The sanctuary contained
a small shrine, which was used as a receptacle for the small
statue of the god on the sacred bark. The *Great Temple of
Amon at Karnak* (Ill. 25), the largest of all, acquired size
through additions of pylons, courts, and halls in front of
existing ones. This temple was begun during the Middle
Kingdom, but its latest pylon is from the Ptolomaic period,
perhaps 1700 years after the founding of the temple. This
pylon, the largest ever constructed (but never completed),
had walls 49 feet thick. In front of it stretched an avenue of
ram-headed sphinxes, as rams were sacred to Amon. The most
spectacular part of the temple is the gigantic hypostyle hall
(Ill. 26) with 12 central nave columns, 69 feet high and 12
feet thick. Columns of the lower order are 9 feet in diameter
(Fig. 1). The central columns rise above the sides to form the
clerestory with openings in the walls to illuminate the nave.
Massed together, the 134 columns take up so much space
that the interior effect is one of a forest of stone. The columns,
carved with hieroglyphics and originally brilliantly decorated,
must have been extraordinarily impressive. The paintings relate to gods and the kings.

From the temple entrance, one passed through colonnaded
courts, open and sunlit, into the dimmer hypostyle hall,
through more halls, each decreasing in illumination and
height, to reach the sanctuary, which was almost totally dark.
The effect was calculated to create a feeling of awe. The mys-

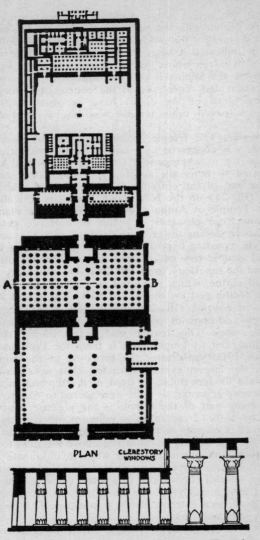

PLAN   CLERESTORY WINDOWS

Ill. 25 The Great Temple of Amon at Karnak.
After Simpson (1929)

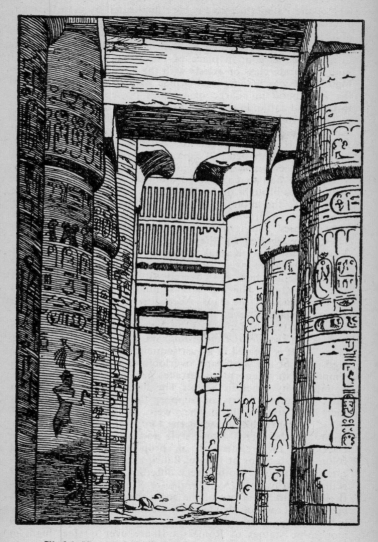

Ill. 26 Hypostyle hall at Karnak. *After Simpson (1929)*

tery of the Paleolithic cave is here duplicated by man through
a tremendous expenditure of effort. Here we see a more elaborate expression of the magic found in the Stone Age caves.
Ceremonies are performed by king and priest and addressed
to a particular god; in place of the Stone Age sorcerer, we
find a separate class of priests with the king at their head. The
high priest was a sacerdotal prince with political power, and
the priesthood in charge of temples possessed great wealth
in land and cattle, in slaves and servants.

The temple of Amon at Luxor near Thebes varies in some
aspects from its namesake at Karnak. Colossal statues of
Ramesses II stand between the columns of the great court
(Fig. 2); finely shaped bell capitals, superior in design to those
at Karnak, crown a row of columns that were intended for
a hypostyle hall that remained unfinished, interrupted by the
disturbances brought on by Ikhnaton.

Obelisks, the monoliths which stood in pairs before the
pylons, are square in plan, with tapering sides covered with
hieroglyphics and terminating in a metal-covered pyramid.
They were erected by the ruler in celebration of festivals.
Two obelisks at Karnak, erected by Queen Hatshepsut
(XVIII Dynasty), were of pink granite from Assuan on the
Upper Nile and had tops covered with electrum, a mixture of
gold and silver. The one still standing is 97 feet high and
8½ feet thick at the base. According to the inscription, the
two were made in seven months.

Another type of temple of the New Kingdom is the partially rock-cut *temple of Deir el-Bahri* built by Queen Hatshepsut
(Fig. 3). It is located in a vast semicircular valley, against the
high cliffs of the west bank overlooking ancient Thebes. This
temple, in three enormous terraces partly cut out of the rock,
is unlike any other in Egypt. The limestone columns which
flank the great courts or support the ceilings of the halls
each have sixteen flutes. They were formerly called "proto-
Doric" because, like those at the tombs of Beni Hassan, they
resembled the Greek Doric style and are comparable to the
Greek in the refinement of proportions. Hathor-headed
columns also occur at Deir el-Bahri, as some parts were dedicated to Hathor. Another very different temple of this period
is illustrated by the *Great Temple of Abu-Simbel* by Ramesses
II. It is entirely cut out of the rock; the façade, over 100 feet
high, is cut out of the face of the sandstone to suggest the
typical pylon terminating in a cavetto cornice. Four seated
monolithic statues of Ramesses II are over 60 feet high; in
size they compare with the great hypostyle hall of Karnak.
Two interior halls have eight and four piers, each carved
with figures of Osiris, as at Luxor. Rectangular and blocklike

in outline and proportions, the heads are carved with special attention to detail; the total effect is monumental. Rows of monkeys at the top of the pylon refer to the eastern lands, where monkeys were thought to live, ready to greet the rising sun.

The kings of the Middle and New Kingdoms gave up the pyramids as unsafe for burial. Beginning with the XVIII Dynasty, royal tombs were concealed in the less accessible Valley of the Kings opposite Thebes and separated from the mortuary temple. In times of strife, these rock-cut tombs were also robbed of their gold and treasure, forcing the priests to hustle the royal mummies from one hideout to another. Ramesses III had to be reburied three times.

Egyptian architecture developed few ornamental details; capitals (Ill. 27) are the most significant single features.

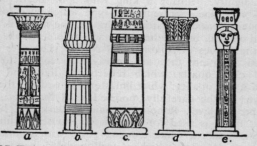

Ill. 27 Types of columns: (*a*) campaniform; (*b*) clustered lotus column; (*c*) simple lotus column; (*d*) palm column; (*e*) Hathor-headed column. *After Hamlin (1909)*

Typical are the lotus capitals, representing bud or flower, the palm-leaf capital, and also the Hathor-headed, or Isis, capital. Painted decoration used color to excellent effect in designs based on the lotus and papyrus, the solar disk, the vulture with outspread wings, and the sacred beetle, the scarab. Hieroglyphics were incised in the stone, but other decorations were applied in color and relief after the walls had been covered with a thin layer of plaster (Fig. 1). Austerity, combined with grace and elegance, gives Egyptian ornament a unique place in Western art.

Sculpture in the Round. The cult of kings who became gods after death probably led to the development of sculpture, which did not exist as an art for its own sake. Monumental sculpture in large stone statues represents gods, kings, and nobles. In colossal form, on occasion, god or king statues fused with the architecture, as in the *Osiris piers* at *Luxor* and the seated memorial statues of *Ramesses* at *Abu-Simbel* in expressions of unity, endurance, and strength. Statues often look as if they had been carved in a front and side elevation like a building. Compact volume is emphasized and feeling of the original stone block is retained. In monumental sculpture in the round, there is no movement to speak of and there are no groups; emotional expression is restrained.

Old Kingdom. Portrait statues during the Old Kingdom were idealized to an extent, so that the individual is represented at his best; deformities and old age were seldom represented. The seated statue of *King Chephren* (Khafre) (diorite, 67 inches high, Cairo) from the valley temple of the *Second Pyramid* is a distinguished example of one of the few remaining statues of the pyramid period. The royal falcon of Horus appears behind the headcloth. The features express impassive, gentle dignity, befitting a king who upon death becomes a god. This statue represents the type which was followed in subsequent periods. In stone sculpture, the figure is rectangular and cubical, but the head is made to look lifelike (Fig. 4), as in the statues of *Rahotep and Nofrat*. The eyes are given detailed attention; they are engraved in copper to hold the iris of clear quartz, which reflects the light and gives the head a living quality; white limestone is used for the white of the eye. In the carefully modeled head the ears are set at their proper level. Rahotep is painted dark red, his wife is lighter; black is used for his hair and mustache and for her wig. She wears a white clinging gown with shoulder straps, and a cloak from which a well-modeled hand protrudes. With variations, the seated posture of this masterpiece is repeated in all periods. In the standing figure facing forward, one leg is set out in front, and the soles of both feet are on the ground. Several V Dynasty figures of *Ranofer* of painted limestone (Cairo and the Gulbenkian Collection of the National Gallery of Art, Washington, D. C.), about life-size and less than life-size, represent this frontal type so characteristic of Egyptian art. Attached to a stone slab in back, they are in the round, practically freestanding. Arms may be extended, held close to the body, or bent holding emblems. Generally speaking, standing and seated figures in the round conform to what has been called a law of frontality (Julius H. Lange). When first discovered, a wooden figure of *Ka-aper* (V Dynasty, 44 inches high) so impressed the workmen as a type they were familiar with that they exclaimed "Sheik-el-Beled" (Fig. 5) due to the resemblance the figure bore to their own village headman. The head, with beautifully carved features, double chin, and thick neck, is highly individualized.

The squatting type, seated on the ground cross-legged, is illustrated in the famous *Seated Scribe* (Ill. 28) of the Louvre (Paris), the educated man of the V Dynasty. His cheeks, inset eyes, and hands are carefully modeled, but the heavy calves less so. His expression of alert attention is noteworthy. In Egypt, a sculptor was "he who makes live," a statue, a "living image." Priests' learning through inscriptions of magic formulas and sculptors' art combined to produce images "to satisfy the heart of gods." Old Kingdom sculpture remained conservative but highly competent. Though this tended to limit experimentation, it did not preclude development in later periods. The Egyptians themselves looked upon the Old Kingdom as their period of highest achievement.

Ill. 28 Seated Scribe, Louvre. *After Lübke*

Middle Kingdom. The XII Dynasty has left a number of distinguished portrait statues in hardstone, which have an insistent appeal. They are distributed among the great collections in Cairo, Berlin, London, Paris, New York, and Boston, and are well illustrated in recent publications (*see* Bibliography). A black granite human-headed sphinx, found at Tanis now in Cairo, is associated with the Hyksos invasion; it shows a deeply-cut muscular face, believed to represent *King Amenemhet III.* An obsidian head on loan at The National Gallery of Art in Washington, D. C. (Gulbenkian Collection), is a masterpiece of sculpture (Fig. 6), strong of feature, highly individual, and imbued with a brooding sadness. It is a fragment apparently from a figure, *Sesostris III,* (?) known from numerous statues. Greek art, striving for other goals, has nothing comparable.

New Kingdom. This period has yielded more monuments than any other period. During the XVIII Dynasty, a pleasant animation, greater softness in modeling and elaboration of detail replace the tragic severity of some Middle Kingdom statues. Youth and age were differentiated in the portraits of private individuals. Such statues were no longer concealed in the tomb chambers, but were placed in the open. New types appeared, and statues were installed within the enlarged temple precincts. Sculpture became so varied that one can hardly speak of a single style. With the ascent to the throne of Amenhotep IV, who adopted the name of Ikhnaton, monothe-

ism, dedicated to a worship of the sun, became the state
religion. In relief, we see *Ikhnaton*, raising his arm toward
the sun disk with rays ending in hands (Ill. 29). An unprece-

Ill. 29 Ikhnaton and his family. *After Lübke*

dented realism temporarily revolutionized art. It is shown in
Ikhnaton's long head, projecting chin, and prominent cheek-
bones. In his mortuary statue (Louvre), the style appears
more restrained. His wife, *Queen Nefertiti* (Fig. 7), is best
known from the painted limestone bust in the Berlin Museum
(28 inches high, excavated 1912–1913 at Tell el-Amarna).
Her elongated neck is in keeping with her individual headdress. Delicacy of modeling makes this bust one of the fine
works of Egyptian art; it is dated around 1375 B.C. and may
be a life study. The art of the XIX Dynasty, which followed
Ikhnaton's rule, returned gradually to earlier traditions, but
something remained of the relaxation of the Amarna period.
It is felt in the grace and delicacy of the granite seated
statue of *Ramesses II* at Turin.

Reliefs. A relief of *Ikhnaton fondling his infant daughter* (Berlin) and others (Ashmolean Museum, Oxford), showing the human side of the royal family heretofore depicted on the level of gods, represents a type unknown either before or after Amarna.

For a wealth of reliefs of all periods, the reader must be referred to numerous illustrated works now available. Fine reliefs have survived from the III Dynasty, such as the wood panel of *Hesire* and hunting reliefs from the tomb of Ti at Saqqara, of the V Dynasty. Other reliefs of the XII through the XVIII Dynasty give an impression of the accomplishments of Egyptian art in this field. Animals are correctly observed and sensitively reproduced. The suave elegance of the official court art style of the XVIII Dynasty is illustrated in a small limestone *relief of a Pharaoh* (Fig. 8). Every line of the smiling profile is part of an ornamental pattern, calculated, refined, and delicate. A surface design enriches the crown, surmounted by the uraeus, with its superimposed coil fitted into the linear design.

Painting. Egyptian painting is known from tombs of the Old Kingdom (Medum), the Middle Kingdom (Beni Hassan), and particularly from the New Kingdom rock-cut tombs of the nobles west of Thebes. Of over 400 tombs that have been numbered, about 100 are significant artistically (André Lhote). Among them, the tombs of *Rekhmire* (Ill. 30) and

Ill. 30 Mistress and servants, tomb of Rekhmire. *After Schäfer* (1932)

Nakht (Ill. 31) are notable for variety and beauty of color and line. The paintings are in horizontal friezes about 12 to 18 inches high, one above the other. The important figure of the deceased is about 4½ feet high and the background is filled in with hieroglyphic legends executed in the style of the paintings. The figure (Fig. 9) is represented with shoul-

ders in front view and legs and head in profile, though men at work (Ill. 21), dancers, musicians, wrestlers, and acrobats, are often in complete profile; the eye without exception is always in full front view. This suggests that the eye was important to indicate life. Profile views of living persons were not drawn until the VI Dynasty (Heinrich Schäfer), which suggests a disinclination to use profiles even for lesser persons. Only the representation of action favored a relaxation of the rule. As profile fingernails and toenails were not avoided (Schäfer), lack of skill was not the reason for avoiding side-view eyes. On occasion, even an unusual posture is attempted, as in the back view of the central figure of the maid in Rekhmire's tomb (Ill. 30). It is likely that the combination of profile and front view was considered as doing complete

Ill. 31 Musician, tomb of Nakht. *After Schäfer (1932)*

justice to the living person, robbing him of nothing essential. We presume that this habit was based on magic and developed as a compromise that assured maximum safety for survival. Representation is flat and avoids perspective and foreshortening, which would make objects look smaller and thus would detract from the desired monumental effect (Ill. 22). Composition and movement were undeveloped in comparison with later periods, but individual figures are often lively and graceful (Ill. 31). Egyptian painting with a limited palette of colors in flat tints achieves spectacular results. Clinging costumes and pleated loincloths contribute to the linear effect, and the lithe figures (Ill. 31) are outlined in a darker color. In the best examples (Fig. 9), line as pattern and brush stroke reveals a beauty of its own. The Amarna influence is also felt in painting (*Northern Palace, Tell el-Amarna*); the fragmentary condition of the wall paintings suggests that they were naturalistic and did not confine themselves to registers and single walls, but treated the scene as a unit covering all walls. Such an enlarged space conception, embracing the world as a unified whole, is perhaps a reflection of a new spirit that resulted from the sun worship.

Until recently, the world knew little of Egyptian painting, as the tombs themselves had to be visited to be appreciated. In 1930, a Metropolitan Museum of Art exhibit of remarkably accurate copies (made by Norman de Garis Davies and his wife) of some of the XVIII Dynasty tomb paintings came as a revelation. Since then good color reproductions have also become available (*see* Bibliography). Some restorations have been made of the paintings themselves, which have shown a tendency to disintegrate after the tombs have been opened.

Crafts. A great variety of forms and materials were used in cutting stone in the various periods. During the prehistoric period hard basalt as well as soft alabaster was cut by hand into large thin vases, hollowed out and highly polished. The use of hard stone declined during the dynastic periods, as soft alabaster was preferred. Gold was so common that the picture of a collar of beads became the hieroglyphic for gold. Casting in cire perdu (lost wax process), chiseling, and soldering were well understood. Some magnificent jewelry (gold pectorals from Dahshur, twelfth century, B.C.) are of openwork gold plate, engraved and set with colored stones, carnelian, turquoise, and lapis lazuli. One of Sesostris II (Cairo) shows two hawks between the royal cartouche; a headdress of gold threads is decorated with delicate flowers and berries of lapis lazuli set in gold sockets. Bracelets, daggers, and axes show different techniques, including inlay. Silver, then known as "white gold," came into use later than gold, but hammered copper was used in vases with cast spouts. A life-size copper statue of *King Pepi and His Son* is the best-known early work made of hammered plates riveted together.

The sensational discovery (1922) of the untouched treasures of *Tutankhamen's Tomb* (end of XVIII Dynasty) gave us a complete picture of the arts and crafts of his period. Here for the first time the world was confronted with a unique gold sarcophagus enclosing the mummy and a gold portrait mask of the king, a part of the outer coffin. The reddish glitter of the gold is enhanced by colored inlay of the mask's blue striped headdress. The lavish use of gold, elaborately chased and embellished with superimposed cloisonné work, reveals the crafts in a high state of perfection. Mask and coffin were made by the craftsmen in the short period, a few months, between death and funeral (Howard Carter). In a gold enameled wood statuette the youthful king is shown throwing a javelin. Four statuettes of goddesses carved in wood and overlaid with gold are extraordinarily free and graceful. The back panel of the carved wood throne, overlaid with sheet gold and inlaid with colored faïence glass and semiprecious stones, shows king and queen in easy, unconventional attitudes. Painted caskets with battle scenes in an Egyptian style convey to the contemporary viewer something of the spirit of fifteenth-century Italian painting. Jewelry, head rests and tomb furniture, carved bedsteads, chairs, stools, chests, and couches have rarely been equaled in their refined taste and exquisite craftsmanship.

Ancient Egyptian art was once looked upon as rigid and formal because the style adhered to conventions rather than visual truth, but the art of our own period has helped us to appreciate styles that are not based on naturalism. Even the few monuments here selected are convincing proof that Egyptian art ranks among man's major achievements.

Fig. 1 Hypostyle Hall, Temple of Amon at Karnak. *Courtesy Trans World Airlines*

Fig. 2 Ramesses II, Temple of Amon, Luxor. *Lehnert and Landrock*

Fig. 4 Rahotep and Nofrat, Cairo Museum. *Lehnert and Landrock*

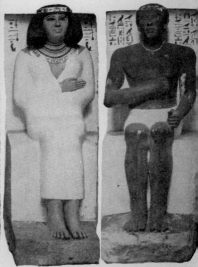

Fig. 3 Rock-cut Temple of Deir el-Bahri of Queen Hatshepsut. *Lehnert and Landrock*

Fig. 5   Sheik-el-Beled, wood, Cairo Museum. *Lehnert and Landrock*

Fig. 7 Queen Nefertiti, Berlin Museum. *Staatliche Bildstelle*

Fig. 6 Amenemhet III. *National Gallery of Art, courtesy C. S. Gulbenkian (loan)*

Fig. 8   Relief of a Pharaoh. *National Gallery of Art, courtesy C. S. Gulbenkian (loan)*

Fig. 9 Banqueting scene, copy. *Egyptian Expedition, Metropolitan Museum of Art*

Fig. 10 Monster in crystalline limestone (magnesite), Elamite, late prehistoric period. *Guennol Collection, Brooklyn Museum, courtesy Alastair B. Martin*

Fig. 11 Statuette, standing male figure, Sumerian, *c.* 3000 B.C. *Metropolitan Museum of Art, Fletcher Fund, 1940*

Fig. 12 Stele of Naramsin, Akkadian period, *c.* 2340–2180 B.C., Louvre. *Archives Photographiques*

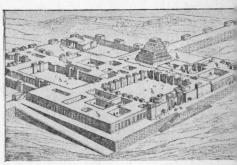

Fig 13 Palace of Khorsabad. *After restoration by Perrot and Chipiez*

Fig. 14 Gudea, Neo-Sumerian period, 2125–2025 B.C. *Copyright British Museum*

Fig. 15 Winged being and the arms-bearer of the king, alabaster relief, Assyrian, *c.* 850 B.C *Metropolitan Museum of Art, gift of John D. Rockefeller, Jr., 1932*

Fig. 16 Bronze bit, Luristan, Persia. *Courtesy Nelson Gallery and Atkins Museum Nelson Fund, Kansas City, Mo.*

Fig. 17 Cupbearer, reproduction, Cretan fresco from Knossos, 1500–1350 B.C. *Metropolitan Museum of Art*

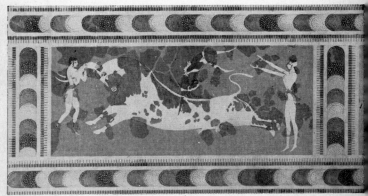

Fig. 18 Bull vaulting, Cretan fresco from Knossos. *Metropolitan Museum of Art, Rogers Fund, 1907*

Fig. 19 Gold cups from Vaphio, reproductions. *Metropolitan Museum of Art, Dodge*

Fig. 21 Votive figure, early fifth century, Acropolis Museum, Athens. *Alinari*

Fig. 20 Primitive idol, Mediterranean, prehistoric, third to second millennium B.C. *Courtesy Brooklyn Museum*

Fig. 22 Relief from the treasury of the Siphnians, Delphi, Greece, archaic period. *Courtesy Dr. Clarence Kennedy*

Fig. 23 Birth of Aphrodite, Terme Museum, Rome. *Alinari*

Fig. 24 Head of Charioteer of Delphi, Delphi Museum. *Courtesy Dr. Clarence Kennedy*

Fig. 25 Phidias (after): Lemnian Athena, Dresden, with head from Bologna. *Courtesy Dresden Collection of Antiquities*

Fig. 26 Phidias: Three Fates, from east pediment of the Parthenon. *Copyright British Museum*

Fig. 27 Demeter. *Copyright British Museum*

Fig. 28 Polycleitus (after): Spearbearer (Doryphoros), Vatican Museum. *Alinari*

Fig. 29 Praxiteles: Hermes, Olympia, Greece. *Alinari*

Fig. 30 Athena group, Pergamum altar, Berlin. *Courtesy Inter Nationes (Bonn) and Stoedtner*

Fig. 32 Douris: painted kylix. *Metropolitan Museum of Art*

Fig. 31 The Nike of Samothrace, Louvre. *Archives Photographiques*

Fig. 33 Francois vase, Archaeological Museum, Florence. *Alinari*

CHAPTER III

Ancient Near Eastern Art

While Egypt was developing a civilization on the Nile, other
nations to the east and north were also emerging from Stone
Age villages to build cities and unite city states into kingdoms. Those who settled along the great rivers like the Tigris
(northern branch) and the Euphrates (southern branch) or on
islands like Crete gained stability and achieved continuity as
nations. They advanced more rapidly than their neighbors in
Syria (Phoenicians) and in Asia Minor (Hittites). Though
these nations on the periphery also made contributions to
ancient art, they lack the continuity found in Egypt and
Mesopotamia.

Mesopotamia. Mesopotamia, like Egypt, was a leading cultural center of the ancient world before the rise of Greece.
The other nations of this region were influenced by Mesopotamia and passed these influences on to the West. Mesopotamia lacks Egypt's architectural ruins above ground and its
wealth of large stone sculpture. Palaces, temples, and cities
built of sun-dried brick disintegrated and are known from
archaeological restorations begun in the mid-nineteenth century. Stone sculpture, with exceptions, is modest in size; some
of the best pieces do not exceed a few feet. Monumental
rock carvings are from the mountainous countries to the
north and west. Painting is represented chiefly by colored
tiles; gold, by jewelry and decorated weapons from Ur; silver,
by a well-known vase which Entemena, King of Lagash, presented to the temple. Copper is known from statues, as part
of temple furniture. Objects of bronze, as well as reliefs,
heads, and statues have been found chiefly in Syria, Anatolia,
and Luristan (Persia).

Regions and Periods.[4] Sculpture is often identified by the
names of the sites where excavation took place, like Warka,

49

Tell Asmar, Khafaje, Tell Agrab, Ur, Tello, Mari, Khorsabad, Nimrud, and Kuyunjik. Even when arranged approximately in chronological order, names of sites do not by
themselves convey a sense of historical periods, of rulers
and dates, as the kingdoms and dynasties of Egypt do. Racial
or tribal divisions, Sumerians (Sumer), Akkadians (Akkad),
Babylonians (or Chaldeans), Assyrians (Assur), show no
easily defined artistic differences. The Chaldeans were a
caste of priests versed in astronomy and astrology who rose
to power in the late Babylonian period. The southern part of
Mesopotamia is known as Babylonia after the city of Babylon
on the lower Euphrates. Assyria, named after Assur, is the
northern region of Mesopotamia, with its city of Nineveh
on the upper Tigris. Four well-known names in history are
useful as guides to corresponding styles in art: Naramsin,
Gudea, Ashurnasirpal II, and Ashurbanipal. Naramsin was
ruler during the Akkadian period (2340–2180 B.C.); Gudea,
of the New Sumerian period (2125–2025 B.C.), ruler of
the Sumerian city of Lagash; and in the Assyrian period,
Ashurnasirpal II and his son ruled around 850 B.C., and
Ashurbanipal around 650 B.C. Naramsin and Gudea, being
but a few centuries apart, belong to the early period, which
corresponds to the Middle Kingdom in Egypt. Ashurbanipal
precedes the Saite period in Egypt (XXVI Dynasty).

Mesopotamian art developed independently, as was the
case with Egyptian art. Whereas Egyptian art did not spread
beyond the Nile Valley, except to the extent it may have
influenced native African styles, ancient Mesopotamian art
affected a large area, from Armenia to Syria and from the
Persian Gulf to the Mediterranean. In variety, Mesopotamian art is perhaps not equal to Egyptian; statues of gods and
kings constitute about all we have for Mesopotamian sculpture in the round. Sculpture achieved a level of distinction
comparable to Egypt's largely in the early period (Naramsin
and Gudea before and around 2000 B.C.) and in the late
period (historical Assyrian reliefs around 850–650 B.C.). At
least this is our present-day impression; it is perhaps tenta-
tive, as our knowledge of Mesopotamian art is limited to
monuments from isolated excavations.

Sumeria: Prehistoric Period, 4000–3000 B.C. The beginnings of art, as far as known, are here represented by
decorated pottery from Samarra. The insides of plates and
bowls show figures, fish, and birds well distributed and related to the center. They seem to bear no relation to subsequent sculpture. An alabaster vase over three feet high
from Warka represents three superimposed friezes carved in
relief with nude men, stocky and muscular, bearing gifts to

a goddess, as well as rams and plants. Mesopotamian representation emphasizes combat; lions attacking bulls appear on a ewer from Warka, perhaps symbolizing gods engaged in struggle. Other massive forms carved in high reliefs, without background, represent this early experimental stage of Mesopotamian carving approximately contemporary with the I Dynasty in Egypt. A female head in gypsum (flat, eight inches high; Frankfort, Pl. 7) is so fine in the carving of mouth and chin and the oval of the face that it compares with Greek art of the historic period. Hair and eyes were attached and inserted in other materials, probably metal. A small hard limestone monster (3½ inches high) combines the head of a lion with a human body, a compact muscular symbol of fierce, cruel strength (Fig. 10). The specific meaning is uncertain; a mother goddess has been suggested (Henri Frankfort).

Early Dynastic Period: 3000–2340 B.C. Statues of king, priest, or noble were intended for temples, where the statue, charged with an inscribed message, confronted the god. Gods are larger than worshipers; they are identified by an emblem like a lion-headed eagle and have exaggeratedly large eyes. These characteristics of divinity can be seen in the god *Abu,* "The Lord of Vegetation," one of ten white gypsum statuettes found at Tell Asmar near Bagdad. The cylindrical shape and rounded form (Fig. 11) are characteristic of Mesopotamian sculpture, in contrast to the cubical block in Egypt. Color is introduced through the blue lapis lazuli or black limestone of the pupils set into eyeballs of shell; hair is painted black and details are stylized. During the second and third dynasties, the sharply articulated shapes became soft, a delicate smile appeared, and textures of materials were expressed. A magnificent cow's head cast in gold from Ur was once attached to a wooden harp inlaid with shell, lapis lazuli, and red jasper (University Museum, Philadelphia). Among the inlaid scenes which appear on the soundbox of the instrument (restored) is the Sumerian hero Gilgamesh, strangling a bull under each arm. Gilgamesh corresponds to the Hebrew Samson and the Greek Hercules. This harp is one of several objects found; among them are a gold fluted cup of graceful flare (University Museum) and a gold helmet (British Museum).

Akkadian Period: c. 2340–2180 B.C. Sargon of Akkad became the ruler of various city states as a king. His coming to power introduced a new northern group of Akkadians, Semitic people who were not Sumerians. Speaking another language, the Akkadians adopted Sumerian civilization and script; their best-known work is the *stele of Naramsin*

(Fig. 12). This relief (over 6 feet high) glorifies Naramsin, the grandson of Sargon, in victory; he stands at the top of a mountain before his enemy, who is about to free himself from a lance. Naramsin, resting his foot on the slain victims, is larger than life-size; a horned crown and sun disks above indicate his divinity. Against the disorganized foe, the victors march up in a solid group. The artist has succeeded in suggesting an event in a unified composition and with a sense of freedom.

Neo-Sumerian Period: 2125–2025 B.C. Some of the best-known sculpture in the round belongs to another city state, Lagash (or Tello), during its brief period of power. Gudea, the king, is represented in a number of seated and standing figures which resemble each other a good deal. The Naramsin stele have been known for some time, whereas our knowledge of Sumerian art is based on more recent discoveries. The traditional picture of Mesopotamian art as being stern and concentrated on an expression of power, while likely to be modified as new discoveries add to our scant supply of monuments from the Sumerian period, still holds for the Gudea group and the later Assyrian reliefs. It is also true that the pleasant aspects of contemporary life, as evidenced in Egyptian art, are absent from Mesopotamian art. It has no place for the light touch and, like the Old Testament, knows no humor. In Mesopotamian reliefs, kings engage in religious ceremonies and in scenes of battle. In sculpture in the round, the figure stands or sits, in either case motionless. Standing or seated, Gudea presents a powerful physique, calm in feature and posture. He holds his hands clasped and the well-rounded figure is compact and firm. Something of the large open eyes of the earlier statues (Fig. 11) is present here. Head and torso (Fig. 14) emphasize anatomy; the head with its large ears, heavy eyelids, and stylized details is portraitlike. Hands interested the sculptor only so far as they indicated posture. Carved of hard diorite, the Gudea statues are masterful in their perfection of finish. A head is precise in detail and in the carving of the cheeks and the corners of the mouth is subtle.

Statues were proof of the king's devotion to his god, from whom he expected favors. Gudea built temples. From the texts he placed in the foundations of the temples, we learn how the king felt about his god, and the benefits he expected from "the humid winds which bring the rain" for the "fields to bear" and "the dykes and canals to swell," (Frankfort). Gudea ascribed the peace and prosperity of his rule to his good relations with the gods. Unlike Egyptian art, representations of Mesopotamian gods tell us little of religion. Stars, moon crescents, and sun disks suggest that such gods personify the heavenly bodies. Long beards, large eyes, and horns indicate male divinities; it may be that these long beards make the heads look so much alike, even where specific persons are represented. Mesopotamian art, except during Gudea's period, has nothing to equal the individuality of the Old Kingdom art of Egypt.

One monument linked to Babylon that must be mentioned before we turn to Assyrian reliefs is the stele inscribed with the *law code of Hammurabi* of Babylon (1792–1750 B.C.). This great ruler of the period is also known from a black granite head in the Louvre. In his stele, the famous legal code is inscribed in beautiful archaic cuneiform characters rather than pictographs, as in Egypt. Above the stele (7 feet high), is a relief (2 feet high) in which the king is portrayed standing before Shamash, lawgiver and sun god. It is either Shamash or Hammurabi whom we have to thank for the famous *jus talionis,* the "eye for an eye and tooth for a tooth" law, as well as other basic tenets of our legal code of today. This stele antedates the Mosaic law by some 600 years. It was found in 1901–02 on the Acropolis Mount at Susa (Persia), where it was taken as booty of war.

Reliefs. The art of engraved seals is a unique achievement of Mesopotamian art. Some of the best delineation of figure and animal is found in the intaglio engraved stone cylinders from which the clay tablets were produced in relief. Akkadian seal impressions of the period of Sargon represent the nude figure strangling a lion or feeding buffalo from overflowing vases. Man and beast are strong, muscular, and ornamental in details. The rendering of the figure is less constrained by conventions than in Egyptian art, but is not free.

From the early dynastic period (about 3000–2340 B.C.), fragments from a *victory stele* (72 inches high, Louvre), from Lagash (before Gudea) record King Eannatum's purge of his neighbor city of Umma. The infantry is shown marching behind a solid wall of shields over prostrate bodies as vultures in the air make off with the heads of the dead. On the other sides, the god Ningirsu has collected Eannatum's dead enemies in a big net. As a representation of the slaughter of battle, the *vulture stele* is revealing. The artist gives us a realistic account of an historical event, in which the Sumerian gods participated on the side of the victor. Many Assyrian alabaster reliefs of Ashurnasirpal II (around 850 B.C.) and Ashurbanipal (around 650 B.C.) have been found. Individual reliefs of animals like the *Dying Lioness* (British

Ill. 32 Dying Lioness, British Museum. *After a drawing by Harold B. Warren, courtesy Winnifred B. Warren*

Museum, Ill. 32) render the details with sympathy and understanding; they rank among the masterpieces of this style. This sensitive treatment is not transferred to the figure, not even to a lush banqueting scene showing Ashurbanipal and his queen under a grapevine and among palm trees. For all the descriptive detail of the elaborate furniture, the heavily robed figures preserve a stiff formality.

The most extensive demonstration of Assyrian reliefs (Fig. 15) are those which lined the walls of Ashurnasirpal's palace at Nimrud (about 3 feet and 7 feet high). The king is shown as priest, with his officials holding libation cups or with winged griffin demons. In a splendid mythological relief (Ill. 33), a winged god holds a thunderbolt seemingly threatening a fierce dragon. Though in retreat, the dragon, with clawlike hands and snarling mouth, turns his head back aggressively. The god's expression is unperturbed.

In the hunting and battle reliefs (British Museum), whole campaigns and royal lion hunts are in considerable detail. The hunted animals are rendered with extraordinary vigor in a variety of convincing attitudes. The reliefs are low and flat, and depth is not represented; but action is more spirited than in Egyptian reliefs. The style is not the same during the several periods represented by the ruling kings. The reliefs in Sargon's throne room at Khorsabad represent processions suggesting a tapestry effect. The most ambitious Assyrian reliefs represent Ashurbanipal's war against the Elamites and the destruction of their city. In a mighty battle covering several registers, the action spreads in depth as one episode is placed above another, the lower edge forming a baseline in the foreground.

Carved human-headed winged bulls were placed at the barrel-vaulted entrance gates as guardian spirits: twenty-six pairs were found at Khorsabad. These monolithic stone monsters were built into the wall to support brick arches (Ill. 34); towers flanked the gateway. In front view, two legs show, in side view, four, so that five legs appear when seen diagonally. Where two bulls come together, the one in front against the tower, though showing a profile body, also turns his head (Ill. 35). The carving is excellent; muscles are differentiated and veins are indicated. The carvers studiously devoted themselves to bringing out attractive decoration, so that we can speak here of an idealized combination of man and beast.

Walls and towers were important in Mesopotamia. Inscriptions on the gates refer to them as "conquerors of kings" and "foundations of the throne." Bulls and lions were symbols of force and evil, opposed to man and to be conquered by him. Beards, horns, and wings related to kings and gods. The combination of the human heads, emblem of divinity, and the strength of animals symbolized protective power (Ill. 34).

Architecture. The primitive temples of the early period

Ill. 33 Assyrian relief from Ashurnasirpal's palace, Nimrud. *After Lübke*

(3500–3000 B.C.) are known from excavations. The later palace (Fig. 13) with its temple-tower (ziggurat) is but an elaboration of house or temple. The use of sun-dried brick and lack of an abundant supply of timber made for narrow rooms, thick walls, and vaults built over temporary wooden forms. The rooms were grouped around a court. Entrances placed on a central axis were avoided. The extensive use of semicircular barrel vaults introduced a new principle into architecture. Though vaults were known to the Egyptians, they were not used above ground.

Ill. 34 Human-headed winged bull, Khorsabad. *After Lübke*

The characteristic part of one type of temple was a hill, man-made and covered with glazed tiles, with steep battered sides, square or rectangular in plan. A ramp or flight of stairs led to a platform on top. The most famous ziggurat at Babylon, the Biblical *Tower of Babel*, was an eight-stage pyramid, with a continuous ramp leading around it from top to bottom; each stage was in one color. Every town and many royal palaces had such towers. They have survived as low hills in the Mesopotamian valley. The other type of temple was essentially a rectangular room with a pedestal for the god's statue.

The large square court of *Sargon's Palace* at Khorsabad (Fig. 13) measured 300 feet on each side; the smaller courts were for service quarters, and several temples were included in the palace. As protection against floods, palaces were erected on huge platforms. Those awaiting an audience with the king passed by the impressive reliefs of the forecourts and through the gates lined with the human-headed bulls.

The walls of the throne room were covered with brilliant painting in superimposed friezes known from restorations. Reliefs on the stone throne represented Sargon on his chariot above slain enemies, with soldiers piling up pyramids of heads before him (Henri Frankfort).

War was perhaps no worse in Mesopotamian times than in any other period, and kings have often used art for their own glorification. Mesopotamian reliefs differ in this respect; art was used almost exclusively to emphasize the might of the king and the ruthless punishment awaiting the

Ill. 35 Gate, Khorsabad. *After Hamlin (1909)*

rebel. The Assyrian Empire, with its capital Nineveh, was destroyed in 612 B.C.

The Late Babylonian Period: c. 612–539 B.C. After the fall of Nineveh, Babylonia, where Mesopotamian culture had originated, returned to power for approximately seventy years. During Nebuchadnezzar's reign a new technique of using colored glazed tile in relief was created. A frieze of walking yellow bulls and white dragons on a blue ground decorated the walls of the *gate of Ishtar*. Babylonian sculpture was less important.

Persian Art. The late Babylonian rule was replaced by the Persian Empire when Cyrus conquered Babylon (539 B.C.). For about two centuries, the Persian Empire remained undivided in the hands of the same royal (Achaemenian) family. Persian architecture and sculpture used stone and are known from the ruins of palaces built in Persepolis by Darius and Xerxes. The architecture is characterized by slender stone columns in large halls and monumental stairways flanked by relief-carved friezes of dignitaries in stately processions. The Mesopotamian bull motif on top of inverted volutes was used for capitals (Ill. 36). Persia provides one of the first examples of the use of calculated proportions in architecture. Definite proportions between width and height, as 1:2, 2:3, or 3:5, have been found in doors and windows (Marcel A. Dieulafoy). Color and gold were used on lintels

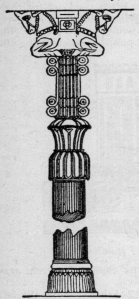

and enameled tiles on walls, as in friezes of archers and lions in the Louvre. Persian reliefs are sober and dignified, calm and serene in spirit, quite different from the aggressive ferocity of Mesopotamia.

Architecture and sculpture were designed for court ceremonials, to reflect the absolute power of the king. Persian art was contemporary with Greek art, which was known and appreciated by the Persian kings, but Persian art remained aloof from any Greek influence. Little is known of its early periods, and nothing, of its fate after the downfall of Persia, when conquered by Alexander the Great. As court art, it came to an end and had no influence on Western art.

Small portable objects of bronze have been excavated at Luristan, in the western mountains of Persia. They include objects of personal adornment; many relate to harnesses (Fig. 16) and chariots, and others suggest a religious use as votive figures. The dates given to the Luristan bronzes vary considerably, as this label has been attached to a variety of bronzes, not all of which necessarily relate to the same period. The Godards date them between 2000 and 800 B.C. The animal motifs are adapted to the objects. They may be abbreviated and simplified, and one animal may change to represent part of another animal. This imaginative and free use of animal motifs is said to be characteristic of Luristan bronzes. There are other specimens that suggest affinities to early Mesopotamian motifs, like winged heraldic bulls placed on either side of a sacred tree motif. The artistic significance of Luristan bronzes is considerable, and they are eagerly sought by collectors.

Ill. 36 Column from Persepolis. *After Hamlin (1909)*

Cretan Art. The newer Cretan archaeology was founded

by Arthur T. Evans, who started excavations at Knossos
(1899). An entire civilization, previously unknown to the
modern world, came to light. The chronology established by
Evans differentiates Early (3000-2000 B.C.), Middle (2000–
1500 B.C.), and Late Minoan (1500–1300 B.C.). The unforti-
fied palace of Knossos (near Candia) was the center of Cretan
civilization. It was rebuilt three times and finally destroyed
about 1400 B.C. Our knowledge of Cretan art and civilization
is an exclusive contribution of archaeology; history had given
us some hints through the early Greek myths of Theseus, the
Minotaur, and the labyrinths of King Minos, inspired by
the complex plan of Cretan palace architecture. In contrast
to other civilizations, this culture is known to us only
through its works of art.

The general picture one gets of ancient Cretan life through
its art is charming. We see flowery landscapes in painted
frescoes; great palaces, stately processions (Fig. 17), dances
and athletic games of skill, but no scenes of warfare, no acts
of violence, nothing to disturb the peaceful bliss of a happy
existence.

The king's palace, not the temple, is of dominant interest;
the king himself seems to have been high priest, and a small
part of the palace contained a sanctuary. Crete had many
palaces; *Knossos* is the best known and the largest. It was
built around 2000 B.C. and lasted for six centuries. This palace
is different from the Egyptian temple; it lacks a central
axis, a symmetrical system, and a monumental façade. It
had pavilions, porches, galleries, and rooms turned away
from the sun apparently to provide for different seasons and
different times of the day. In such livable interiors, the social
forms must have been more natural and human, less artificial
and stilted than was customary in Egypt in the fourteenth
century B.C. or at Versailles in the seventeenth century A.D.

The stone architecture was interspersed with wood piers,
lintels, and columns. Houses varied in height, and the palace
was adjusted to the natural setting; gardens were more like
the Japanese gardens, modeled after nature rather than nature
formalized in the Renaissance and modern manner. Color
extended to the interior; frescoes or painted stucco reliefs
covered the walls, colored ornaments covered ceilings, the
light floors were divided by bands of red stucco and may
have been covered with rugs.

The male dress was simple and shows no change in the
course of centuries; women wore elaborate costumes and
used fine jewelry. The frescoes and colored reliefs represent
slender, thin-waisted figures (Fig. 17) or festivals with many

people and processions of youths bringing presents or trib-
ute. Others represent large nature scenes, flowers, fish, marine
animals, deer, monkeys, and birds. A well-known painting
represents a bull vaulting (Fig. 18), in which the athlete
grabs a galloping bull and somersaults over his back.

Cretan art seems more natural than Egyptian art because
its motifs are from nature, but it is not based directly on
nature and does not represent nature through perspective
and foreshortening. The difference between informal Cretan
art and conventional Egyptian art is fundamental; no doubt
the Cretan informality was connected to religious beliefs
which are unknown to us.

The Cretans had paintings, but did not develop monumental sculpture, though they must have come in contact
with such sculpture in Egypt; Cretan costumes and funnel-
shaped vases appear in Egyptian XVIII Dynasty tombs. Temples and large-scale human figures representing gods are
missing in Crete, and there is no differentiation of size between the king and his subjects. Cretan art did have sculpture on a small scale in votive figures, as in the well-known
ivory-and-gold statuette of the snake goddess (about 6 inches
high) in the Boston Museum of Fine Arts. The Cretan religion emphasized goddesses rather than gods, an earth goddess of fertility rather than a sky god of thunder and light-
ning.

The crafts were highly developed, as in votive offerings
intended for small chapels, and in carvings, chairs, chests,
and gaming boards. Utensils and vessels for profane and
cult use were made in quantities. The beauty of the material
itself is appealing, and all commonly known materials were
used: gold, silver and copper with inlays, as well as ivory,
faïence, glass, and stones of various kinds. Cretan art also
excelled in the miniature carvings of gold rings and seals.
Ceramics were highly developed and existed before there
were palaces. Pottery of the Palace Period already had color
with stylized ornament on a black ground (Ill. 37), but
pottery decoration used only animal and plant forms, not the
figure. Finally, there must have been textiles to provide the
dress goods for feminine fashions which appear on paintings and statues.

Cretan art seems more European than Eastern, though
compared to Greek art this European character is still slight.
While Crete was enjoying a high state of civilization, Egypt
had completed one great period of bronze during the Old
Kingdom, but Europe was still in the Megalithic age.

Mycenaean Art. Just as Cretan archaeology is known largely through the work of Evans, so Mycenaean, or pre-Greek art, is based on the excavations of Heinrich Schliemann (1874–1890, Mycenae, Tiryns, Troy). Mycenaean civilization was based on bronze, as Homer says, though he lived in the age of iron. Homer's *Iliad* takes its themes from the deeds of ancestors, and the myths deal with the ancient cities of Mycenae, Tiryns, Thebes, Orchomenos, Pylos, and Athens (Acropolis).

About 1600 B.C., Greek tribes were warring against each other and building great fortresses; neither Cretans nor Greeks built such structures. This new Mycenaean architecture, unlike C r e t a n work, is megalithic in character: c y c l o p e a n blocks were used for walls and gates, as at T i r y n s and Mycenae, and vaulted beehive tombs were constructed.

The Mycenaean palace featured the living quarters of the ruler, the Men's Hall or megaron, which was larger and higher than all other rooms of the palace. The megaron originated from the cell, which was also to develop into the cella (or nave) of the Greek temple. Mycenaean art adopted the Cretan use of colored stones, wooden columns, piers and entablatures of wood, and perhaps flat roofs. The interior fresco decora-

Ill. 37 Palace style vase from Knossos, Crete. *After Evans and Hoernes (1925)*

tions of the megaron were by Cretan artists, using friezes of figures, bull vaulting, warfare, and hunting scenes. Cretan goldsmiths and gem cutters were employed in Mycenaean metalwork and jewelry.

Mycenaean architecture is here illustrated by the *Lion Gate* of Mycenae (Ill. 38). It was originally (about 1200 B.C.) the entrance gate to a fortified palace. Two posts support a heavy lintel, and the space above the lintel is filled in by a slab (10 feet high) carved like a coat of arms with two lions (now without heads) facing a column. The carving is of about the standard of Mesopotamian art, and the column seems copied from Crete. Gold disks and coffin ornaments and death masks (Athens, National Museum) show geometric and spiral designs and octopus motifs. Bronze daggers inlaid with gold and silver and decorated with hunting scenes seem to illustrate the metalwork mentioned in the *Iliad*. Two cups (Fig. 19) from Vaphio (south of Sparta), each made of two sheets of gold, represent Mycenaean gold work at its best. The craftsmanship is excellent; the outside is hammered in high relief (*repoussé*) to represent a capture of wild bulls. The cups, probably imported from Crete, represent an excellence not reached in Greek art until the fourth century B.C.

About two centuries after the destruction of Cretan civilization (1400 B.C.), the Mycenaean palaces, with their monumental wall paintings, had disappeared. In their place were primitive villages and a meager pottery. The splendid Mycenaean culture was followed by a new primitive beginning which, seven centuries later, flowered in classical Greek art. There is no parallel in the later development for such a break in tradition, which had resulted from the complete obliteration of the high-level Mycenaean civilization.

Ill. 38 Lion Gate from Mycenae, Greece. *After a drawing by Harold B. Warren, courtesy Winnifred B. Warren*

CHAPTER IV

Greek Art

Significance. Except for a present-day renewal of interest in Egyptian art, no preclassic style has had so prolonged an influence on the art of Europe, particularly from the Renaissance on, as Greek art. The specifically Greek influence was limited to certain periods of Greek revivals; more often it was Greek art as modified by the Romans—a classic influence which began with the rediscovery of Roman art in Italy. In the present day, when classic art has ceased to be a source of inspiration to modern art, the interest has turned to the Greek archaic period. Nevertheless, a few basic shapes and characteristic motifs have endured for over two thousand years.

In the field of aesthetics and art criticism a concept of beauty in art, based on order and revealed in harmony, rhythm, and balance, owes much to the Greeks. The classic influence on Western culture is not restricted to the arts, but appears also in literature and philosophy. Even modern science has a kinship to Greek thought and the beginnings of scientific thinking. Johann Winckelmann, through his interest in classical archaeology (1763), laid the foundation for the academic study of art history, basing his studies on Roman copies of Greek originals. It was left to the publications of his successors, H. Brunn (1857–59) and Adolf Furtwängler (1893), to clarify the underlying Greek contribution. The fascination which Greek art had for the nations of the West, though intermittent, is unparalleled; it rivals that of Egyptian art in duration.

General Character. Greek art is unique in that it limited itself to a few motifs that were developed to a final perfection. Basic to Greek thought are its intense preoccupation with man and its striving for rational interpretations. This interest in man found visual expression in sculpture, and a seeking after a consistent logic is demonstrated in architecture. Of all the sculptural styles anywhere, only Greek sculpture devoted itself exclusively to the development of the human figure. In a change from stylization in the archaic period to realism in the Hellenistic, nature gradually penetrated sculptural form. This change of style was less a matter of increase in skill or a development in taste than a shift in the artist's emphasis. The ornamental objectives of the archaic sculptor no longer interested his son, nor did the grandson merely perpetuate the style of his father: each of the major periods developed its own "ideal of beauty," to use this term for the German *Kunstwollen*. As the Platonic philosopher sought reality in the idea, so the Greek sculptor, from the archaic period on, worked from his conception of the human form to achieve his ideal. A Greek, in referring to himself, thought of his body. The concept of his soul came only after Socrates, and made itself felt in the sculpture of the fourth century, as exemplified in Praxiteles. The healthy body was raised to a higher level, as if to improve upon nature through art. It was late in Greek history before realism appeared.

Greek architecture developed disciplined styles, in which every part conforms to a restatement of a basic norm. Although the Persians may have used a limited system of proportions, they never developed such all-inclusive principles.

In artistic representation, as shown in painted vases, the Greeks were the first to arrive at an unprejudiced manner of dealing with reality. This all-pervading aspect of the Greek genius was due to their respect for what is factual and does not contradict observation. The Egyptians may have been as aware of the facts of vision, but preferred to ignore them in painting. Other nations adopted correct visual representation but the profile eye, wherever found in drawing outside of Greek art, was the result of Greek influence (Heinrich Schäfer).

The Greeks humanized their major gods and represented them in art as human beings, without wings or animal heads. The animal world survived in their associations with certain gods, as in Athena's owl and Hera's swans. Nature in Greek art was limited in scope and brought within the restraining influence of conventions.

Early Historical Background, 1400–650 B.C.[5] The brilliant Mycenaean civilization, having come to an end around 1200 B.C., was succeeded by a primitive culture. According to tradition, Dorian tribes infiltrated Greece from the north (1100 B.C.); Herodotus called them Hellenic, the name by which the Greeks referred to themselves. Some time before 700 B.C.

the inhabitants of Greece spread to Sicily and southern Italy. By 600 B.C. the expansion had reached Marseilles and Spain and north to the Bosporus and east to Asia Minor. Everywhere independent city states were founded, held together by a common religion and a consciousness of being of the same race. Great religious festivals were celebrated at Olympia, Corinth, and Delphi, where athletic and musical contests took place. These city states produced monumental sculpture connected with temples, particularly during the late seventh century and the early sixth century, the archaic period of Greek sculpture.

Before that period was reached, smaller, more primitive statues, so-called idols, had been produced everywhere on the Mediterranean islands. Two main types that existed at the same time have been differentiated (Valentin Müller). One, the "spread style," shows the figure with arms and legs spread out away from the body; the other, "block style" (Fig. 20), is solid and compact, with less separation of arms and legs from the body. Both types contributed to the formation of the archaic Greek style, but neither had developed far enough to include real movement or any serious attempt at anatomy. Monumental Greek sculpture originated during a period when the block style was dominant. This style came to Greece from Asia Minor, Syria, and Egypt.

Sculpture: Archaic Period, 625–480 B.C. Sculpture in Greece was religious before it became secular. Statues were used as votive offerings to the gods and as tomb figures. Though architecture also benefited from decorative sculpture, the early figures were simply placed in the temples; they were not part of the temple structure. The figure of *Nicandra* (Ill. 39) is an example of one of these freestanding statues. The frontal position is typical of all early sculpture, and in this case is not necessarily the result of Egyptian influence. The block style is retained; the hair falls over the shoulder, the arms are part of the block, rounded only along the edges. At some later period this figure was used in the pavement of a road, which partially accounts for the mutilation of the head.

The archaic period developed sculpture in the round in the standing nude male, draped female, and clothed sitting figure. The nude male type is illustrated in a series of athletes, the so-called *Apollo statues*. A fine example is in Munich, the *Apollo of Tenea* (Ill. 40). These figures suggest Egyptian sculpture, with their stiff, constrained postures, the left foot set forward flat on the ground; but the artists tried to bring out the essential parts of the anatomy. The shoulders are broad, the chest is developed, and the legs are properly related to the torso; even details like kneecaps are attempted. Realism is carried as far as the intent and skill of the sculptors permitted. In spite of stiffness, the Greek figure has a certain tension that suggests life; the bulging eyes and the hair arranged in a pattern of ringlets are typical. It is important to note that Greek sculpture was painted even during the best period.

Sculpture was produced in various local schools, but with Athens the Attic school became outstanding, fusing Dorian

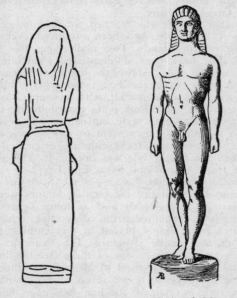

Ill. 39 *(upper left)* Nicandra statue. *National Museum, Athens*
Ill. 40 *(upper right)* Apollo of Tenea, Munich. *After Lübke*

and Ionian styles, as in the famous *Maidens* of the Acropolis. This series of over thirty draped statues was discovered in fragmentary condition, having been used as filling material after the Persians destroyed Athens (480–479 B.C.). One day, fourteen statues were taken out of the ground, where they had been buried in neat rows. The drapery is in pleated folds and painted with restraint (Fig. 21). The hairdress is arranged in rows of curls and braids, eyes curve up, and the lips attempt animation with what has come to be known as the "archaic smile." The long parallel folds of the mantle and short zigzag pleats of the tunic form a charming and effective ornamental pattern. These are a few typical examples of the hundreds of archaic figures and single heads that have been excavated.

The small island of Siphnos enjoyed prosperity during a period before 525 B.C. due to the income derived from its gold and silver mines. The Siphnians erected a *treasury at Delphi* and employed good sculptors on the relief-carved frieze. Form is made to appear more rounded and bulging than it really is (Fig. 22). In the static figures drapery clings to the contours and becomes ornamental; line, shape, and mass are emphasized with a sophisticated calculation. In this monument, one of the most effective of archaic sculpture, the style reaches its culmination. It is this phase of Greek art that has inspired some modern sculptors.

The fragmentary marble figures from the *temple of Aphaia* on the island of Aegina, representing a battle between Greeks and Asiatics, date from the end of the archaic period (*c.* 500–480 B.C.). Discovered before the age of scientific restoration, they were restored by the Danish sculptor Bertel Thorwaldsen, who was so proud of his competence that he said he could no longer distinguish between the original parts and his own (erroneous!) restoration. To fit into the triangular pediment, standing, kneeling, and lying figures were arranged in a symmetrical, balanced manner, although each figure is individually posed. The nude figures suggest the heroic age and reflect the Dorian school of sculpture's interest in anatomy. They are fully rounded and finished, even in back, which could not be seen; but their posture is static and lifeless. Athena, standing in the center, is more archaic than the others, as the artist hesitated to take liberties where religion prescribed adherence to conventions.

The pedimental figures of the *temple of Zeus* (*c.* 465–457 B.C.) show sculptural developments. Some fairly well-preserved figures were found where they had fallen when the temple was destroyed by an earthquake. The more advanced west pediment contains some exceedingly fine work, severe in facial expression, but free in action and flowing in the clinging drapery. In the convincing struggle between centaurs and Lapiths (Greeks), the frozen immobility of the Aegina figures has been overcome.

Transitional Period: 480–450 B.C. During this brief period, Greek sculpture culminated in the freedom of the period of Phidias and the Parthenon and the personalities of the sculptors began to emerge. We do not always know the names of the sculptors, but stylistic differences stand out more clearly. The works of the Great Period are known largely from Roman copies. We must therefore distinguish between Greek originals and Roman copies in marble, often made after Greek originals in bronze. This problem does not exist with archaic sculpture as archaic works are usually originals discovered through excavation, which began only in the nineteenth century.

Of the several transitional sculptors known by name or by works, Myron (active 480–445 B.C.) is the best. His most famous work, the bronze *Discus Thrower* (*Discobolus*), exists today in several Roman copies; the one in which the athlete turns his head is the correct version. Often several Roman copies of the same Greek original exist; they vary in quality, due to the changes introduced by the copyist. Our illustration of Myron's masterpiece (Ill. 41) is from a cast which

combines the head of one copy with the body of another. The figure is composed in one plane, like a relief, and though it is anatomically correct, something of the decorative effect of the archaic period is retained in it.

A studied search for beauty is revealed in the relief of the so-called *Ludovisi Throne* representing the birth of Aphrodite, who rises from the sea assisted by two attendants (Fig. 23). Rounded forms and delicate relief are effectively contrasted. The ripple of transparent drapery is a device invented by the artist. A firsthand observation of nature is shown in the realistic pebbles under the feet. An extravagant play with drapery as an attractive pattern is seen in a seated *Enthroned*

Ill. 41 Myron: Discobolus, Lanzelotti Palace, Rome. *Courtesy British Museum,* Guide to Greek and Roman Antiquities (*1908*)

Goddess (Berlin). Stern dignity characterizes the *Charioteer of Delphi*, an idealized bronze statue commissioned by the victor in a chariot race, and set up at Delphi (Fig. 24). The original was first modeled in clay, which permitted a linear treatment, whereas marble favors soft transitions. The clay medium explains the sharp ridges in the eyelids, with the lashes cut into the edge, and the outlines of the lips, which contrast with the smooth surface of cheeks and chin.

The Second Half of the Fifth Century B.C.: *Phidias and Polycleitus.* Very little is known of the Greek sculptors themselves. Phidias reached his climax under the administration of Pericles in connection with the artistic adornment of Athens. His celebrated statue of *Athena Parthenos* was erected in 438 B.C. This figure, about 40 feet high, was constructed, using bronze, silver, colored marble, gold and ivory, over a wooden core. The original statue has long since been destroyed; it is known chiefly from a small Roman copy, the *Varvakeion statuette,* though the copy has but a faint glimmer of the original's majesty. The Athenians regarded their goddess as the symbol of the state, reassuring Athens through her wealth, her weapons and alliances, and inspiring fear in her enemies, although self-assured peacefulness rather than threatening hostility appears to have been the impression intended. Our modern world has nothing comparable to show, either as art or as a symbol.

The seated statue of *Zeus* at Olympia, of about the same size, was made of even more precious materials. Its dark marble, ebony, and precious stones intensified the color effect. No copies have been preserved (except minor representations on coins and gems), but the impression of grandeur made on those who have left us descriptions was overpowering. We are told that all grief and misfortune were forgotten when standing before this statue. "A singular magic of peace, gentleness and kindness emanates from this statue, and faith itself is strengthened." Only a few works in Western art have comparable emotional effects on the observer or achieve such depth of religious feeling.

Phidias's life-size *Lemnian Athena* was in bronze; a Roman copy in marble shows the youthful goddess bareheaded. Originally, she stood on the Acropolis, a spear in one hand and her helmet in the other. Though serene, she is also gentle, as if showing concern for the Athenians over whom she was watching. Compared to the Charioteer of Delphi, the posture is more relaxed, the drapery not quite so severe (Fig. 25).

Leaving the architecture of the Parthenon for a later discussion, we turn to the exterior sculpture of the eastern pediment. Of the architectural sculpture the pediments were made last, after the dedication of the temple. Plutarch tells us that "everything was made under Phidias's direct charge." Even if Phidias did not carve the figures, he must have designed them. The subject of the east pediment, *the birth of Athena,* has often been told, and lack of space prevents our retelling it here. In the impressive group of the so-called *Three Fates* (Fig. 26), we do not know who is represented; this name is but one of the many suggested. Adolf Furtwängler believed that the right figure held a spindle in her left hand, pulling the thread with her right. Each figure is shown in a different stage of rising, forming a closely knit group. In these grandly relaxed figures, drapery emphasizes anatomical structure, nevertheless giving the impression of natural folds, as if laid on while damp. In the right figure, thin folds fall around the arm and transparent broad folds drape themselves around the breast, terminating in a ridge at the waist line. Clinging folds describe the arched abdomen beneath and long, deep, sweeping, channel-like folds curve around the thigh. A half-seated, half-reclining youth of the east pediment, the so-called *Theseus,* is carved with breadth and vigor. The verticals of head and neck and left upper arm are counteracted by the low-lying diagonals of the thighs. All ninety metopes of the Doric frieze of the Parthenon were sculptured. The style varies, as no doubt many carvers are represented. The sixteen best-preserved panels represent individual struggles between a Lapith and a centaur. The background was red, the figures blue or green. One of the finest compositions (Ill. 43) shows a wounded centaur held by a Lapith, who is about to stab him. With its related lines, parallel horizontals and diagonals, and contrast of figures against drapery, this metope is a masterpiece of design.

In a section of the frieze (Ill. 42), Poseidon, Apollo, and Artemis are represented as awaiting the arrival of the procession. In the center over the east side, the handing over of Athena's gown—the peplos—is enacted. The total frieze, located on the cella wall high up behind the colonnade

Ill. 42 Phidias: Seated gods, Poseidon, Apollo, and Artemis, Parthenon frieze. *After Seemann*

(Ill. 61), was over 500 feet long, representing in great variation the many participants, including some magnificent horses and riders. The frieze of the Parthenon alone marks Phidias as a great sculptor.

A famous contemporary of Phidias was the sculptor Polycleitus of the Dorian School of Argos. He worked in bronze, and his style has been recognized in three well-known Roman copies, *The Spearbearer* (*Doryphoros*, Fig. 28). *The Fillet-*

Ill. 43 Wounded centaur, metope from Parthenon. *After Lübke*

binder (*Diadumenos*), and an *Amazon*. Sculpture has reached a stage of freedom and ease in the posture of the figure; archaic stiffness has vanished and anatomy is mastered in all its details. Polycleitus is known for three things: (1) he was the sculptor of athletes, (2) his heads are placid and stolid, and (3) he used a scale of proportions known as a "canon." The palm of the hand is four times the breadth of a finger, the length of the foot is four times the breadth of the palm, the breadth of the shoulders is four times the breadth of the head, and the height of the figures is seven times the length of the head. *The Spearbearer* demonstrates this canon. The off-balance pose, placing his weight on the advanced right foot with the left knee bent, is a significant departure from frontality. Order, regularity, and repose are distinctive characteristics of Polycleitus' work. A more slender figure with greater movement is shown in his *Fillet-binder* (British Museum), and the standing figure is further elaborated in *The Wounded Amazon*.

The Fourth Century, 400–323 B.C.: Scopas, Praxiteles and Lysippus. The three best-known Greek sculptors besides Myron, Phidias, and Polycleitus are Scopas, Praxiteles, and Lysippus, who lived in the fourth century. Although we know Scopas was born on the island of Paros, we know practically nothing of his life. In contrast to the serenity expressed in the sculpture of Phidias, the style associated with Scopas expresses grief and pain in distorted features and violent action. There are a few original works that have been attributed to him, sculptural remains from the Mausoleum of Halicarnassus in Asia Minor (British Museum) and several battered heads excavated at Tegea (Athens, National Museum). These heads are flat on top and have short faces. The deep-set eyes with a heavy roll of flesh descending and projecting from the forehead give the heads an expression of intensity. Wherever these characteristics appear in Greek sculpture, Scopas's influence is believed to be present. The deep-set eyes and an expression of sadness are found in a seated statue of *Demeter* (Fig. 27), the goddess who mourned the loss of her daughter, Persephone, who, in the Greek myth, was abducted by Pluto. A fine statue of a *Maenad,* a dancing and singing female companion of Bacchus, is also associated with Scopas. With head tossed back and arms uplifted, she follows Bacchus in wild abandon. These two, as well as *The Wounded Niobid* (Rome, Terme Museum), also Scopasian, belong among the great works of sculpture of all time. His style was a potent influence during the Hellenistic period.

A great contemporary of Scopas was the Athenian Praxiteles. His style was one of gentle grace and sensuous loveliness, and his fame rivaled that of Phidias. The lofty dignity of the great gods worked by Phidias in gold and ivory was replaced by the grace and charm of the lesser divinities carved by Praxiteles in marble. He used more extensively the motif of the lowered head as a device for an expression of sentiment, and a slight *s* curve with the weight of the body supported on one leg. The line of the shoulders inclines slightly, the hair is fluffy, the forehead high, the face oval shaped, and the eye is given a long sweep. Occasionally the delicate modeling of the cheeks shows a dimple. Such Praxitelean traits were also passed on to the Hellenistic period. In ancient times the reputation of Praxiteles rested on his *Eros* and his *Satyr,* both known to us only from copies. The *Satyr* was made famous by Hawthorne's novel *The Marble Faun.*

Praxiteles has a particular significance for us, as he may be the only one of the great sculptors of Greece who is represented

Fig. 34 Satyr swinging a maiden, beaker, *c.* 450 B.C. *Berlin Museum*

Fig. 35 Painted lecythus. *Boston Museum of Fine Arts*

Fig. 36 Model of Parthenon. *Metropolitan Museum of Art, bequest of Levi Hale Willard, 1883*

Fig. 37 Erechtheum, north porch, Acropolis, Athens. *Alinari*

Fig. 38 Griffin head, Greek, seventh century, B.C. *Courtesy Walter C. Baker Collection, New York City*

Fig. 39 Pipe players, tomb of the Triclinium, Corneto. *Courtesy Swindler*, Ancient Painting, *Yale University Press (1929)*

Fig. 41 Baths of Caracalla, interior. *After W. Bäumer*

Fig. 42 Model of Pantheon, Rome. *Metropolitan Museum of Art*

Fig. 40 Apollo of Veii, Villa Giulia. *Anderson*

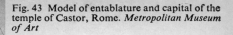

Fig. 43 Model of entablature and capital of the temple of Castor, Rome. *Metropolitan Museum of Art*

Fig. 44 A peasant driving a cow, Munich. *Staatliche Antiken Sammlung (Kaufmann)*

Fig. 45 Relief of Tellus from *Ara Pacis*, Rome. *Anderson*

Fig. 46 Triumphal procession, relief from Arch of Titus, Rome. *Anderson*

Fig. 47 Roman family portrait, relief, marble funeral slab, first century A.D. *Ny Carlsberg Glyptotek, Copenhagen*

Fig. 48 Portrait bust from Palmyra, third century A.D. *Ny Carlsberg Glyptotek, Copenhagen*

Fig. 49 The Battle of Alexander and Darius, mosaic. *National Museum, Naples*

Fig. 50 The Aldobrandini Marriage, Vatican Museum. *Alinari*

Fig. 51 Coptic textile. *Courtesy Detroit Institute of Arts*

Fig. 52 Portrait of a man from the Fayum, Egypt, second century A.D., encaustic painting on wood. *Metropolitan Museum of Art, Rogers Fund, 1909*

Fig. 53 Sarcophagus of St. Theodore, Ravenna. *Alinari*

Fig. 54 Church of Hagia Sophia, Istanbul. *Courtesy Pan American World Airways*

Fig. 55 Enthroned Madonna and Child, Byzantine, thirteenth century. *National Gallery of Art, Mellon Collection, 1937*

Fig. 56 Frieze of female saints, section, mosaic, S. Apollinare Nuovo, Ravenna. *Alinari*

Fig. 57 Basilica of S. Vitale, nave, Ravenna. *Anderson*

Fig. 58 Emperor Justinian and His Court, mosaic, S. Vitale, Ravenna. *Alinari*

Fig. 59 Christ, Virgin and archangels, mosaic, apse, church of Cefalù, Sicily. *Alinari*

Fig. 60 Last Judgment, detail, mosaic, basilica of Torcello, Venice. *Alinari*

Fig. 61 Marriage diptych, ivory, late fourth century. *Victoria and Albert Museum*

Fig. 62 Madonna and two saints, Byzantine ivory, tenth century. *Courtesy Dumbarton Oaks Collection, Washington, D.C.*

Fig. 63 Christ, enamel on gold, Byzantine, eleventh century. *Metropolitan Museum of Art, gift of J. Pierpont Morgan, 1917*

Fig. 64 Bronze plaque, Sarmatian, Ordos region. *Courtesy Gazette des Beaux Arts (Sept. 1952) and Alfred Salmony*

Fig. 65 Visigothic fibulae, gilt bronze and glass paste or semiprecious stones, sixth century A.D., Spain. *Walters Art Gallery, Baltimore*

Fig. 66 Lombard fibula, sixth century A.D., Austria. *Courtesy Naturhistorisches Museum, Vienna*

Fig. 67 Ornamental page with letters Chi Rho, Lindisfarne Gospels. *Copyright British Museum*

Fig. 68 Ornamental page with letters Chi Rho, Book of Kells. *Courtesy Trinity College, Dublin University, and "The Studio" Ltd. Detail*

by an original, his larger than life-size marble statue of
Hermes with the infant Bacchus (Fig. 29). During antiquity
this was not considered to be a major work of Praxiteles', and
Hermes was just barely mentioned by Pausanias, who saw the
statue at Olympia, where it was actually found (1877). A tree
trunk often indicates a Roman copy in marble, which, being
heavier than the Greek original of hollow bronze, needs added
support. In this case the tree could be a part of the composition as a support for *Hermes's* mantle. In his right hand,
Hermes is believed to have held a bunch of grapes. His face,
with flat cheeks and a faint smile, is not turned toward the
infant; instead he is looking dreamily into the distance. This
emphasis on casualness is characteristic of Praxiteles. The
high polish and the carving of the marble to express softness
and subtle gradations without stressing individual muscles
came as a revelation when first viewed. This statue established
a standard by which to measure the quality of Greek originals,
if it is an original. It has also been believed to be a Roman
copy after Praxiteles' bronze original.

In the *Aphrodite of Cnidus*, best represented by a Roman
copy in the Vatican, Praxiteles achieved a culmination of
female beauty. To motivate her nudity, Praxiteles represented
the goddess as about to enter her bath. The sculptor is said to
have carved a nude figure for Cnidus and a draped one for
Cos, neighboring cities in Asia Minor. Nicomedes, King of
Bithynia, desired to own the nude Cnidian version so much
that he offered to pay the public debt of Cnidus in exchange,
an offer the Cnidians rejected.

Lysippus, a contemporary of Praxiteles', appears to have
been very prolific as a sculptor of bronze. He introduced a
new type by making the body slender and the head one-
eighth of the total height of the figure. His statues are said
to have possessed a delicacy and lifelike quality. His most
famous work is an athlete called *Apoxyomenos*, who is portrayed (Ill. 44) cleansing himself after a wrestling match. The
extreme delicacy claimed for the bronze original is missing
in the marble reproduction (Vatican), but it does show the
detailed rendering of the hair, the small head and slender
proportions. Lysippus also made numerous portraits of Alexander the Great, known from marble busts in the British
Museum and the Louvre. One of the finest sculptured works
of the fourth century is known as the *Alexander Sarcophagus*
(Istanbul) from Sidon, though Alexander was not buried in
it. It is distinguished in several ways, but particularly for its
delicate use of color in sculpture. The battle and hunting reliefs show varied hues of purple, violet, yellow, blue, and

shades of red and brown. The moldings above and below the
carved panels are a repertoire of the finest Greek architectural motifs, executed with exquisite finish.

Hellenistic (323–146 B.C.) *and Greco-Roman Period (146*
B.C. *to about 1* A.D.). Alexander the Great conquered the
Persian Empire, and so brought its countries into intimate
contact with Greek civilization. New and larger cities outside of Greece became centers of commerce and of art; Alexandria in Egypt, Antioch in Syria, and Ephesus and Pergamum

in Asia Minor. Athens continued as
the center of classic art, but no longer played a leading part, and Alexandria continued the tradition of
fourth-century Greece. The greatest
contribution came from Pergamum
and Rhodes. Pergamum became pre-
eminent due to the enlightened patronage of the local dynasty of Attalid
kings, beginning when Attalus called
in Greek sculptors to make statues
to commemorate his victories over
the Gauls in 241 B.C. The sculptors
founded the most vigorous school of
Hellenistic sculpture, the first school
of Pergamum. *The Dying Gaul*
(Ill. 45) is represented as mortally
wounded and reclining on his shield,
resigned to death. Great skill is dis-
played in the anatomy; differences
of textures, i.e. in hair and skin, are
indicated, and the surface is highly
polished. In its expression of pain
and its realistic treatment, the statue
is characteristic of the Hellenistic

Ill. 44 Lysippus: Apox-
yomenos, Vatican,
Rome. *After Lübke*

period.

Under Eumenes II, the son of Attalus, Pergamum was
made into one of the most beautiful cities of antiquity (197
B.C.). On its fine Acropolis were public buildings, temples, the
celebrated library, and the huge *Altar of Zeus,* one of the
seven wonders of the ancient world. On a great quadrangular
base, over 100 feet in width, the altar itself stood on a platform in an open court, surrounded by colonnades. Two friezes
decorated the structure; the larger frieze on the base, representing a battle between gods and giants, is the most extensive
and characteristic example of Pergamene art. About one-half
of this frieze was preserved, and after decades of painstaking
work, reconstructed in the Berlin Museum, where it stood

until the fall of Berlin in the Second World War. Giants and gods are interwoven in a closely packed, vigorous composition, overwhelming in its richness and complexity. One of the best preserved is the group in which Athena seizes the hair of a young giant (Fig. 30). Some of the destruction, as in the missing or badly fractured heads, has been attributed to iconoclasts of the early Christian period, who identified the altar as the seat of Satan.

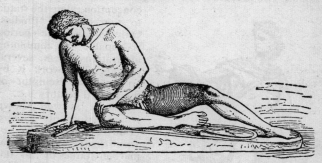

Ill. 45 Wounded and dying Gaul, Capitoline Museum, Rome.
After Lübke

A genre figure, like the *Old Market Woman* in the Metropolitan Museum, is in the spirit of Hellenistic art, and unthinkable at any earlier age. The *Apollo Belvedere* (Ill. 46) is a Roman copy in marble of a bronze original. In his left hand, he held a bow and perhaps also an arrow; in his right, he held a laurel wreath tied with ribbons. The lower arm bent forward symbolized the healing power of the god, and his light vigorous gait indicated, according to Adolf Furtwängler, that *Apollo* was not following the flight of an arrow, but looking about in all directions, as the saving and healing god who wards off evil. An earlier age turned to this statue to demonstrate everything that was thought to be fine in Greek sculpture. Modern criticism has reacted against such extravagant praise; with our more comprehensive knowledge of Greek sculpture, there is no need to single out this statue as an embodiment of all classical beauty. The well-known *Artemis of Versailles* (Louvre) has the same slender proportions and energetic stride.

No work of Greek sculpture has attained such popularity as the *Venus of Melos* (Louvre) and for some it is the finest Greek statue known (Ill. 47). It was discovered in 1820 in a grotto on the island of Melos, in two parts which fitted together. Many attempts have been made to restore it. The left arm may have rested on a column and the right hand may have held the garment (Fürtwangler). According to another view, the left hand held a shield of Ares, used as a mirror. Typical of an eclectic period, the pose expresses a compromise between draped fifth-century and nude fourth-century figures. The smiling mouth and the eyes fixed on the distance are like Praxiteles; the smallness of the head derives from Lysippus. The breadth of modeling and a certain grandeur of conception relate the statue to the style of Phidias. Only an eclectic period is capable of combining inspirations from several periods. The work is by an unknown sculptor of the second century B.C.

Ill. 46 Apollo of Belvedere, Vatican, Rome. *After Lübke*

Almost as well known is a statue of *Victory* (Louvre), *the Nike of Samothrace,* an original marble statue by an unknown sculptor (Fig. 31). It had been set up in the open country to commemorate a naval victory fought in 306 B.C. The statue is generally admired as one of the most powerful works of sculpture in any period. *The Victory* is represented as standing on the prow of a ship, her right hand holding a trumpet, her left, a trophy. The motif is known from a coin, and the prow itself is set up in the Louvre. The treatment of drapery resembles that of the Parthenon sculpture; the thrust of the uplifted chest and right shoulder stretch the transparent folds across the abdomen, and the unbent right knee is set firmly against the onrushing wind. So convincing is the impression conveyed by the posture of the figure that the absence of arms and head is hardly noticed. The statue is now believed to be of the Greco-Roman period.

In 146 B.C. Corinth and Carthage were conquered and Greece became a Roman province. Greek statues were taken by the conquering Roman generals, who ransacked Athens, Olympia, and Delphi and carried off the great masterpieces

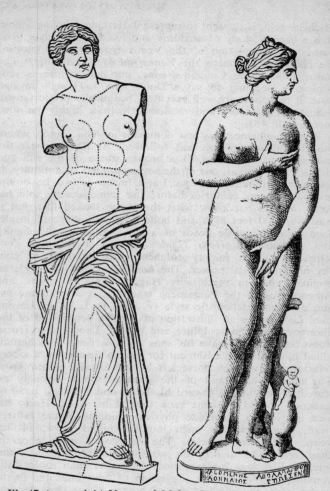

Ill. 47 *(upper left)* Venus of Melos, Louvre. *After Seemann*
Ill. 48 *(upper right)* Venus dei Medici, Uffizi, Florence. *After Lübke*

for the decoration of the public buildings and private villas of Rome. Nero is said to have taken 500 bronze statues from Delphi alone, and there were still enough left for Pausanias to write about. When original works could not be procured, the Romans employed Greek artists to produce copies; these artists are known as the Neo-Attic school. *The Torso Belvedere*, signed by Apollonios of Athens and admired by

Michelangelo, is thought to represent Hercules playing a lyre.
It is a careful study of anatomy and has life and vigor. The
best-known adaptation of the Venus type by a sculptor of
the Neo-Attic school is the *Venus dei Medici* (Uffizi). The
statue follows the Cnidian *Venus*, but her gesture is self-
conscious, seeming to say, "Don't look!" Though in bad
taste, it is technically well executed, beautifully proportioned,
delicate in contours and modeling, with a highly polished
surface (Ill. 48).

Roman influence was less dominant in Asia Minor, where
the Hellenistic tradition was followed. At Rhodes near the
harbor stood (c. 280 B.C.) a bronze statue of the sun god
Helios, *the Colossus,* one of the seven wonders of antiquity. It
fell in an earthquake (224 B.C.) and, broken in two, lay on the
ground for nine centuries before the remains were sold for
scrap. We do not know what the statue looked like, but it
was over 100 feet high and hollow, with a staircase inside.
Two colossal marble heads of a late date show the dignity
and mildness of *Hera (Ludovisi)* and a bearded *Zeus
(Otricoli),* whose mighty forehead was intended to convey his intellectual power. The *Laocoön* group (Ill. 49), an
original work in marble by Hagesandros, Polydoros, and
Athenodoros in the Pergamene tradition, is an extreme example of late Hellenistic style (c. 150 B.C.). G. E. Lessing
used *Laocoön* as an illustration of Virgil's description of the
difference between sculpture and poetry. Laocoön, a Trojan
priest, in trying to save his sons from serpents was himself
killed by them as punishment for having desecrated a sacred
offering, the wooden horse left by the Greeks before Troy.
The outstretched hand of the younger son is wrongly restored; it should fall toward his head, and the right hand of
Laocoön should be bent back toward his head. Every device is used to dramatize physical pain, as in the father's
head, bent back, his open mouth, knitted brow, swollen
veins, and tense muscles. The realism is more apparent
than real. The snakes do not strike like real serpents,
but bite like dogs, and are more decorative than zoologically
convincing. Without any suggestion of guilt indicated in the
group itself, the effect is one of horror rather than tragedy,
perhaps as a result of the concepts of the sixteenth-century
restorers.

Painting. All works of the great painters Apelles, Zeuxis,
and Polygnotus have perished, but we know of them
through literature. Greek authors have more to say about
these painters than about Phidias. The best evidence as to
the periods of the great painters comes from the drawings
and compositions on vases.

Between the Mycenaean period and the first purely Greek style in vase painting, the black-figured style of the sixth century, there are two more primitive styles; the geometric style from 1100–700 B.C. and the so-called orientalizing style

Ill. 49 Laocoön group, Vatican, Rome. *After Lübke*

of 700–600 B.C. Greek vase painting falls into three roughly chronological groups which somewhat overlap: the black-figured, the red-figured, and the white-ground style. *The Warrior vase* portraying a woman bidding farewell to departing warriors, is an example of the Mycenaean period before 1000 B.C. The style of this vase represents the end of a naturalistic tradition.

The Dorians brought with them a rectilinear geometric style in decoration (Ill. 50). The term Dipylon culture, named after the first discovery in Athens near the Dipylon gate, has been applied to the geometric vases of Attica, large terra-cotta vases placed over tombs. In brown and black, the patterns are carried out in horizontal stripes, meander bands, triangles, zigzags, squares, rhombuses, and chevron patterns. Birds and animals are introduced as part of the abstract type of decoration; the figures themselves are symbols of man in the abstract. There is no trace of naturalism; the Dipylon style is a purely geometric style of European and northern origin, handed down from Neolithic times and merged with Mycenaean and oriental influences.

The orientalizing style of the seventh century represents a move from east to west, from Phoenicia, Egypt, the Ionian cities of Ephesus and Rhodes to Greece. The ornamentation shows oriental motifs like the lotus and the palmette, fabulous monsters like griffins and sphinxes, Mycenaean spirals and natural plant motifs. Vacant spaces between the animals were filled in by dots, rosettes, zigzags, and other designs. Processions of decorative animals (Ill. 51) are introduced and the decoration is more varied and more skillful than in the geometric style.

With the appearance of figures, the eye is a convenient detail by which to check on the trend toward naturalism. In

Ill. 50 (*upper left*) Dipylon ware, British Museum. *After British Museum catalogue (1908)*

Ill. 51 (*upper right*) Corinthian vase with frieze of animals, Louvre. *After Collignon*

the course of a century and a half, from about 625–475 B.C., the drawing of the eye changed from straight front view to the correct profile view.

Other noteworthy groups of vases precede those of the black-figured style. A typical example is the so-called *Arkesilas Kylix* (cup) of the Louvre (*c.* 570 B.C.), portraying King Arkesilas II of Cyrene seated on his throne on the deck of a ship. Silphium, the most important export article of Cyrene, is being weighed on scales and carried by men to the hold of the ship. From the end of the seventh century is a famous pinax, shaped like a soup bowl, of Ionic design (Ill. 52), made in Rhodes and exported from Miletus.

Ill. 52 Combat of Menelaus and Hector over Euphorbus. *After British Museum catalogue* (*1908*)

Two warriors, Menelaus and Hector, dominate the composition, which is striking in its lights and darks. There is a considerable amount of oriental filling ornament, and in the upper center two eyes are included to ward off evil; a guilloche border is at the bottom.

Archaic painting shows the same vigor and freshness as archaic sculpture. Vase painting emphasizes man and his doings in warfare, athletics, dancing, and drinking; the artists tell the myths and Homeric legends more as if these were tales of their contemporaries rather than tales of their ancestors. The use of many colors on a small area disappears in the sixth-century black-figured style, and the clay becomes a warm reddish surface against which the figures stand out in a simple contrast of black with a metallic luster. Attention is concentrated on drawing; decoration, invention, and profile figures are new achievements in this period.

The outline and elongated volute handles give a stately character to the famous *François vase* (Fig. 33). The painter Klitias introduced a degree of refinement in the figure drawing which marked Athenian vase painting as superior.

From the top down, we have (1) Calydonian Boar Hunt, (2) Funeral Games for Patroclus, (3) Procession of Gods to the Wedding of Thetis, (4) Troilus persuaded by Achilles, (5) Base: Battles of Pygmies with Cranes. Archaic traits are in evidence; profile shoulders and frontal views are used, as well as the "bent knee" formula to convey an impression of swift motion. The drawing is rectilinear and angular, particularly noticeable in the horses.

Greek art came into its own with the black-figured style. As in sculpture, vase paintings reflect the conflict of the artists between stylized formality and natural appearances.

Ill. 53 Epictetus kylix, British Museum.
After Furtwängler and Reichold

The leading masters of the fully mature archaic style were Exekias and Amasis. In this severe style the figures are restricted to a frame instead of spreading over the whole surface of the vase. A masterpiece of all periods is the *Kylix of Exekias*, showing Bacchus sailing a boat, his grapevine growing boldly and gaily from a heap of earth inside

Ill. 54 Euphronius: Heracles and Antaeus krater. *After Baumeister*

the boat. It is a charming fantasy, imbued with the Greek spirit of carefree abandon and appropriate to the god of wine. Another masterpiece by Exekias is the amphora representing Achilles and Ajax playing draughts (Vatican). The shape shows a gradually swelling profile; neck and body merge without break. Black silhouettes are enhanced by ornamentation, which turns the clothes into delicate patterns, making them look like woven sheets of thin gauze. In hands and feet, these elegant shapes diminish into tapering ends.

The red-figured style is well represented by an Epictetus kylix (Ill. 53) with interior central medallions in which the painter shows great skill. Naturalism is seen in the lively poses, the turn of the dancing girl's head, and the zigzag folds over the shoulder of the flutist. An important kylix, signed by the great master Euphronius (Ill. 54), shows Heracles' struggle with the giant Antaeus. The figures are large in scale; there is considerable interior drawing outlining the muscles and well-drawn feet and hands, as in the upturned right hand of Antaeus. Euphronius was the ranking master of the so-called severe style. He was both a potter and

Ill. 55 Pan-Master: Death of Acteon krater, Boston Museum of Fine Arts. *After Furtwängler and Reichold*

painter, and often signed his vases in both capacities:
epoiesen (made) and *egrapsen* (painted). A beautiful kylix
by Douris shows two women putting away their clothes
(Fig. 32). Freely undulating line in the slender figures is
combined with a quality of precision and contrasted with
the bundles of folded clothes; the eye is in near profile. On a
bell krater by the so-called Pan-Master (Ill. 55), the influence
of Phidias and Polygnotus is present. Artemis points an arrow at Acteon, who spied on her while bathing. Although
Artemis' left foot is foreshortened, the stiff postures and
complicated drapery are archaic. One vase (Fig. 34) shows a
little girl in a swing being pushed by a satyr. The scene represents part of a spring festival when the spirits rose from the
earth and had to be pacified; the gust of air caused by the
motion of the swing was thought to be cleansing. In another
red-figured amphora (Ill. 56) the swallow of spring appears;
the man on the left greets her coming with the words, "Look
at the swallow"; the youth on the right says, "There she is";
and the bearded man exclaims, "By Heracles!" The return of
spring was celebrated by songs and commemorated by painted
vases. Something of the charm and dignity of the Parthenon

Ill. 56 The swallow of spring amphora. *After Baumeister*

frieze reappears in two maenads (Ill. 57) and in an amphora
by the so-called Achilles Painter (*c*. 450 B.C.). This drawing
seems to exist solely to provide pleasure to the eye.

Vases with a white background show the same progress in
skill of drawing as appears in the red-figured style. A
group of white-ground lecythi, cylindrical vases with high
narrow necks, show funeral customs. Most of them are
Athenian, and, like
other vases, many were
exported. A well-known
example in Boston (Fig.
35) shows a dead war-
rior standing before his
tomb; on the other side
is a maiden about to
present a funeral offer-
ing. Her drapery was
once painted over the
nude figure in a pig-
ment that has disinte-
grated. For sensitive
drawing as well as for
sentiment, it is one of
the masterpieces of
drawing of all time. As
vases have been recov-
ered from tombs, it is
presumed that they
were placed there to be
used in a future life af-
ter death. Some were

Ill. 57 Two maenads from an amphora. Cabinet des Médailles, Paris.
After Furtwängler and Reichold

found deliberately broken, a custom familiar to other cultures; this seems to be a projection of death to the object
broken, thus establishing a bond between the man and
his possessions. Shapes similar to those found in tombs
no doubt were used in life. The kylix was a drinking cup;
the amphora was used for storing wine and liquids; the three-
handled hydria was for water; and the krater was a mixing
bowl. These are a few of perhaps twenty known shapes
(Ill. 58).

Architecture: Archaic Temples. The Mycenaean Bronze
Age had no temples, but the temple was developed to a high
state of perfection during the period of Pericles and, once
perfected, remained unchanged. The cella of the temple is
derived from the megaron, the men's hall of the old Mycenaean palaces, as palaces would naturally be thought proper
for the gods. The Doric style was that of the Greek mainland.
The other style of Greek architecture, the Ionic, was intro-

Amphora

Pelike

Volute Krater

Loutrophoros

Calyx Krater

Column Krater

Bell Krater

Stamnos

Psykter

Hydria

Lebes Gamikos

Lebes

Lekythos

Squat Lekythos

Oinochoe

Kantharos

Kylix

Stemless Kylix

Skyphos

Aryballos

Alabastron

Pyxis

Ill. 58 Shapes of Athenian vases. *Guide, Greek Collection, Metropolitan Museum of Art*

duced to Athens from the islands and Asia Minor. The Doric order in stone was evolved partly from wood architecture and partly through innovations that were initially worked out in stone. These archaic temples have been preserved only in ruins in Greece (Olympia, Corinth), in southern Italy, in Sicily, and on the island of Corfu. Sicily has several temples at Selinus, one of which (Temple B) was the largest Greek temple of antiquity. In the tympanum Temple C appears to have had a huge *Gorgon's Head,* 9 feet in diameter and made of terra cotta. The limestone was sheathed with terra cotta in red, black, and buff to produce an effect of massive vigor and brilliant color.

The Acropolis of Athens. Architecture reached its highest development on the Acropolis (*acros,* "high"; *polis,* "city"), the upper fortified part of the city of Athens, during the administration of Pericles (450–430 B.C.). Civic buildings were not developed, as the Greeks lived an outdoor life. The ruins of the *Parthenon,* once the most perfect Greek building, are famous today and a major tourist attraction. Ictinus and Callicrates were the architects. The finest example in the Ionic style is a smaller temple, the *Erechtheum* (421–405 B.C.). The *Propylaea* (437–432 B.C.), the monumental entrance to the Acropolis, was never completed. The placing of the temples (Ill. 59) was informal; for instance, an uneven spot near the edge was selected for the Erechtheum because that ground was sacred. As a result, the Erechtheum was built on two levels and three porticos were combined, demonstrating an unexpected elasticity of Greek architecture. Models of modern restorations of the Acropolis give a total impression of the buildings. The Greek temple, like the Egyptian, was not intended for a congregation; the cella was a place for the statue of the god. How the interior was illuminated is not clear—probably through the open door.

Doric Order. All Greek architecture used the post-and-lintel system. The Doric columns, fluted and without base, support the entablature and the roof, which was covered with marble tiles and had a gable, or pediment, at either end. The structure will be clear from a study of the illustration (Ill. 60). The original effect of the Parthenon (Fig. 36), in addition to its basic design, owes something to the appeal of the finely grained marble, to the added use of color, and to subtle curves of lines that ordinarily would be straight. The stylobate, the topmost of the three steps on which the columns rest, rises in the center about 2¾ inches on the ends and 4 inches on the long sides. The profile of the column tapers and is slightly curved (entasis) and so is the echinus (*see* Ill. 60); the columns lean inward; the angle columns have a

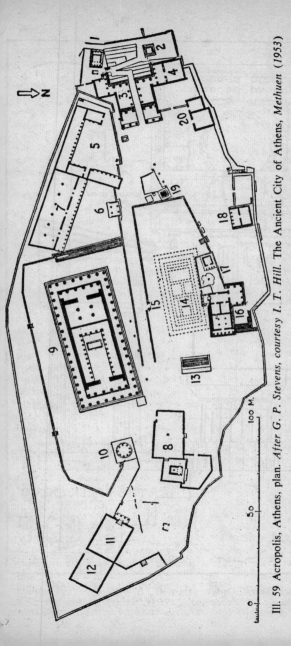

Ill. 59 Acropolis, Athens, plan. *After G. P. Stevens, courtesy I. T. Hill. The Ancient City of Athens, Methuen (1953)*

1. Niké Temple. 2. So called Monument of Agrippa. 3. Propylaea. 4. Picture Gallery. 5. Sanctuary of the Brauronia Artemis. 6. Propylon. 7. Chalkotheki. 8. Precinct of Zeus Polieus and Boukoleion. 9. Parthenon. 10. Heroon of Pandion. 11. Service. 12. Service. 13. Great Altar of Athena. 14. Old Temple of Athena. 15. Propylon. 16. Erechtheum. 17. Pandroseum, Temple of Pandrosus, Sacred Olive Tree, Cecropium. 18. Dwelling of the Arrephori. 19. Promachos. 20. Service Building (?)

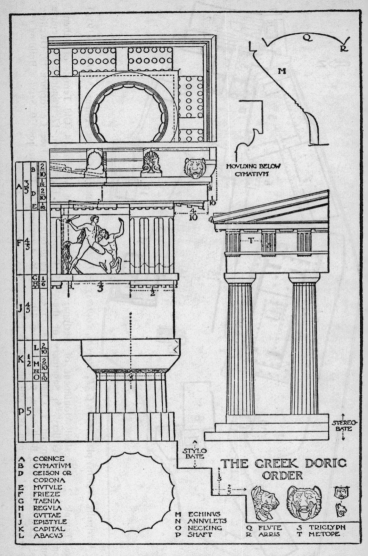

MOVLDING BELOW CYMATIVM

THE GREEK DORIC ORDER

A CORNICE
B CYMATIVM
D GEISON or CORONA
E MVTVLE
F FRIEZE
G TAENIA
H REGVLA
I GVTTAE
J EPISTYLE
K CAPITAL
L ABACVS

M ECHINVS
N ANNVLETS
O NECKING
P SHAFT

Q FLVTE
R ARRIS
S TRIGLYPH
T METOPE

STYLOBATE

STEREOBATE

Ill. 60 Greek Doric Order. *After H. L. Warren,* The Foundations of Classic Architecture *(1919), courtesy Winnifred B. Warren*

double inclination; the face of the cornice, the abacus (*see* L Ill. 60), and the moldings lean out. These curves and inclinations are not obvious, but can be detected; they have been measured in modern times (Francis C. Penrose), and have been described by Vitruvius in the Roman period. The explanation offered is that the curves offset the optical illusion of sagging given by straight lines; it may be simply that the Greeks found curves to be pleasing. The Ionic order curves are less emphatic.

The Greeks experimented with proportions of height to width, reaching the finest solution on the exterior of the Parthenon (Fig. 36). Greek architecture aimed at external appearance suggestive of unity and strength; interior design and architecture's capacity to create effects of great spaciousness remained undeveloped. Columns were left unadorned as structural members to carry the superstructure (Ill. 61). Only those parts that carry no weight, the tympanum of the pediment and the metopes, were sculptured. A logical appeal to reason found its expression in dealing differently with the structural parts—structure and decoration do not fuse: the columns have flutes but no carving and there are purely decorative parts such as the sculptural and painted decorations. The lintels are structural, hence uncarved; the triglyphs are structural and have grooves like the flutes of columns. Logic and clarity were the controlling principles; there was no mysticism. Construction was as highly developed as design. Columns consisted of drums ground and doweled together; metal clamps were used, but no mortar.

At the time of Emperor Justinian (*c.* 450 A.D.), the Parthenon was made into a Christian church and altered accordingly. In 1453 the church became a Turkish mosque and a minaret was added. In 1687, in a war between Venetians and Turks, the Venetians blew up the buildings, which had been used to store powder, causing a fire. Early in the nineteenth century, Lord Elgin acquired fifteen metopes and a few figures from the east pediment for the British Museum, where they have been preserved. All medieval and Turkish additions were cleared away when Greece became free of Turkish rule (1836).

Ionic Order. Compared to the sober Doric, the Ionic (Ill. 62a) is luxuriant; it has more parts, is more slender in proportions, and has a scroll, or volute, capital. Moldings are carved instead of painted, as in the Doric. The Ionic frieze was sculptured, but had no metopes nor triglyphs. Columns had bases and shafts and more flutes separated by narrow bands called fillets (Fig. 37). The Ionians occupied Asia Minor and Attica on the Greek mainland, and in

Ill. 61 Parthenon, sectional view. *After British Museum catalogue*
(1908)

Athens the Ionic style was refined and simplified. The vertical volute capital was used by the Persians (Ill. 36); in
Greek art the volutes were placed horizontally. Several theo-
ries have attempted to explain the origin of the Ionic capital, such as coils of rope, metal and plant forms; it has been
related to Egypt and Babylonia, but an indigenous Greek
development has also been claimed.

The *Erechtheum* mentioned above has been attributed to
Mnesicles and has been called the most beautiful example
of the Ionic order. It certainly became the most favored,

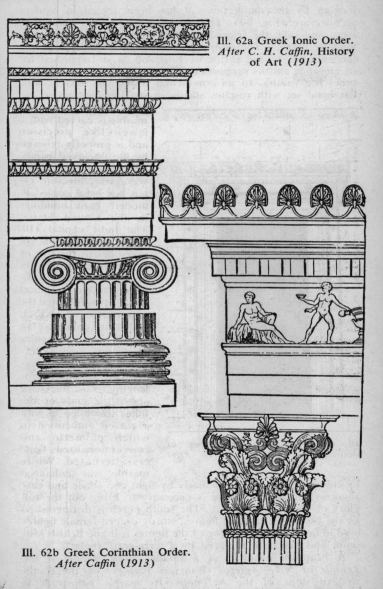

Ill. 62a Greek Ionic Order.
After C. H. Caffin, History
of Art (*1913*)

Ill. 62b Greek Corinthian Order.
After Caffin (*1913*)

judging by the many times it has been copied in modern architecture (Fig. 37). The corner capital shows volutes on front and side; the frieze is in dark blue marble, the rest, in Pentelic marble. The doorway in the wall behind the porch, the entrance to the shrine of Poseidon, is distinguished for its elegance and its proportions (height about two and a third times the width). In its ornamental frame (Ill. 63), a wide flat band set with rosettes stands in striking contrast to the inner moldings. The marble is carved with a jewelrylike precision and is properly relieved by flat uncarved bands. This most famous doorway in architecture often has been copied in modern bank buildings in the United States. The Ionic capital (Ill. 62a) is admirable in every detail; the eye of the volutes probably had gilded bronze disks c e m e n t e d in place; metal strips followed the convolutions, which ended in palmettes to fill in the triangular spaces left in either corner. The so-called egg-and-dart moldings show lengthy ovals; the space above the ends of the flutes was filled in with a carved anthemion in which palmetto and conventionalized flowers alternated. White marble was enhanced

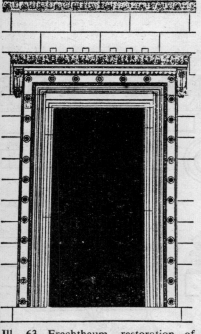

Ill. 63 Erechtheum, restoration of doorway, north porch, Athens. *After Lawrence (1957)*

by color and gilt and particularly by light and shade and cast shadows; brilliant sunshine is necessary to bring out the full glory of Greek architecture. The south porch is distinguished by the use of six caryatid figures, sturdy draped female figures used in lieu of columns. One of the figures is in the British Museum and has been replaced by a terra-cotta replica.

A beautiful example of a smaller Ionic temple is the *Temple of Nike Apteros (Wingless Victory)* on the southwestern slope of the Acropolis. Its marble balustrade is carved in relief with winged Nikes. The finest example, *Nike Tying Her Sandal* (Acropolis Museum), rivals the *Three Fates* in the exquisite drapery revealing the form underneath. In addition to the ones here discussed, there are perhaps a dozen Ionic buildings, mostly temples, in Greece, on the islands and Asia Minor.

A variation of the Ionic order is the bell-shaped Corinthian capital, which is enhanced by sharply defined acanthus leaves. It is probably the most elaborate single architectural ornament ever developed in Western art. The Corinthian capital was first used in Athens in the small circular choragic monument of *Lysicrates,* designed as a sumptuous pedestal for a bronze tripod won as a prize at a Bacchanalian festival in 334 B.C. The name of the monument perpetuated the sponsor of the winning team of the patron of art rather than the winners of the tripod or the architect.

Gems, Coins, and Metalwork. Gems were cut in intaglio, from which impressions were struck in wax or metal for seals. Semiprecious stones were used, as they were hard enough to stand wear but could be cut with simple tools. In antiquity seals served in place of modern locks and keys to safeguard property and as signatures at a time when few people could write. Dexamenos of Paros of the fifth century B.C., the most celebrated gem cutter, was as famous for gems as Phidias was for sculpture. Gems recapitulate in miniature the stylistic development from the archaic through the Roman period. Though small, they were engraved with exquisite finish in a style that often suggests the breadth of sculpture; and like sculpture, gems have their masterpieces. The subjects from mythology and daily life use animals and the human figure and repeat the same types. A heron spreading his wings is engraved on one side of a carnelian with delicacy and precision, and is well related to the oval shape.

For variety of invention and beauty of design, Greek coins are often superior to modern coins. A die was cut in a hard metal; the coin was then struck from the die by driving the coin into the die with a hammer blow. The relief was higher than it is nowadays, but since the coins were not uniform in size, they could not be stacked. Each Greek city had its own coins showing a head, a figure, or some attribute of a god.

Bronze was used more commonly in ancient than in modern times, not only in sculpture, but also for utensils and household furniture, vases, tripods, mirrors, and pins (safety pins called fibulae). Often these objects were beautiful in shape and elaborated with reliefs or incised designs. An extraordinary bronze in the Walter C. Baker private collection, a head of a griffin from a seventh-century cauldron, combines the vigor and elegance of the archaic period at its best (Fig. 38).

The use of precious metals, which was already highly developed in Mycenaean art, was brought to a new high of perfection during the Hellenistic and Roman period. All technical processes were employed in silverware found at Boscoreale (Italy) and at Hildesheim (Germany). Silver plates and silver vessels found at Hildesheim (1867) probably belonged to a traveling table service of a Roman nobleman of the Augustan period. A large mixing bowl (Ill. 64) about

Ill. 64 Silver mixing bowl from Hildesheim, Berlin Museum.
After Lübke

18 inches high is one of the finest of the set. Two stylized griffins at the base are part of a pattern of delicate tendrils that spread across the whole surface. Little cupids perched astride the tendrils are attacking marine animals. The style is in the Hellenistic manner of Alexandria, except for the naturalistic tendrils and leaves, which are in the taste of the Augustan period.

Conclusion. Greek art was long regarded as having produced models that hardly could be surpassed. Though no longer imitated, Greek art is better understood today than ever before and, as a result, our appreciation of Greek art rests on a firmer foundation.

Various explanations have been offered for the conditions that made Greek art possible. Perhaps the climate gave the people something of the hardiness of the North combined with the relaxation that characterizes the countries of the East. The topography of mountains and valleys may have encouraged in the inhabitants a spirit of independence without isolating the settlements. Their closeness to the sea made the Greeks enterprising travelers to other countries, and love of sports gave sculptors an opportunity to observe the human body and increase their knowledge of anatomy. The simplicity of Greek dress, the availability of excellent marble, and the beauty of the country are often mentioned as favorable influences. Religious festivals and a common culture gave the Greeks a sense of solidarity and pride, and fostered competition as well. But climate, natural beauty, and fine marble existed before Greek art came into existence and continued after it had run its course. Moreover, a similar background is found in other regions which produced no comparable development in art.

We must look for additional causes; the small city state is one. Attica was smaller than the state of Rhode Island, and Athens at the time of Pericles had about 40,000 citizens in a total population of between 200,000 and 300,000. Athens was a self-governing community; citizens took an interest in public affairs, and even religion was subservient to the needs of the state. Greece never developed a powerful priesthood, as in Egypt. The development of free thought culminated in philosophy, in literature, and in a cult of beauty, and gave background and content to the visual arts. In all cultures, the arts reflect the intellectual climate; they do not by themselves create it. How the talents of artists are utilized depends on the culture, which in Greece emphasized the free development of all human potentialities, including the arts.

It also happened that Pericles was fortunate in having surplus funds available, as Athens had been the treasury of the Delian League. These funds were freely used to beautify the city. If we think of freedom of thought as a basic condition which combined with other favorable circumstances, we may come closer to understanding why, in the course of a few centuries, the arts developed in such a spectacular fashion in Greece.

CHAPTER V

Etruscan and Roman Art

Etruscan Art (800 B.C.—Empire Period). The ancient Etruscans settled in central Italy and at one time dominated most of Italy. Though conquered by the Romans, they were not wholly integrated with Roman culture until the period of the Empire. Their origin, like their language, has remained obscure; the most plausible theory is that they came from Asia Minor, though some authorities have claimed a northern or a native Italian origin. Before the Etruscans were absorbed in the general population, they developed an art of their own, in which the most potent influence was Greek. According to the nineteenth-century point of view, Etruscan art was provincial Greek art; the trend today is to accord to Etruscan art a measure of individuality, without denying a Greek contribution. Some Etruscan contributions to Roman art were the semicircular arch, stone masonry using large blocks usually without mortar, and the temple raised on a platform and with a deep porch in front.

Painting. Except for painted terra-cotta plaques, Etruscan paintings have survived only on the walls of underground tombs; they once existed in public and private buildings as well. Of the many paintings in the Etruscan cemeteries of Tarquinii (near Corneto) and Chiusi, only a few have been preserved. The most flourishing period was in the two above-mentioned cities, though there are other places with painted tombs, such as Orvieto, Vulci, and Caere. Some were known at the time of the Renaissance; others have been discovered and studied since, particularly during the nineteenth century. In certain instances paintings have been successfully lifted from the walls and transferred to museums.

The tomb was the "eternal home" of the soul, which, according to Etruscan beliefs, survived after death and had to

be provided for. The earlier paintings show scenes of daily
life, banquets and dances in which the dead man participates.
The paintings probably imitate those of the houses of the
living in order to provide the owner with the pleasant things
of life. During the later period, the subjects of the paintings
relate to a land of the dead, a counterpart to the Greek
Hades.

The tomb paintings are original paintings by the best artists, native Etruscans or Greeks, and not imitations of well-
known Greek masterpieces. Therefore they vary in style according to the period; the early seventh- and sixth-century style is archaic and, like Greek art, shows an orientalizing influence. A painting from the Grotta Campana at Veii
(Ill. 65) shows a polka-dotted horse, sturdy Doric-like figures,

and a hunting leop-
ard. The space is
filled with ornamen-
tal plant motifs, as
in the orientalizing
style of Greek vase
painting. The same
influences that came
to Greece from Asia
Minor also were felt
in Italy (Etruria);
hence the stylized lo-
tus tendrils filling in
the vacant spaces.

Ill. 65 Etruscan wall painting from
Veii, Grotta Campana. *After Martha*

The freer fifth-
century style is well
illustrated in the decorations from the Tomb of the Triclinium
(*c.* 470 B.C.), transferred to the Museum of Tarquinii. One
painting is of a banqueting scene; others from the side walls
show dancers. A dancing pipe player (Fig. 39), surrounded
by birds and flowers, is represented in profile with the eye in
front view. The flowing curves, bold and self-assured, give this
figure a buoyancy which is unlike anything Greek or Egyptian.

Sculpture. We know the name of one famous Etruscan
sculptor, Vulca of Veii of the sixth century B.C., who also
worked in Rome. The Etruscans preferred terra cotta and
bronze to stone and marble for sculpture and architectural
decorations. One of the best-known sculptures is the *Apollo
of Veii,* a painted terra-cotta figure (*c.* 500 B.C.), a decoration
from the apex of a pediment (Fig. 40). It was this use
of figures on the roofs of temples which caused the Roman
author Vitruvius to call Etruscan temples "top-heavy."

The pleated drapery recalls the contemporary Greek Ionian style of the *Maidens of the Acropolis*, but the modeling is more vigorous and the forward step, energetic, so that this figure has been called the *Walking Apollo*. Color, black hair, ivory drapery, and a dark-brown flesh tint add to the effectiveness of the statue.

The Etruscans were known for their metalwork, bronze sculpture, and jewelry. The *Orator* (Florence, Archaeological Museum), of the fourth century B.C. or later, may represent a Roman. It was made by an Etruscan artist, perhaps as a votive figure (Massimo Pallottino). The portraitlike head of this statue, as well as another portrait, *L. Junius Brutus,* indicates the Etruscans' famous capacity for realistic portraiture. However, as Greek artists also worked for the Romans, archaeologists often differ as to whether a work like the Brutus head is Etruscan or Greek.

Imperial Roman Art, 31 B.C.*–313* A.D.; *Emperor Augustus to Constantine*. Roman art existed during the Republic, but it was Octavius, the first Roman emperor, under the name of Augustus, who made over Rome "from a city of brick to one of marble." Monumental architecture was fully developed during the Empire, and sculpture took on a Roman flavor during his reign. With Constantine, three centuries later, Christianity became the state religion, and the subject matter of art became Christian, although the style continued in the Roman manner.

Roman art was exported to the provinces as far north and west as Scotland and Spain and as far south and east as North Africa and Syria; it was definitely Roman art, even though it was originally based on the Etruscan and Greek counterparts.

Architecture: Forums. The most characteristic expression of the Romans was architecture, and the most original aspect of Roman architecture was the concept of a building as a complex and spacious interior. In addition, the Romans developed the planning of many buildings to form a monumental group, related by means of a major axis and often minor axes as well. The forums from the *Forum Romanum*, the earliest, to the forum of Trajan (110–114 A.D.), the most magnificent, became centers of public life and places of trade and political assemblies. Up to the time of Julius Caesar the *Forum Romanum* had shops and was used as a market place. Under the Empire, shops and markets were cleared out and it became the center for law courts and other civic activities. All the forums in Rome had at least one temple; the Roman forum had six, in addition to other buildings, a platform for orators (rostrum), triumphal arches, columns, and many statues. The plan of the forum of Trajan, designed by Apollodorus of Damascus, somewhat resembled the Egyptian temple plan, but was more varied. A broad court with columns on three sides and semicircular exedrae on two sides for shops was followed on the same central axis by a basilica and a temple. A monumental arched entrance replaced the Egyptian pylon. Where real estate is expensive, uneconomical use of land is not long tolerated. Nero's well-known fire in Rome appears to have been a slum clearance project, and later his own famous *Domus Aurea* (Golden House) was demolished to make room for the Colosseum.

The region of the imperial forums (*Fora Caesarum*) has been uncovered (since 1932) and is today crossed by the Via delle Fore Imperiale. Of the forums, incidental ruins which exist today are columns, which have been found among the debris of demolished houses which once covered the area and have been re-erected. Systematic work on recovering the ruins of the Roman forum started in 1871, on individual buildings, as early as 1803. The original pavement of the Trajan forum is still unexcavated, some 20 feet below the present street level.

Dwellings. Domestic architecture included the palace; the villa, or country house; the *domus*, or ordinary house; and the many-storied apartment house (*insula*). Excavations at Ostia show that the well-to-do lived in duplex apartments with living rooms and dining rooms two floors high (T. F. Hamlin). There were balconies and large windows with glass in the more expensive houses and transparent mica in the more modest ones.

The excavated ruins of Roman imperial palaces have brought to light an elaborate complex of rooms, courts, temples, libraries, baths, peristyles, fountains, terraces, and covered passageways adorned with statues, columns, marbles, and mosaics. The most extensive palace ruins are those of the *Palace of Emperor Diocletian* (284–305 A.D.) at Spalato, the modern Split, in Dalmatia on the Adriatic coast. Within the still magnificent ruins, live today one-fifth of the population of Split. The ruins of *Hadrian's villa* near Tivoli outside Rome cover hundreds of acres.

Remains of Roman houses have been found in many parts of the Empire, but the most complete are at Pompeii, as in the *House of Pansa*. All chambers in the one-story house opened upon interior courts, which provided light. The front of the house, facing toward the street, was given over to shops. The interior walls were wainscoted with marble or covered with painted decorations. Many of our modern comforts such as plumbing and heating were anticipated in Roman dwellings.

New Types of Buildings. The requirements of an empire and a metropolis like Rome developed new types of buildings on a larger scale than had ever been realized before. The five-aisled basilica used colonnades and perhaps wooden roofs, as in the basilica of Trajan's forum. The post-and-lintel system employed by the Greeks was elaborated by the Romans. They placed columns on pedestals to gain height, and invented flattened wall columns called pilasters and so-called engaged columns which, merging with the wall behind, projected from the wall by more than half the column's diameter. The more revolutionary Roman structures included temples with spacious interiors made possible through the use of barrel vaults, great baths with central halls erected on groin vaults, and circular vaulted temples like the Pantheon, now a Christian church. To these must be added places of amusement, theaters of nearly semicircular plan such as the Theater of Marcellus (23–13 B.C.), amphitheaters like the Colosseum, circuses like the Circus Maximus, triumphal arches, and finally tombs like Hadrian's (138 A.D.), now Castel Sant' Angelo. For these new types the Romans developed a more practical type of construction that did not depend on trained craftsmen but left much to unskilled labor, thus making it possible to build in the Roman manner in any part of the Empire.

Construction. This construction was made possible through the use of the ground arch, the vault (Ill. 66–68), and the

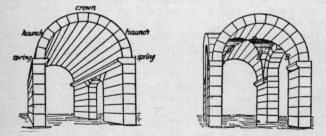

Ill. 66 (*upper left*) Barrel vault. *After Hamlin (1909)*
Ill. 67 (*upper right*) Groined vault (*g, g,* groins). *After Hamlin (1909)*

dome on a circular base. Generally the material was concrete faced with brick, though cut stones of enormous size were also used, particularly in Syria at Palmyra and Baalbec. Concrete was most common for massive structures, as it was economical and saved labor. As raw materials for concrete, Italy had—in addition to stone—lime and a volcanic product, pozzuolana, which made an excellent cement. Small vaults were cast in concrete on wooden molds called centerings; large vaults were built with light ribs of brick, and the concrete was filled in between the arches (Ill. 68) forming a monolithic mass. The Romans used heavy walls as abutments, often needlessly, as the concrete vault was like a lid which exerted no outward thrust, in the manner of a masonry vault.

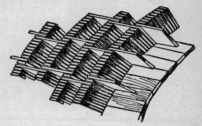

The Romans, among the world's best engineers, built roads and bridges like the great bridge at Alcantara in Spain (617 feet long, 180 feet high) that are in use

Ill. 68 Brick ribs of barrel vault. *After Simpson (1929)*

today. Water was brought to Rome from the mountains through fourteen aqueducts. The finest example in southern France is the famous *Pont du Gard* near Nîmes. Three tiers of arches, one above the other, conduct the water across the river valley 150 feet below. Such structures were not only utilitarian and constructed as if to last for eternity, but they were also well proportioned and had a monumental grandeur which has won them universal admiration.

There is no single Roman building which combines the best aspects of Roman architecture as the Parthenon embodies the Greek. As major achievements, we may cite the Pantheon, the Baths of Caracalla, the vaulted Basilica of Constantine, and the amphitheater of the Colosseum.

The Pantheon, Built during the Reign of Emperor Hadrian (117–138 A.D.). The creation of vast interior spaces was the greatest Roman engineering triumph. The Pantheon (Ill. 69) was the largest circular structure ever built until modern times,[6] and one of the most remarkable buildings in the world. Until Michelangelo built the dome of St. Peter's in Rome, the Pantheon was the largest interior without obstructing supports. It consists of an immense rotunda 142 feet in diameter and 140 feet high. Walls 20 feet thick support a hemispherical dome with a circular opening at the top 28 feet in diameter. This opening provides the only illumination. The single barrel-vaulted entrance has a huge bronze door, originally gilded. Niches of variegated marble within the thickness of the walls now contain altars; originally they were for statues of gods. Our section shows the interior as it was when it was first built. Each of the rectangular and coffered or re-

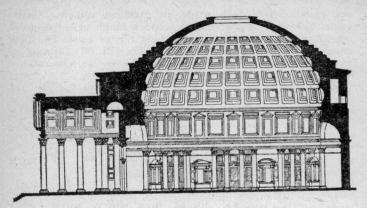

Ill. 69 Section of the Pantheon. *After Simpson* (*1929*)

cessed panels of the dome was once decorated with a bronze
rosette and with moldings in gilt stucco. The walls were lined
with rich marbles; the green porphyry and white marble at
the attic level has since been replaced with stucco. With
some exceptions, the decoration was applied to the brick walls
in the typical Roman manner of surface decoration. No other
type of decoration was possible; modern architecture separates structure from ornamentation in the same way.

The portico of the exterior (Fig. 42) was originally a gateway to the garden of Agrippa. It was partially salvaged to
become the front of Hadrian's new circular temple. The frieze
still contains the name of Agrippa, son-in-law of Augustus.

A model of the restored Pantheon (Fig. 42) gives an impression of its original splendor. The marble and granite columns with Pentelic marble capitals contrasted with the gleaming white marble stucco which covered the building. A sculptured and gilded four-horse chariot (quadriga) and other
statues were placed above the portico and in front of the low
dome. Sculpture also included the gilt bronze pedimental figures within the steep gable, and gilt bronze roofing tiles added
to the lavish effect of the exterior. Today the Pantheon, though
complete in structure, is disappointing in the exterior, like a
wedding cake without its frosting. Instead of being hemmed in
by buildings, as is the case today, the Pantheon stood in a
circular piazza. It was also raised seven or eight feet above
the pavement, whereas today one enters from street level.

The Empire had public baths in towns from the Rhine to
the Sahara, and from the Atlantic to the Persian Gulf. Hot
baths, as well as outdoor swimming pools and colonnaded

courts, were part of many bathing establishments. An elaborate system of wall and under-floor spaces and flues conducted the heat, and storage tanks provided water for warm and hot baths. To ingratiate themselves with the people, Titus, Domitian, Trajan, Caracalla, Diocletian and Constantine vied with each other to construct ever larger and more magnificent baths. The Baths of Diocletian, the ruins of which still occupy many city blocks in Rome, are said to have accommodated 3200 bathers. "Of ordinary baths such as those found in Pompeii, there are said to have been in Rome over eight hundred" (Anderson and Spiers). Paris, Trier (Germany), Bath (England), Timgad and Leptis Magna (North Africa), and other cities have remains of Roman baths, some of them rivaling those of Rome itself.

Baths of Emperor Caracalla (211–217 A.D.). The most famous Roman baths are those begun by Caracalla (212 A.D.) and completed by Alexander Severus (223 A.D.). Even the ruins, the most extensive in Rome, though now bare and roofless, are impressive. For an appreciation of the original we must turn to the restoration (Ill. 70 and Fig. 41).

The great central hall or *Tepidarium,* a kind of lounge, (Fig. 41 and 2 in Ill. 70), was the nucleus around which a variety of halls, open courts, niches, and hemicycles were related. A main axis through the swimming pool (1, *Frigidarium,* Ill. 70), the great hall, and the circular hot bath (9, *Caldarium,* Ill. 70) divides the block into two symmetrical parts. This block was raised on a platform 20 feet high, leaving space for furnaces and service areas underneath. We cannot be certain of the use of each room, but the restored plan suggests the function of almost every section. What are here labeled private baths (14, Ill. 70), others have interpreted as shops. The main block, exclusive of surrounding areas, was about the size of the Pennsylvania Railroad Station in New York City and larger than the House of Parliament in London. The *Caldarium* had a diameter of 116 feet and may have been domed; the *Tepidarium* consisted of three groined vaults (108 feet high) illuminated by clerestory windows above the roofs of adjoining halls. The thrust of the groin vaults was concentrated on huge monolithic granite columns (38 feet high and over 5 feet in diameter), and resisted by transverse walls behind carried as buttresses above the roof.

This system afforded an unencumbered spaciousness which neither the hypostyle halls of Egypt nor the temples of Greece possessed. The gilt-coffered vaults covered with ornamental stucco, the use of the Corinthian order, the panels of colored and white marble for wall facings, and the pictorial mosaic floors with figures of gladiators, athletes, and motifs from

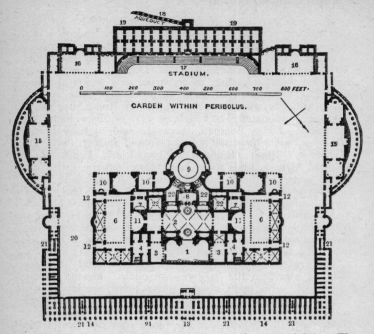

Ill. 70 Baths of Caracalla, plans. *After Anderson and Spiers,* The
Architecture of Greece and Rome (*1937*)

REFERENCES

1. Frigidarium.
2. Tepidarium.
3. Halls.
4. Apodyterium.
5. Ditto.
6. Peristyle Halls.
7. Hot Baths.
8. Antechamber
   or Laconicum.
9. Caldarium.
10. Special Baths for Athletes.
11. Hemicycles.
12. Entrance to Baths.
13. Principal Entrance of the Thermae.
14. Private Baths.
15. Lecture Rooms, Libraries, and Porticoes for Promenading.
16. Palestrae.
17. The Stadium.
18. The Marcian Aqueduct.
19. Reservoirs.
20. Ancient House discovered on Site.
21. Staircases to Private Baths.
22. Internal Courts.

mythology, must have produced an effect of unparalleled
splendor. Decoration was applied, but not entirely as a ve-
neer, as structural columns and entablatures were securely
built into the walls.

The *thermae,* or bathing establishments, were more than

baths; they were places for recreation. A Roman of the Empire could spend a day at one of several of the major thermae to attend lectures, play games, meet friends, or take a Turkish (sweat) bath, if he did not care for the more common ways of bathing, which were also available.

Basilica of Maxentius (306–312 A.D.*) and Emperor Constantine (316–337* A.D.*).* This building was begun by Maxentius, the rival of Constantine, but was completed by the latter, to become the first vaulted and fireproof basilica. In Roman times, basilicas served as law courts and places of business. The design repeated on a larger scale (325 feet by 85 feet) the Tepidarium halls of the thermae. Three groin vaults, originally 117 feet high, flanked by barrel-vaulted aisles, stand to this day. The decoration must have been in the style of the thermae. The monumental ruins were greatly admired by later architects and furnished inspiration for the building of the Church of St. Peter's.

The Colosseum. The Colosseum, the best-known ruin of the Empire, still retains much of its original appearance (Ill. 71). An amphitheater seating from 40,000 to 50,000 people, it was oval-shaped in plan, with four tiers of stone seats supported by stone piers and concrete vaults rising from the arena where the bloody gladiatorial combats took place. The network of cells, dens for wild animals, and underground passages are now visible. Though the Colos-

Ill. 71 Colosseum, Rome, cutaway view and façade. *After Lübke*

seum was for centuries used as a convenient source for building materials, a portion of the exterior travertine façade is left to show how the Roman orders, Doric, Ionic, Corinthian, were superimposed in three stories as engaged columns. Each order had a complete entablature and enclosed a round arch; in the Colosseum, the arched openings led to vaulted aisles and stairs. This scheme became so common that it received the name of the Roman arch order and became a part of the Western architectural tradition.

Triumphal arches and columns were another Roman contribution to Western architecture. Of the many arches which existed in Rome, the Arch of Titus (71–82 A.D.), the Arch of Septimus Severus in the Roman forum, and the Arch of Constantine near the Colosseum are still standing in good condition. Of these, the Arch of Titus is the simplest and best proportioned. The triumphal column of Trajan in Trajan's forum is of colossal size (140 feet high). It has a spiral band of reliefs winding around the shaft representing the Dacian (Rumanian) campaigns.

Roman temples were for statues of the gods, but they might also house statues of famous generals (*Mars Ultor*). They were not intended for congregations, and sometimes even functioned as public treasuries (*Temple of Saturn*) or as offices for weights and measures (*Temple of Castor and Pollux*). The finest of all, the *Temple of Venus and Roma*, was barrel-vaulted and had columns on all sides. The best-preserved temple, the *Maison Carrée*, is at Nîmes in southern France; it is raised on a platform, with a deep porch in the Etruscan manner and freestanding columns engaged on the sides. The *Maison Carrée* is as well proportioned as any Greek temple; it was admired by Thomas Jefferson and is thus related to the Classic Revival in the United States.

Roman architecture developed variations in Syria. At Palmyra streets were lined with porticoes of Corinthian columns. *The Great Temple of the Sun* at Baalbec, with its entrance portico, court, and great quadrangle, covered as much ground as the whole forum of Trajan. Under Greek influence, carving in Syria took on a flat surfacelike character.

Architectural Decoration. The Romans elaborated the Corinthian order: moldings were carved, the entablature was enriched with carved brackets called modillions and with rectangular blocks called dentils placed underneath the cornice (Fig. 43). The bell-shaped Corinthian capital was filled in with scrolls and foliage completely concealing the background. The Romans also added Ionic scrolls to the Corinthian capital above the rows of leaves, creating the "composite" capital. A heavily foliated scroll, carved in a continuous band for friezes and pilasters, was enriched with tendrils and rosettes. Figures, grotesques, griffins, vases, and masks were often combined with acanthus leaves, and festoons and eagles were used. These decorations were carved on marble and molded in stucco. Such stucco reliefs used on ceilings are among the most attractive creations of Roman art. A whole new category of ornamentation, varied and inventive, was created; it later furnished inspiration to Renaissance and modern art. The most common examples are the Roman architectural moldings (Ill. 72).

Reliefs. Pictorial reliefs were developed in Hellenistic centers, as in Alexandria, and continued during the period of the Empire. These reliefs are virtually pictures in stone, and were used for interior decoration of houses and public buildings. A scene from daily life, *A Peasant Driving a Cow* (Fig. 44) of the Augustan period (M. Bieber), is carved in high relief in the foreground and low relief in the background. The historical reliefs made for the *Altar of Peace* (*Ara Pacis*) in Rome represent official Roman state art. The altar was commissioned to commemorate the return of Augustus after he had "pacified Spain and Gaul." The carved panels represent the imperial family advancing toward the sacrificial scene held once a year in honor of the goddess of peace. Figures heavily robed in togas crowd the space to suggest figures standing in front of others that fade into the background (Florence, Uffizi). This suggestion of several planes in the relief to indicate depth, a Roman innovation, has been called "illusionism" (Franz Wickhoff). The heads are believed to be portraits; the figure with the toga slung over his head is Augustus, as high priest (Pontifex Maximus); he is followed by a child (Lucius) and Livia, his third wife. Realism did not extend to the children, who were made to look like miniature adults.

In the less formal design of another large relief (Fig. 45) from the *Ara Pacis,* the children on the lap of Mother Earth (Tellus) are like little chubby cupids. Behind her, a seated figure personifies water, another in front of her personifies air; together with fruits and vegetation, the group symbolizes nature's abundance. The carving of *Tellus* is in the tradition of the Parthenon pedimental figures; the two subordinated figures on a slightly smaller scale are a bit lifeless compared to the fine relaxation of the main group. The illusionist style was continued in the reliefs from the Arch of Titus, which was erected to commemorate the Palestinian campaign of 71 A.D. In one of the two reliefs, the table of the shewbreads and the seven-branched candlestick (Menorah) are represented as being carried from the Temple as trophies of war (Fig. 46).

Portrait Sculpture. The custom of keeping in the atrium of

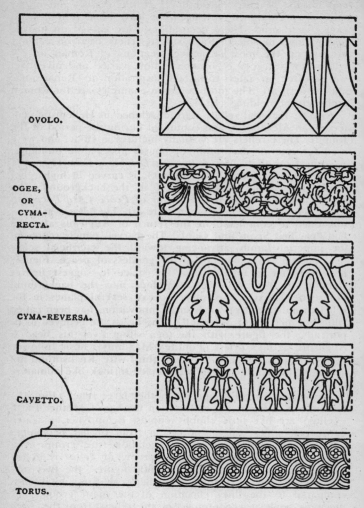

Ill. 72 Roman moldings and their ornamentation. *After G. W. Rhead* (1905)

the Roman house wax masks (*imagines*) of the ancestors encouraged a literal style in portrait sculpture (Fig. 47). This
style was supported by the realistic tradition of Etruscan

art. A realistic trend based on imitation of wax death masks was tempered by Greek idealism. The *Augustus of Prima Porta* (Vatican) shows an idealized Doryphoros-like pose. Barefooted and bareheaded, he stands with one foot advanced and with one arm raised, as if addressing his army. He wears an elaborately decorated cuirass. The miniature *Amor* on a dolphin at his feet is symbolic of Aphrodite, the goddess of love, to whom the imperial dynasty traced its origin. A portrait statue of a *Roman Lady* (Capitoline Museum) reclining in an armchair (Ill. 73) combines an easy, natural pose with a calm, contemplative dignity. The Hellenistic style shown in this statue was popular with Hadrian and his successors. *The Bronze Equestrian Statue of Marcus Aurelius*, restored and without its original base, now stands in Rome on the Square of the Capitol (Piazza del Campidoglio). Aurelius is seated on a massive horse with his arms outstretched, a gesture which has been interpreted, perhaps wrongly, as one of benevolence, a posture appropriate for

Ill. 73 Seated Roman lady, Capitoline Museum. *After Lübke*

the Stoic philosopher and author of the well-known *Meditations*. This work, ancestor to numerous equestrian statues of later periods, owes its preservation during the Middle Ages to the fact that it was believed to represent Constantine, the first Christian emperor.

The production of statues, heads, and busts of emperors and prominent citizens was an industry for which we have no close modern parallel. Every Roman of prominence was expected to have an image of the emperor in his house. Busts of women were made to provide movable hair, so as to be able to keep up with the changes of fashion. Statues without heads were turned out in quantity; trained artists were then commissioned to supply the individual heads. It became the fashion to have oneself represented as a god, for example as Apollo or Venus. Busts of gladiators and courtesans were placed in temples; those of scholars and playwrights, in public libraries and market places.

The wax mask favored a stark but lifeless realism (Fig. 47). Greek Hellenistic influence produced restrained but more lifelike portraits (Ill. 74), and the late period of the third century produced stylized heads which had large eyes with carved irises and hollowed-out pupils (Fig. 48).

Ill. 74 Agrippa, Louvre.
After Baumeister

Painting and Mosaics. What has been preserved in this field does not lack variety; portraits, figures, landscape, and still life are represented in subjects from mythology, the theater, and everyday life. This includes fresco wall decorations, paintings on marble panels, as well as wood panels of mummy cases found in quantities in Egypt. Mosaics were also used pictorially to suggest realistic paintings, using small tesserae in many colors (*opus vermiculatum*) to suggest gradations of form. The most famous is *The Battle of Alexander and Darius* (Fig. 49). It was probably imported from Alexandria or the Aegean Islands and laid as a pavement in Pompeii, in the House of the Faun.

The Pompeiian frescoes give a comprehensive impression of wall decoration as it had developed in four styles up to the year 79 A.D. The final stage is delicate and graceful, at times fantastic or seminaturalistic. Large background areas are painted in flat tones, chiefly vermilion, black, blue, and green. This "Pompeiian style" has influenced later periods in art, particularly in the United States.

The style of painting, to differentiate painted panels from architectural, shows an easy command of figure drawing, light and shade and a slight use of cast shadows. Depth is suggested by receding lines which simulate perspective, but are not scientifically correct. The walls seemingly open up through painted windows, through which one sees open courts and fanciful architectural structures of an open and airy appearance. The paintings are themselves set in panels within the painted decoration, which covers the entire wall. These panels are now in the Naples Museum, in Pompeii itself, and in Rome. The emphasis is on the figures; we should call the style decorative. As the technique is fresco, it could hardly be expected to attain the full visual effect of consistent illumination, which was only made possible after the introduction of oil painting. A well-known work is the *Aldobrandini Marriage,* named after its first owner, Cardinal Aldobrandini (Fig. 50). Discovered around 1605, it has long been admired and copied by such artists as Rubens, Van Dyck, and Poussin.

The individual heads from the Egyptian mummy cases came from a colony of Greeks in lower Egypt (Fayum). The technique is impressionistic in the thick surface of paint. The pigments were mixed with wax and set by passing a hot iron over the painting. In this encaustic wax process, the heads are broadly modeled in light and shade, have large dark expressive eyes, and appear to be portraits of individuals (Fig. 52).

Conclusion. Roman art has achievements in its own right, independent of its Greek heritage. Four centuries of comparatively peaceful development had led to great wealth in the hands of a few. This concentration of power, based on slave labor, made possible an unprecedented artistic development. No modern city compares architecturally with the magnificence of imperial Rome.

The decline of the Empire is revealed in what happened to the city of Rome and the surrounding *campagna.* Deterioration set in by the fourth century; the barbarian invasions only contributed to the total destruction, which was largely brought on by the Romans themselves. The temples were neglected after the introduction of Christianity; columns and capitals were removed individually as needed in Christian basilicas. Marble of every kind, including much sculpture, was burned in the lime kilns merely to provide raw materials for new construction. Practically every pagan public building was converted; the Colosseum bristled with churches before it was finally ruined in an earthquake in the fourteenth century. Even so, an individual building like the Temple of Concord was not destroyed until the Renaissance. Eventually Rome was reduced to the status of a provincial town of 20,-000 inhabitants. In the once proud Roman forum, where senators and emperors had settled the affairs of the world, cattle grazed among the ruins.

CHAPTER VI

Early Christian
and Byzantine Art:
100 A.D. - 1453 A.D.

Historical Background. As Christianity spread through Europe in the centuries after Constantine, the classic art of antiquity became the Christian art of the Middle Ages. The Church inherited the classical civilization and gave art a Christian content, but changed the style only very gradually. The millennium between 300 and 1300, between the disintegration of Roman art and the culmination of the Gothic, is the period of medieval art. The new styles, which grew up beyond the Alps as well as in Italy, reflected the integration of these more primitive people into the advanced culture of Rome. A result of this contact of the still undeveloped Teutonic culture with classic civilization was the so-called "Carolingian Renaissance" of Charlemagne (771–814), who temporarily united the various Frankish tribes under one ruler. The beginning of the Romanesque style after 1000 A.D., some 700 years after Constantine, in countries which had once been Roman provinces, brought the newly emerging nations of France, Germany, and Britain into the forefront of Western art. The intervening period is in the nature of a bridge from Roman to Romanesque art rather than a void between periods, though the centuries between 500 and 800 are commonly referred to as the Dark Ages. Even so, this slowing down of cultural development was not so much of a break in tradition as the period that separated Mycenaean from classical Greek art.

Though all medieval art is Christian, the term Early Christian is applied to the early centuries, particularly the period in Rome and Italy from 300 to 800. Byzantine art is the Christian art of the Near East. After the death of

Emperor Theodosius, the Roman world was divided into a western and an eastern empire (395 A.D.); in 476 A.D. the western (Italy) came to an end, but the eastern continued until it was overthrown by the Turks in 1453. In 330 A.D. Constantine renamed Byzantium "Constantinople" and made it his capital; this city was the great cultural and artistic center of Christianity up to the time of the Renaissance. Byzantine art grew out of the same background as Early Christian art, and at times can hardly be separated from it. The contributions absorbed from the eastern provinces of the Empire, fused with a classic heritage, eventually gave Byzantine art an individuality of its own.

The Art of the Catacombs. Christianity became the state religion (313 A.D.); the ancient gods no longer satisfied the religious needs of the age. The Christian emphasis on the immaterial world of the spirit gave art a new meaning, but not a new style. This is evident in the painted decorations of the Christian subterranean burial places, or catacombs, of Rome. Catacombs occur elsewhere, but those in Rome are the most famous. The use of such underground galleries, some 550 miles of cemeteries barely a yard wide cut out of the tufa along the highways, was not peculiar to the Christians, but an oriental custom. Concealment was not their purpose; the plots were reserved for burials and served as places of refuge only during periods of persecution. Shafts opening up to the surface provided some light, though lamps were used. Catacomb burials declined after Constantine and ceased during the first quarter of the fifth century.

The style of the early fresco decorations of the first half of the second century is in the manner of the fourth style of Pompeian wall decoration. These architectural decorations, for the most part painted ceilings, continued with variations of style during the centuries before Constantine.

As the Christians were interested in the soul's salvation after death, they were not disposed to introduce into their tomb paintings that fullness of life represented by classical art. Considering the poor illumination and the fact that these paintings were rarely seen, almost any picture that conveyed the idea might have been deemed acceptable. As paintings were looked upon as visual prayers rather than as works of art, they could be sketchy. We need not assume that the early Christians were always poor people who had to be satisfied with mediocre paintings, or that the style of the catacomb paintings reflects a general decline of Roman painting. Certain stories from the Old and New Testaments that were developed during later periods are present in a simplified form in the catacomb paintings. A painted fresco of the mother

and child motif suggests the involved compositon of Raphael's
Madonna of the Chair.

We may use the catacomb of *S. Lucina* as an example of
the Christian modification of Pompeian decoration. We must
look to the corner figures representing a beardless young
man carrying a lamb on his shoulders (Ill. 75) and a woman

Ill. 75 Ceiling painting, catacomb of S. Lucina,
Rome, detail. *After Springer (1898)*

with uplifted arms. The former is the symbol of the good
shepherd of the Twenty-third Psalm, who leads his sheep
"through the valley of the shadow of death," and the shepherd of the parable (Luke 15:4-6), who finds the lost sheep
and "layeth it on his shoulders, rejoicing," and Christ Himself, the "good shepherd" who "giveth his life for the sheep."
The female figure is the symbol of the soul. Her uplifted
hands represent the Biblical expression for the attitude of
prayer, called orant by archaeologists. This attitude was used
in one of the early relief carvings of the crucifixion on the
doors of Santa Sabina in Rome (*c.* 432 A.D.). A realistic representation was avoided, as this form of punishment, reserved for criminals, was popularly held to be shameful. The
ridicule to which the early Christians were subjected is illustrated by a drawing (second century) substituting an ass's
head in the crucifixion, inscribed "Alexaminos adores his
God."

Ill. 76 Sarcophagus of Junius Bassus, Vatican. *After Lübke*

Catacomb paintings do not represent events fully and in all details; they refer to stories that were well known and could be reduced to a figure or two or to an emblem. The ship symbolized Christ (Ill. 77), the anchor, hope (Ill. 78). The dove stood for the soul and, being a bird, follows familiar symbolism used before the Christian era. Other symbols were the palm branch for victory, the grapevine for Christ, and the peacock for immortality. These are a few of the many symbols common to early Christian and later medieval iconography.

Symbols appear in their typical form also on terra-cotta and bronze lamps and on glass, which had become plentiful by the fourth century. The bottoms of the so-called gold glass plates found in the catacombs show symbolic figures engraved in a film of gold, protected by a layer of glass. A married couple (Ill. 79) appears in a center medallion with the words of a toast "Drink! Live!" These were probably household dishes, the bottoms of which were left pressed into the stucco as memorials or for identification. The figures are posed to illustrate a particular miracle or scene: the raising of Lazarus, Adam and Eve, the sacrifice of Isaac. Subjects like these were commonly used and have been related to later funeral liturgies that deal with Biblical descriptions of divine deliverance from death. The thought seems to be

that almighty God, who had wrought miracles, could also be
relied on to deliver the soul from death.

Sculpture. After catacomb burials declined, elaborately
carved marble sarcophagi were used for wealthy Christians,
not only in Italy, but also in France, Spain, and other countries. Some 500 have been preserved in Rome, around 300 in
France. Several styles used in cosmopolitan Rome are believed

Ill. 77 (*upper left*) A ship, engraved gem. *After British Museum Guide* (*1921*)
Ill. 78 (*upper right*) Anchor, fish and dove, engraved
gem. *After British Museum Guide* (*1921*)

to have been introduced from eastern centers like Alexandria,
Antioch, and others in Asia Minor. The carving itself was
most likely executed in Roman shops, as in the sarcophagus
used for Junius Bassus, a Roman consul (d. 359 A.D.). The
carved front shows two rows of five niches each; in our
illustration (Ill. 76) only the central niche and the two on
the right side of the center are included. In the upper left
niche, a beardless Christ hands the Gospel to St. Peter or St.
Paul in the so-called *traditio legis.* Representing an advanced
stage of sculptural development, the carving is elaborate and
conveys the meaning of each episode.

A type of sarcophagus more in the Eastern spirit of Byzantine art was made in Ravenna during the fifth century, as in
that of St. Theodore (Fig. 53). Monograms of Christ within
wreaths are carved as ornamental reliefs on the rounded lid,
and on the front are symbolic peacocks and grapevines. The
two monograms in the center of lid and front are formed
by the first two letters of the Greek word for Christ, the
chi and *rho* (*ch* and *r*). The alpha and omega, first and
last letters of the Greek alphabet, to the expression "I am
Alpha and Omega, the beginning and the ending, said the
Lord . . ." (Rev. 1:8-11; *see also,* Rev. 21:6; 22:13). The
monogram within a wreath was the imperial emblem the Em-

peror Constantine used at the top of his standard (*labarum*).

Except for sarcophagi, there was less need for religious sculpture in early Christian art. Some works probably existed, but have not been preserved. The best known type of half life-size statue represents the Good Shepherd and was probably taken over from the catacomb paintings. Of ten known statues, the best one (Lateran Museum) represents the figure with lamb and milk pail on a sling, executed with classic dignity. The Christian emperors continued the custom of having themselves represented in life-size statues.

Architecture. The early Christian church or basilica was the only new type of building which resulted from the recognition of Christianity. The Christian basilica was probably the solution to a new problem; housing a congregation for a religious service. Such buildings had not existed before; the Roman temple had furnished the god (statue) with shelter, the altar outside the temple provided sustenance (sacrifice).

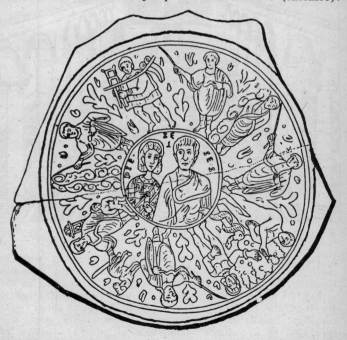

Ill. 79 Healing of the paralytic, raising of Lazarus, Adam and Eve, the sacrifice of Isaac, the water from the rock. *Courtesy Lowrie*, Monuments of the Early Church, *Macmillan (1901)*

Ill. 80 San Clemente, nave, Rome. *After Springer* (*1898*)

The large monumental hall of the law courts with its
semicircular apse is repeated in the plan of the religious
basilica; the atrium of the Roman house is repeated in the
atrium of the basilica, a forecourt with a central fountain
for Baptism. The early churches built by Constantine were
rectangular halls in which a central nave (*navis,* ship) was
separated by colonnades from side aisles. The *basilica of
San Clemente* in Rome still shows the original interior arrangement (Ill. 80). The high navè walls resting on the

Fig. 69 Ornamental page with Madonna and Child, Book of Kells. *Courtesy Trinity College, Dublin University, and "The Studio" Ltd.*

Fig. 70 Basilica of S. Ambrogio, nave, Milan. *Alinari*

Fig. 71 Cathedral and Campanile, Pisa. *Brogi*

Fig. 72 Carving from Oseberg ship find. *Courtesy Oslo University Museum*

Fig. 73 Durham Cathedral from north-west. *Marburg*

Fig. 74 Christ in Majesty, Catalonian fresco from church of S. Maria de Mur. *Boston Museum of Fine Arts.*

Fig. 75 Saint Gregory with Three Scribes, ivory book cover, West German, ninth-tenth century. *Courtesy Kunsthistorisches Museum, Vienna. Photograph, National Gallery of Art*

Fig. 76 Utrecht Psalter, Psalm CVII, (108), section. *Courtesy E. T. De-Wald,* The Illustrations of the Utrecht Psalter, *Princeton University Press (1932)*

Fig. 77 The Fleet Crossing the Channel, Bayeux tapestry, section.
Archives Photographiques

Fig. 78 Gold and jeweled book cover, ninth century A.D. *Courtesy Pierpont Morgan Library, New York City*

Fig. 79 St. Luke in Ecstasy, manuscript illustration. *Courtesy Staats Bibliothek, Munich*

Fig. 80 Adam and Eve, Exultet Rolls. *Copyright British Museum*

Fig. 81 Chalice of Abbot Suger, St. Denis, sardonyx, *c.* 1140. *National Gallery of Art, Widener Collection, 1942*

Fig. 82 Expulsion scene from bronze door of Hildesheim Cathedral. *Courtesy Inter Nationes (Bonn) and Stoedtner*

Fig. 83 Antellami: The Descent from the Cross, Parma Cathedral, 1178. *Alinari*

Fig. 84 *Maiestas Domini,* south portal, church of St. Pierre, Moissac. *Stoedtner*

Fig. 85 Bronze crucifix from Werden, Lower Saxony, eleventh century. *Courtesy Inter Nationes (Bonn) and Bavarian National Museum*

Fig. 86 Guglielmo: Creation and Fall of Man, relief, Modena Cathedral, 1099. *Alinari*

Fig. 87 Cathedral of Notre Dame, west facade, Paris. *Archives Photographiques*

Fig. 88 Cathedral of Chartres, west facade. *Courtesy French Government Tourist Office*

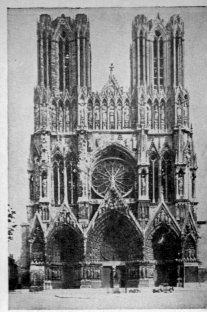

Fig. 89 Cathedral of Chartres, rose window, nave. *Courtesy French Government Tourist Office*

Fig. 90 Cathedral of Rheims, west facade. *Courtesy French Government Tourist Office*

Fig. 91 Cathedral of Amiens, nave. *Clarence Ward*

Fig. 92 Cathedral of Amiens, vault of choir. *Clarence Ward*

Fig. 93 Cathedral of Amiens, west façade. *The Sargent Co.*

Fig. 94 Cathedral of Coutances, west facade. *Archives Photographiques*

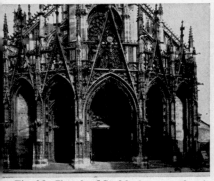

Fig. 95 Church of St. Maclou, west façade, Rouen. *Archives Photographiques*

Fig. 96 Exeter Cathedral, nave. *Courtesy Central Office of Information, London*

Fig. 97 King's College Chapel, Cambridge. *Marburg*

Fig. 98 Gloucester Cathedral, cloisters, fan vaults. *Courtesy Judges Ltd., Hastings, England*

Fig. 99 Henry VII Chapel, Westminster Abbey. *Courtesy British Information Services*

Fig. 100 Cathedral of Halle, nave. *Stoedtner*

colonnades had clerestory windows above the side aisles. A semicircular vaulted apse at one end with a marble bench provided seats for the clergy, with a chair or throne in the center for the bishop. As the clergy came to require more space, a slightly projecting transept (bema) was added. The altar in front of the apse was placed over the tomb of the martyr to whom the basilica was dedicated. The tomb itself was in a crypt on a lower level. Four columns supported a marble canopy (ciborium or baldachino) over the altar. Space in front of the altar, reserved for the officiating clergy, was enclosed by a marble railing. Two pulpits (ambones) on the sides completed the built-in church furniture, all of marble and enhanced by colored marble mosaic.

The total interior effect is well illustrated in the *basilica of St. Paul (San Paolo fuori le mura)*. It was built by Theodosius in 386, but was destroyed by fire in 1823. In its restored condition, it is one of the most impressive churches in Rome. Unlike the classic temple, the Christian basilica developed the interior and left the exterior unadorned. The colonnades, diminishing in perspective, concentrated attention on the altar; the nave arcade shows Corinthian columns supporting arches in the late Roman manner rather than horizontal architraves. The space above the colonnade and below the clerestory, the triforium, was reserved for colored mosaics, as well as the space above the triumphal arch which terminated the nave. The open timber ceiling showing the trussed roof construction was at times enclosed by an ornate ceiling. The effect was one of colored surface and airy spaciousness varied through the views that unfold through the openings of the colonnades, one behind the other in the five-aisled basilica. Such an expansion of view was well suited to the spirit of the Christian religion, which addressed itself to all people everywhere and also focused on heaven and eternity (Ill. 81).

From the point of view of structure, a lightly constructed hall with a wooden roof was no rival of the groin-vaulted basilica which Constantine completed. The more laborious and more expensive vaulted construction was avoided, probably because new structures were in immediate demand. Constantine himself built two large and splendid basilicas in Rome: St. Peter's, which is no longer standing, and St. John Lateran which has been so altered as to be unrecognizable. Constantine's basilicas were built of new materials, but later basilicas made use of materials taken from pagan buildings *(San Lorenzo fuori le mura)*. Eventually basilicas and subsequent churches were oriented to face the west, the apse being at the east in the direction of Palestine.

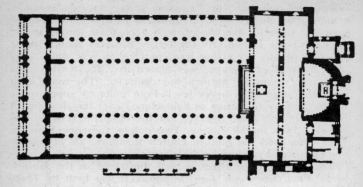

Ill. 81 S. Paolo fuori le mura, plan, Rome.

Mosaics. The apse of the basilica became the favored place for mosaic decoration. Christ, bearded following the Eastern (Syrian) custom and surrounded by his disciples, appears seated in the manner of an emperor on a throne in the apse of the fourth century *church of Santa Pudenziana* in Rome (Ill. 82). The background shows buildings which no longer exist; the empty cross is a symbol of death and sacrifice; the whole scene was meant to suggest heavenly Jerusalem. Two women with wreaths may be allegories of the Christian church and the Jewish synagogue or they may be the daughters of Pudens, who donated the church. The symbols of the evangelists from Revelation appear in the sky as winged half-figures: Matthew as angel, Mark as lion, Luke as ox, and John as eagle. This is believed to be the earliest appearance of these symbols in art. The background suggests space, the draped figures, rounded form; the style is pictorial, reminiscent of classic art. Even though the mosaics have been altered and restored, the general effect is probably original. Since mosaics received their most elaborate development in Byzantine art, we shall return to them in connection with that style.

The Byzantine Style. Byzantine art was controlled by religion more rigidly and for a longer period than any subsequent style in the history of Western art. The Church determined the subjects and prescribed rules as to how they were to be given visual expression. The unreal and visionary character of Byzantine art at its best was due to the influence of the Church, whereas the splendor and refinement directed its appeal to the cultivated tastes of court and nobility.

Until fairly recently, critics of Byzantine art looked upon it as lifeless and static, not unlike Egyptian art. Both styles have in common duration and inflexibility—in both cases more apparent than real—based on a belief in immortality. To change the style of works of art that were considered sacred would have seemed impious. Such feelings encouraged a conservative spirit and a disinclination to experiment. Art was limited in its capacity to suggest the spiritual; dematerialization could go only so far, particularly as the human figure and occasional motifs from both nature and the man-made world had to be introduced to tell the story of the Gospel. Lofty domes encrusted with mosaics of sacred images on a gold ground represented ultimate achievements. Also, since Byzantine art included all countries of the eastern Mediterranean and used different materials and techniques, some variations were unavoidable. External conditions of the Empire hardly affected the style, but only provided greater wealth for the enrichment of art. The individual styles of great artists made themselves felt in artistic quality rather than in easily recognizable differences. Names of painters are known from the late period, when signatures appeared. In the last period, the stories of the Gospel were interpreted realistically; a change of the religious spirit vivified content, but did not greatly change style (D. Talbot Rice). In the course of a long history even a religious art did not remain static.

Origins. Of the several elements that fused in the formation of Byzantine art, a Hellenistic trend can be differentiated

Ill. 82 Christ enthroned in the New Jerusalem, mosaic, S. Pudenziana, Rome. *After Springer (1898)*

from an Eastern one. The Hellenistic made for delicacy and
for idealization in the treatment of the figure. The frontal
pose, a trend to realism to denote strength, and an emphasis
on the head, as in the representation of Christ, came from
the Syrian East. The dome on a square plan and a non-
representational element in relief carving have been linked
to northern Persia (Altai-Iran) and to silks, ceramics, and
metalwork derived from southern Persia and Mesopotamia.
Byzantine architecture, sculpture, and decoration were also
influenced by Rome, Italy, and Asia Minor.

Periods. The first two centuries of Byzantine art after the
transfer of the capital to Constantinople were a period of
formation. This was followed in the sixth century by the
first Golden Age under Justinian (527–565 A.D.). Here belong
two major achievements, the building of the Church of the
Holy Wisdom (Hagia Sophia) and the codification of Roman
Law, Corpus Juris Civilis. Between 717 and 843, the period
of iconoclasm (image breaking), no representation of the Divine was permitted in religious art. This resulted in an increase of Eastern influence, which favored floral and geometric motifs and emphasized texture and color. A second
Golden Age included the period from the end of iconoclasm
(843) to the Latin conquest of Constantinople (1204) in connection with the fourth crusade. Existing mosaics, ivories,
textiles, and metalwork, including enamels, are mostly from
this period, as similar works from the first Golden Age had
been destroyed during the iconoclastic period. A late period
under the dynasty of the Palaeologi (1261–1453), the "Byzantine Renaissance," produced mosaics and mural painting of a more lively, pictorial spirit. Those of the small
church of *Kahrieh Djami* (Constantinople) are stylistically related to Italian art.

Meanwhile, the Russians had accepted Christianity with
the conversion of Vladimir of Kiev (989). Byzantine art,
orthodox Christianity, and the concept of sovereignty by
divine right in the image of the Byzantine emperor spread
to Russia. (For the expansion of Byzantine art to Russia and
its development in subsequent periods, the reader is referred
to recent publications in English mentioned in the Bibliography.)

Architecture. Byzantine architecture was chiefly ecclesias-
tical, though the city walls and the vaulted cisterns supported
on columns (1001 columns in the cistern of Bin-bir-direk) of
Constantinople were vast engineering structures, and the Imperial Palace was a number of pavilions, rather than a single
structure. The basilica was developed on a central plan
which might be octagonal (San Vitale, Ravenna), circular
(Aix-la-Chapelle or Aachen), a near square (Santa Sophia),

or the shape of a Greek cross. The church on a central plan
prevailed during the second Golden Age, and produced many
small stone churches like the *Little Metropolis Church* at
Athens (*c.* 1150), which measures only 25 by 38 feet. Some
highly original churches carried the stone into the roof tiles
over the central dome, which was raised to appear externally
as a low tower (Akthamar). All emphasize the vertical axis
around a central dome, as at Hagia Sophia. In the Greek
cross plan, each of the four arms of the cross has a lower
dome of its own not externally visible in small churches. The
plan of the Church of the Holy Apostles in Constantinople
was imitated in the churches of St. Mark's (1063–1071) in
Venice and St. Front at Periguex (1120) in southern France.

Byzantine architecture received its most monumental expression in Constantinople in the Hagia Sophia founded by
Constantine, wholly reconstructed by Justinian in 532, and
dedicated with impressive ceremonies in 537. Anthemius of
Thralles and Isidorus of Miletus were the architects. Architecturally its dome on a square plan (Ill. 83 and 84) marks an
advance over the Pantheon dome on a circular plan. The
lightly constructed dome rests on four massive piers (Ill. 83)
carried across the vaulted aisles on arches. The piers or buttresses and arches are shown in the section (Ill. 83), and the
arches appear on the interior as well as on the exterior

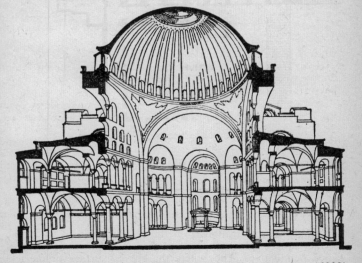

Ill. 83 Hagia Sophia, section, Istanbul. *After Simpson* (*1929*)

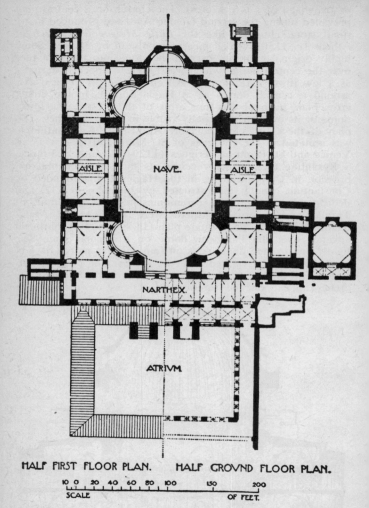

Ill. 84 Hagia Sophia, plan, Istanbul. *After Simpson* (1929)

(Fig. 54). The transition from the circular base of the dome to the square plan is accomplished by spherical triangles called pendentives. They carry the curved surface of the less than semicircular dome to the points from which the arches spring. The exterior is left undecorated, though slender towers

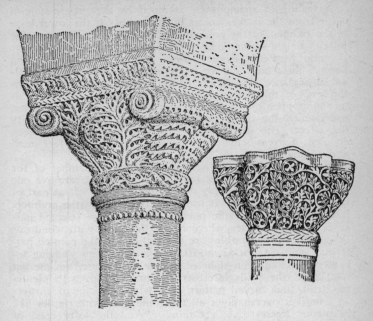

Ill. 85 Capital, Hagia So-phia, Istanbul. *After Moore*

Ill. 86 Capital, San Vitale, Ra-venna. *After Simpson* (*1929*)

(minarets) built by the Turks improve the effect. The interior was sumptuously decorated with veined marble slabs and glass mosaics above the ground story.

Monolithic columns from classic buildings were imported; columns of dark green variegated (*vert antique*) marble were used in the nave arcade, columns of Egyptian porphyry, in the niches. The Roman entablature with its projecting mem-bers and heavily carved moldings developed into flat bands. Arches rise directly from a basket-shaped capital; a delicate pattern of shallow, crisp carving, suggesting acanthus and floral motifs, covers the surface of the capital and stands out, light against dark (Ill. 85 and 86). This style of Byzan-tine carving recalls a type of lacelike surface carving in Syria, as in a section of a frieze from Mschatta (Berlin Mu-seum), where this section formed part of a now ruined palace wall (fourth to seventh century). Windows in the side walls and at the base of the dome furnish illumination, and a varied grouping of columns, arches, and niches produce a contrast of light and deep shadow.

A feeling of spaciousness is aided by the progression of color from the darker colors in the marble at the lower level to the richness of the gold-covered vaults above. Even so, the interior height of the dome (180 feet) is exceeded by the later domes of St. Peter (Rome) and St. Paul's (London). In Hagia Sophia, the whole interior in its majestic simplicity is apparent at a glance. The height of the columns above and below the level of the gallery is kept to a modest scale. This adds to the impression of height, climaxed by the huge arches, over which the dome flows in a gentle curvature to unify the effect. The grandeur of this interior has never been equaled; it overwhelms the individual, making him feel small and insignificant.

Paul the Silentiary, a court official and a member of the literary circle of Emperor Justinian, recited a descriptive ode on Hagia Sophia, probably within the church itself as part of the opening ceremony. It translates the ideas of the architect into the language of the poet. Here are a few selected passages: *Atrium:* "Everywhere the walls glitter with wondrous designs. . . . The marbles are cut and joined like painted patterns . . ."; *Carved Spandrils:* ". . . the mason weaving together with skill thin slabs of marble, has figured on the flat surface of the walls intertwining curves laden with plenteous fruit, and curved pattern of a winding chain of clusters . . . until it overshadows all the stone near with ripples like beauteous tresses . . ."; *Capitals:* "And the lofty crest of every column, beneath the marble abacus, is covered with many a supple curve of waving acanthus—a wandering chain of barbed points all golden, full of grace . . ."; *Mosaic:* "Now the vaulting is formed of many little squares of gold cemented together. And the golden stream of glittering rays pours down and strikes the eyes of men, so that they can scarcely bear to look. One might say that one gazed upon the midday sun in spring, what time he glides each mountain height . . ."; *Altar:* "And on columns of gold is raised the all gold slab of the holy table, standing on gold foundations, and bright with the glitter of different stones . . ."; *Lighting:* "No words can describe the light at nighttime; one might say in truth that some midnight sun illumined the glories of the temple . . . long twisted chains of beaten brass come together as they fall towards the ground . . . and finish in unison on a circle. And beneath each chain he has fitted silver discs, hanging circlewise in the air . . . these discs, pendent from their lofty courses, form a coronet above the heads of men . . . pierced by skillful workmen that they may receive shafts of firewrought glass and hold light on high for men at night. . . . And whoever gazes on the lighted trees with their crown of circles feels his heart warmed with joy . . . all care vanishes from the mind . . . the whole heaven, scattered with glittering stars, opens before them, while the night seems to smile on their way."

Iconography. As the representative arts expanded in mosaics, mural painting, book illustration, ivories, and enamels, certain prescribed types were adhered to for Christ, the Virgin, angels, prophets, apostles, and evangelists. The earlier classic representation of Christ, youthful and beardless, was replaced by a more aged type with long hair, black beard, and yellowish skin. This grave and solemn Christ was meant as a realistic representation of a man typical of Palestine. After the Council of Ephesus (431 A.D.) had proclaimed the Virgin Mary mother of God (*Theodokos*), she was represented in art between the sixth and twelfth centuries with an oval face and a serious expression. Several attitudes were used: (1) standing, holding the Child in her left arm, her right held out in prayer, known as *The Hodegetria* (she who points the way); (2) standing, holding the Child close, *The Kyriotissa* (mistress); (3) bust length, arms raised as an orant, *The Blachernitissa* (named after a church in Constantinople); (4) standing as an orant without Child; (5) seated on a throne, holding the Child on her knees or blessing (Fig. 55); (6) nursing the Child. These types were repeated without change. A long white beard and bald head became standard for St. Paul, a short beard defined St. Peter; long curly hair and black beard, St. John the Baptist; archangels took on the elaborate armor of Roman emperors. Blue and cherry-red were used for Christ, at times combined with gold; blue and claret-red for St. Paul, yellow and light blue for St. Peter, and blue for the Virgin. By the sixth century, the representations of the Annunciation, the Adoration of the Magi, the Baptism, the Ascension, and other stories from the Gospels had received their definitive form in the mosaics of the sanctuaries of Palestine. Through the influence of the pilgrims who visited the Holy Land from the West, the topics represented in Palestine were accepted for Christian art everywhere.

Mosaics. Color, the use of gold grounds, luminosity, and flatness are characteristic of mosaics. The surface of wall mosaics is slightly uneven, depending on how each colored glass or mother-of-pearl tessera is imbedded in the mortar. With colors ranging from light to dark, variations in the reflection of light produce a glitter, increased in the curved surfaces of apses and domes, which accounts for the luminous quality of mosaics. Mural paintings, sometimes referred to as frescoes, were cheaper substitutes for mosaics, and on occasion mosaics replaced earlier paintings. Except for differences of techniques, the styles are basically the same. Only the religious mosaics have been preserved; there were also secular mosaics, but they no longer exist except in the Palace at Palermo (Sicily).

Mosaics are as important for Byzantine art as sculpture is for Greek art or painting, for the art of the Renaissance. Wall mosaics were used in churches to "glorify God by beautifying His home" (D. T. Rice), to instruct the illiterate, and to add to the total splendor of the service. Some well-known Byzantine mosaics are located in Santa Pudenziana and other churches at Rome, at Ravenna (Italy), in Hagia Sophia and the Church of Kahrieh Djami (Istanbul), in the churches of the monastery of St. Luke at Stiris (Phocis, Greece), at Daphni (near Athens), at Torcello, and in St. Mark's (Venice), in the cathedrals of Cefalù, Monreale, and the Palatine Chapel (Palermo) and elsewhere (arranged approximately in chronological order). Mosaics were commonly used between the fifth and eleventh centuries; they were replaced by wall paintings in Constantinople, in Yugoslavia, at Mistra (Greece), in Russia, and in other places.

Ravenna. A sense of classic naturalism is retained in the rocks, shrubs, woolly sheep and the informal posture of the youthful Christ, holding a cross, symbolized as the royal Good Shepherd in the lunette of the *Tomb of Galla Placidia* (404–450 A.D.). The symbolic meaning is indicated by the sheep turning their heads toward the shepherd. The deep blue mosaic vault overhead, interspersed with designs, suggests the glittering "tent" of the heavens. These are among the best and most complete of the early mosaic decorations.

No indication of space remains in the mosaics in the *basilica of Sant' Apollinare Nuovo,* completed by Justinian after he had reconquered Ravenna from the Ostrogothic King Theodoric. The side walls between the clerestory windows and nave arcade are covered to a height of ten feet with mosaics in broad expanses of green, gilt, and white, treated as flat-surface decoration. On one side, a frieze of female martyrs (Fig. 56), led by the Three Kings bearing gifts, advance toward the Virgin and the Child enthroned between guardian angels. Each martyr, in a long-sleeved, bejeweled costume, carries her crown of martyrdom in her hands, displaying it like a treasure against the background of her white veil. Palm trees and lilies, symbols of immortality and of victory over death, separate the figures. On the other side, male martyrs in white dalmatics advance toward the enthroned Christ. The elongated figures face to the front; the men are of sturdy build and have individualized heads; the women, graceful in their flowing costumes, show less rigid postures. The uniformity of dress was meant to indicate that all are equal before God (André Grabar).

The best known of all mosaics are those of the choir of *San Vitale* (540–548 A.D.). From vault to pavement, in a closely woven pattern chiefly of green, purple, and delicate grays, mosaics and veined marble slabs cover every surface. The decoration of floral motifs, acanthus scrolls, medallions, and figures conveys a sense of an over-all preciousness, as a radiance of color from every direction envelops the beholder. The aisle windows admit daylight, which reflects from vaults and walls as a warm glow and makes a luminous background for the dimmed choir. Unlike the reasoned clarity of the Parthenon or the grandeur of Hagia Sophia, the mosaics of San Vitale depend on an effect of color, based on an insistent and all-embracing continuity of mosaic and marble encrustation (Fig. 57).

Two panels achieved world renown. One represents Emperor Justinian, church dignitaries, and a palace guard (Fig. 58) as standing within the sanctuary of San Vitale (Otto von Simson), on the right side of Christ in the apse, and Empress Theodora and her court ladies about to enter on the left side. Each sovereign bears a bowl of gold as a votive offering to the church. The halos around their heads are emblems of power used in Roman art for gods and emperors. In Christian art halos became marks of sanctity for Christ, the Virgin, and the saints. Theodora's headdress gleams with gold and mother of pearl, the border of her gown shows the Three Magi, indicating that, like the Magi, the royal court also brings gifts to Christ. The slightly larger than life-size elongated figures merge in a tapestrylike pattern, though it is not necessary to look upon mosaics as imitation of textiles. Flat and "dematerialized," they seem to float in the air; they are above reality, and thus closer to the divine. The heads, treated as portraits, indicate that the mosaics are historic, hence very real in their imperial authority. Standing, an imperial couple is crowned by Christ (ivory of Romanus II and Eudoxia); kneeling before the throne of Christ, Leo VI receives holy wisdom (mosaic at Hagia Sophia). The Emperor receives directly from God both authority to rule and wisdom.

In the vault of the apse, Christ appears seated on a sphere between angels, about to present the martyr Saint Vitalis with a crown. Bishop Ecclesius stands by with a model of the church for presentation to Christ. Beneath the apse stood the altar, which was concealed in orthodox churches by the *Ikonstasis,* a screen shutting off the sanctuary from the nave. The ever-recurring celebrations of the Mass, symbolic of Christ's sacrificial death, are related to other choir mosaics representing a sacred repast from the Old Testament in Abraham entertaining the Angels, and the idea of sacrifice in

Abraham sacrificing Isaac. The basic theme of the San Vitale mosaics is the redemption of mankind through Christ, the triumph over death through sacrifice (Grabar André). The emperor and his court unite with Christ, the Ruler of the universe, and His saints in a ceremonial ensemble. Art is here a visual expression of the imperial doctrine supplementing the dogma of the Church by placing Emperor and Church as equals under Christ, the Supreme Ruler. In honoring God, Justinian here sets himself a memorial and affirms his authority in associating himself with Christ. The Byzantine emperor considered himself "the Chosen of God, His Vicar on Earth"; he was "God inspired, prince equal to the apostles" (Charles Diehl, 1957). Gudea of Lagash was on intimate terms with his god, the kings of Egypt were raised to divinity after death, and the exalted grandeur of the oriental rulers is brought out in these mosaics.

Hagia Sophia. The mosaics of the dome postdate the otherwise contemporary and iconographically more elaborate mosaics of San Vitale. They owe their effectiveness to the simplicity of the design of huge, well-proportioned crosses against the vast expanse of gold ground. Other mosaics were gradually added, independently of each other, as ex-votos, or thank offerings, made to repay a fulfilled vow for divine or saintly favors. These mosaics, formerly plastered over by the Turks, have been restored only recently under the direction of the late Thomas Whittemore. Their arrangement in the main body of the church became customary after Hagia Sophia; Christ in the dome as *Pantocrator* (Ruler of all), the Virgin in the apse, and prophets and saints on the nave walls represented in frontal poses on a gold ground. The figure of St. John Chrystostom (tenth century), in white relieved by blue and gilt, large in scale to be effective at a distance, has dignity and power. A more meticulous, delicate drawing appears in the two bowed heads of the Virgin and St. John the Baptist from a *Dëesis,* in which Christ as judge stands between the Virgin and St. John, who plead for mankind. In their troubled expression both heads indicate a deep concern. Most of these mosaics, as well as the following ones, except for the late mosaics of St. Mark's, Venice, illustrate the period of the second Golden Age.

St. Luke at Stiris, and Daphni near Athens. The mosaics of the monastic church of St. Luke at Stiris of the early eleventh century abound in flat planes, sharp edges, and defined contours. A severe linear style suggests more than the usual constraint, in forms that appear compressed into frozen immobility. At Daphni, a less ascetic style shows a well-modeled nude in the figure of Christ in the Baptism, but a forceful and serious Christ in the bust of the Pantocrator in the dome (*c.* 1100).

Sicily. The *cathedral of Cefalù* shows a further elaboration of the same Pantocrator type of Christ placed in the mosaic (twelfth century) of the apse, as the church has a basilican plan. The upper part of the apse is filled with the huge bust of Christ; in his left hand he is holding the Book, inscribed in Greek (left-hand page) and Latin (right-hand page), beginning with *"Ego sum lux mundi"* ("I am the light of the world"); with his right hand he makes the sign of blessing. The dark, somber Palestinian type of face with long wavy hair, black beard, and blue-and-gilt mantle is treated as a linear pattern in which every fold is exquisitely developed to bring out form as well as line (Fig. 59). Immaculate in detail, the total impression is commanding to express the divine "energy" of the "image of God." The ancient Egyptians' idea of the colossal statue to denote superhuman power reappears in a Christian setting. Below Christ, in a smaller scale, is the Virgin as an orant between two archangels.

Greek artists from Constantinople executed the mosaics for the Norman King Roger II, who had taken Sicily from the Moslems. Like his successors, he was a devout Christian and prolific builder; his buildings of Sicilian-Romanesque architecture combine the Moslem, Byzantine, and Norman styles. The Cefalù mosaics bear a resemblance to the cycles of mosaics of *Monreale* (late twelfth century). The royal chapel at *Palermo* (*The Palatine Chapel*) contains mosaics of rare beauty, among which the *"Entrance into Jerusalem"* is a fine example.

Torcello and Venice. The *basilica of Torcello* near Venice has in the apse a fine mosaic of the Madonna standing and holding the Child (twelfth century). Her figure, blue against gold, stands alone; empty space is used to achieve the monumental effect unique to Byzantine art. *The Last Judgment* (Fig. 60) on the opposite west wall contains, among its many scenes, one depicting sinners in hell. Two angels tend the fires of hell, while little blue devils are busily tugging at the heads above the flames in order to push them back. Turbans on some heads indicate that Moslems were fair game, properly consigned to hell; others wear crowns or look like persons of rank—a telling example of artists wreaking vengeance on sinners in high places. The artists did not invent the conception of hell as a lake of fire and brimstone into which the devil and his followers were to be thrown on the Day of Judgment. It was based on the Book of Revelation, was taught by the theologians, and described by Dante in his *Inferno.*

In the *church of St. Mark's* in Venice, the north narthex has thirteenth-century mosaics in a descriptive and realistic style, Italian rather than Byzantine in spirit. *"The Miracle of the Quail"* tells the story (Exodus 16) of the feeding of the children of Israel in the desert.

Book Illumination. There are two basic types, the roll, derived from classical art, and the bound book, or codex. Three kinds of workers contributed their labors: the calligrapher wrote the text; the chrysographer, the chapter headings; and the painter produced the miniatures. An example of the roll type is the *Joshua roll* at the Vatican Library (fifth–sixth or tenth century). The story of Joshua is told in a continuous friezelike series of delicately tinted drawings, with the text written beneath. The style is in the classical tradition of freely dispersed figures modeled in light and shade. The Rossano Gospel, *the Codex Purpureus* (sixth century), on a reddish-purple background, shows figures with accessories set out like props on a stage. In later manuscripts (ninth–eleventh centuries), paintings of figures and landscape against a gold ground occupy full pages. The manuscript style is more varied than that of the mosaics, and concentrates on splendor. These elaborate works are in the Bibliothèque Nationale of Paris, in the Vatican Library, and in church treasuries.

Sculpture, Stone Carving, and Ivories. Works of sculpture preserved in various museums are less plentiful; a prejudice against "graven images" discouraged figure sculpture. Two well-known types of sarcophagi have been discussed: stone carving in capitals and architectural decoration has been mentioned in connection with Hagia Sophia. Various transitional types of capitals show the development from the Roman Corinthian to the surface-carved Byzantine type. The so-called wind-blown acanthus capitals of the basilica of Sant' Apollinare in Classe (fifth or sixth century) and the melon-shaped capitals with interlaced carving of San Vitale are of particular interest. Here a beveled block was used on top of the capital, the impost block as a transition from a wider arch to the top of a column of smaller diameter. Later, as at Hagia Sophia, the capitals themselves became virtually carved impost blocks, square on top.

Reliefs carved in ivory are more like drawings in relief than works of figure sculpture, and were not discriminated against. They were, in fact, well suited to the expensive tastes of the luxury-loving Byzantines. Ivory was used for the decoration of furniture, as in bishops' chairs, for jewelry caskets, mostly from Constantinople, book covers, and diptychs, which were covers for writing tablets with wax sheets for inscription on the inner surfaces. Over fifty so-called Consular Diptychs from the third to the sixth century

(Roman, Early Christian, and Byzantine) are known. The pure Hellenistic style of Alexandria is illustrated in one leaf from a marriage diptych (Fig. 61) of the late fourth century, which bears the name "Symmachorum" (Victoria and Albert Museum; the other half of the diptych is in the Cluny Museum). A young woman before an altar drops incense into a flame. Drapery suggests the form beneath; a linear pattern adds a note of delicacy and, in addition, demonstrates exquisite craftsmanship.

The well-known episcopal chair of Maximian of Ravenna was probably commissioned by him after 548 in Constantinople (Otto von Simson). The chair is entirely covered with carved ivory plaques, originally thirty-nine, showing scenes from the Old and New Testaments. Figures of St. John the Baptist and the four evangelists are combined above and below with vines and scrolls enclosing peacocks, stags, lions, and other animals. The carving is vigorous and combines various influences. The muscular, rugged types of the plaques representing the story of Joseph suggest Syrian and Persian influences as practiced in an Egyptian workshop (Charles Diehl).

The religious ivories of the second Golden Age are most typically Byzantine. They depict Christ, the Virgin, groups of figures, or scenes from the New Testament. The center panel of a triptych shows the coronation of Romanus II and Eudoxia by Christ (959 A.D.) The base suggests the dome of Hagia Sophia (Bibliothèque Nationale). One of the finest is the *Harbeville triptych*. In the center (upper panel), the enthroned Christ is between St. John the Baptist and the Virgin in the scene of the *Dëesis;* five apostles and eight saints fill in the other panels.

Ivory plaques of the standing Madonna holding the Child show an extraordinary refinement of design and workmanship (Fig. 62). The drapery became a precise and delicate surface pattern with an emphasis on aloofness from reality, detaching the figure from everyday life. Such cool perfectionism suggests the spirit of Greek art without its sensuous living quality. In such ivories, no other medieval style matches the Byzantine for austerity and elegance.

Metalwork. Byzantine silver is known from various finds as far apart as Great Britain (Traprain Treasure), Rome (Esquiline Treasure), and South Russia. The famous silver *Chalice of Antioch,* discovered in 1910, is covered with decorative reliefs, a closely spaced grapevine enclosing twelve seated figures and Christ giving the law to the apostles. It may have belonged to a fourth-century basilica, but there is no evidence that it goes back to the time of Christ. Silver vessels were mostly for use in the church. A fine cast-bronze triptych, of the eleventh or twelfth century, showing the enthroned Madonna and Child between saints, is in the Victoria and Albert Museum. Embossed book covers, crosses and reliquaries, intended for the preservation of sacred relics, were attached to a base, as the ornamental figures, hammered out of thin metal, needed a support. Small religious images are included among the icons, a term used to denote a sacred object on a portable plaque of wood, stone or metal. The art of enameling was highly developed between the tenth and twelfth centuries, in the cloisonné technique. Cloisons, wirelike partitions, outline the drawing and were soldered edgewise to the metal, usually gold. The background was filled in with enamel paste made from powdered glass, which, upon the application of heat, was fused to the metal. This laborious technique required skill and precision. It resulted in a type of design that depended on simple but expressive contours (Fig. 63). Small enamel plaques were applied to larger objects such as choir screens. The most famous altar screen is the *Pala d'Oro* (table of gold) of St. Mark's, about 6 feet high and over 9 feet wide, set with many small enameled plaques and precious stones. The plaques were made in different centuries by artisans from Constantinople and repeatedly restored (Charles Diehl). The Treasury of St. Mark's contains the largest collection of Byzantine enamels, including plaques, caskets, and chalices.

Textiles. Linen fabrics, with designs in wool thread applied in tapestry fashion, have been recovered in quantity from Coptic (Christian) tombs in Egypt, where the dry climate preserved them. In the fourth century, Christian subjects like the Adoration of the Magi replaced the pagan subjects. The designs are highly conventionalized (Fig. 51), recalling the manner of ancient Peruvian textiles. Designs were also applied to textiles through "resist" dyeing. Wax was placed over the design, and in dyeing the whole piece red or purple, the wax "resisted" the dye, so that only the background took the color, preserving the design in the natural color of the cloth.

Woven silk textiles achieved a high degree of perfection. Persia may have learned silk-weaving from China, and Persian motifs became common. Among such motifs are animals, birds, and fantastic beasts, riders and horsemen shown back to back in pairs and enclosed in medallions separated by the ancient tree motif. According to Joseph Strzygowski, the figured silk textiles were themselves imported from Sassanian Persia, whereas Falke believes that the technique of silk-weaving was developed in Egypt, and reached Constantinople from there. After the Arab conquest of the Near East,

Islamic textiles also used Sassanian-Persian motifs, adding to the difficulty of attribution.

About 552 A.D., according to legend, the secret of silk cultivation was sold to Justinian. Thebes and Corinth became centers of silk production and an imperial factory which had a monopoly on imperial purple was established at Constantinople. Silk textiles were used as hangings, and some were made into costumes. After the iconoclastic period, royal costumes were set with precious stones. Textiles were traded to the countries of the West and given as royal presents, ranking in value with gold. The purely Byzantine textiles are distinguished by their monumental character. In addition to their pronounced aesthetic quality, Byzantine textiles became important during the Middle Ages for their influence on designs in other materials, even in other countries; sculpture, painting, metalwork, and pottery often owed particular motifs to designs on Byzantine textiles, which were imitated.

Conclusion. Early Christian and Byzantine art was an original development in which the classical heritage of the West fused with new contributions from the East. An emphasis on the human figure and nature was replaced in Byzantine art by abstraction and symbolism to suggest the supernatural rather than to imitate the concrete and visual. This change of style resulted from a new point of view brought in by the introduction of Christianity. It expressed itself in all the arts and gave a unified expression to Byzantine art.

Domed churches developed interiors in a new type of building quite unlike the pagan temple. The classical orders were merged in a new kind of decoration that aimed at contrasts of light against dark. Painting, aiming to create an illusion of space, was replaced by flat mosaics without substance or weight, and an expression of aloofness and serenity prevailed in religious ivories and in the arts of metal. Craftsmanship rather than originality was sought after. A closer approximation of nature as a new objective appeared in the last period, paralleling similar trends in Italian art.

A weakening of government in Italy, due to the decline of the Empire, resulted in a transfer of imperial power to the East, which was less affected by threats of barbarian invasions. Ancient civilization, preserved in Constantinople, was passed on to nations of the West. The Byzantine Empire was but the first of the nations on the periphery of the Roman Empire to take its place in history. It was followed by the emergence of new nations to the west and north of Italy, which developed the Romanesque and Gothic styles.

CHAPTER VII

Early Medieval
and Romanesque Art:
100 B.C. - 1150 A.D.

Periods. We may divide the span of two millennia from the end of the Bronze Age (1000 B.C.) to the end of the Romanesque (1150 A.D.) into three parts: (1) The Early Iron Age (1000 B.C.–100 B.C.), still prehistoric before the preliterate cultures came into contact with the Romans; (2) Roman Provincial and Migration Period art (*c.* 100 B.C.–*c.* 800 A.D.), which came to an end with Charles the Great; (3) The Carolingian Renaissance and Ottonian style, which developed into the mature Romanesque (*c.* 800–1150) and produced a wealth of monuments in all countries.

The Early Iron Age, 1000 B.C.–100 B.C. When northern Europe was last mentioned (p. 26), it was still in the Bronze Age. This was followed by the Early Iron Age divided into an earlier Hallstatt and a later La Tène period. The Hallstatt period is named after a cemetery in the Austrian Tyrol and La Tène, after an excavated military post on Lake Neuchâtel in Switzerland. The La Tène culture (*c.* 500 B.C.–100 B.C.) covered central Europe from the British Isles and southern Scandinavia to the Black Sea. The Celts (or Gauls) inhabited western Europe south of the Rhine-Danube line. Celtic burial sites have yielded many kinds of metal objects, including weapons, wheels from chariots, twisted metal collars called torques, plaques, brooches, pins, and mirrors. Occasionally the Celts buried their chiefs with their chariots, complete with horses and harness. Fine examples have been excavated in France and in Britain, such as the embossed and enameled shields of Witham and

Ill. 87 Back of bronze mirror from Desborough. *After British Museum guide to Iron Age antiquities (1925)*

Thames (British Museum). A bronze mirror (Ill. 87) from Desborough shows the La Tène type of design at its best, combining lively vigor with elegance and refinement. Its basic scroll and palmette elements belong to many periods; in this case contact with Greek art contributed to the development of the self-assured mastery of La Tène design. The art of about the same period in eastern Europe is represented by a gold belt plaque from the Black Sea region.

It shows a fantastic animal resembling a boar without tusks fighting with a serpent. Enamel inlay once filled the triangular shape of the ear. The plaque at Leningrad, like one formerly in the Eumorfopoulous Collection (Fig. 64) is attributed to the Sarmatians, an Asiatic tribe that replaced the Scythians to whom they are believed to have been related. From such contacts the Goths presumably took over such motifs as the eagle, which appears in later Visigothic fibulae.

Art of the Migration Period, 370–800 A.D. The Teutonic tribes that became involved in the migrations inhabited central Europe between the Rhine-Danube line in the west and Vistula in the east. The migrations began in 370, when the Huns forced the Goths of the north shores of the Black Sea to migrate to the west. One of the incidents of this movement was the capture of Rome by the Visigothic king, Alaric (d. 410). As these Teutonic tribes had no written history, we have little information on the premigration period. Some hints are given through heroic literature in which folklore and historic personages are combined, as in the Anglo-Saxon *Beowulf,* attributed to the eighth century, and the *Niebelungenlied,* which received its literary form in the eleventh century. The Ostrogoths, like the Visigoths. Lombards, and Vandals, were Christians of the Arian confession. Only the Franks had accepted the Roman Catholic form when Clovis, founder of the Frankish Empire, was baptized (496).

Crafts. The art of the Migration period consists of portable objects, such as ornaments for personal use or adornment. They have been found in graves, but some of the finest were in treasure deposits where they had been concealed for preservation. A well-known deposit is the famous *treasure of Petrossa,* linked to the Visigoths. It is now in Bucharest, and contains golden dishes, ewers, openwork baskets, and fibulae. Another gold find from eastern Hungary at Nagy Szent Miklos uncovered twenty-three golden vessels (Vienna Museum). Golden crowns of the Visigothic kings—Svinthilia (621–631) and Reccesvinthus (649–672)—were discovered in Spain (now at Madrid and in the Cluny Museum, Paris). They had been given to churches as votive deposits, and then removed during the Moslem invasions and concealed for safe keeping. Some of the finest crowns were discovered in 1858 in the tomb of a priest at a place called Guarrazar near Toledo.

The brooch, or fibula, and the buckle received the most sumptuous elaboration. Brooches were worn by men and women, but women wore them in pairs. In its long history, the fibula had evolved many types before it was further developed by the Teutonic people. Its simplest form was much like our modern safety pin. Plate brooches made of gold or other metals and inlaid with garnets or enamel are typical of migration ornaments, as illustrated in two Visigothic eagle fibulae (Fig. 65) found in Spain (sixth century). This combination of gold and garnet inlays prevailed throughout the whole region; there are no pronounced stylistic differences. The hilt of the sword (Bibliothèque Nationale, Paris) of the Frankish chieftain Childeric (d. 481) is important as a dated piece of a known historic person. Its jeweled mountings are in the style of the Visigothic fibula. Surface patterns were based on chip carving executed originally in wood, or featured animal motifs. According to one point of view, this type of Migration art—gold with inlays—is an expression of Germanic taste, though influenced by Roman art. Alois Riegl believed that the style was a Roman invention, and that the objects were made in Roman factories and exported to the provinces. An "artistic intent" (*Kunstwollen*), or, in other words, a change in taste on the part of the later Roman Empire resulted in a preference for color in isolated units. The effect was intended for a distant rather than near view; impressions of color were preferred to an appreciation of form (Riegl). Whether it was made by Germans or Romans, the style is primitive in its repetition of chevrons, crosses, lines, and dots, as in a Lombard fibula (Fig. 66), and is unlike earlier classic ornament.

Architecture. Only a few examples have been preserved of Migration architecture, the most important being *Theodoric's tomb* in Ravenna, representing the Ostrogothic Kingdom in Italy (493–555). It was built during Theodoric's lifetime; he died in 526. Because of the small size of the two-storied polygonal structure of cut stone, it could be roofed over by a flat dome 36 feet in diameter carved from a single block of Istrian stone. More lid than dome, this method of covering a tomb recalls the dolmens of prehistory. What little carving has been preserved suggests wood carving translated into stone. Narrow slits in the walls made for a dim illumination for the stone sarcophagi, which stood in recessed niches; the staircases were added in the eighteenth century. Bronze grilles, once used for the second-story gallery, appear to have been removed to Aachen by Charles the Great for use in his own palace chapel.

For two centuries Italy endured a second Germanic occupation under the Lombards (568). Held inferior to the Goths in artistic interest, the Lombards contributed a type of stone-carved surface ornament, braided and interlaced, used for panels, railings, and altars. Examples are preserved in churches in Lombardy, particularly at Ravenna and Cividale.

The Visigoths also left a few architectural monuments in Spain and southern France, where they had established the Kingdom of Toulouse (418). Visigothic rule in France lasted less than a century, as it was overthrown (507) by another Teutonic tribe, the Salian Franks. In Spain, Visigothic power endured until the Moorish conquest (711). Thus Spain was a Roman province for six, and a Visigothic Kingdom for two, centuries. Romans, Visigoths and Moslems left their mark on Spanish art. Two Visigothic architectural monuments in Spain are of interest. A small basilica, *San Juan Bautista*, built at Baños de Cerrato in Valencia near Valladolid in 661 during the reign of the Visigothic King Reccesvinthus—the same king who left us his crown—shows a horseshoe arch, a type of arch usually ascribed to Moslem architecture. This slightly different type of horseshoe arch appeared half a century before the Moslem invasion of Spain. If it was not a Visigothic invention, it reached the West from the East independently of Moslem influence. In the extreme north of Spain, in the province of Asturias, never occupied by the Moors, there is a small church called *Santa Maria* at Naranco near Oviedo. Though only 12 feet wide, the church or hall has a ribbed tunnel vault, an unusual feature for so early a church (dated 848). Such advanced construction did not appear elsewhere until the Romanesque period. Throughout this period, styles have little to do with races. Names like Visigothic or Lombard have become attached to those finds discovered in the regions where Visigoths and Lombards lived.

Early Art in Britain and Ireland: Manuscripts and Stone Crosses. After southern Britain had become a Roman province (43 A.D.), the Celtic mirrors and shields that lent such distinction to the late La Tène style in Britain gave way to Roman art. The Roman period is now represented chiefly by architectural remains, tombstones, and mosaic pavements. After the Romans had withdrawn from Britain, the arrival of the Saxons forced the Christian church to retire to Ireland. The pagan Jutes, Angles, and Saxons developed the "Migration style" industrial arts, as in square-headed metal brooches and disk brooches set with garnets and pearls in the cloisonné technique.

Irish Manuscript Ornamentation. A style of manuscript ornamentation, called Nordic in contrast to the southern classic Roman, is represented in its most intense expression in the books of Durrow (seventh century), of Lindisfarne (*c.* 700), and of Kells (*c.* 800). They are Gospels, written on vellum, their ornamental pages without text. The ornamental style of the *Book of Durrow* is uncompromisingly massive and metallic, and shows no interest in the human figure. St. Matthew is like a panel for a grille in red, yellow, and green, with symbolic feet and a disk for a head; the border consists of interlaced ribbons curled into loops with birds' heads, their long beaks closed around their own tails. Though wholly orderly, the impression is one of an impenetrable maze. There is no trace of a human element; closely packed braided figures on another page are set against rectilinear ironlike grilles. Spirals shoot off trumpets and ribbons, all in a tight mesh filling the rectangle held in by a broad border of similar structure. As T. D. Kendrick has shown, the style of the *Book of Durrow* was a local development derived from late Roman British mosaic pavements (Dorset and Somerset), from enameled and metallic ornaments, and even from Coptic or Syrian sources. "It is basically the art of the British Church, introduced into Ireland at the time of the flight to the west before the advancing Saxons" (Kendrick). A development of the Irish art of the *Book of Durrow* appears in the more sumptuous decorations of over thirty ornamental pages of the *Lindisfarne Gospels* of the monastery of Lindisfarne near Durham. The ornament is reduced in scale to "a tightly woven web," in which the animal heads in complicated patterns are more natural and convincingly real and birds take on realistic details. In this advanced stage of ornamentation, a climax is achieved in the two letters *Chi Rho,* the sacred monogram of Christ (Matthew 1:18), which in the Latin text begins with *Christi autem generatio sic erat* (Fig. 67).

The ultimate of extravagant ornamentation appears in the most famous of Irish manuscripts, the *Book of Kells*. The whole page here is given over to the *Chi Rho*; only one other word appears below (Fig. 68). The size of the pages is 13 by 9½ inches, having been cut when the book was rebound (*c.* 1800). Each of the four Gospels has its own initial page. Ornamental motifs of great variety and richness combine into a closely packed pattern where the principles of dominance and subordination find a brilliant application. The Irish interlace appears in countless variations. Large circles as major accents are reduced to smaller circles and to still smaller filling ornaments; shapes that seem to expand freely are gracefully swept back into controlled areas. These elaborations of line and shape are enlivened with color applied in small areas. Each color is fresh and brilliant and retains its own identity, as may be seen in a facsimile edition published by Trinity College, Dublin, where the original is kept. The ornamental style of the Celtic manuscripts on occasion introduced the human figure, as a Madonna and Child in the *Book of Kells*, but the figure is so ornamentalized that its ugliness is repellent (Fig. 69). It is this lack of comprehension of the human figure that contrasts the Nordic with the Classic style, in which the figure is all important.

Stone Crosses. This element of figure sculpture is present in the Northumbrian stone crosses at Ruthwell and Bewcastle. *The Ruthwell Cross* is a tapering shaft of red sandstone over 17 feet high. Opposite sides have each five figure reliefs and carved vine scrolls containing birds and animals. In one panel, Mary Magdalene at the feet of Christ raises an arm, an attempt at action beyond the experience of the carver. In the frontal figure of Christ, the lumpy drapery composes into a dignified total. The idea of story-telling figure sculpture was imported; the style is Anglo-Saxon, the cross type of monument, probably Irish. At a time when there was little monumental stone sculpture in western Europe, it is noteworthy to find it in the extreme West, which had little experience in this medium. It is possible that the ancient menhir cult was of some aid in the missionary work of the Church in introducing the carving of stone crosses.

Carolingian and Romanesque Art, 750–1050 A.D. Of the Teutonic tribes which participated in the migrations, the Franks prevailed in the end. After Charles the Great had changed his capital from Paris to Aachen, the German-speaking part of the Frankish Empire gained importance, and, in 842 the Oath of Strasbourg, the earliest extant document written in French rather than Latin, was proclaimed. After Charles's death, his empire was divided in 843 at the Treaty of Verdun, the beginning of France and Germany as separate nations. During his rule (771–814), Charles the Great started a cultural movement that looked to sixth-century Ravenna for guidance. Charles placed Alcuin (782–796) in charge of organizing the arts for the purpose of furnishing instruction through pictorial means. The primary objective was educational rather than aesthetic. The Carolingian Renaissance produced a few architectural monuments in France and Germany which prepared the ground for the Romanesque. The later Ottonian period was dominated by the German emperors, Henry I, three Otto's, and Henry II (d. 1024). The true patrons of the arts during this period were powerful ecclesiastics, princes of the Church like Archbishop Egbert of Trier, Bishop Bernward of Hildesheim, and Abbot Odo, who founded in 930 the monastic order of

Fig. 101 Burgos Cathedral, nave. *Mas*

Fig. 102 Collegio San Gregorio, exterior, Valladolid. *Mas*

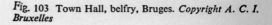

Fig. 103 Town Hall, belfry, Bruges. *Copyright A. C. I. Bruxelles*

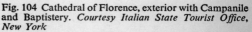

Fig. 104 Cathedral of Florence, exterior with Campanile and Baptistery. *Courtesy Italian State Tourist Office, New York*

Fig. 105 Church of St. Mark's, west façade, Venice. *Courtesy Pan American World Airways*

Fig. 106 Canaletto: View of the Ducal Palace, Venice. *National Gallery of Art, Kress Collection, 1939*

Fig. 108 Cathedral of Chartres, archivolts, west façade, south portal. *Archives Photographiques*

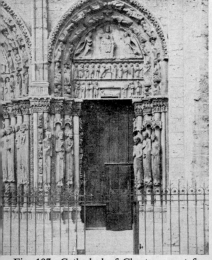

Fig. 107 Cathedral of Chartres, west façade, south portal. *Giraudon*

Fig. 109 Annunciation and Visitation groups, west façade, central portal, Rheims Cathedral. *Giraudon*

Fig. 110 Charles V, Louvre. *Giraudon*

Fig. 111 Claus Sluter and Claus de Werve: The Well of Moses, Abbey of Champmol, Dijon. *Giraudon*

Fig. 112 Jan Borreman. Retable of St. George, wood, Musée du Cinquantenaire, Brussels. *Copyright A. C. I. Bruxelles*

Fig. 113 The Holy Trinity, alabaster, English School, late thirteenth century. *National Gallery of Art*

Fig. 114 Visitation of Mary, Bamberg Cathedral. *Stoedtner*

Fig. 115 Tilman Riemenschneider: Saint Burchard of Würzburg, detail, wood, Franconian. *National Gallery of Art, Kress Collection, 1945*

Fig. 116 Madonna with Child from Dangolsheim, wood, *c.* 1470, Berlin Museum. *Staatliche Bildstelle*

Fig. 117 Herman and Regelindes, Naumburg Cathedral. *Stoedtner*

Fig. 118 King Stephen, Bamberg Cathedral *Stoedtner*

Fig. 119 Hans Brügge-mann: Christ in Purgatory, altar, detail, cathedral of Schleswig. *Landesamt für Denkmalpflege, Schleswig-Holstein*

Fig. 120 Bernt Notke: Saint George and the Dragon, after the reproduction in St. Catherine's Church, Lübeck. *Courtesy Angelsachsen Verlag, Bremen*

Fig. 121 Lady with the Unicorn, tapestry, Homage to the Betrothed, Cluny Museum, Paris. *Archives Photographiques*

Fig. 122 Yolande de Soissons kneeling before a statue of the Virgin and Child, manuscript psalter, French (Amiens), thirteenth century. *Courtesy the Pierpont Morgan Library, New York*

Fig. 123 Limbourg Brothers: The Very Rich Hours of the Duke of Berry, April, detail, Condé Museum, Chantilly. *Archives Photographiques*

Fig. 124 The Wilton Diptych: Virgin, Child and Angels; King Richard II, St. Edward and St. John the Baptist, left panel. English, *c.* fourteenth century. *Copyright National Gallery, London.*

Fig. 125 Stephan Lochner: Madonna in the Rose Arbor, Wallraf Richartz Museum, Cologne. *Marburg*

Fig. 126 Martorell: St. George and the Dragon, 1430. *Courtesy Art Institute of Chicago, The Charles Deering Collection*

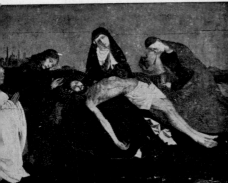

Fig. 127 Pietà from Villeneuve-les-Avignon, *c.* 1485, Louvre. *Archives Photographiques*

Fig. 128 Duccio: Madonna and Child with Saints and Angels, section, Cathedral Museum, Siena. *Alinari*

Fig. 129 Simone Martini and Lippo Memmi: Annunciation, Uffizi, Florence

Fig. 130 Giotto: Joachim and the Shepherds, section, fresco, Arena Chapel, Padua. *Alinari*

Fig. 131 Ivory diptych, Milanese School, fifteenth century. *National Gallery of Art, Widener Collection, 1942*

Fig. 132 The Trinity, gold and enamel morse, detail, Burgundian or French, *c.* 1400. *National Gallery of Art, Widener Collection, 1942*

Cluny, which became a leading artistic and cultural center. Much of Carolingian art was still of the portable variety, book painting, goldsmiths' work, and ivory carving. Sculpture in the round hardly existed; an exception is a bronze equestrian statuette, traditionally accepted as representing Charles the Great (Musée Carnavelet, Paris).

Architecture. Carolingian architecture hardly compares with the Romanesque and Gothic; the actual remains are not impressive. The basilican plan developed from a *T* shape into a Latin cross plan. Piers replaced columns in the still unvaulted interiors. A plan of the famous Benedictine monastery of Saint Gall has been preserved, consisting of the church and many buildings conceived as a complex self-supporting community. It is unknown whether this plan represented the actual monastery or was only a project in the planning stage. The most important Carolingian monument was the *Palace Chapel of Charles* at Aachen, inspired by San Vitale in plan, but not in interior effect. The modest dome, less than 50 feet in diameter, is divided into eight sections to correspond to the octagonal plan. Imported columns were used, as well as the above-mentioned bronze grilles (p. 141) from Theodoric's tomb in Ravenna; no mosaic decoration has been preserved. Until the Romanesque period, this chapel was the most important building in northern Europe since the Roman period.

After the year 1000, building activity throughout Europe increased, resulting in Romanesque architecture. It has been claimed the end of the world was expected in that year, and that when the "zero hour" passed and the fear was dispelled, there was a renewed interest in the future, which led to increased building. Ecclesiastic architecture was the most important, though Romanesque architecture also developed the castle. Classic, Byzantine, and native elements contributed to the development of local styles. All Romanesque styles used the round arch; a desire for fireproofing buildings led to vaulting. Labor was unskilled compared to the highly developed craftsmen of classical antiquity. Except in parts of Italy, stone rather than marble was used. Italy had three styles, the Lombard, the Tuscan of central Italy, and the south Italian and Sicilian. Germany had mainly one style, the Rhenish, closely related to the Lombard style.

Lombard Style. Since Lombardy had been taken over by the Franks after the defeat of the Lombards, there were close political ties between Germany and Italy, which are reflected in Lombard and Rhenish Romanesque architecture. A famous band of masons, the Comacini (named after an island in Lake Como), are believed to have spread the Lombard style to other countries. The Lombard style developed the most advanced structural system, but not the largest or most impressive churches.

The great invention of Lombard architecture was the rib vault. In contrast to the monolithic Roman concrete vault, the Lombard vault was constructed of separate stones that formed projecting ribs on which the "web," the stone ceiling, rested, so to speak (Fig. 70). The projecting (or salient)

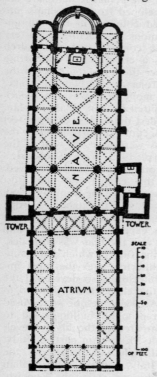

arches divide each square vaulting bay into four parts. Each bay has two diagonal arches, two transverse arches spanning the nave, and two wall arches, one on either side of the nave. Five of these ribs come together on each of the four piers that mark the corners of each vaulting bay. At *San Ambrogio* at Milan (Ill. 88) this pier is a compound pier, which means that each of the five vaulting ribs has its own separate part in the compound pier, the thrust of each rib transferring to its own pier. To resist this thrust, a projecting buttress is placed opposite each pier and appears on the exterior like a piece of wall set at right angles to the nave. At San Ambrogio neither nave nor piers are impressive, because a second-story aisle conceals the buttress and takes away the light, making the nave dark and gloomy. In Gothic architecture, this system, developed and carried to greater heights, produced spectacular results. Romanesque vaults, as in San

Ill. 88 San Ambrogio, plan.
After Simpson (1929)

Ambrogio, are higher in the center than at the transverse arches. As the diagonal ribs are semicircles and the diagonal of a square is longer than one side, each vault has a domical effect. This means that each vault is a unit by itself and the nave ceiling, divided into pockets, is without a unified effect. One large pier alternating with one smaller pier, as two bays of the aisle correspond to one nave bay, is known in architectural terms as the alternate system.

Externally the Lombard style used corbel tables as horizontal bands in the same way in which Roman architecture used cornices. (*Corbel tables* are projecting courses of masonry, carried on corbels or brackets, often connected by arches.)

Ill. 89 Modena Cathedral, exterior. *After Lübke*

The classic pilaster became a pilaster strip of no definite proportion, and open arcades appear under the eaves (Ill. 89). Due to thick walls, Romanesque portals were developed into recessed carved archivolts, which are the molded bands carried around the arched opening and continued to the ground in carved jambs. Capitals showed a variety of shapes, at times

revealing a relationship to classic forms, as in borders o
painted or carved acanthus leaves. The plainest type wa
cubical; in it the pure classic tradition disappeared completely
and nothing was left of the precision workmanship tha
characterizes Greek or Roman work. The façade of *Sa
Michele* at Pavia is haphazard in its use of carving, as i
meant to display existing sculpture rather than to decorate
San Zeno in Verona is exceptionally light and elegant, com
bining marble with reddish sandstone. A specialty of Veron
is the Lombard porch in front of the portal with column
resting on the backs of lions.

Tuscan Romanesque. The Tuscan Romanesque style o
Florence and Pisa became the most Italian of Romanesqu
styles, just as the language spoken in Tuscany became th
Italian language of the country. The Italian characteristic
were a neglect of vaulting (only the aisles were vaulted)
of columns in place of piers, an effect of color in masonr
used in stripes through alternating light and dark marble an
the use of marble and mosaics for decoration, showing th
Byzantine influence. The Tuscan style shares the blind ar
cades, corbel tables, and pilaster strips with the Lombar
style.

The outstanding example of this style is *Pisa*. The Cathe
dral, Campanile, and Baptistery (Fig. 71) were built at th
height of Pisa's commercial supremacy, between 1063 an
1188. The *Cathedral* is entirely of marble; on the interior
there are alternating bands of yellow-white and dark green
The five-aisled basilica-type plan (312 feet long) has vaulte
aisles, but the nave has a timber roof. The interior effect i
unified and festive and, in comparison with northern Roman
esque, light and airy. The west façade is made ornamenta
by a blind arcade and four superimposed open galleries
Called a "screen façade," it does not represent an attemp
to express the interior of the building. The columns of th
galleries are not always above one another, and on the side
the blind arches vary in height. John Ruskin praised th
irregularity of the arches as a refinement, but Goodyea
claimed it was accidental, due to the settling of marsh
ground. Often the detail is superior to the total effect. The
bronze lamp of the choir of Pisa Cathedral is said to have
inspired Galileo's pendulum experiment (1581)—the freely
suspended pendulum swinging in a plane—proving that the
earth rotates about its own axis.

Italian bell towers, campaniles, are often detached, as ir
Pisa's famous *leaning tower*. It probably settled during build
ing operations, and was then continued in a leaning position
or it may have been intended as a leaning tower, as there are

others besides Pisa. The tower has thick walls and is safe, as the center of gravity falls within the area of the plan. The lean was used by Galileo in his experiment with free fall using shot and cannon balls. Begun in 1174, the tower was completed 176 years later in 1350 by Tommaso Pisano. The third structure of the group, the circular *baptistery,* was begun in 1153, but completed in the Gothic style with crockets and gables.

Florence participated in the Romanesque and is represented by *San Miniato,* built on a hill overlooking the city. Refinement and emphasis on color by using marble inlay on the exterior in the form of geometric design differentiates the Florentine from the Pisan Romanesque. Elaborate mosaic pavements in light and dark are a unique feature. The exterior of the octagonal *Baptistery* of Florence shows an approximation to classic architecture in space division and the use of Corinthian capitals. Its double shell dome (not externally visible) influenced Filippo Brunelleschi in his design for the elegant cupola of the Cathedral of Florence. The Baptistery floor is covered by an inlaid pavement of white, dark green, and red marble, arranged in small pieces to form "rippling patterns which suggest running water . . . an allusion to the four rivers of Paradise, which are mentioned in the service for blessing the baptismal waters" (Lethaby). All children born in Florence were baptized in the *Battistero* or Church of San Giovanni Battista, to which Dante refers as "his beautiful San Giovanni" (*mio bel San Giovanni, Inferno,* xix, 117). To its bronze doors we return later (pp. 198, 230).

Sicilian Romanesque. Mentioned before in connection with mosaics, Sicilian Romanesque architecture is noted for its imaginative fusing of four styles. The plans are of the Early Christian basilican type, the mosaics are Byzantine, the stilted arches and interlacing designs on the exterior, as at Monreale, are Moslem, and twin towers, as at the west façade of Cefalù, are Norman.

German and Scandinavian Romanesque. In the large Rhenish churches of Speyer (Ill. 90), Worms (Ill. 91) and Mainz, the Romanesque achieved a unified national expression; the Lombard vaulted system was linked to picturesque exteriors. *Speyer* has vaults that are organic (nave 108 feet high) except for the missing diagonal ribs, and *Worms* has all ribs of the alternate system. The most impressive interior is *Mainz* (nave 88 feet high), where the vaults were built later and use some pointed arches. Exteriors are varied through round telescoped towers and a lantern over the crossing, grouped to make for magnificent silhouettes. Worms and Mainz have choirs east and west, the eastern for the bishop, the western for abbot and monks. The entrance portals had to be on the sides and are inconspicuous. Open galleries within the thickness of the wall, borrowed from Pisa and Lucca, add to the picturesque effect of Rhenish Romanesque churches (Ill. 92).

Essentially, Romanesque exteriors are massive; solids predominate over voids and, externally, apses, lantern, and transept towers produce effects of monumentality. The German is the most homogeneous of Romanesque styles.

The German Romanesque style was carried to the Scandinavian countries; the *cathedral of Lund* in Sweden of the twelfth century is in the Rhenish style, built of local sandstone. Norwegian Romanesque churches were subjected to English influence, particularly in the *cathedral of Trondheim*, though it is now largely a Gothic structure. Stone architecture was introduced from other countries in connection with Christianity, which came to Scandinavia in the eleventh century, but a wood style was indigenous to all northern countries. Slavic and Germanic countries build in wood, laying

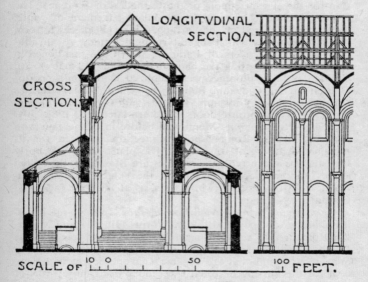

Ill. 90 Speyer Cathedral, section. *After Simpson (1929)*

the logs horizontally, as in American log cabins introduced by the Finns and Swedes. The early Saxons in Britain and the Norwegians set logs vertically, as in the stave churches in Norway. Steep roofs were common, due to the heavy snowfall of northern climates; the round arches were imitated in wood to fill in as decorations between posts, and the Nordic animal-and-ribbon style of wood carving was used on the portals, as at Urnaes and Tind (Ill. 96). Gable ends were carved in shapes of dragons that recall the carved dragon heads of the prows of Viking longboats.

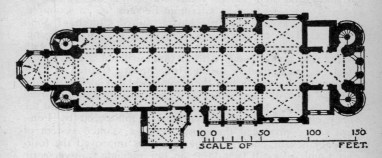

Ill. 91 Worms Cathedral, plan. *After Simpson (1929)*

The *Oseberg ship,* a royal yacht of about 850 A.D. belonging to Princess Asa, daughter of King Harald Redbeard, was accidentally discovered (1903) on the western bank of Oslo Fiord. The Princess had been buried on her ship with all the movable utensils of the household, a wagon, four sleds, chests, beds, armchairs (all carved), as well as tents, rugs, mats, wood pails, needles, thread, spinning and weaving equipment, gold, silver, and all the ship furnishings. For the first time, the existence of Norwegian wood carving was definitely proven, with examples illustrating several different styles and individual artists. The typical animal motif was well executed in a ferocious beast (Fig. 72) carved by the so-called "Baroque Master." The Oseberg ship (64 by 16½ feet), in an excellent state of preservation, is now at the Oslo University Museum.

An earlier boat (75 by 10½ feet, with 15 rowing benches) had been filled with weapons and sunk as a victory sacrifice in the fifth century, after being used by the Saxons to invade England. Excavated in 1863 in the moors of Schleswig, this ship is in Kiel, Germany.

Scandinavian ships differed from other contemporary boats in that the bow and stern rose higher above the water than did the vessel amidships, and both ends were pointed. The breadth of beam and curving ends give these ships a great sweep and elegance of line, considered both from the point of view of structural logic and as an abstract design.

French Romanesque. France developed variety with at least seven style groups, centered from south to north in

Provence, Auvergne, Languedoc, Aquitaine, Burgundy, Normandy, and Ile de France. Barrel vaults and Corinthian capitals are typical of the style in *Provence,* as in the above-mentioned *Saint Trophíme* (Arles) and *Saint Gilles* (Gard). *Auvergne,* north and west of Provence, has barrel vaults for the nave and half barrel vaults for aisles; the church of *Notre Dame du Port* at Clermont-Ferrand is an example. *Languedoc* has the five-aisle barrel-vaulted church of *Saint Sernin* at Toulouse with a lofty lantern over the crossing. North of Languedoc and west of Auvergne is *Aquitaine* with *Saint Front* at Perigueux with its domes; if not a copy of St. Mark, it is a derivative of the Holy Apostle Church at Constantinople. *Burgundy* had the magnificent five-aisled, double-transept groin-vaulted *abbey of Cluny,* which was destroyed during the French revolution, the *cathedral of Autun,* and the abbey church of *Vézelay. Normandy,* influenced by Lombard vaults, produced the most inventive vaulted system of all Romanesque churches. The Normans improved the four-part Lombard vault by adding an intermediate transverse rib from the intermediate pier, thereby dividing the vault into six cells instead of four. This system was used at Caen in the

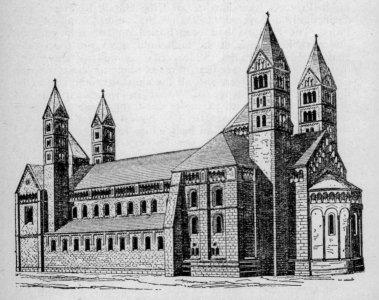

Ill. 92 Speyer Cathedral. *After Mathaei*

Ill. 93 Abbaye-aux-Hommes, vaulting system. *After Moore*

church of the *Abbaye-aux-Hommes* (Ill. 93 and 94), with half barrel vaults over the aisle. In the smaller church of *La Trinité* at Caen using the same six-part vaults, a series of arches under the aisle roof set at right angles against the outer walls transmit the thrusts to pier buttresses. The transmission of thrust through a flying buttress, though still of a primitive type, was an important invention of Norman Romanesque.

English Romanesque. After England had been conquered (1066), Norman churches were built in England that were more massive than those in Normandy. In contrast to the organic vaulted system of Normandy, the English churches were built with wooden roofs. Even the finest of the English Romanesque cathedrals, *Durham* (Fig. 73, Ill. 95),

Ill. 94 Abbaye-aux-Hommes, west façade. *After Moore*

though vaulted, did not use the system in its most advanced
version, as the intermediate piers had no transverse ribs, but
only diagonal ribs which sprung from corbels. Piers were
extremely heavy; carving was massed, as at Iffley, or the interior was left bare.

In *Ile de France* small Romanesque churches such as
Morienval and *Beauvais* (*St. Étienne*) represent vaulting
at its most advanced stage, foreshadowing the Gothic. At
Morienval the transverse rib is stilted to bring the arch to the

level of the diagonal ribs, making a level ceiling possible. The diagonal rib at Morienval (north aisle) has no rib, but a pilaster strip in the compound pier to take the diagonal. In the aisle around the choir, called the ambulatory aisle, the transverse ribs are stilted and pointed, which is the Gothic method of solving the vaulting problem.

Spanish Romanesque. The Spanish Romanesque is a modification of the southern French of Auvergne and Languedoc; *Santiago* at Compostela resembles Saint Sernin at Toulouse. Roofs were flatter and sculptured decoration became profuse.

Romanesque architecture led consistently into the Gothic style, as the smaller churches of Ile de France demonstrate. This was but one of its characteristics; essentially Romanesque architecture was many sided and expressed the abilities of many regions.

Mural Painting. The age of Charles the Great (768–814) coincided with iconoclasm in the East (717–843). Charles took a reasonable attitude; he condemned image veneration, but encouraged images for purposes of decoration. Little remains of Carolingian wall paintings, but some are known from nineteenth-century reproductions on canvas. Of the many murals that once existed in the churches of the monasteries of Reichenau (Lake Constance), some fragments from a church at *Oberzell* give an impression of the pre-Romanesque style.

Murals from Romanesque churches have on occasion been recovered in fragments after removal of the overpainting of later periods. The paintings in the chapel of the Castle of Znojomo in Bohemia, dated 1134, were discovered in this way in 1949. A series of figures of

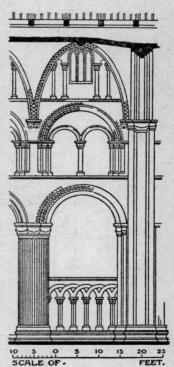

Ill. 95 Durham Cathedral, bay of nave. *After Simpson (1929)*

SCALE OF ,   FEET.
10 5 0   5   10   15   20 25

ancestors of the local feudal lord have a portraitlike quality, somewhat obscured by the heavy outline technique used. The murals of the early twelfth century of the Church of Saint Savin in France (Vienne) are well known. In such scenes as St. Michael on a white horse confronting the dragon or Christ entering Jerusalem, the flat tone and outline style uses earth colors against blues and greens.

Of Spanish Romanesque murals, the early twelfth-century frescoes in the little Catalonian church of *Santa Maria de Mur* are among the best preserved. These frescoes, painted *al secco,* were disintegrating on the wall when they were transferred, in an operation of extraordinary delicacy, to a new back, and reinstalled (*c.* 1921) at the Boston Museum of Fine Arts. The monks probably hoped, by decorating their church, to attract pilgrims returning from the famous shrine at Santiago de Compostela. The bones thought to be those of St. James the Elder had been taken to Santiago de Compostela, which rivaled Rome and Jerusalem as a goal for pilgrims. Roads through the south of France were repaired, bridges built, and monasteries established in aid of this traffic, which was a factor contributing to the spread of the Romanesque style.

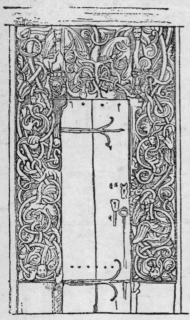

Ill. 96 Portal of church at Tind, Norway. *After Lübke*

In the Santa Maria de Mur mural, Christ in Majesty in the shell of the apse is seated on a cushioned throne (Rev. 4:2) within a *mandorla,* an almond-shaped emanation of light surrounding the whole figure of Christ, against a background of whirling stars (Fig. 74). He blesses with His right hand and holds the open book in His left, as in the mosaics. The twelve disciples are painted life-size in a zone beneath Christ; St. Paul replaces Judas Iscariot. The style reflects the Byzantine tradition; the delicately modeled drapery of the mosaics here becomes broad, massive, and flat, but the stern features are strangely elegant. The colors are red, ocher, cobalt, and black. The composition of Christ surrounded by the symbols of the four evangelists is believed to have been based on a manuscript illumination, *The Commentary on the Apocalypse,* by the monk Beatus of Liebana (786). The Beatus illustrations are flat, more pattern than picture, the figures rigid, angular in movement and without modeling. Like the Irish manuscripts, the Beatus manuscript reflects a severely ornamental and unclassic trend in medieval art.

The Bayeux Tapestry. Closely related to mural painting is this so-called tapestry, which is really an embroidery in wool thread on a linen strip less than 20 inches wide and 230 feet long. It tells the story of the historical events that culminated in the Battle of Hastings (1066), when William, Duke of Normandy, conquered England. For centuries it was exhibited at Bayeux Cathedral (Normandy) at the Feast of Relics. Its artistic interest is equaled by its historic importance. The style is vivid and executed with extraordinary skill. Action is clearly expressed, even in facial expressions, though there is no perspective or suggestion of form through light and shade. Suggesting the modern cartoon strip, events are told pictorially in historical sequence to appeal to an illiterate audience; for the learned, legends in Latin accompany each scene. One artist must have designed all parts, which may have been executed by as many as eight different groups of embroiderers. The so-called "laid, couched, and outline stitch" technique was used with particular skill. Whether it was produced in England or Normandy is not clear; arguments have been advanced for both. Perhaps the most recent investigations favor an English (Canterbury) origin, between 1066 and 1077, at the direction of Bishop Odo for the dedication of Bayeux Cathedral. It has been suggested that the underlying moral of the events illustrated may well have been that those who break a solemn oath taken on sacred relics come to a bad end. Harold, Earl of Wessex, was defeated and killed at Hastings. He had sworn allegiance to William, Duke of Normandy, and then had himself made king of England in place of William, to whom the last English king, Edward the Confessor, having no heir of his own, had promised the English throne. The tapestry is a rich source of information on Norman ships (Fig. 77), costumes, armor, warfare, and incidental details; stylistically it fits in with illustrations in manuscripts of the same period.

Illuminated Books. Among the greatest but least-known works of medieval art are the extravagantly illustrated and richly bound Bibles, psalters (Book of Psalms), missals and sacramentaries (used in the Mass), antiphonaries (sung passages), and lectionaries (read passages). These liturgical books were written in ornamental script on vellum (calfskin) or parchment (sheepskin) and bound in gold, jeweled covers (Fig. 78) or in carved ivory panels (Fig. 75). The arts of the painter, sculptor, and goldsmith united to achieve the utmost of splendor. These books were commissioned by princes and church dignitaries, and created by artists who were dedicated individuals, giving their best as a proof of piety. The Gospels, such as in the *Echternach Codex* (between 962 and 1056), were used in ritual to symbolize the presence of Christ. It was "placed on the neck and shoulders of the person to be invested as a symbol that Christ himself is the head of the person about to become head of the Church" (Peter Metz).

Full-page manuscript illustrations or illuminated initials virtually represent Carolingian and Romanesque painting, as panel painting was probably not yet fully developed and few frescoes have been preserved. Manuscript illustrations often show stylistic resemblances to larger works of sculpture and painting; the small-scale illustrations influenced the larger media. Romanesque like Byzantine art did not look to nature for models, but copied or adapted earlier works of art. In contrast to Byzantine art, Romanesque manuscript painting developed many local styles. The creative centers were in the northwest corner of Europe from Lower Saxony south to Lorraine, Ile de France, and across to England.

For the Carolingian style, the *Utrecht Psalter* (Fig. 76), now in Utrecht, but produced at Rheims, is a basic work. Whatever could be illustrated in the psalms was sketched in brown-ink miniatures, including many contemporary items—birds and animals, men in many situations, and elements of landscape. The fluid, sketchy, and energetic style of the 108 pages makes it an important work of art in its own right; it influenced much of later manuscript illumination. Roger Hinks calls the linear black-and-white technique of the *Utrecht Psalter* (eighth to tenth century) "a free-lance performance" in contrast to most other Carolingian manuscript illustrations, which follow the Palace School. The following text for Fig. 76 is from E. T. DeWald, *The Illustrations of the Utrecht Psalter*, Princeton University Press, 1932, Folio 63 verso: "The beardless, cross-nimbed Christ-Logos is seated in a mandorla supported by four angels . . . To the left, rays from a personification of the sun fall upon the psalmist who, carrying a harp, a lute, and a measuring rod, is walking in front of a cross-surmounted tabernacle. . .

('Awake psaltery and harp, I myself will awake early,' verse 3, *2*; and 'I will measure out the convallen tabernaculorum,' verse 8, *7*). In the center of the picture, King David is standing within a walled enclosure and holding a pair of shoes in his right hand ('over Edom will I cast out my shoe,' verse 10, *9*). To his right in the middle of the enclosure three men are seated, Gilead, Manasseh, and Ephraim (verse 9, *8*). Further to the right, over against the wall, Moab is holding up a cup, the *'lebes spei meaé'* (verse 10, *9*). Outside the wall another man is measuring the ground with a rod. At the extreme right a portion of another walled town is shown. In the foreground to the left is a group of 'our hosts' (verse 12, *11*)." "It was the liberating influence of the School of Rheims as in the *Utrecht Psalter* that prevented Romanesque art from becoming labored and formal" (Hanns Swarzenski, 1954). For the Ottonian Period around 1000, the *Gospel of Otto III* of the Reichenau School is a representative example. Depth of feeling and a highly imaginative rendition are illustrated in the painting of the evangelist *St. Luke in Ecstasy* (Fig. 79).

England developed an exuberant style of her own in the Winchester miniatures, which are rich in lively ornamentation. Italy, in the *Exultet Rolls* (Fig. 80), created a more natural figure style of illustration, firm and decorative without the emotional expression of the northern schools. These rolls were produced in the Benedictine monastery of Monte Cassino in southern Italy. The available reproductions of these manuscripts unfortunately are few (*see* Bibliography); a welcome addition to this hitherto neglected field is *The Golden Gospels of Echternach*, published in book form in 1957.

Goldsmithery and Metalwork. Book covers, altar frontals, portable altars, baptismal fonts, bowls, boxes, candlesticks, crosses, croziers, reliquaries, patens, chalices, and aquamaniles, as well as bronze doors, jeweled crowns, and related objects constitute the art of Church treasures, which are by no means "minor arts." In early primitive cultures, gold was associated with the sun, and thereby acquired a divine significance; precious stones were believed to have magical powers. In the medieval view, the more precious the material and the more painstaking the craftsmanship, the more pleasing the work appeared to God as an expression of the dedication of the maker. The artist did not labor for money, the use of which was still restricted in an economy tied to the soil, nor did he work for personal glory, as pride or *superbia* was sinful. Art, like virtue, was practiced for the love and greater glory of God, not for the sake of the prestige of artist or donor; each man, be he craftsman or bishop, had his station in life assigned to him by God. The Middle Ages submitted to the power of art as a demonstration of God's power, not of the artists' superiority. Thus an impersonal element is characteristic of medieval art.

With these motivations in mind, we may appreciate what is back of the extraordinary richness of gold and jeweled book covers. With figures in *repoussé* (Fig. 78), the crucified Christ is mourned by sun and moon, the Virgin and St. John and two holy women (lower panels), and four angels (upper panels). Rarely have precious materials been exploited to such splendid effect. The plain surface of the immaculate back panel and the delicate texture of the *repoussé* of the figures create a pleasing contrast. The tension is increased and, with a violent emphasis, the four central clusters and the broad bands of the jeweled border burst into a climax of splendor. This "most finished specimen of Carolingian goldsmiths' work in existence" (*Illustrated Catalogue,* The Pierpont Morgan Library, 1940) was made at Rheims or St. Denis about 870. The copper chalice with applied silver nielli at Kremsmünster (Ill. 97) is of about the same date, as it was presented by Duke Tassilo of Bavaria (748–788) and his consort. The linear animal ornamentation of the Nordic style is typical of England. Niello is a black compound of silver, lead, copper and sulphur, which is applied like an enamel to silver. The chalice from Saint Denis (Fig. 81), was made almost three centuries later (*c.* 1140) for Abbot Suger. The cup is made of a single piece of translucent sardonyx of antique origin; rim, handles, shaft, and base are silver gilt set with rubies, emeralds, jades, and pearls. Medallions embossed in gold decorate the base. Though still massive and sturdy, the proportions are lighter and the design more elegant than the Tassilo chalice.

Enamelwork, in which the effect is essentially one of line engraved in copper enamel against blue, achieved a dramatic expression in the work of Nicholas of Verdun. His so-called *Verdun Altar* (1181) at Klosterneuburg near Vienna shows fifty-one enameled panels in champlevé, representing scenes from the Old and New Testaments. In each framed panel an ornamental figure composition, such as *Samson and the Lion* (Ill. 98), stands out against the blue enamel. The action is convincing and yet constrained; the expression of exertion is felt in the total posture, but not in hands and feet. The unwieldy engraving technique made it difficult to carry expression that far.

Romanesque bronze casting achieved pre-eminence during the eleventh and twelfth centuries in Lower Saxony. Hildesheim, under Bishop Bernward (d. 1022), took the lead with the bronze doors of St. Michael, later transferred to the *cathedral of Hildesheim*. The doors were cast solidly, rather than in separate panels attached to wood. In the *Disavowal Scene*, the Lord points a finger at Adam who points to Eve who in turn points to the Serpent. In the *Expulsion Scene* Adam is already fumbling at the gate, ready to leave (Fig. 82). The Latin inscription reads: *"An(no) Domini MXV B(ernward) Ep(iscopus) dive mem(orie) has valvas fusile(s)"* [In the year of our Lord 1015 Bernward, Bishop of Blessed Memory (erected) these bronze doors]. Through gestures and ac-

Ill. 97 Chalice of Tassilo at Kremsmünster. *After Lübke*

tion, meanings are brought out. The motifs, the mushroom-like trees and the modeling under the drapery, are largely borrowed from the miniatures of the School of Echternach. The slight figures in their bends and twists were derived from the manuscripts of the School of Rheims. The nude parts, including the heads, are more plastic than the draped portions. When the artist felt the roundness of form, he used full relief; to make room for the halo, the head of God is bent out of the plane. Elements that were derived from the artist's own experience are combined with suggestions that

Ill. 98   Samson and the Lion from Verdun altar, Klosterneuburg.
After Lübke

came to him from what he had seen in illustrations (Alcuin Bible). The abbreviated figures are placed against the empty background like illustrations in a book. The psychological interpretation is stronger than the formal rendering, which is still experimental. Without experience in sculpture, a primitive but spontaneous style sufficed; art itself was a mystery. One master artist probably designed the panels, which several craftsmen modeled in preparation for the casting in bronze.

The pictorial style of the door became sculpturesque in a slightly later (1022–1038) bronze column. It is 14 feet high and has a spiral frieze in the manner of *Trajan's Column;* it served as a candlestick at Easter.

A work sympathetic to contemporary taste is the bronze crucifix in the Abbey church of Werden, Westphalia (last quarter of the eleventh century) of the same Saxon School. A stylized body, about two-thirds life-size, is related to a sensitively modeled head with sharp ridges of brow and nose,

bulging eye and drooping mouth. The head is emphasized as
seat of the spirit (Fig. 85). A major work is the bronze lion
which Henry the Lion had erected at Brunswick (1166).
Though stylized in structure and details, the lion still retains
an expression of untamed ferocity, his mouth open, tail lowered, and legs firmly planted. These examples are but a few
of the well-known bronzes that still exist.

Ivory Carving. Carolingian and Ottonian (ninth and tenth
century) sculpture is represented by ivory carvings in form of
book covers. In an ivory book cover, later used as the wing
of a diptych (Fig. 75), the acanthus-leaf border and treatment of drapery are in the classic spirit. St. Gregory is seated
in a niche, bent over, eagerly writing the opening words of
the Mass, inspired by a dove symbolizing the Holy Spirit on
his shoulder. On a lower register three scribes are individualized in posture and in facial expression. The shallow cur-
tained niche, elaborated with architectural motifs, creates a
frame which is packed with closely spaced sturdy figures with
round heads and bulging eyes. This tendency to compactness
and concentration also characterizes much of Romanesque
art. It is apparent in a set of twelfth-century ivory chess figures discovered on the Island of Lewis (west of Scotland). The
largest figure, although only four inches high, is truly monumental, a massive block on which details are engraved as
surface decoration.

Stone Sculpture. The Carolingian Renaissance concerned
only one section of northwest Europe; Romanesque sculpture
in stone, largely architectural, included the whole of western
Europe from Italy to Britain.

Carving in the round was re-established in Italy by Lombard sculpture of the early twelfth century, Italian sculpture
having been under Byzantine influence since the sixth century. On the façade of the Modena cathedral, a new primitive school of sculpture is represented in a relief showing the
Creation and Fall of Man (Fig. 86). From left to right are
these scenes: the Creator, holding a book, in a *mandorla*
held by two angels; Adam, sluggish and with bent knees,
receiving life from God who, somewhat larger, stands erect
beside him; Eve rising from the prostrate body of Adam at
God's command; and Adam and Eve after the Fall standing
beside the Tree of Knowledge and the Serpent. The heavy
forms were derived from Ottonian manuscripts; an inscription and date, "Wiligelmus, 1099," translated into Guglielmo,
points to a German origin, which is not surprising, since the
German emperors claimed dominion over Lombardy. The
bulky Lombard carving appears more refined in the later relief *The Descent from the Cross* from the pulpit of Parma

Cathedral by a Master Benedetto, known as Benedetto Antellami (Fig. 83). The delicately arranged drapery folds probably reflect direct French influence, or else the fact that French and Lombard artists were inspired by the same models, perhaps Byzantine ivories.

An entirely different style is expressed in animals in combat or hunting and battle scenes, in capitals and on carved bands, as on the façade of San Michele at Pavia. Beasts devouring men and other animals have suggested interpretations that call attention to "aggression, sadism," and "mass neurosis." The idea that the subjects originated in the imagination of the carvers, as if they represented a kind of sublimation, if not an actual expression, of neurotic states, is based on a misapplication of contemporary psychology. The basis for such themes already existed, if not in a literary tradition or in folklore, in other art forms of the portable variety. The motifs came presumably from the East, where they existed in ancient Mesopotamian and later Scythian and Sarmatian art.

Due to the artistic interests of another German emperor, Frederick II, who was partly of Italian descent, a local style of sculpture that might be mistaken for Roman work was produced at the imperial castle at Capua. Except for this single imitation of the ancient Roman style, the term Romanesque implies little that is reminiscent of Roman art.

The portals of Romanesque churches in Burgundy were embellished with sculpture, encouraged by the monastic order founded at Cluny (910). Some capitals included secular subjects, such as the labors of the month, scenes from the life of aristocrats and peasants, trades and amusements.

Southern France or Lombardy has long been considered as having influenced Romanesque sculpture in other European countries. According to another point of view (A. Kingsley Porter), the style was international and was derived from sculpture on the pilgrimage road to Santiago de Compostela, which linked Lombardy, southern France and Spain. The supreme examples are the sculptured portals of Moissac (Languedoc), of the Cluniac Abbey of Vézelay and the portal of St. Lazare at Autun (Burgundy).

At Moissac (Fig. 84) dated from 1115 to 1150, the Apocalyptic Vision of the throne of God in heaven (Maiestas Domini) is represented in the tympanum, the space above the portal. Christ crowned, in large scale, is flanked by the symbols of the evangelists and an angel holding a scroll on either side and the twenty-four crowned elders in three superimposed rows. They hold harps and golden vials full of odors "which are the prayers of saints" (Rev. 5:8);

cloud bands, originally painted, separate the rows. The modeling is in flat, broad surfaces, the folds of the undergarments are heavily pleated. Angels are elongated and curved, and the elders twist each in a different way to suggest animation. The linear design, with its flourishes derived from similar mannerism in the pen-drawn miniatures, injects a fervor of its own. The jamb figures of St. Peter and Isaiah are among the most effective in medieval sculpture, exalted in movement and of great breadth.

The tympanum with the *Last Judgment* at *Autun* contains the most attenuated and free treatment of the human figure. In the center, Christ sits in judgment, St. Peter below leads a little soul (personified as a child) toward heaven; an angel lifts another into heaven above. St. Michael weighs the souls, as one devil pulls down the scales and another demon throws the damned into the mouth of hell. On the lintel below, the dead rise, the condemned twist in agony; those to be saved are comforted by angels.

Because the south of France had been a flourishing Roman province where classical antiquities furnished models, a more classic style of sturdy figure was developed in Provence, as at St. Trophîme at Arles and at St. Gilles.

In Spain during the eleventh century, local schools of sculpture grew up in the provinces of León, Aragon, and Castile. In León, the style was characterized by large heads and hands and clumsy drapery. A particularly sensitive style was developed in the cloister of San Domingo de Silos as in *Christ and the Two Disciples on the Road to Emmaus*, the date of which is uncertain. It has been suggested (A. Kingsley Porter) that the extreme refinement of this relief was due to the fact that it was carved by Moorish captives working under Christian direction. Catalonia furnished some very attractive wood sculpture during the twelfth century, and isolated examples of the Romanesque wood sculpture have also been preserved in other countries.

Conclusion. The first millennium of the Christian era (100 B.C.–1150 A.D.) produced for the most part works of portable art. Indigenous stone buildings belong essentially to the last part of this period, the Carolingian and Romanesque periods (800–1150). Architecture, relief sculpture in stone and ivory, goldsmiths' work, bronze casting, mural and book painting were the fields in which Romanesque art excelled. Sculpture in the round and panel painting were as yet undeveloped. Art was closely linked to religion; a secular art existed, but fewer examples have been preserved. Provincial styles developed, due to the absence of a single authority to supervise regions that were only beginning to achieve a national unity. The style of late antiquity and of Byzantine art merged with a northern Germanic contribution to produce local styles. A Roman Classic element was most noticeable in Italy and southern France, a northern Germanic in northwestern Europe, including Germany, Britain and Scandinavia. Whatever models of ancient or Byzantine art happened to be available influenced styles locally. Though the personality of the artist was not emphasized, the artist often remaining anonymous, great art was the creation of the individual artist, not the result of a group's activity.

CHAPTER VIII

Gothic Art

1150 - 1400

Significance. The word *Gothic,* as applied to a style, was meant as an expression of contempt when it first came into use during the Renaissance. Gothic art was rejected as barbarous, and the style, quite erroneously, was linked with the Goths, even though they had long been absorbed in the population and no longer existed as a nation at the time the cathedrals were built. The eighteenth century also lacked understanding for the Gothic. Voltaire wrote "what unhappily remains of the architecture of those days," and Rousseau said of the Gothic cathedrals that they were "a disgrace to those who had the patience to build them." It was not until the nineteenth century that Gothic architecture became popular; like Greek architecture, it has had its revivals. Gothic style cathedrals, begun in this century, are still being completed.

The Gothic style is unique; though details may show a lingering classical influence, the total impression of the Gothic is the antithesis of Greek art. Historical styles of Western art from the end of the Middle Ages to the beginning of modernism are indebted, directly or indirectly, to either the Greek or the Gothic periods.

Economic Factors. Gothic cathedrals towered high above the roofs of the surrounding towns. Their size seems out of proportion to the small towns that built them. We have no exact figures on the number of inhabitants of medieval towns, but a town of six thousand was considered of good size. In the eighteenth century, Chartres had only ten thousand inhabitants; when Chartres Cathedral was begun, it was probably large enough to hold the whole population of the town.

167

Where did the funds come from to keep so many crafts-men employed? This question has been answered by a reference to the growth of towns due to increased commerce by land and by sea, to the increase of royal power in France and England, to the Crusades, and to various contributing cultural developments. Though medieval towns developed from the administrative centers of an episcopal diocese taking in the surrounding countryside, and though pilgrims added to the congregations, such discrepancies between small towns and large cathedrals are still amazing. Out of an estimated five thousand inhabitants of Noyon around the year 1200, only two thousand actually came within the jurisdiction of the town (Charles Seymour).

It has been claimed, incredible as it may seem, that between 1180 and 1270 eighty cathedrals and nearly five hundred abbeys were built in France (Abbé Bulteau, quoted by Otto von Simson). Cathedrals were not built by slave labor as in Egypt; moreover, where figures are on record, the number of workmen at any one time does not seem to have been large. Each mason had several helpers and was assisted by carters, carpenters, ironworkers, and other laborers. In an age that could accumulate only enough financial support for the cathedral's building fund to last at best from one year to the next, the income to support the work came mostly from voluntary contributions of many people, often from deathbed donations.

Sale of indulgences accounted for some income. In the case of the Church of St. Victor at Xanten, one-third of the cost of the construction for the year 1487 came from that source. The south tower of the cathedral of Rouen was known as the *Tour de beurre* (butter tower) because the construction was paid for by money collected from indulgences to eat butter during Lent. A "good indulgence" was expensive; in 1398 at the cathedral of Milan it cost 500 florins (Bioto, quoted by Pierre de Colombier).

Contributions were often in the form of livestock; the records of the year 1387 for Milan cathedral mention the receipt of horses, mules, a donkey, a cow, and sheep. At Autun in 1294 a shop near the church portal sold such contributions for cash. The Queen of Cyprus sent gold cloth and a duchess, jewels.

When all Europe was united through the Christian church, funds were also collected abroad. Cologne sent emissaries to England to help raise funds for its cathedrals. The Cistercian Order used its international connections for drives, and Cistercians were considered to be effective fund raisers. In the beginning of the twelfth century, the city of Laon paraded its relics throughout France and England to publicize the need for support; the possession of relics helped to encourage contributions.

Siena had a law compelling each citizen who owned beasts of burden to bring a load of marble to the cathedral site each year; the bishop allowed one indulgence for each load delivered. Santiago de Compostela made ingenious use of its pilgrims. On arrival at Triacastela (Galicia), each pilgrim was handed a block of limestone to be carried to Castaneda, where the lime kilns were located. Where there were Roman ruins, this material was salvaged and used.

Religious Enthusiasm. The construction of such large buildings would never have been possible had it not been for the religious enthusiasm of the times. A powerful emotional drive and willingness to sacrifice were essential to the success of these ambitious projects. Hope for salvation rather than a concern for art prompted many to heed the call for contributions. The customs of chivalry and the worship of the Virgin, which gave many cathedrals the name "Cathedral of Our Lady" (*Notre Dame*), characterized the period. On the other hand, fear and insecurity contributed to such phenomena as the wild excesses of flagellations and to the hopeless misery of the masses, who saw in the near future the coming of the Antichrist, the end of the world, and the Day of Judgment. The so-called "cult of carts" illustrates a phase of the extravagant religious fervor of the times. A letter of the Norman Abbot Haymo describes an event occurring at Chartres in 1144: "Rulers, princes, prelates . . . bound by straps to carts and like beasts of burden drag to the asylum of Christ loads of wheat, oil, mortar and wood. . . . A thousand or more men and women yoked to one cart in silence, except for confession of faults . . . and holy prayers for forgiveness of sin. . . ." (Porter, *Mediaeval Architecture,* vol. 2, Yale University Press, 1909). Abbot Suger thought such labors of little practical benefit, the real work in the construction of the cathedral being done by trained craftsmen. Still, the fact that man's emotions are capable of constructive as well as destructive ends is well illustrated by the change of spirit of the people of Chartres after the fire of 1194, which destroyed the cathedral and the town. It was first believed that the disaster was sent by the Virgin as a sign of displeasure, particularly since the sacred relic, the tunic of the Virgin, was believed to have perished. When the relic was discovered unharmed in the crypt, the intense grief and feeling of guilt turned to joy and determination to rebuild the church. The people now felt that the Virgin herself had permitted the destruction of the old basilica "because she wanted a new and more beautiful church to be built in her honor" (Otto von Simson). The Gothic cathedral has even been interpreted, though not convincingly, as a literal representation of the heavenly Jerusalem as described by St. John, and, from a psychoanalytical point of view, as an attempted unconscious repression of a female element.[7]

Patron and Architect. Every building operation had to be supported by some agency that would organize the work, hire an architect and be ready to pay for materials and labor. The state had performed that function in Athens and Rome, and kings and priests, in ancient Egypt and Mesopotamia. The monasteries took charge of Romanesque church building and the bishops performed that duty during the Gothic period. Viollet-le-Duc's idea that the Gothic was a popular expression of the free communes has not been substantiated by the documents. Charles Seymour has pointed out that at Noyon, which was agricultural and primarily a religious community, the contribution of the commune to the construction of Noyon cathedral does not appear to have been important. In Italy and occasionally in other countries the town municipalities took charge of erecting the cathedrals. While the kings seldom took on the full responsibility for building a cathedral, many were important contributors, as in the rebuilding of Chartres. King Louis IX was the patron of Sainte Chapelle, and the King of England, Henry III, of Westminster Abbey.

Stability and beauty were thought of as being based on perfect proportions as they were demonstrated in the universe itself, an idea which goes back to Plato. God, the Creator of the universe, was personified in Gothic art with compass in hand, and by using the laws of geometry, the architect was following the example of the Creator. Much stress was laid on the doctrine of proportion in the medieval philosophy of Augustine and Boethius, but such speculation finds no support in medieval literary references to existing cathedrals. On the other hand, recent research has produced some new evidence; Ernst Levy has demonstrated by a number of exact measurements on the south tower of Chartres Cathedral that the Gothic architect may well have applied his theoretical belief in the efficacy of geometry. This study revealed that the width of the tower was made the length of one side of an octagon, the center of which coincided with the center of the tower. No modern architect would base a design on such a preconceived system of proportions, but the medieval mind played with proportions and recognized in numbers a mystical resemblance to Christian belief. The octagon might conceivably have been preferred because it has twice as many sides as the square, which recalled the four evangelists. Otto von Simson found that the architect used the proportions of the golden section in deciding on the dimensions of the different parts of the nave piers. The actual measurements were too close to the figures obtained by arithmetical means to have been accidental. Visual harmony was related to musical harmony, and both, to the mystery of redemption. Such matters may have been of no concern to the mason, but rather to the architect. It is not quite clear how fixed the architect's duties had become by the thirteenth century, as such medieval terms as *magister operis* (master of the work) were used loosely to include financial and administrative duties as well. The architect rarely lived to see the completion of his plans. Time was of little importance; the work transcended the individual.

Origins. The great Gothic cathedrals are located in the northwest part of France in the region around Paris, Ile de France. The system of rib vaults started in the small churches and was applied to a larger church, the Abbey of Saint Denis, in 1140. Architecturally speaking, this region had been backward compared to the south of France, where the large Romanesque churches were located.

Periods. The Gothic period has been divided into three parts: Transitional and Early Gothic (1150–1200), High Gothic (1200–1300) and Late Gothic (1300–1550). Due to the gradual development and the length of time it took to complete a cathedral, many show some mingling of styles from Early to Late. Of the large French cathedrals, Notre Dame (Paris), Chartres, and Bourges were begun in the twelfth century, as were Noyon, Senlis, Soissons, Laon, and Le Mans. Rheims and Amiens are of the thirteenth century; the Palais de Justice and several churches at Rouen, Abbeville (St. Wulfram), and the façades of Troyes and Tours represent the Late Gothic.

General Character. The linear tendency and other elements of the Gothic style originated in architecture and were applied to sculpture and painting. National characteristics were subordinated to a general expression shared by all the countries except Italy, which was less hospitable to the Gothic than the rest of Europe. Variety within the style is also typical; the Gothic was capable of unexpected solutions.

Structure and decoration were more of a unit in Gothic cathedrals than in Greek temples. Ornament seemed to grow out of the stone and the sculptured figure merged into the total structure. Through the elimination of large wall surfaces and the appearance of stained-glass windows, sculpture and colored light defined space and, at the same time, re-

lated the congregation with the world beyond the cathedral
walls. No other style made translucent colored light serve
artistic ends.

What the early Christian basilica aspired to, the Gothic
cathedral brought to a climax. The blending of the religious
and the aesthetic impulse inspired by Gothic architecture
was expressed by Abbot Suger about his own St. Denis:
"When the house of God, many colored as the radiance of
precious stones, called me from the cares of this world, then
holy meditation led my mind to thoughts of piety, exalting
my soul from the material to the immaterial, and I seemed
to find myself, as it were, in some strange part of the universe, which was neither wholly of the baseness of the
earth, nor wholly of the serenity of heaven, but by the
Grace of God I seemed lifted in a mystic manner from this
lower toward the upper sphere."

Unlike Greek architecture, no single cathedral included all
points of excellence. Amiens had the finest nave; Chartres
and Notre Dame of Paris, the most spectacular glass; Rheims,
the most inspiring west façade; Le Mans, the finest
chevet-apse; and Beauvais, the loftiest choir.

The plan of the French cathedral was compact; transepts
projected but little beyond the nave. Chartres, Rheims, and
Amiens have a five-aisle choir, and the apse was developed
with radiating chapels. A logical system was developed in
the rib vault in a way that often seemed to deny that stone
had solidity and weight. Rationality and emotionalism found
expression in the cathedral. The medieval scholastic combined geometry with theology, as in the use of the equi-
lateral triangle to demonstrate the mystery of the Trinity.
Logic and speculation were combined in medieval thinking;
the logic of thrust and abutment were used in nave construction while speculation on the terrors of the Last Judgment
was set forth in the tympanum of the portal.

Structural Frame. A glance at the plan of a Gothic cathedral (Ill. 99, 100, 101) shows compound piers at each corner
of a rectangular vaulting bay and isolated buttresses in place
of the continuous walls of the Romanesque cathedral. The
cross section (Ill. 102) shows the piers as well as the outside buttresses which, it has been claimed, reinforce the
structure like props. According to this theory, advanced by
Viollet-le-Duc and his followers, thrust and counterthrust
gave stability to a framed skeleton construction (Ill. 103).
Actual experience with vaults did not support any such
theory; the vaults did not crash when a buttress was demolished, as happened on occasion, because the stones were
laid in mortar and the stone skeleton achieved a monolithic

character. By using the pointed arch for the rib vaults, the crown of the vault became level, as pointed arches of different spans could be carried to the same height. It may be, however, that the builders were as much intrigued by the

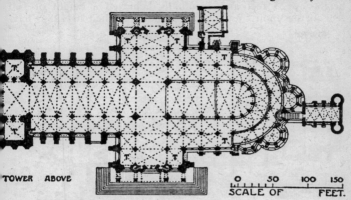

TOWER ABOVE

SCALE OF FEET.

Ill. 99 Chartres Cathedral, plan. *After Simpson* (*1929*)

aesthetic appeal of pointed arches as by their structural advantages.

Development. Wall surfaces were reduced between buttresses to make room for windows that gained in width and height to accommodate the stained glass, which was held in by iron bars. When the windows became too wide for iron

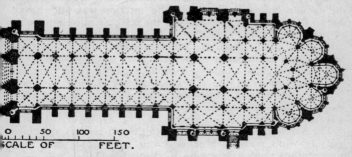

SCALE OF FEET.

Ill. 100 Rheims Cathedral, plan. *After Simpson* (*1929*)

bars to hold the glass, the opening was subdivided by stone bars and the use of tracery was developed, using pointed arches, geometrical shapes and a great circular "rose" window at the clerestory level in the west façade and in the transepts.

In the Late Gothic, a free flowing type of design was used for
"Curvilinear" (English) and "Flamboyant" (French) styles of
tracery. A trend toward ever greater nave heights marks the
development of the style. Beauvais was to surpass Amiens in
height by 25 feet and eventually achieved a height of 160
feet in the choir, but the choir vaults crashed in 1284, hav-

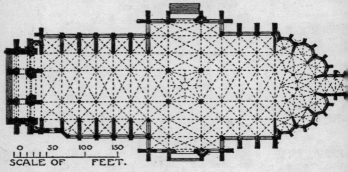

Ill. 101 Amiens Cathedral, plan. *After Simpson (1929)*

ing stood for twelve years. Though they were rebuilt later,
a nave was never constructed.

Of the many churches that bore the name of the Virgin,
the cathedral of *Notre Dame of Paris* is the best known.
The design of the west façade (Fig. 87) is marked by a
calm, severe simplicity; perfect symmetry was not the goal,
as may be noted in the gallery of kings that stretches across
the façade below the towers. The interior was still heavy,
due to the massive round piers in the nave arcade reminiscent
of the Romanesque style. Stained-glass windows became the
cathedral's chief glory, the saturated reds and blues of the
earlier glass contrasting with the lighter hues of later glass.
The colored glass windows were like paintings in light, all
that is left to us of the rich color effects of both nave and
exterior. Vaults and piers were originally painted, and color
was used on the exterior, where the most lavish decoration
was found.

The *Sainte Chapelle* of Paris, a thirteenth-century structure,
had its walls painted blue and red with gold stars in a
nineteenth-century restoration by Viollet-le-Duc.

The west façade of *Chartres* (Fig. 88) retains much
solid wall surface from the façade of the original Romanesque church. The western rose window (after 1180) shows
plate tracery in which the design appears in the openings, as
if cut out of the wall surface (Fig. 89). These solids were
developed and given a shape when bar tracery appeared.

The north tower was built 300 years after the south tower, and was finished in 1515 in the Flamboyant style. The contrasting styles of the towers illustrate the passage of centuries; whole generations lived between the beginning of a cathedral and its completion. The earlier parts were respected for reasons of sentiment, but each period made additions in the style of its own day. The south tower is adjusted to the simplicity of the Romanesque façade; it is nearly unique in having a spire. The design of the spire, on an octagonal base, is well related to the square tower, the transition from square to octagon being skillfully handled. The architect of Chartres was esteemed in his own day, but his name was among those records that have been lost.

The finest part of *Rheims* (1212–1400; seven different building periods) is its soaring façade (Fig. 90), a supreme achievement which ranks with the great masterpieces of architecture of all times. The total effect is emphatic and orderly; delicacy and refinement are combined with force.

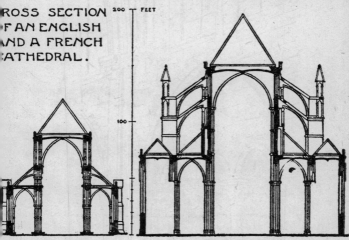

CROSS SECTION OF AN ENGLISH AND A FRENCH CATHEDRAL.

200 FEET

100

SALISBVRY. AMIENS.

Ill. 102 Salisbury and Amiens cathedrals, sections. *After Simpson (1929)*

In spite of many divisions, including portals, figures, and buttresses, a strong contrast of light and shade holds the elements together. The rose window with its radiating bar tracery immediately above the central portal is in the best possible position and is unequaled in any other cathedral. There are no walls; the structure dissolves into shafts, piers and

Ill. 103 Church of St. Leu d'Esserent, vault. *After Moore*

colonnettes. The jambs of the recessed portals consist of
carved archivolts, pointed arches and pointed gables forming
a mass of delicate stonework. Octagonal towers are related
to the sculptured gallery below through canopied niches at
the corners. The damage the façade and roof suffered during World War I has been skillfully repaired. The side eleva-

Fig. 133 Jan van Eyck: Annunciation to the Virgin, detail. *National Gallery of Art, Mellon Collection, 1937*

Fig. 134 Jan van Eyck: Giovanni Arnolfini and His Wife. *Copyright National Gallery, London*

Fig. 135 Rogier van der Weyden: The Nativity, Augustus and the Tiburtine Sibyl, and the Magi, Bladelin altar. *Berlin Museum. Photograph, National Gallery of Art*

Fig. 136 Hugo van der Goes: Portinari Altarpiece, central panel, Uffizi, Florence. *Alinari*

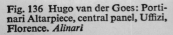

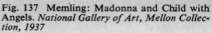

Fig. 137 Memling: Madonna and Child with Angels. *National Gallery of Art, Mellon Collection, 1937*

Fig. 139 Fra Angelico: The Last Judgment, detail, center panel. *Berlin Museum*

Fig. 138 Gerard David: Rest on the Flight into Egypt. *National Gallery of Art, Mellon Collection, 1937*

Fig. 141 Andrea del Castagno (?): Portrait of a Man. *National Gallery of Art, Mellon Collection, 1937*

Fig. 140 Masaccio: The Expulsion of Adam and Eve, Brancacci Chapel, Carmine Church, Florence

Fig. 142 Giovanni Bellini: Madonna with Saints, Frari Church, Venice. *Böhm*

Fig. 143 Giorgione: Sleeping Venus, Dresden. *Courtesy Inter Nationes (Bonn) and Stoedtner*

Fig. 144 Fra Filippo Lippi: Madonna Adoring the Child. *Berlin Museum. Photograph, National Gallery of Art*

Fig. 145 Botticelli: Portrait of a Youth, detail of hand. *National Gallery of Art, Mellon Collection, 1937*

Fig. 146 Botticelli: Birth of Venus, Uffizi, Florence. *Anderson*

Fig. 147 Leonardo da Vinci: Last Supper, Milan. *After Seemann*

Fig. 148 Raphael: Sistine Madonna, Dresden. *Anderson*

Fig. 149 Raphael: Galatea, Farnesina Palace, Rome. *Anderson*

Fig. 150 Botticelli: Birth of Venus, detail. *Brogi*

Fig. 151 Leonardo da Vinci: Madonna of the Rocks, Louvre. *Alinari*

Fig. 152 Leonardo da Vinci: Mona Lisa, Louvre

Fig. 153 Michelangelo: Temptation and Expulsion, Sistine Chapel ceiling, Vatican. *Anderson*

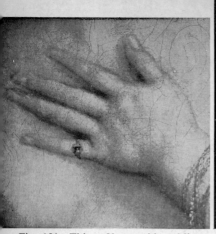

Fig. 154 Titian: Venus with a Mirror, detail. *National Gallery of Art, Mellon Collection, 1937*

Fig. 155 Titian: Assumption of the Virgin, Frari Church, Venice. *Böhm*

Fig. 157 Veronese: The Finding of Moses. *National Gallery of Art, Mellon Collection, 1937*

Fig. 156 Tintoretto: Presentation of the Virgin in the Temple, detail, S. Maria dell' Orto, Venice. *Böhm*

Fig. 158 Correggio: Holy Night, Dresden. *Deutsche Fotothek*

Fig. 159 Ghiberti: Bronze doors, Baptistery, Florence. *Alinari*

Fig. 160 Jacopo della Quercia: Creation of Eve, S. Petronio, Bologna. *Alinari*

Fig. 161 Donatello: Annunciation, S. Croce, Florence. *Alinari*

Fig. 162 Desiderio da Settignano: Marietta Strozzi, marble bust. *National Gallery of Art, Widener Collection, 1942*

Fig. 163 Verrocchio: Lorenzo de' Medici, terra cotta bust. *National Gallery of Art, Kress Collection*

Fig. 164 Michelangelo: Monument of Giuliano de' Medici, Florence. *Alinari*

Fig. 165 Cellini: Salt cellar of Francis I, gold, cast, chased and enameled. *Courtesy Kunsthistorisches Museum, Vienna*

tion of Rheims, with its elaborate parapet and its row of
buttresses loaded with niches and pinnacles, is also effective.
Transept towers were started, but never completed. Jean-le-
Loup was the architect of the cathedral.

Amiens Cathedral (chiefly thirteenth century) in its nave
(Fig. 91) unites clerestory and triforium and allows the vertical line complete dominance; of the vaulting shafts, only
the transverse ribs are carried to the floor. A carved band
below the triforium emphasizes the immaculate severity of
the nave, which depends for effect on its architectural lines.
The proportion of voids to solids is reduced to a minimum,
unlike the hypostyle hall at Karnak, where the massive columns greatly reduce the space between supports. A glance up
into the vaulted ceiling of the choir (Fig. 92) reveals the
structural system, the large clerestory windows, the triforium
gallery, and the arches of the nave arcade. In side view
the high nave dwarfs the façade, as the towers barely sur-
mount the nave roof (Fig. 93). The monumental sculptured
portals project and are of major interest. Robert de Luzarches
was the original designer.

Laon Cathedral (begun in 1165) has six towers, an Eng-
lish-type plan, and a west façade which is fantastic in its
massive voids and complex structures. Carved oxen look
down from the towers, in honor of the animals that dragged
the stones to the building site.

The façade of *Coutances* in Normandy has a strange,
fairyland quality. Halfway up past the arched buttress is a
lonely region, removed from the huge portals at the street
level. The change in scale and the use of many small openings and turrets in the tower account for the effect (Fig. 94).

Late Gothic Architecture in France. By the end of the
thirteenth century, the style had reached maturity in the
great cathedrals. During the fourteenth century, the trend
to verticality increased, ribs became lighter and tracery more
frail, and with the fifteenth century a new decorative system,
the Flamboyant, developed. Lines in tracery became wavy,
flamelike, concave and convex profiles alternating. Lacelike
effects were obtained in openwork gables and spires. Delicacy rather than strength was aimed at; the churches Saint
Vulfram at Abbeville and St. Ouen at Rouen are examples.
Rouen, formerly the capital of Normandy, is rich in Gothic
architecture. One of the finest of French Flamboyant,
St. Maclou at Rouen (Fig. 95), was not completed until the
Renaissance. On the west façades of the early sixteenth
century, stone achieved a lacelike delicacy. Architecture was
turned into a vast relief in which architectural details were
made into a frame for sculpture. The south tower (1497–

1509) shows pointed arches in pairs, repeated in superimposed
stories and overlaid with a network of delicate panels, shafts,
and gabled niches; cusps, crockets, and finials soften all lines
that terminate a section.

In the south of France *Angers* and *Albi* cathedrals have
wide naves (about 60 feet at Albi) and often no aisles. They
were built of red brick, were vaulted, and used pointed arches,
but differed in plan and exterior from the northern type.
This modified Gothic style was also applied to domestic and
municipal architecture. Half-timbered construction replaced
stone, so that the upper gabled and carved stories could be
projected out over the street.

The fortified thirteenth-century French château is illustrated by *Coucy,* now in ruins, and by *Pierrefonds,* remodeled
by Viollet-le-Duc on a late fourteenth-century castle, with
eight towers and walls 15 to 20 feet thick. The *house of
Jacques Coeur* (finance minister of Charles VII), at Bourges,
is a handsome example of the Gothic city mansion of the
fifteenth century (Ill. 104).

Gothic Architecture in England. Though English Gothic
was influenced by French Gothic, it developed its own style.
It was less interested in thrust and abutment; heavy walls
served as sufficient abutments as in the Romanesque, and
so the buttress never developed as in France. The English
cathedral was often located in a rural environment. It emphasized the horizontal, developed towers, had square east
and west ends and double transepts. The naves were narrow
and not so high as in France; Salisbury was small compared to Amiens. In the English vaulting system, ribs
were used for decoration and multiplied extravagantly. The
west façades conformed to no single prevailing type, but
emphasized the wall that confronts, rather than the portals
that invite.

The English Gothic styles are conveniently divided into
"Early English" (thirteenth century), "Decorated," also called
"Geometric" or "Curvilinear" (fourteenth century), and
"Perpendicular," also called "Tudor" (fifteenth century). The
shape of arches and the style of the tracery differentiate
these styles. The most homogeneous English cathedral in the
Early English style is *Salisbury,* begun in 1220, the same
year as Amiens, and completed in 1258. The "lancet" shaped
openings were high and narrow, and the tower over the
crossing became an important feature. Canterbury, Lincoln
and Wells also had important parts in the Early English style.
Canterbury Cathedral, built by a French architect, William
of Sens, shows French influence in twin western towers and a
French choir. Dark (Purbeck) marble shafts were used in

the nave; its great length and the central tower are English characteristics. *Lincoln Cathedral* has a screen façade, Norman in the lower section, and massive square towers finished in the Perpendicular style. The angel choir is an excellent example of the Decorated style, the name referring to relief-carved angels between the triforium arches. *Westminster Abbey* also shows French influence in the west façade, the chevet-apse, the high nave (*c.* 100 feet), and exterior flying buttresses. Among the characteristic features of the English

Ill. 104 House of Jacques Coeur, Bourges. *After Roger Smith*

Gothic are ornamental vaults, chapter houses, lady chapels, and large east end windows. In the nave and choir of *Exeter Cathedral* of the Decorated period, many ribs spring from each support, forming long triangular spaces easily filled in (Fig. 96). These tierceron vaults meet in a single continuous ridge rib. In *King's College Chapel* in Cambridge (Fig. 97) these spreading ribs are connected by minor ribs called

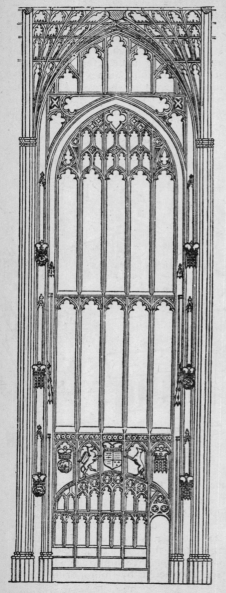

liernes (Ill. 105), and at *Gloucester Cathedral* cloisters (Fig. 98) the ribs are of a uniform curvature and form concave conoids. At the summit of the vault, patterns of tracery are linked to the conoids. In the *Henry VII Chapel* (Fig. 99) at Westminster Abbey the most sumptuous fan vaults have elaborate stone pendants suspended from the two sides and the center of the vault. Decorative wall paneling, three and four centered arches with square hood moldings above and parapets and deep buttresses on the exteriors are characteristics of the Perpendicular style. These vaults, as well as the fan vaults that radiate from a central column to the sides of the polygonal chapter house ceilings, are the most ornate the Gothic style developed. The cathedral chapters erected separate meeting halls, the offices of the cathedrals, as at Lincoln, Westminster, Salisbury, and Wells. Decorative stone vaults had a counter-

Ill. 105 King's College Chapel, vaulting bay, Cambridge. *After Simpson (1929)*

Ill. 106 Eltham Palace Hall. *After Roger Smith*

part in the exposed timber roofs supported on trusses. The largest trusses are the so-called hammer-beam trusses with intermediate uprights on brackets extending from the wall (Ill. 106). Elaborate stone vaults and wooden truss roofs are distinctly English contributions. The damp climate of Britain has left it mark on the exterior stonework of medieval buildings, and the scouring effect of the wind and weather is also evident on the buildings on the Continent. The corrosion that has taken place over the centuries is shocking when seen for the first time.

Gothic Architecture in Germany. The Gothic did not have a consistent development in Germany, but was taken over from France; a term for German Gothic was *opus francigenum* (French work). Some early churches represent a compromise between German Romanesque and French Gothic. Bamberg, Naumburg, Münster, Strasbourg, and Freiburg are

in this group. It has been said that the largest French cathedral is in Germany, as Cologne is an adaptation of
Amiens, though it differs in details. It was left unfinished
until 1842; after the original plans had been found, the completion of the cathedral was carried through, inspired by
popular support. In our own day, the city rallied again to re-
pair the damage done to the cathedral in the Second World
War. The Minster of Ulm (1377–1529) did not complete its
single tower (528 feet high) until the nineteenth century. A
specifically German custom was the use of open, pierced
spires, as at Cologne, Freiburg, Strasbourg, Vienna, Regens-
burg, and Ulm.

The most original of the German Gothic churches are the
hall churches (*Hallenkirchen*). These three-aisled churches
have aisles with vaults as high as the nave, such as *Saint
Elizabeth* at Marburg (1235–1283) and *St. Lorenz* (1445–
1472) at Nuremberg. The surfaces of barrel vaults were
covered with a network of decorative ribs, as in the *church
of St. George at Dinkelsbühl* (1448–1492) or the *cathedral
of Halle* (begun 1529, Fig. 100). In these churches, the piers
rise uninterrupted by capitals from floor to vault, the shafts
of the compound piers continuing into the ribs of the vault;
nave aisles and choir are unified. This late type of hall church
represents an original development with little relation to the
French type.

In north Germany and the Baltic provinces, brick was
adapted to the Gothic and produced fine churches with tall
narrow windows and ornamental step-gable ends. The thirteenth-century Cistercian monastic church of *Chorin* is more
Romanesque than Gothic, its broad expanse of wall surface
subdivided by narrow pointed arches, massed to emphasize
verticality. *Pelplin* is a fourteenth-century Cistercian church
in which the unadorned brick wall is featured almost for the
sake of its own stark simplicity. Ornamental gables and ornamental brickwork are used for contrast and emphasis.
The city hall of Königsberg is one of many that apply
brick Gothic to a municipal building. The German Gothic
varies from a close imitation of French to original solutions,
which represent an expansion of the Gothic idea. Comparable civic buildings in western Germany were of stone and
had ornate step-gables, as in the City Hall of Münster (Ill.
107).

Gothic Architecture in Spain. Spain adapted the Gothic of
France and on occasion also took suggestions from German
cathedrals, but the Spanish Gothic has a vitality of its own.
The climate favored small openings and roofs that were less
steep than in northern countries. On the exterior, smaller
openings left larger wall surfaces for profuse carving, which

was contrasted with plain walls. In Seville roofs were quite flat and piers, widely spaced. Spanish interiors were gloomy and the size was obscured by having the choir (*coro*), west of the crossing, shut off by a screen from the nave. Other Spanish peculiarities were the *capilla major*, the apsidal chapel, bound by the ambulatory and screened off from the church, and the *retablo*, the great carved screen back of the altar. Moorish influence determined the rectangular mosque plan of *Seville Cathedral*, which was the second largest of any Christian church measured by floor area.

Ill. 107 City Hall, Münster. *After Seemann*

The Gothic lasted longest in Spain, where new cathedrals were started in the sixteenth century. Spain had fewer Gothic churches because parts of the country were occupied by the Moors until the late fifteenth century. Moorish mosques were consecrated as Christian churches, as in the case of Cordoba Cathedral. Even so, Spain has a number of large Gothic cathedrals, of which *Burgos*, with its elaborate furnishings, is the outstanding example (Fig. 101). Burgos has seven bays, a pentagonal apse, and heavy cylindrical piers at the crossing for the support of a high lantern (*cimborio*). The vault of the lantern, which has windows to admit light, has a star-like spiderweb tracery ceiling. Smaller churches often show a mixture of Gothic and Moslem (Moorish) motifs in the so-called *Mudejar* style. Mudejars were Moors who remained in Spain after the reconquest. A late Gothic or Renaissance style of ornamentation with

Moorish delicacy goes by the name of *estilo plateresco*, plateresque, or silversmith's style. The dormitory of the University of Valladolid, the *Collegio San Gregorio* (Fig. 102), shows an exuberant mingling of the Late Gothic details and Moorish arches. Heraldic motifs in relief combine with figure sculpture in extraordinary richness. A Spanish palace of the fifteenth century, the palace of the Duke of Infantado *(Palacio del Infantado)* at Valladolid, shows iron grilles set against plain walls decorated with shell motifs, the emblem of St. James (Santiago). The shell was derived from the shells Christ and the pilgrims carried as drinking cups.

Netherlandish: Belgian and Dutch Gothic Architecture. The Netherlands followed the French Gothic in its cathedrals, of which those at Brussels and Antwerp are the finest examples. Compared to Ile de France, the cathedral towns of Flanders, whose level country has a French character, were less important than other towns which had developed out of commerce. Secular architecture produced the more imposing monuments, as in the *cloth hall of Ypres* (1200–1304), the earliest and most impressive. Destroyed in 1914, it has been rebuilt. With its steep roof, its unbroken façade 440 feet long, and a massive tower with corner turrets, it combined simplicity with a striking impression of strength. The principal upper floor, made for storage and for the buying and selling of cloth, had an open timber roof. Bruges (Fig. 103), Ghent, and Malines had similar halls. The *town hall of Louvain* is particularly ornate, the architecture taking on a sculpturesque quality. The belfry of the *town hall at Bruges* (about 352 feet high) combines elegance with an expression of strength that reflects the proud defiance of the independent medieval merchant city.

Gothic Architecture in Italy. Compared to the Gothic as it developed in the northern countries, the Italian variety is the least Gothic of all. France influenced Italy during the Gothic period as Italy influenced France during the Renaissance. The system of vaulting that began at Sant' Ambrogio in Milan and in San Galgano did little for Italy. The classic feeling for spaciousness stood in the way of a development of an Italian structural Gothic. The Italians made the Gothic into something that was classic in spirit even where the details were Gothic.

Roofs were flattened and naves were made wider. The square nave bays produced high nave arcades and eliminated the triforium; windows were kept small, wall surfaces remained prominent. In place of buttresses, iron tie rods were used on the interiors to counteract the thrusts. Italian Gothic falls into easily differentiated groups: (1) the typical Italian church of the type of San Francesco at Assisi, of Siena,

Orvieto, and Florence cathedrals and the church of Santa
Maria Novella in Florence; (2) the Venetian Gothic as represented by the Ducal Palace, parts of St. Mark's, and palaces
on the Grand Canal; (3) the imported Gothic of Milan
Cathedral; (4) municipal buildings as in Florence and Siena.
The mother church of the Franciscan monks, *San Francesco
at Assisi,* was the result of Cistercian influence, but the
church, built by the Tyrolese architect Jacob of Meran, looks
more Romanesque than Gothic (completed 1253). Built on a
hill, it has an upper and a lower church, and is best known
for its frescoes, painted by Giotto. The rose window and
the pointed arches, due to French influence, are the Gothic
features. The single-nave hall-type church was adopted because the sermon received emphasis in the Franciscan service. *Siena Cathedral,* designed by a sculptor, Giovanni Pisano, is a dazzling creation of red, black, and white marble,
in which no parts seem to have been left uncarved. The present nave was planned as a transept, with a still larger church
to follow. Building was interrupted in 1348 by the plague;
the nave was never completed, though parts exist today as a
ruin on the south side. The present groin-vaulted nave of
white-and-green banded marble incrustation has round arches
and a hexagonal dome over the crossing. The inlaid marble
mosaic pavement is ornate and interesting, but it is kept
covered over.

Orvieto Cathedral, designed by Maitani, has perhaps the
most colorful façade in architecture, the hues varying from
light cream to nut-brown in glass mosaic and marble. A
direct front view is the most effective; it is essentially a
pictorial composition and more unrelated to the interior
than most Gothic façades. It was finished during the
Renaissance.

The cathedral of Florence (Fig. 104) *Santa Maria del Fiore,*
was planned by Arnolfo di Cambio to be larger than any of
Italy's other cathedrals. Its nave, about 450 feet long, is
almost as long as Milan, but has only four bays and is
spacious and bare. The pointed arched and ribbed vaults are
the only Gothic elements; tie rods are used and stiff
acanthus-leaf capitals are applied to square piers. The exterior is paneled in white, pink, and green marble; the façade
is of the late nineteenth century. The dome belongs to the
Renaissance, and the detached campanile follows a design
of Giotto's (1334). It is a work of great distinction, fine in its
rhythmic progression in the size of the openings toward the
top. Its effect also depends on the white and colored marbles,
mosaic inlay and carvings.

Milan Cathedral (1386–1416), begun late and finished
during the early Renaissance, has been much criticized. The

upper portions belong to the seventeenth century, the unfinished façade was worked on again under Napoleon. Unlike other Italian cathedrals, it has no color, being built of white marble. More northern than Italian, it combines German workmanship and modified French details. The vast five-aisled nave (50 feet wide) and three-aisled transept are said to hold forty thousand people. The façade has Renaissance windows; the south elevation is a forest of pinnacles, as the perpendicular trend is carried through with a vengeance. The three large windows of the apse are the largest stained windows ever designed. The interior is one vast dim space, unobstructed and impressive; capitals nearly twenty feet high make a rich band across the nave.

Secular Architecture in Italy during the Gothic Period. As in the Netherlands, the growth of the towns due to commerce and the beginnings of industry produced a new middle class, the burghers, who were not peasants, nobles, or priests. Some of these towns became city republics, like Florence and Venice; others were ruled by despots, such as the Visconti of Milan. Municipal buildings and palaces of nobles produced new types of architecture.

The *Palazzo del Podesta* (Chief Magistrate) of Florence became known in the sixteenth century as *Il Bargello* (Sheriff), as it served as a prison and the seat of the chief of police. It now houses the collection of the Museo Nazionale. Begun by Arnolfo di Lapo, it has a severe, fortresslike appearance, a fine interior court, and a projecting fourth story for defense. The two-light pointed arch windows indicate that the building belongs to the thirteenth century. The *Palazzo Vecchio,* by Arnolfo di Cambio (1298), was built for the heads of the seven greater guilds (wool, silk, cloth dyers, bankers, apothecaries, leather dressers, judges and notaries). The heads of these guilds, the "consuls," were the magistrates of the city. Square battlements were representative of the Guelphs, the papal and republican party; the swallow-tail battlements of the tower were added by the opposing party, the Ghibellines, who supported the Empire. The *Loggia de' Lanzi,* a spacious vaulted arcade representing the only section finished of one planned for the whole square, is the best known and finest of the vaulted arcades of Florence and Siena; it is now an outdoor museum.

Siena's *Palazzo Pubblico* (Begun c. 1287) is almost delicate compared to the robust Florentine style. The building's façade follows a slight bend in its plan, giving the whole area a shell-shaped effect; Italians did not insist on regularity. The slender tower is a more graceful and elegant counterpart of the contemporary tower of the Palazzo Vecchio of Florence.

By the end of the thirteenth century, Venice had become

the center of international trade due to its strategic geographic position. In addition, Venice was the largest grain market of Italy and was also the main source of salt. The city was ruled by an aristocracy of commerce which allowed the burghers and the Church a limited participation in government. By the middle of the fifteenth century, Venice had become a city of easy, comfortable living and a center of great architectural splendor.

The *Palace of the Doges* (*Palazzo Ducale,* 1424–1442, by Giovanni Buon Talenti and his sons), facing the Piazzetta, adjoins St. Mark's which, together with the Piazza and its campanile, form a justly famous architectural landmark. The charm of the Ducal Palace is in its open arcade in two stories. The two façades (Fig. 106) are of about equal length. The rose-and-white colored marble of the wall contrasts with the effect of light and shade in the sculptured arcades below. The capitals by Lombard stone carvers and the Porta della Caritas connecting the Doges' Palace to the Church of St. Mark's are extravagant in the richness of the carving and the elaboration of architectural motifs, mingling the flamboyant Gothic with suggestions of the Renaissance. The capital of the southwest corner toward the lagoon was particularly admired by John Ruskin, who wrote that it was "in the workmanship and grouping of its foliage" the finest he knew in Europe (*Stones of Venice*).

The *Church of St. Mark's* (Fig. 105) goes back in its present plan to 1063, when an earlier and smaller basilica was converted into a central-type church. Its foundation belongs to the second Golden Age of Byzantine art. The present Greek cross plan has five domes, one on each arm and a larger (40 feet in diameter) dome in the center; windows at the base of the dome furnish the illumination. Its bulbous-shaped domes, wood and lead covered, are for external effect and bear no relation to the lower internal brick domes. The impression of the exterior is based on a series of five arches resting on green marble and porphyry columns massed in superimposed groups within the portal jambs. Crests and crockets, polished surfaces of variegated marble, and colored mosaics create a fantastic variety of shapes, colors, and textures. Mosaics against a gold ground cover the vaults of the narthex and interior domes. An iconostasis with fourteen figures, the Apostles, the Virgin, and St. Mark separates the raised apse from the crossing. Many of the columns, of which there are said to be 500, were imported, and they vary from the Byzantine to the Corinthian type. Many reliefs and various statues from different periods have been built into St. Mark's. Perhaps the most significant single attraction is the group of four bronze horses placed above the central portal. They are Hadrianic, probably from a triumphal arch, and were taken to Constantinople, but returned by the Crusaders (1204) and placed on St. Mark's. The criticisms that have been made against St. Mark's are the bulbous domes, the late pictorial mosaic pictures, the expanse of glass of the upper central window, and a lack of structural logic. None of these points have ever detracted from its glamor as having the most fascinating façade of any Christian church.

The jewel of the palaces facing the Grand Canal is the *Ca d'Oro*, now restored and used as a municipal museum. In its free mingling of flamboyant tracery in vigorous form with surface carving in delicate panels and border, this façade has been a favorite of students of architecture everywhere.

Gothic Sculpture: General. Gothic sculpture was either carved out of the same stone from which the cathedral was built or was applied to rood screens, tabernacles, retables, tombs, choir stalls; in the Late Gothic, portrait sculpture appeared. Theologians selected the topics, and the interpretation in each case was one that was commonly accepted, rather than the personal invention of the artist. A freer choice of subjects seems to have prevailed in ornamental carvings as in choir stalls. The use of emblems continued; Moses was represented by holding the tables of the law; a king was characterized by his crown; and a monk, by his gown. Saints were differentiated as representing types of character, rather than individual portraits. Those who suffered martyrdom by decapitation were represented as holding their heads in their hands. Otherwise saints held the instruments of their martyrdom. Traits that shock our sensibilities were accepted by the Middle Ages; the confidence that eternal bliss was awaiting the martyr must have counteracted the horror of the means by which his entry into heaven was assured. Styles of individual carvers vary and the styles of drapery indicate periods in Gothic sculpture, just as development of anatomy dates Greek sculpture. No names of carvers from the thirteenth century have been preserved, but names of the fifteenth- and sixteenth-century sculptors are well known.

Countries. France was the leading country in sculpture as in architecture; she influenced Germany, which also developed her own styles. Italy developed her own version, while the Netherlands depended on France, and Spain, on French and Moorish influences. English sculpture is usually conceded to have been less important than her architecture, which may be due to the fact that fewer works have been preserved rather than to any lack of talent for sculpture.

Architectural Carving. In connection with vaulting, the capitals developed original types which were based largely

on Byzantine forms. The early period
preferred simple bud-like forms, crisp
and vigorous and studied from nature;
later the style became more naturalistic,
as in the *Vintage* capitals of Rheims. The
foliage was applied; it no longer grew
out of the capital. The gutters ended in
open-mouthed heads of fantastic animals
or gargoyles, through which the rain
water was thrown away from the building. Other carved monsters or grotesques
look down from the towers and galleries
of Notre Dame of Paris.

*Sculpture in France, Burgundy, and
the Netherlands.* The west portals of
Chartres were consecrated to the glorification of Christ, who occupied the tympanum of the central portal, surrounded
by the beasts of the Apocalypse. The
south portal was dedicated to the Virgin
and Child (Fig. 107), the north, to the
Ascension. The portal figures, representing the ancestors of Christ, project from
columns forming the splayed jambs of
the portals; this type of jamb decoration
became typical. The seemingly archaic
frontal postures of the figures are adjusted to the width of each column. The
strict parallelism of the delicately pleated
drapery folds (Ill. 108) suggests the
Byzantine influence, as in almost contemporary mosaic figures of the Palatine
Chapel at Palermo. The personification
of the liberal arts, represented in the
archivolts of the south portal (Fig. 108),
may have been a part of the influence of
the Chartres School of Theology. The
many thousands of carved and painted
figures were not left to the carvers to
select, but were based on a unified plan
which illustrated a specific part of human
knowledge—divided, during the Middle
Ages, into natural, scientific, ethical, and
historical knowledge. Victor Hugo has

Ill. 108 Jamb figure, west façade, Chartres
Cathedral. *After Moore*

said aptly that medieval man had no important idea that
he had not expressed in stone (quoted by Emile Mâle),
but the sculpture as such usually interests us more than
the particular kind of knowledge illustrated. The stones
were usually carved before they were set in place, but
the figures were not signed. Some
scholars claim to be able to differentiate the styles of the chief
masters from the work of their assistants.

The thirteenth-century style is
well represented by the Virgin and
St. Elizabeth of the *Visitation* (Fig.
109) on the central portal of the
west façade of *Rheims*. The Virgin,
resembling a Greco-Roman matron, is contrasted with the aged
Elizabeth. Classical statues seem to
have furnished the inspiration for
this group. A smiling angel placed
beside the Virgin in the *Annunciation* shows the thirteenth-century
style at its best. Another smiling
angel turns toward St. Nicaise,
standing by; the drapery is in
broad, soft folds. *Amiens*, during
the thirteenth century, produced an
idealized style. On the central portal of the façade, Christ pointing
heavenward is truly *le Beau Dieu*,
mild and serene (Ill. 109). He
holds the Book of Life and
tramples on the lion and dragon.
The drapery at Amiens is full and
less clinging than at Chartres. This
central portal has a double row of
reliefs within a quatrefoil under
the statues of the apostles. Virtues
are represented as seated women
holding shields, and the figure of
Force holds an unsheathed sword.
Otherwise the virtues are more uni-
formly dull; virtue seemed to be less
susceptible to interesting interpretations than vice. Gentleness is

Ill. 109 Christ, *le Beau
Dieu*, west façade,
Amiens Cathedral. *After
Lübke*

represented by a lamb; but Cowardice, by a knight running from a hare; Rebellion, by a man snapping his fingers at a bishop, and Arrogance, by a lady kicking a serv-

ant. Another series illustrates the months placed beneath the signs of the Zodiac. February is represented by an old man warming himself at the fireside; his boots, removed for comfort, stand beside him.

After the middle of the thirteenth century, the figure is represented with more action; the weight is shifted and rests on one leg, the other foot is drawn back (Ill. 110), as in the Virgin of the north transept of the Cathedral of Notre Dame. One of the best known is the Madonna holding the Child from the south transept of Amiens (*Vierge Dorée, c.* 1288). The smiling Virgin, crowned as the Queen of Heaven, turns toward the Child, who holds a sphere as an emblem of sovereignty; this side sway in the posture gives the figure a slight curve, which became the characteristic expression of the fourteenth century. A note of animated realism appeared during the second half of the thirteenth century in the *Last Judgment* on the central portal at *Bourges*. As St. Michael holds the scale for the weighing of good and bad deeds, the devil gives the scales a downward push. Satan took on a bestial ugliness; devils have a human face on their stomachs to signify that "the seat of intelligence had been placed in the service of the lesser instincts." The jaws

Ill. 110 Virgin, north transept, cathedral of Notre Dame, Paris.
After Moore

of hell became the jaws of Leviathan, a monster who shoots flame from his mouth and smoke from his nostrils. In the top frieze, Christ is enthroned in judgment and the souls are taken to the lap of Abraham.

During the fourteenth century, the motif of the smiling Virgin and Child of the great cathedrals was carved everywhere in statuettes in stone, wood, and ivory, and sculpture enlarged its repertoire by adding portraits and tombs. Detached from the cathedral structure, sculpture became realistic, as in the statues of Charles V (1324–1380) and his wife Queen Jeanne de Bourbon, now at the Louvre. Charles, who recovered his kingdom from the English, was a clever diplomat and a patron of the arts. He is represented with a slight stoop, a long nose and perhaps with an expression of sly craftiness (Fig. 110). The courts of the kings of France in Paris and the dukes of Burgundy at Dijon became art centers. Through marriage, Burgundy and the Netherlands were united under the dukes of Burgundy, the Netherlands furnishing the court at Dijon with craftsmen.

The fifteenth century was dominated by a Dutchman, Claus Sluter, the outstanding Late Gothic sculptor. His style is represented at the Abbey of Champmol near Dijon by statues of *Moses and five prophets,* grouped around a well. Each figure holds a square leather box (phylactery) showing an inscription predicting the sufferings of Christ. These forceful figures with hollow faces and wrinkled foreheads emerge from contorted masses of drapery. They have a savage energy that represents the climax of the naturalistic tendency of the Late Gothic (Fig. 111). The same energy was lavished on the *tombs of Philip the Bold and John the Fearless,* designed by Sluter and executed by others. These two tombs (now at Dijon) suggest the bier on which the body was placed for funeral ceremonies. The bases are black, the surrounding figures of the mourners (*pleurants*), of white marble. Duke Philip, massive featured, lies crowned with folded hands; two kneeling angels hold his helmet, and his feet rest against a lion. The mourners, weeping, have their heads and bodies concealed under raised cloaks and heavy, broken folds; the craftsmanship is excellent.

French sculpture of the end of the fifteenth and early sixteenth century abandoned the emotionalism and the realism of the Claus Sluter School. Michel Colombe's tomb of Francis II of Britanny and his wife, in Nantes Cathedral, is of the same massive type, with the recumbent figures on a raised marble bier, but it is sober and dignified in spirit. Detached statues of the four cardinal virtues, Strength,

Temperance, Prudence, and Justice, stand in the corners in contemporary costume. The imported white-grained Italian marble encouraged a precision in details, and the full drapery does not obscure the figure. The Italian Renaissance style is indicated in the niches containing the apostles.

Decorative sculpture in sepulchral slabs (Tournai), in metalwork (Dinant), and in wooden retables (Brabant and Antwerp) were manufactured in shops for sale throughout Europe. Retables were carved screens with shallow recessed niches formed by Gothic arches and tracery and made into a stagelike setting for groups of small figures, detached and carved in the round. The Passion and scenes from the life of the Virgin or of saints were represented. Jan Borreman (c. 1479–1522) was the best known of Flemish wood carvers of this period. We illustrate his *retable of St. George* (Fig. 112). Holland, in comparison with Belgium, occupied a less prominent place, but exhibited in her sculpture a homely realism, which is developed into a major style in seventeenth-century Dutch painting.

Sculpture in England, Germany and Austria, Italy and Spain. Figure sculpture in England covered façades in superimposed rows, as at the cathedrals of Salisbury, Lichfield, Wells, and Exeter. Destruction during the Reformation, from civil war and the climate, has still left enough to show that English sculpture was not inferior to Continental sculpture. The carved spandrels of the arches in the transept ends of Westminster and in the triforium arches of Lincoln, the *Angel Choir* or the standing *Madonna and Child* of the doorway to the chapter house at York Minster are representative examples. Not all the original 255 figures covering the façade of Wells Cathedral have been preserved; those of Exeter are badly corroded. The fine Purbeck limestone was used in thirteenth-century naves, but stone, bronze, alabaster, and wood became the favorite materials. A school of "Alabasters" produced sepulchral sculpture, knights in armor recumbent on an architectural base, as in the figure of *Edward II* at Gloucester. An alabaster statuette of *the Holy Trinity* at the National Gallery of Art (Fig. 113) represents the style. Of the bronze figures, the Queen Eleanor by William Torel in Westminster Abbey is one of the best, and in wood carving, finely carved choir stalls are those at Ely Cathedral.

German sculpture of the thirteenth century includes two main groups, the Saxon group, with Bamberg and Naumburg cathedrals, and the Rhenish group represented by Strasbourg Cathedral. A close connection in style between Bamberg and Rheims indicates that the sculptor of Bamberg was

familiar with the sculpture of Rheims. The fully developed
Gothic style of the *Visitation* group from Rheims, when compared to the *Visitation* group of the cathedral of *Bamberg*
inspired by Rheims, brings out the difference between the German and the French style. In both cases the Virgin holds a
book in her left hand and extends her right outward. At
Rheims the motive seems natural and intelligible from all positions. The head is slightly turned, and the hands stop at different levels. In the corresponding figure at Bamberg, the backward bend of the right leg and right arm, though clear in side
view, is lost in front view (Fig. 114). The French sculptor alter-
nates smooth and folded parts of the drapery, the German
artist envelops his figure with an even mass of closely
spaced folds. The process of combining a side view with a
front view as we have it in the first half of the thirteenth
century resulted, in the second part of the century, in truly
organic and plastic sculpture in the series of figures from
the choir of *Naumburg* representing the *Founders*, who
had, a century before, contributed funds for the building of
the cathedral. The drapery hangs in broad, loose folds, well
separated from the figure. In these figures of great stability
and power, the German Gothic reached its full bloom. In
the group of *Herman and Regelindes* (Fig. 117), the woman
is smiling, the man, sad; such expressions are devices to
suggest animation rather than characteristics of individuals,
as to the artist the founders were but names in a document. In the *Bamberg Rider* (Fig. 118) the man's eyebrows
are straight and angular to suggest masculine strength and
energy.

The motif of the supporting and the free leg was a problem which engaged the sculptors through the Middle Ages.
In the *Strasbourg Ecclesia*, and the *Chartres Visitation*, this
contrast is only slightly indicated in a gentle walking pose
which shows the influence of Chartres. The full development
of this motif may be seen in the statues of *Virtue Killing Vice*,
both at *Rheims* and on the west façade of *Strasbourg*,
where the loose and firm leg are clearly differentiated.

From the Romanesque to the Renaissance, sculpture re-
peats the cycle from linear to plastic and from curved to
angular; as one form exhausts itself through overfamiliarity,
it is replaced by its contrasting element.

During the fifteenth century, Bavaria produced an outstanding sculptor in Adam Krafft, a stone carver of Nuremberg. His figures are short and dumpy (Ill. 111), carved in
broad surface and simple folds. In his *Seven Stations of
the Cross*, he carved in relief the seven most noteworthy
incidents on the way from the house of Pilate to Golgotha.

In each one the contrasting expressions of friend and foe are well brought out in features and gestures.

Much of German and Austrian sculpture of the fifteenth and sixteenth centuries was in wood, though some masters carved in both wood and stone, as did Tilman Riemenschneider (*c.* 1460–1531) of Würzburg. His style is well

Ill. 111   Adam Krafft: Station of the Cross, Nuremberg. *After Lübke*

illustrated in the sensitive portraitlike half-length figure of *Saint Burchard* of Würzburg (Fig. 115). Gothic wood carving without color existed in oak choir stalls and pulpits. Veit Stoss (d. 1533) of Nuremberg (Franconian School), Jörg Syrlin the Elder (*c.* 1430–1491) of Ulm (Swabian School), Michael Pacher (*c.* 1435–1498, Tyrolean School) and Hans Brüggemann (*c.* 1480–1540) of northern Germany were known as wood carvers.

Most Gothic wood carving was planned for color, to harmonize with the colorful church interiors. The wood was undercut and hollowed out to such an extent that the carving lost all sense of weight. The background was blue, the carved surface was covered with white ground (gesso), which gave the tempera color an enamel-like luster; leaf gold was used for accents. Borders, precast in gesso, were glued on, as well as precious stones, pearls, and rock crystal. This type of polychrome wood carving must be seen from the front like a painting; the parts turned away from the spectators were given less attention. Essentially, the methods used in tempera painting on wood panels were also used for wood carvings. With the final application of a coat of varnish, the altarpiece was finished and its completion celebrated at the expense of the church which had ordered the work. According to a document, Hans Leinberger and his helpers, on completion of the altarpiece for the church of Moosberg in lower Bavaria, were served 64 measures of wine (Hubert Wilm).

The Late Gothic period produced a wealth of carved and painted statues and altarpieces. One of the great works of this period is the famed *Madonna with Child* from *Dangolsheim* in Alsace (Fig. 116). Every device was used to impress the beholder with the significance of the Divine Child. Without loss of naturalness, a skillful arrangement of the drapery focuses attention on the Child, discreetly drawing attention away from the head of the Virgin, a forceful Germanic type, imbued with a sense of veiled triumph. Drapery, broad and massive, breaks in angular folds without completely obscuring the figure.

A very sympathetic type of Madonna is the *Madonna as Protectoress* (c. 1480, region of Lake Constance; Berlin Museum). Enclosed within her outspread mantle is a huddled group of kneeling men and women seeking refuge. Her expression, gazing into the distance, seems to suggest that she too is seeking protection.

The Netherlandish wooden retables that were also exported to Germany may have aided the development of a north German wood carver Hans Brüggemann (c. 1480–1540). His chief work is the carved wood altar of light-colored unpainted oak in the cathedral of Schleswig. According to tradition, this large altarpiece, over 45 feet high and with wings, was completed after seven years (1521). The incidents from the passion of Christ (Fig. 119) are represented in the complicated broken drapery style of the Late Gothic, and are based on Dürer's small woodcut *Passion*.

Bernt Notke (c. 1440–1507) of Lübeck on the Baltic brought North German wood carving to an unprecedented climax in his monumental group of *St. George and the Dragon* (over 9 feet high). Commissioned as a votive offering, it was installed in the Nicolai Church in Stockholm in 1489. The figure of the princess forms a separate statue. St. George is in gilt armor set with red and green stones, and on a light gray horse; having broken his lance, he has raised his sword in one mighty swing. The fantastic dragon is fitted with real elk horns. The rearing horse, frightened and repelled by the spiky monster, is overlaid with rich sculptured trappings, which suggest that Notke might have been trained as a goldsmith. Without benefit of classical models which inspired Verrocchio and Donatello, Notke arrived at an entirely different effect out of the native Gothic tradition (Fig. 120).

Nuremberg after 1500 was the center of artistic activity dominated by Albrecht Dürer. Some of her artists belong to the Gothic, others to the Renaissance periods. Besides Adam Krafft and Veit Stoss, Nuremberg had a third artist of major rank, Peter Vischer the Elder (*c.* 1455–1529). His father was the founder of a bronze foundry; his sons carried on his work and represent the Renaissance style in Nuremberg. Vischer's most important work was the bronze *tomb of St. Sebald* in Nuremberg in the church of the same name. An architecturally conceived open arcade structure, elaborated with sculpture, served as a baldachin for an ancient silver sarcophagus of the saint. The twelve apostles standing on colonettes beside the piers suggest in their broad drapery an awareness of the Italian Renaissance style. The most impressive of all Vischer's works are two larger than life-size bronze statues, Kings Arthur and Theodoric in armor for the *tomb of Emperor Maximilian*.

In *Italian* Gothic sculpture, Nicola Pisano (1205–1278) carved a fine hexagonal pulpit on Gothic arches for the Baptistery of Pisa. Each of the six sides has a sculptured relief. In the *Adoration of the Magi* (Ill. 112) the heavy figures in bold relief are based on the style of Roman sarcophagi; the Virgin, resembling a Roman matron, faces the

Ill. 112 Nicola Pisano: Adoration of the Magi, pulpit, Pisa Cathedral. *After Leitfaden*

kneeling Magi, who are as yet without individuality. The closely packed composition is skillfully carried out with no traces of archaism. Grouped columns separate the panels. A later octagonal pulpit by Nicola's son Giovanni Pisano in St. Andrea at Pistoia and a later pulpit made for the cathedral of Pisa introduce an element of emotionalism; his figures are either tender or intense. The teachings and activity of the Franciscans were responsible for this emotional approach, and sculptors and painters carried this theme into art. Giovanni's style parallels the French Gothic sculpture and may have influenced Giotto.

Perhaps the best known of Italian Gothic sculptors was Andrea Pisano (*c*. 1270–1348), who represented the Pisan style in Florence. In his bronze door of the Baptistery of Florence, reliefs illustrate in figure compositions the story of St. John the Baptist, and allegorical virtues are inscribed in rectangular panels. Andrea also furnished reliefs for Giotto's campanile. Tino da Camaino developed the Italian type of Gothic sepulcher, as in the *tomb of Maria of Hungary* at Naples (S. Maria Donna Regina), and Lorenzo Maitani may have carved the lovely scenes from Genesis on the façade of Orvieto Cathedral, one of the finest works of Gothic sculpture.

Spain, like the rest of Europe, was influenced by France and developed a wealth of Gothic sculpture in connection with portals and tombs and with the reredos behind the altar. Spain is less well known to travelers than Italy or France and its art treasures have not received the wider attention their quality and quantity deserve. Through painting of the later periods, Spanish art has achieved its proper appreciation by an international audience because many of these paintings are owned outside of Spain.

Gothic Painting. Even though painting did not come into its own until the Renaissance and Baroque periods, Gothic painting was diversified. Painting fused with sculpture in the carved and painted wooden altarpieces of Germany and the Netherlands. Rather than mural painting, the northern Gothic developed stained glass, which may be considered as an art in its own right. Though it owed its essential effect to color, a painter added brush work in black to define details. The fact that such later painters as Jacquemart de Hesdin, André Beauneveu, and Froment were also glassworkers suggests that the artists who designed the stained glass for Chartres were painters. Stained glass must be seen in the original; the intensity of daylight adds to colored glass a degree of saturation above the limitation of pigment, which depends on reflected light.

Tapestries were another outlet for painting, as painters

furnished the original designs in color from which the working drawings, or cartoons, for the weavers were made. The craft developed in France and Flanders. The underlying structure of tapestries consists of the horizontal warp threads and the vertical weft threads, which bring out drawing, design, and color and cover the warp completely. The weft is carried only as far as the color extends, making the design an integral part of the textile. Also peculiar to tapestries are hatches, vertical streaks of color resembling the teeth of a comb, which form transitions from one tone to another.

Tapestries were used for decoration and to curtain off parts of interiors. They lined the walls in castles and were hung between the piers in churches. During religious festivals, coronations, royal marriages, or formal entries into cities, tapestries lined the streets; they often formed the background to spectacular events of history.

The most important surviving examples of French fourteenth-century tapestries are the *Scenes from the Apocalypse* (Angers Museum). Though not entirely complete, they are also among the oldest European tapestries. They were commissioned about 1375 by Louis I, Duke of Anjou, for his castle, and were finished in the early fifteenth century. For over two centuries, they were at the cathedral of Angers, where they were hung on feast days. The scenes follow closely the vision of St. John as told in the Revelation of St. John. A celebrated set of late fifteenth-century tapestries (*c.* 1495) comprises the six tapestries of the *Lady with the Unicorn* (Fig. 121). In one of the set, a lady and a servant stand in front of an open tent, flanked by a lion for bravery and a unicorn for purity, on a deep-blue ground against rose-red. Bearing the legend "A Mon Seul Desire," it has been named *Homage to the Betrothed*. For refinement, elegance of design, and richness of harmonious color, this set represents the pinnacle of late medieval tapestry design.

Illuminated Manuscripts. The brilliant effect of the glass windows of the cathedrals had a parallel in the dominant reds and blues against a gold background on parchment of the painted illustrations in the French *illuminated manuscripts* of the thirteenth century. Architectural details were carried into the manuscripts, as in a psalter once owned by Yolande of Soissons (Morgan M729), where Yolande is represented as kneeling before a statue of the Virgin and Child (Fig. 122). In the *psalter of Saint Louis* (Bibliothèque Nationale, Paris), dated 1256, figures are like parts of a stage set, acting out incidents from scripture. These dainty little figures are modeled in light and shade, and though not anatomically correct, they have an easy freedom and substance that make them seem alive. The world of the artist's own period is carried into the illustrations from the Old Testament. In a thirteenth-century French manuscript illustrating 183 events, from Genesis to the life of David, the figures are the knights in armor of medieval France. King Saul, addressing his army, wears a crown, and is clad in chain mail, and medieval cavalry is fighting with broadswords and lances. (The Pierport Morgan Library, New York. M638.)

In the fourteenth century, Jean Pucelle, the outstanding miniature painter, developed a refined style that influenced illumination for two centuries. From five to six manuscripts have been attributed to his atelier, the most important being the *Belleville Breviary* (1342). Text and decoration became a unit, and included small miniatures in frames as well as freely disposed figures on the lower border. Pucelle no longer used solid gold backgrounds, but an ornamental frame around the text of sprigs, leaves, insects, flowers, and birds in gilt and color. Book illumination flourished in Paris while the Hundred Years' War between France and England was going on. King Jean II le Bon (1350–1364) and King Charles V the Wise (1364–1380) attracted miniature painters to Paris, and Duke Jean de Berry was an active art patron.

The Book of the Hours, known as *Les Très Riches Heures,* was painted by the three Limbourg brothers (Pol, Hermann and Jean) for the Duke of Berry. This precious book was painted in thin body color on parchment; it stands at the head of all Books of Hours. Of the 129 pages, twelve illustrate the labors of the months, which include landscapes (Fig. 123). Fashionably gowned court ladies pick flowers on the green for the month of April. The illustration for January shows the Duke's banqueting hall with richly dressed courtiers; the one for December, a boar hunt with a ducal castle in the background. One must linger over these exquisitely finished paintings; they require careful inspection to reveal their charm fully. The stage of development represented here combines seemingly primitive characteristics with a sophisticated elegance based on line and ornamental pattern in costume. The aristocratic persons are highly stylized to best show off their fine costumes, but peasants go about their work in more natural postures. What appears as a difference of styles also denoted social distinctions of class.

Pol Limbourg was the Duke's *valet-de-chambre* and André Beauneveu, sculptor, architect, painter, and illustrator, occupied a place of honor and trust at the ducal court. Painting in France during the second half of the fourteenth century was a luxury available only to the king and the nobility. The Duke's passion was collecting works of art and keeping artists busy. He traveled from one of his seventeen

Fig. 166 François Clouet: "Diane de Poitiers." *National Gallery of Art, Kress Collection (loan)*

Fig. 167 El Greco: The Virgin with Saint Inés and Saint Tecla. *National Gallery of Art, Widener Collection, 1942*

Fig. 168 Bosch: The Millennium or The Garden of Earthly Delights. *Prado*

Fig. 169 Pieter Brueghel the Elder: Summer. *Metropolitan Museum of Art*

Fig. 170 Dürer: Portrait of Hieronymus Holzschuher. *Berlin Museum. Photograph, National Gallery of Art*

Fig. 171 Dürer: Four Horsemen of the Apocalypse, woodcut. *Courtesy L. J. Rosenwald*

Fig. 172 Dürer: Melencolia, engraving. *National Gallery of Art, Gallatin Collection*

Fig. 173 Holbein: Portrait of George Gisze. *Berlin Museum. Photograph, National Gallery of Art*

Fig. 174 Grünewald: The Crucifixion, Isenheim Altar, Colmar, Alsace. *Bruckmann*

Fig. 176 Altdorfer: Alexander Battle, section. *Courtesy Bavarian National Collection*

Fig. 175 Cranach the Elder: Rest on the Flight into Egypt. *Berlin Museum. Photograph, National Gallery of Art*

Fig. 177 St. Peter's, aerial view, Rome. *Courtesy Pan American World Airways*

Fig. 178 Cranach the Elder: Portrait of a Saxon Lady. *Courtesy Stuttgart State Gallery*

Fig. 179 Chateau of Chambord, France. *Courtesy French Government Tourist Office*

Fig. 180 Louvre, aerial view, Paris. *Courtesy French Government Tourist Office*

Fig. 181 Goujon: Reliefs of water nymphs, Fountain of the Innocents, Paris. *Archives Photographiques*

Fig. 182 Tomb of Louis XII and Anne of Brittany, marble, St. Denis. *Archives Photographiques*

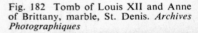

Fig. 184 Sperandio: Bronze medal of Giovanni II, Bentivoglio. *National Gallery of Art, Kress Collection*

Fig. 183 Vase in the form of a dragon, rock crystal, Milanese workshop of the Saracchi. *National Gallery of Art, Widener Collection, 1942*

Fig. 185 St. Peter's, facade, Rome. *Courtesy Pan American World Airways*

Fig. 186 St. Peter's, altar with baldachino by Bernini, Rome. *Alinari*

Fig. 187 Bernini: The Ecstasy of St. Teresa, S. Maria della Vittoria, Rome. *Anderson*

Fig. 188 Bernini: Louis XIV, bronze bust.
National Gallery of Art, Kress Collection

Fig. 189 Pozzo: Entrance of S.
Ignazio into Paradise, section,
church of S. Ignazio, Rome.
Alinari

Fig. 190 Caravaggio: Death of the
Virgin, Louvre. *Alinari*

Fig. 191 Tiepolo: Cleopatra's Banquet,
section, fresco, Palazzo Labia, Venice.
Böhm

Fig. 192 Günther: Group of the Guardian Angel, Bürgersaal Church, Munich. *Hirmer*

Fig. 193 Velázquez: The Maids of Honor (*Las Meninas*), Prado. *Mas*

Fig. 194 Velázquez: Pope Innocent X. *National Gallery of Art, Mellon Collection, 1937*

Fig. 195 Goya: La Maja Desnuda, Prado. *Museo del Prado*

Fig. 196   Montañes: The Virgin of the Immaculate Conception, polychrome wood Seville Cathedral. *Mas*

Fig. 197   Rubens: Castor and Pollux Seizing the Daughters of Leucippus, Munich. *Courtesy Bavarian National Collection*

Fig. 199   Van Dyck: Queen Henrietta Maria with Her Dwarf. *National Gallery of Art, Kress Collection, 1952*

Fig. 198   Rubens: The Felt Hat. *Copyright National Gallery, London*

châteaux to another, accompanied by tapestries and furnishings. In several of his castles, he supported resident artists. A painted book might be started by one artist at Mehun-sur-Yèvre, where Beauneveu was active, and taken to Poitiers for Jacquemart de Hesdin to finish. The Romanesque illustrator worked for the Church and the glory of God, the Gothic book painter for the pleasure of a wealthy patron.

The Sienese painter Simone Martini came to Avignon in Provence (1339) to work for the papal court, which had taken up residence there (1309–1376). This contact of Sienese with French art contributed to the formation of a courtly style of art which became international but had its center in Burgundy. French miniature painting combined with Sienese painting in a cult of decorative splendor, a preference for slender figures, for garden and landscape settings and realistic court costumes, as in the work of the Limbourg brothers.

International Style. Each country had its own variation of the so-called International Style. Details are realistic and precise, as if seen in near view and in sharp focus; a strange mingling of the artificial and the real. One of its most attractive examples is a late fourteenth-century panel painting by an unknown artist, the celebrated *Wilton Diptych* (Fig. 124). Its miniaturelike delicacy and grace have earned it universal praise. On the left panel are King Richard II (kneeling), St. Edward the Confessor (with ring), St. Edmund, and St. John the Baptist. The Virgin holding the Child and surrounded by angels occupies the right panel. Sweetness and splendor are reflected from all participants; the supposedly rugged St. John the Baptist, in spite of his beard and disheveled hair, expresses the same blissful innocence as the attending angels. The Wilton Diptych has been attributed to France, Italy, Bohemia, and England. One inclines to the English attribution; it "looks" English. It is so proper and well mannered; no Lochner would have invented these well-groomed kingly saints.

A Bohemian version of the International Style (*c.* 1350) combines Sienese and Byzantine elements with motifs from Giotto in an original manner in a panel in the Berlin Museum. Stephan Lochner (d. 1451) represents the International Style in Cologne in the fifteenth century. One of the most attractive of his several altarpieces is his *Madonna in the Rose Arbor* (Fig. 125). His flavor of sweetness and splendor is German in character and less ethereal than the Wilton Diptych. The Madonna is seated in the midst of adoring and music-making cherubs under a rose arbor, as angels hold up a curtain to form the background. The Lord, not unlike a benevolent Santa Claus, looks down upon the scene. It has been said that all this partakes more of the character of a vision than of reality. In Spain, Luis Borrassa (d. after 1424) was the pioneer of the International Style; Bernardo Martorell of Catalonia (and the Master of St. George, if they represent two persons) incorporates in his style some of the realism of Flemish, as in the panel of *St. George and the Dragon*. It is one of the most attractive of all examples of court art (Fig. 126); it reproduces a miniature of the same theme (Jacquemart André Museum, Paris).

An unusual panel (Fig. 127) that does not fit in with other Gothic paintings is the well-known *Pietà* from Villeneuve-les-Avignon, dated about 1485 (Louis Hourticq). The gaunt figures, the kneeling donor, St. John, the Virgin and St. Mary Magdalene, the bruised and broken dead body of Christ, as well as the sensitive drawing against a gilt background, combine in a design that is powerful and expressive. The monumental grouping suggests a link to sculpture, as if a carved group had been translated into a painting; the artist is unknown.

Gothic Painting in Italy, 1300–1450. Though the traditional center of Christian art had been Constantinople, the roots of modern painting stem from Italy, from the local schools of Siena and Florence. Monumental wall painting continued to be influenced by miniatures, which passed from one country to another.

Duccio (di Buoninsegna) of the late thirteenth and early fourteenth century continued the Byzantine tradition vivified by the northern Gothic. A Byzantine type of Madonna with long nose and small mouth is seated on a throne carried by angels down from heaven in the so-called *Rucellai Madonna*, which Duccio painted for the church of Santa Maria Novella. The throne is slightly turned to one side, the head of the Virgin is tilted, and the line of the drapery across her knees is irregular. These slight but significant details indicate a trend toward realism. Duccio's Madonna was erroneously attributed to Cimabue by Vasari, the well-known Renaissance biographer of the artists of Italy from Cimabue to Titian and Michelangelo.

Duccio's 92-panel altarpiece for the cathedral of Siena (Fig. 128), with paintings on the front and back, was the most comprehensive altarpiece painted up to that time. On the day it was completed (June 9, 1311), Siena proclaimed a public holiday. With saints arranged in rows on either side of the Virgin, the front is conservative; but some panels on the back, like the *Last Supper*, suggest space. As in Byzantine art, foreground and background are as seen from above; there is no single vanishing point and no real depth of space. Duccio drew exquisitely, but his style lacked the largeness and energy of Giotto's.

Simone Martini (1283–1348) was the greatest painter of the
Sienese school. His fame was equal to Giotto's and he was
favored by popes and kings. As stated above, his work at
the papal court of Avignon contributed to every Gothic style
in Europe. He must have learned from Duccio, even if he
was not his pupil. In his large fresco of the *Madonna in
Majesty* (1315) for the Palazzo Consiglio in Siena, Simone
retained the almond-shaped eyes, but his style is more stately
than that of the gentler Duccio. In suggestion of bulk, Simone is inferior to Giotto, but superior to Duccio. His lovely
Annunciation (Fig. 129), painted with the assistance of Lippo
Memmi (side panels), embodies the mystic spirit of Siena.
Mary, shrinking, receives the Angel Gabriel's "announce-
ment" of so exalted a mission as a miracle. In this Annunciation, we have the full glory of Simone's decorative and
highly linear style, a pattern of sharply silhouetted contours.
Individual passages are of great beauty, as in the swirl of the
mantle of the angel. Simone's feeling for grace is indicated
in the airy spaciousness of the composition with plenty of
room around the figures rendered as flat decoration against
a gold background.

Ambrogio Lorenzetti (d. 1348), the younger brother of
Pietro, introduced a civic topic, *The Results of Good and
Bad Government*, in his frescoes in the Palazzo Pubblico at
Siena. For the choice of subject, civic virtues and the
blessings of peace, there are few parallels in art history. Allegorical figures are used, such as Peace and Concord, but
there is also attractive illustration in scenes of artisans at
work in the streets of medieval Siena and of farm laborers
outside the city threshing with flails, to symbolize good
government. More than thirty genre scenes represent early
examples of mural landscapes. The individual scenes by
themselves are superior to the total composition.

The allegorical and descriptive style of Ambrogio is continued in the fresco of the *Triumph of Death* in the Campo
Santo of Pisa, where mounted courtiers, bent on pleasure,
are stopped in their path by three corpses in their coffins. In
another scene, *Worldly Pleasures,* Death with batlike wings
descends upon a gay party of merrymakers. Such brutal
realism becomes understandable against the background of
the Black Death, the plague of 1348–1350 that swept through
Italy.

The Gothic spirit of the International Style lived on in
Italy during the first half of the fifteenth century in Stefano da
Zevio (d. 1451), Lorenzo Monaco, Gentile da Fabriano, and
Pisanello. These painters represented religious themes in an
aristocratic setting through gorgeous costume and brilliant
color, but also included realistic and picturesque detail. In

Gentile da Fabriano's *Adoration of the Magi* the procession of the Wise Men could have taken place in Florence itself on one of its feast days; the foreground is crowded with kings in sparkling costumes and men on horseback, the procession wending its way through the background. This altarpiece was painted in 1423 for the Strozzi Chapel in the Church of Santa Trinita.

Pisanello (d. 1455) of Verona, a follower of Gentile da Fabriano and well known as a medalist, demonstrated the decorative character of the International Style. In a *Portrait of a Lady*,[8] character is completely submerged in the emphasis on the linear quality of her profile, on ivorylike flesh tints and on fashionable costumes and jewelry.

Having followed Sienese painting and the International Style of Gothic painting in Italy down to the middle of the fifteenth century, over a century after its beginning, we now return to Florence and the period around 1300.

Giotto, the founder of the Florentine school, was more progressive than Duccio, who stood at the end of a millennium of the Byzantine tradition. Giotto was an archaic painter from the beginning of a new development which continued into the painting of our own period. The whole of fourteenth-century Italian painting was influenced by Giotto, without advancing beyond the stage of development he represented. Giotto's style is a figure style in which landscape functions only as a collection of symbols; individual modeling is included, but there are no cast shadows. His naturalism is not based on an objective study of nature, but in part on the sculpture of Giovanni Pisano; he took suggestions from nature, but did not work from the living model. Giotto was an excellent composer, with dramatic ability to bring out his story. He profited from ancient frescoes that were still in existence in Rome, which he visited in 1300. He also learned from the best painters of his day, from Cimabue in Florence and Cavallini in Rome. Giotto as a progressive realist was readily accepted by his city. His style, concrete and factual, may seem prosaic; his figures belong to a sober workaday world. Such a matter-of-fact spirit in art was compatible with the practicality of business. The humanizing emotional approach of the Franciscans had found artistic expression in Giotto's frescoes of the life of St. Francis; the early ones are in the upper church of San Francesco at Assisi and the later ones, at Santa Croce in Florence.

Of the several series of frescoes painted by Giotto, the most representative are the frescoes in the Arena Chapel, Padua, commissioned by Enrico Scrovegni. As Enrico's father, Reginaldo, had been a usurer and also appeared in hell in Dante's *Divine Comedy*, the frescoes were probably meant as an act of expiation to restore honor to the family name.

Incidents from the story of Joachim and Anna, to whom eventually a child, Mary, the mother of Jesus, was born, are included in the Arena Chapel frescoes. The story is not Biblical, but a legend regarding the ancestors of Christ. In the part of the story here represented, Joachim had returned from the temple, where his offering had been refused because he was childless (Fig. 130). Rather than return home, where his humiliation was known, he sought refuge with his shepherds in the "desert places among the mountains." The scene is one of barren emptiness, the human actors stand near the foreground, as on a shallow stage. The old man, a bulky figure, stands listless with bowed head, while the shepherds wonder at their master's grief; the action is restrained, but Joachim's dejection is portrayed with deep insight. The sprightly dog makes Joachim seem all the more rigid.

Giotto's massive figures and rocky ledges look solid, as if carved out of the same material. The colors are tints of reds for drapery and of greens for rocks; there are no cast shadows, sheep are like toys, and trees are small clusters. A touchable world belongs to the childhood experiences of each one of us. It also belongs to man's early experience in painting, for Giotto may be said to represent the childhood of modern painting. Giotto neglected feet and drew hands and wrists too small, as beginners do; his knowledge of anatomy was slight.

The Fresco Technique. In Giotto's time and for at least two centuries after him, in wall decoration the painting was applied on the fresh plaster. This technique was called fresco, meaning "fresh." The powdered pigments were mixed with water and united chemically with the lime of the plaster, but had to be applied before the plaster had dried. All colors dried lighter than they appeared when wet, so that fresco painting kept the wall light in tone. The fresco technique was well suited to painting at this early stage; it aimed at broad effects, and had not yet matured sufficiently to worry about complexities and elaborations that the fresco medium could not have solved.

Practice of Painting. The painter considered himself a craftsman; he worked in a shop (*bottega*) and belonged to the guild of the druggists (*medici e speziale*) who made the colors he used. A painter, like an architect, worked only on commission; someone had to make a contract with him to decorate a chapel in fresco or to paint a Madonna or a saint on a wooden panel in tempera. A master trained assistants, who did much of the work; he designed the wall or panel and supervised its execution. Every large church had a dozen or more altars which called for paintings, a small portrait, or a chapel illustrating the saint's life and miracles. In that respect, Florence was not different from other Christian cities except in having civic pride and wealth above the average; hence she could well afford the expense of engaging many artists.

An Italian painter of the fourteenth century, Cennino Cennini, has left us a contemporary source in his instruction book on technical aspects of painting. Every step is carefully explained in the manner of a craft. He advises to use always the best materials; "Even if you do not get paid, God and our Virgin will make it up to you in peace of mind and health of body." Some of Cennini's information seems picturesque; he tells us that, for the faces of young people, the paint must be mixed with the yolk of an egg of a city hen, as it is lighter in color than that of a country hen, which is good only for the faces of older persons. Cennini gives us the proportions of a man, but not of a woman, for he says: "There is not one of them perfectly proportioned."

Crafts: Needlework, Wood, Ivory, and Gold. The crafts continued to serve the church, but during the fifteenth century secular uses achieved about equal importance. England and Florence excelled in pictorial needlework for altars and choir mantles, the finest of which were made by artisans in the cities rather than by nuns. Carving was applied to paneled chests and cupboards, occasionally to chairs, and more rarely to tables. The ornamental forms developed in architecture were applied to utensils regardless of materials, but with due regard to quality, to materials and to the use of the object; utility as well as beauty was important.

The fourteenth-century ciborium, a copper-gilt vessel with hinged lid surmounted by a cross, was meant for keeping and distributing the Sacred Host; its graceful shape recalls the stone finials of Gothic architecture. The decoration, depicting scenes from the life of Christ, is in blue-and-red enamel, filling in the background from which the copper has been removed; hence this type of enamel is known as champlevé. Limoges in France was a center of production of copper-gilt enamel. (National Galley of Art, C-3.)

A panel (Fig. 131) from a late Gothic carved ivory diptych, perhaps made in Milan, has two hinged panels which open like a book. Each is like a sheet of lace, framed by the bold designs of the inlaid certosina borders, so called after Certosa, a monastery near Pavia, which was known for its inlay work. Such diptychs served the devotional needs of an individual. The larger compositions illustrate the life of Christ from the Nativity to the Marys at the Tomb; the apostles are in the center, and angels are on the margins. The pierced background is blue and gilt, and there are gilt halos and crowns. Heads are raised or turned to suggest expression, the hands of the kings really hold their gifts, features are indicated, and the drapery is deeply carved in overlapping folds. The ivory is cut to threadlike thinness, but the action is clear, particularly in the angels in the side niches playing musical instruments.

A Late Gothic morse, a gold and enamel clasp with which ecclesiastics fastened the cope, represents the *Trinity* (Fig. 132); it is a masterpiece of the art of a Burgundian or French goldsmith around 1400. The love for realistic details is shown in the finely modeled head of God the Father with His wrinkled forehead, in the emaciated Christ, and in the twisted leaves of the pearl border; though of a bewildering richness, the workmanship is astonishingly precise. This is the naturalism of the early fifteenth century which, in stone sculpture, produced the *Well of Moses* at Champmol near Dijon (Fig. 111).

Opaque and translucent enamels, gold, and pearls provide a contrast of color; in the costliest materials, several techniques are combined. The medallion of the *Trinity* is embossed; sheets of gold are hammered and tooled into shape and covered with colored translucent enamel. Applied work is used in the several leaf borders, and chasing wherever there are depressed lines, as in the narrow bands separating the wider borders. Chasing differs from engraving in that lines are incised without removing any metal.

Conclusion. Gothic art brought the trends of northern Europe to a brilliant climax. The classic traditions of the south were absorbed in a new and original style, based in part on inspiration from nature. Through the church and monastic orders, the Gothic style was spread throughout Europe. Architecture tended to unify the arts, impress its form on other materials, and minimize national differences. Architecture, sculpture, and painting were often practiced by the same artist. The actual performance depended on craftsmanship, but the selection and planning of the subject matter were determined by the commissioner, usually the church. The interpretation followed traditions which the artist accepted willingly. In the later Gothic, the religious appeal tended to merge with an aristocratic emphasis, as in painting of the International Style, and with a popular approach in the Florentine school in such painters as Giotto and Ambrogio Lorenzetti. In architecture, stained glass, and tapestries, the Gothic set standards that have been universally acclaimed.

CHAPTER IX

Renaissance Art:

1400 - 1600

The term "Renaissance" means rebirth of the art of classic antiquity. Strictly speaking, the Renaissance might be more correctly dated 1400–1520, but we have included mannerism, or eclecticism, much of Michelangelo, and of the Venetian School. Vasari first applied the term Renaissance to the art of Cimabue. Renaissance art was primarily the art of Italy, though it spread to other countries and was most successfully adapted in France. Netherlandish painting of the fifteenth century, concurrent with the Early Renaissance in Italy, developed independently, except for minor influences of one country on the other.

Netherlandish Painting of the Fifteenth Century. In the fifteenth century, the Low Countries, the Holland and Belgium of today, were united. We speak of Flemish artists, though most of them did not come from Flanders, but from one or another of the other provinces and duchies. In painting, the Netherlands was second only to Italy, and in some respects was Italy's equal or superior. The Vasari of the Netherlands is the biographer Carel van Mander, who wrote in 1604; the leading modern critic was Max J. Friedländer.

The outstanding painters of the fifteenth century, contemporary with Masaccio in Italy, were Hubert and Jan van Eyck, with whom, Van Mander says, "Netherlandish painting began." There are no precedents for the quality of the well-known and often-discussed and illustrated *Ghent altarpiece,* the great early work of the Van Eyck brothers, but Jan, who outlived Hubert, left other works.

The Van Eyck Technique. Netherlandish painting developed out of miniature painting. It used oil as the medium on oak panels covered with gesso. Fresco painting existed,

208

but has disintegrated due to the dampness of the climate.
Van Mander says the Van Eycks "invented" oil painting;
actually painters in the fourteenth century had used oil, but
they had failed to produce outstanding works of art in that
medium. Oil had been used as a medium in painting draperies, but not flesh colors. The exact methods used by
the Van Eycks are not known; their so-called oil technique,
which was probably an oil-tempera technique, continued in
use until it was replaced by the technique of Rubens. In the
oil technique, light penetrates the surface and is reflected
from whatever layers beneath have opaque pigments. This
gives a suggestion of depth and, in addition, in the middle
values, a greater intensity of color.

The Style of the Van Eycks. Through the oil technique, a
sense of natural illumination was achieved, though as yet
without a full visual effect. A love of detail emphasized differences of textures and produced effects that in sharp definition seem microscopic, beyond the facts of actual appearances as seen in nature. The figure was individualized and
portraiture became one of the triumphs of the style, but
drawing remained hard, stiff, and angular.

The "Modes" of Painting. A system of differentiating
styles in painting was developed by Denman Ross and Arthur
Pope. As defined by this system, Van Eyck used the "mode
of relief," which deals arbitrarily with facts of vision found
in nature. In place of a consistent illumination, as we become aware of it when confronted by nature, the lights and
darks are varied to suggest relief, but without denying the
flat surface of panel or canvas. Virtually all painting that we
have dealt with so far and much that is before us belongs to
this "mode of relief" type, unless it belongs to the simplest
of all modes, the "mode of line and flat tone," as illustrated
in Greek vase painting. The next level, the "Venetian mode,"
we shall deal with presently, and the "mode of full visual
effect" was accomplished in some paintings of Van Eyck's
and particularly in Vermeer's paintings in the seventeenth
century.

Jan van Eyck's *Annunciation* (Fig. 133) is a sober interpretation of the appearance of the angel to the Virgin. The
angel's massive cope, weighted down with a jeweled border
and a huge morse or clasp, in its hard, metallic quality is
unmatched by anything else in the painting. The stool
serves to set the Virgin back into space, the lilies are like
wax, and a book before the Virgin appears as if seen
through a magnifying glass. The figures and the foreground
are in full visual effect, whereas the background is in the
mode of relief. Space is not continuous; the background is

attached to the foreground, it does not flow out of it. The
linear perspective is inaccurate, but painting attains a super-
reality in objects represented as if in near view. Yet, in Van
Eyck's world of facts, details also have a religious meaning.
In the pictorial floor tiles, Samson pulls down the temple and
David kills Goliath to save the Jewish people; both incidents
are symbols of the salvation of mankind by Christ. The three
windows in the back, which look so much like real glass,
symbolize the Trinity; a dove above the Virgin's head symbolizes the Holy Spirit.[9] The angel wears a crown and carries
a scepter, emblems of royalty referring to the future king of
the world. Van Eyck's *Giovanni Arnolfini and His Wife*
(Fig. 134), dated 1434, commemorates a marriage ceremony,
indicated by the joining of hands, by the raising of the man's
right forearm, and by the single burning candle in the chandelier, indicating the presence of God (Erwin Panofsky,
1953). Marriage could be entered into by a couple without
a priest. The marvelous precision of detail is strikingly illustrated in the chandelier, the mirror reflecting the couple
from the back, the leaded glass window, the wooden clogs,
and the dog, symbol of fidelity. Illumination from front and
rear defines form and suggests space and comes close to
achieving a consistent visual effect. The *Van der Paele altarpiece* at Bruges is extraordinary in its detailed splendor, and
its insistence on effects of texture. The *Madonna with Chan-
cellor Rolin* (Louvre) is reticent and impressive in its all-
pervading atmosphere of serene tranquillity and heavenly
devotion. Attention is drawn to the Christ Child, but an
effect of spaciousness unites the open loggia with the Meuse
River, the city Liége, and the distant mountains (Lejeune,
1956). Van Eyck had no equals though Petrus Christus in
Bruges should be mentioned. All Flemish painters emphasize
detail, but Van Eyck's successors also portray sentiment.

Rogier van der Weyden, the best known painter of Tournai and Brussels, was more influential than Jan van Eyck.
Rogier was trained at Tournai in the School of Robert Campin, known as the Master of Flémalle (d. 1444). Campin
had been forgotten until works, such as a triptych (*Mérode
altar*) now at the Cloisters of the Metropolitan Museum of
Art and two side panels in the Prado Museum (*Weil altar*,
1438), were rediscovered by Hulin de Loo. Both represent
well-furnished Gothic middle-class interiors with figures
placed in the foreground; the rooms recede to the rear in
sharply converging lines, distorted as on a photograph taken
with a wide-angle lens. Rogier van der Weyden's *Descent
from the Cross* (Prado), painted in the manner of a carved
altarpiece, skillfully arranges the ten figures with restrained

expressions of grief in a tightly packed composition. The panel constituted an admired and often-copied landmark of northern painting. The *Bladelin altar*, 1452 (Berlin) is named after the donor who founded the town of Middleburg, presumably represented in the background of the central panel showing the *Nativity* (Fig. 135). The ruined shed with its lone column referring to the column of the Passion on which Christ was flogged, the adoring angels, and the background are forced into a pictorial unity which lacks spatial continuity. Religious symbolism identified the ox with the New Testament and the ass (in the background and not visible in most reproductions) with the Old Testament. In the left panel of the *St. John altarpiece* (Berlin), the infant St. John is brought by St. Elizabeth to his father. It was painted perhaps after Rogier's return from Italy. Space extends backward in a less abrupt, more natural manner. In Van der Weyden's *Portrait of a Lady* (National Gallery of Art), we see the details almost before we see the picture, as if the total impression had to be gathered in piecemeal. The hands are all fingers, bunched together so tightly that they lose the human character and look more like vegetables. Drawn with precision, the veil allows forehead, hair, and ear to show through. Compared to Van Eyck's style, Rogier van der Weyden's is flat and linear.

Dierik Bouts from Holland had a style resembling Rogier's, but more rigid. His *Last Supper* represents the event as he had seen it dramatized in the mystery plays. It is exquisite craftsmanship, but placid and without expression. The scene is frozen in a vein of harsh realism that has cast shadows but no atmosphere.

Hugo van der Goes (1440?–1482) painted the *Adoration of the Shepherds* for Tommaso Portinari, the Medici agent in Bruges (Fig. 136). In a novel interpretation, Hugo introduced three groups of adoring angels, as well as a group of shepherds. Each shepherd is an individual portrait and registers prayerful devotion, loving sympathy, or startled curiosity in his own way. They are characterized as rugged, even uncouth, persons from the lower classes, intended to contrast with the saints and angels. Though of lowly origin, the shepherds too are deserving of salvation; the sincerity of their facial expression atones for their rough appearance. The emaciated appearance of the Christ Child in Netherlandish painting deliberately emphasizes helplessness. The Portinari family is represented on the side panels.

Rogier's most famous pupil was Hans Memling of Bruges (d. 1494). Memling's style is best in repose. His childlike innocence, soft modeling, and smooth, enamel-like tones suggest the Rhenish style of his German youth; his slender figures are taken from Rogier. In the *Madonna and Child with Angels* (Fig. 137) a gentle religious ceremony takes place; the angels attend the Mother and Child like ladies-in-waiting surrounding a princess. A mystic prophecy is being revealed in a mood that is playful and serious at the same time. One angel holds out the apple that symbolizes Adam and Eve's disobedience. Grapes, the symbol of the wine of the sacrament, appear in the carved border of the arch. The apple and grapes suggest the fall and redemption. The Child reaches for the apple and his finger points to the open book, to the passage foretelling the coming of the Messiah. The Virgin was idealized, her ethereal expression revealing her spiritual qualities. In the decorations of the stone arch, King David with his harp and Saint Simon the Apostle, opposite, awaken and lift their hands in wonder; cupids in the capitals watch the ceremony below. In each spandrel, an angel holds up a globe, the world over which Christ is to rule. This is a quiet celebration that starts the Infant Jesus on His mission to save mankind. The music-making angels symbolize the music of the spheres, for it was believed that the heavenly bodies in motion created harmonious sounds. Shakespeare, in *The Merchant of Venice* (Act V, Scene 1), refers to this celestial music: "There's not the smallest orb which thou beholds't But in his motion like an angel sings . . ." Devotion and art are closely interwoven; the figures are related to the lines of the architectural background, the angels' wings out in front of or behind the arches, depending on the position they occupy in space, and major attractions, like the heads, are firmly set into the pattern. The panel was perhaps intended for the private chapel of a Flemish nobleman. The castle in the background with moat and drawbridge could be his ancestral estate.

After Memling, Gerard David became the leading painter of Bruges; his figures are solid and he does not have Memling's sentiment. David was a conservative painter who was rediscovered in the nineteenth century. His *Rest on the Flight into Egypt* (Fig. 138), has harmonious color, delicate drawing, unified space, and a meditative mood. Soft blues stand against grayed tans in the foreground and sky. The tunic under the blue mantle is accented in red. The flesh tints of the child show through a gauzelike material. Note the mother's hand and the child's knee and his small feet with toes pointing in different directions. The outer mantle, spread out over the ledge, forms a veritable still life of folds breaking horizontally and vertically. The woven basket, the grasses and ferns in the foreground, show the desire of the artist to do his utmost in a loving and painstaking study of every detail. Nature is neat and orderly; individual plants appear as silhouettes in the immediate foreground. Joseph, in the middle distance, is knocking nuts off a tree with his staff. The Middle Ages had ignored the visual world as unimportant, but now it was conceded, in the Netherlands as in Italy, that the world was also a manifestation of the divine. Rocks, water, and hills were no longer represented as stage props, but as parts of the natural environment, though the Virgin and Child continued to be the important elements in the landscape.

The Cultural Background of the Italian Renaissance. With the beginning of the fifteenth century, stylistic changes in art took on greater significance, and as an expression of individualism in art, the trend has continued ever since. Styles, like handwriting, became differentiated in subtle ways, so that a fifteenth-century Italian painting is datable almost to the decade. Before the Renaissance such comparatively rapid changes of style had been characteristic chiefly of ancient Greek art; now Italy took its place with Greece in producing some of the greatest works of Western art. We may ask ourselves what brought on such a spectacular development of art and to what extent was this due to the culture.

The individuality of the Renaissance artist appears as a novelty, at least since the days of classical antiquity, as little is known about the medieval artist. The Renaissance may be said to extend back to 1300, when the tendencies that matured after 1400 began. The styles of Giotto, Masaccio, and Michelangelo mark stages of development; each one determined the stylistic trend of at least a century. It was the personal genius of such artists as Leonardo or Michelangelo that provided the energy which drove these artists to creation. Technical skill was but one aspect of their endowment, and skill was often shared with others who lacked genius. Religion, patrons, humanistic learning, and the society in which the artist lived affected the art.

Religion as a Source of Inspiration. It is noteworthy that the Renaissance proper, which virtually ended with the Reformation (1517), also produced some of the noblest works of religious art, like Michelangelo's Sistine ceiling, Raphael's Madonnas, some of Dürer's woodcuts and such contrasting painters as Fra Angelico and Grünewald. The unity of spirit that characterized the art of the thirteenth century now gave way to considerable variety, though differences of interpretation still reflected the accepted dogmas of the Church. A deeply humanizing tendency which increased the significance of the artist constituted a common bond.

Renaissance architecture and sculpture also remained dedicated to religion, though with less fervor. Except for St. Peter's, Renaissance churches hardly compare with Gothic cathedrals, and the most impressive sculptural monuments were tombs and memorials of no religious significance.

Patrons. What seemingly differentiated the cities of the Renaissance from our own was a comparatively high demand for art. At one and the same time, there were 84 wood carvers and 70 butchers in Florence (Wackernagel, quoted by Arnold Hauser). However, other facts tend to correct this impression of a high-level art culture widely supported and popularly encouraged. From other information it appears that probably few of the 84 wood carvers were important as artists. Not only the princes of the Church, but also the ruling courts, the communal governments and the heads of foreign states supported the leading artists. Ludovico, 'Il Moro, Duke of Milan and later Francis I, King of France, employed Leonardo. Sigismondo Malatesta, the notorious despot of Rimini, employed Piero della Francesca; and Ludovico Gonzaga, a "petty prince" of Mantua, employed Mantegna; but the most distinguished of all Renaissance patrons were the Medici in Florence.

From 1400–1743, throughout thirteen generations, the members of the Medici family were the most illustrious patrons of art, of learning, and of science in modern history. Eventually the last member of the family bequeathed to the state the family collection, the present-day treasures of the galleries of Florence. Lorenzo the Magnificent employed virtually all the great artists of his day; Verrocchio, Botticelli, Bertoldo, and Michelangelo were his special favorites. Finally, the governments of cities like Siena, Orvieto, Florence, and Venice used artists on public works.

The Social Status of the Artist. During the fifteenth century, the Italian artist was neither a man of means nor a member of the proletariat. He fitted into the economy at a comfortable level. Toward the end of the fifteenth century and during the sixteenth century, the artists' economic status rose. Filippino Lippi became wealthy, Perugino owned houses, Leonardo (while in France), Raphael, and Titian had considerable incomes and lived lordly lives. Toward the end of his life, Michelangelo was sufficiently wealthy to accept no payment for his work on St. Peter's.

Humanistic Learning. The interest in classical antiquity was aroused by the humanists. These literati, members of the intelligentsia, scholars, poets, linguists and, on occasion, artists like Alberti, set the fashion for things classical. They drew support from the state or depended on private gentlemen who kept humanists attached to their households for their intellectual stimulation. Even where the subject matter was ostensibly religious, an interest in classical learning was often involved. Architecture revived Roman vaults and the classical orders, sculpture concentrated on the study of the figure inspired by excavated classical statues, and painting included such classical subjects as Botticelli's *Birth of Venus*, Mantegna's **Triumph of Caesar**, and Raphael's *School of Athens*.

An Economic Interpretation of Renaissance Art. To an extent this preoccupation with the past made that section of art the private preserve of those who had the education to appreciate the setting. Whatever was painted for private palaces hardly benefited the general public. Some doubt has been cast on the idea that the whole populace was art conscious, as expressed in a report that all Florence was enthusiastic about the plan for a cathedral dome (Arnold Hauser). An economic interpretation of the art of the Renaissance may find support in the fact that the International Style was a court style. Giotto, with his glorification of Saint Francis, might have been favored by those who possessed no property, as Saint Francis had married himself to Poverty. Ghirlandaio's way of representing saints made him, according to Heinrich Wölfflin, a good bourgeois, a representative of the middle-class culture. The greater reserve of the High Renaissance style in contrast to the too familiar mingling of the people with the saints in Early Renaissance paintings, according to one interpretation, would indicate a desire to remain aloof from the populace on the part of an exclusive social elite (Von Martin).

Individualism. The striving for knowledge paralleled a spirit of enterprise, which had created a middle class based on commerce and which spread to politics. The power of money of the upper guilds prevailed against the feudal aristocracy and an emphasis on reason invaded the arts; the artist became engineer and scientist. Brunelleschi, an architect and sculptor, solved an engineering problem in the dome of the cathedral of Florence, and the laws of perspective intrigued among others Uccello. The supreme example of the merging of art with science was Leonardo. The worship of the expert gave rise to the discovery of the man of genius, as exemplified in Michelangelo. Art became the creation of an aristocratic personality, and originality, unknown to the Middle Ages, became a virtue. As religion lost its supreme control over various aspects of spiritual life, art became an autonomous expression in its own right. Art continued to serve the purposes of faith, but was judged from the standpoint of art. Unlike medieval art, which meant to elevate man, Renaissance art was to enrich life and delight man.

Italian Painting of the Early Renaissance; the Grammar of Art. Italian painting during the fifteenth century developed four tendencies, each of which dominated the work of the painters of this period: The international, continued from the Gothic, the monumental, scientific, and devotional. Masaccio represented the monumental tendency, and Uccello, Pollaiuolo, Signorelli, Piero della Francesca, and Perugino, the scientific. Painters of the devotional group—the sentimental, narrative, and pageant painters—were Fra Angelico, Fra Filippo Lippi, Benozzo Gozzoli, Ghirlandaio and Botticelli. Artists decorated a wall or the furnishings of a church or palace with a subject not of their own choice. Originality was encouraged to find a new way to express a religious or classical subject, represented as if it were contemporary with the artists' own period. Local styles developed, the Florentine, Umbrian, North Italian and Venetian being the most important. The period of Italian art from 1400 to 1500 laid the foundation for drawing and painting for all subsequent periods, including our own. It concerned itself with such problems as anatomy, composition, perspective, and representation of space, and created what might be called a grammar of visual expression.

Character of Style in Painting. In the "mode of relief" the modeling is shallow and cast shadows are few. There is no real depth, and atmospheric effects are absent; perspective is linear, and drawing is by outline rather than by brush strokes. The primary and secondary colors were used. A kind of realism emphasized isolated objects in sharp outline. Painting was more for surface decoration than in imitation of nature. True, or buono, fresco was used for walls, tempera for panels; oil was gradually adopted, especially by the Venetian School.

The outstanding painter in Florence at the beginning was Masaccio. He set the standard of monumental form and consistent illumination and he softened the contours, enveloping his figures in atmosphere. His use of broad contrasts of light and shade is illustrated in *The Expulsion of Adam and Eve* (Fig. 140), from his frescoes in the Brancacci Chapel of the Carmine Church. His fame rests on these frescoes, which became the inspiration for all painters of the Early Renaissance. Though he died at the age of twenty-seven, he revolutionized Italian painting. In his *Madonna and Child with Four Angels* (London, National Gallery), the heavy-set figure replaces the elongated Gothic type. The elliptical shape of the halo in this painting illustrates the scientific interest of the times. Masaccio's name, which means "bulky or raw-boned," describes his style.

Masolino, Masaccio's teacher, was essentially a fresco painter of the International Style. A panel of the *Annunciation* (National Gallery of Art), representing an interior of gaily decorated architecture, shows that Masolino was more interested in making the walls seem precious than real. His figures are like manikins, with hands like stuffed kid gloves and doll-like heads.

Fra Angelico, a protégé of the Medici, represents a link between the Gothic and the Renaissance. In *The Death and Assumption of the Virgin* (Gardner Museum, Boston), the conservative medieval spirit lives on in the ornamental design and in his feeling for line. In the rendering of the anatomy, as in such details as the lightly veiled Christ Child, however, Fra Angelico became progressive as his style matured. Fra Angelico, a monk, was one of the most intensely religious painters of the Renaissance. The types he invented reflect the bliss and contentment of an inner peace, and his colors are fresh and pure. Vasari tells us that Fra Angelico wept when he painted the crucifixion. However deeply he may have been moved, Fra Angelico was limited in his power to express emotion (Fig. 139).

In the small panel of *Saint John in the Desert* (National Gallery of Art), Domenico Veneziano seized upon the moment when the saint takes off his rich clothes and puts on the coat of camel's hair. The painter used this subject to present a well-shaped figure—more like an athlete than a saint—though the Biblical story says nothing about this change of costume. The figure stands in a rugged and deserted spot under a blue sky. Though Veneziano shows no firsthand acquaintance with the desert, he has improved upon Duccio's version of rocky ledges.

Paolo Uccello is particularly known for his effects of foreshortening in three battle pictures painted for Medici palaces. The figures in their squared, simplified form seem static; to emphasize depth, lances of the horsemen are pointed toward the spectator.

Andrea del Castagno (1390–1437) painted *The Youthful David* (National Gallery of Art) on a tournament shield. The posture is an adaptation from classic sculpture, like a combination of the action of the Apollo of Belvedere and the Artemis of Versailles. Goliath's head is shown resting between David's feet. Drapery folds are deep and the muscles of arms and legs stand out.

In a similar vein a *Portrait of a Man* (Fig. 141), probably by Andrea del Castagno, exemplifies line and form, which are the special province of Florentine art. The folds emphasize

form; the hand, placed in one corner, calls attention to the
expanse of the chest; the arms, cut off by the picture frame,
make it seem as though the space is not large enough to contain so much energy. The engraving of the *Battle of the
Nudes* (Ill. 117) by Antonio Pollaiuolo, has an intensity of
expression in addition to its decorative quality. In the fierce
hacking and stabbing, the artist shows off his knowledge of
anatomy. Piero della Francesca (*c.* 1410–1492) developed an
impersonal and forceful fresco style of solid and fully rounded
form. His frescoes in Arezzo (*The Legend of the True
Cross*) suggest the monumental character of the Giotto-
Masaccio tradition in a later and more elegant version.

The nude figure in convincing movement and perfect anatomy found its greatest exponent before Michelangelo in Luca
Signorelli's (*c.* 1441–1523) frescoes. In his *Last Judgment*
(Orvieto Cathedral), in the plunge of the damned, figures fall
headlong as bodies pile up in a solid wall. Andrea Mantegna
(1437–1502), the leading artist in North Italy during the
second half of the fifteenth century, created a style of archaeological classicism combined with realism that aimed at an
illusionistic effect of depth, based on linear perspective. The
actual carved columns of the frame on his altarpiece at San
Zeno are continued in a painted open loggia of the altarpiece
itself. Antonello da Messina shares with these painters an
unemotional objective style that stresses form. Having acquired a knowledge of the oil technique in Sicily through
northern painters visiting there, he carried this influence to
Lombardy and Venice.

Venetian Painting before Titian. This contributed to the
practice of oil painting by Giovanni Bellini (*c.* 1430–1516) of
the Venetian School. In his *Madonna with Saints* (Fig. 142)
in triptych form, Bellini used Mantegna's scheme of continuing the carved frame into the painted architecture of the
niche in which the seated Virgin is placed on a pedestal. His
is a stately type of Madonna, conceived in the grand style of
fully rounded form (1488), before this type had become general in Florence. In his *Feast of the Gods* (National Gallery
of Art), signed and dated 1514, the setting sun engulfs the
scene so that the costumes glow in a soft light and darker
figures are swallowed in a murky mist. The intermingling of
hues and the variations in the tints determine the color
effect. (The technical problem of Titian's collaboration on
this painting has recently been analyzed in detail by John
Walker.) The painting illustrates the story, based on Ovid, of
the God of Fertility, Priapus, making advances to Vesta,
Goddess of Chastity. Vittore Carpaccio dealt with the *Legend
of St. Ursula* in a narrative spirit of pageantry. At the transi-

tion to the High Renaissance Giorgione (1478–1510) took over Leonardo's soft style and infused his subjects with a mood of dreamy reverie. His *Madonna Enthroned between St. George and St. Francis* at Castelfranco, where he was born, was painted in oil on wood when he was twenty-six years old. The sense of atmosphere, depth and tranquillity creates a new note in Italian painting. His *Sleeping Venus* (Fig. 143), an oil painting on canvas, was the first of a type that was perpetuated by Titian and others. Figures and landscape in sweeping lines are beautifully related, as if "poured out" (Lucretius). Titian added the landscape and a cupid, now painted over, to the canvas left unfinished by Giorgione. Giorgione was also a musician; his *Concert* (Pitti), an oil painting on canvas which may be partly by Titian, shows the effect of music upon the performers. The dreamy self-absorbed expressions in the faces of the cleric and the woman singer contrast with the ardent melancholy of the player at the keyboard. Though the *Pastoral Symphony* (Louvre) has been repainted, Giorgione's poetic mood is felt. We do not know the story that is here told, and the sole content may be in the contrasting effect of clothed and nude figures in a lush landscape setting. In the *Nativity* (National Gallery of Art), there is an air of solemnity as two shepherds kneel with courtly reverence before the Christ Child. Landscape, shepherds, and design suggest Giorgione as influenced by Leonardo.

The Sentimental Trend in Florentine Painting. Fra Filippo Lippi (c. 1406–1469) represents this trend. He led a far from exemplary life; his love affair and elopement with a nun, Lucrezia Buti, helped to earn him a bad reputation, and for a time he lost his Papal stipend. In his *Madonna Adoring the Child* (Fig. 144), the youthful mother kneels before the Child against a deep forest background; the dove and God the Father are above. This graceful type of "Mystery Madonna" in all its lightness and delicacy is his own invention. The voluminous drapery breaks in large folds, massive in contrast to the girlish figure.

Botticelli (1446–1510) was the most celebrated of the early Florentine painters and one of the great artists of all times. The interest in his work is worldwide; one of the best books on Botticelli is by a Japanese scholar, Yukio Yashiro. Botticelli learned from his master, Fra Filippo Lippi; he was influenced by Antonio Pollaiuolo, and he may also have worked with Verrocchio. His frescoes are among those on the walls of the Sistine Chapel, but he is better known for his tempera panels. No other Western artist equals Botticelli in the beauty of his linear decoration. In his *Adoration of the Magi* (National Gallery of Art), the persons in the foreground kneel or show their reverence. Heads are thrust forward and eyebrows lifted; hands are folded in prayer, laid across the chest, or making the sign of the cross. Botticelli, classed with the sentimental-devotional group, also learned from the scientists. He occasionally disregarded the proper construction of figures, but he knew how to draw correctly and beautifully. Heinrich Wölfflin calls attention to Botticelli's figures, which touch the ground so lightly that they seem to be floating. Botticelli's individuality may be seen in a *Portrait of a Youth;* the features are calm, with a touch of melancholy and wistfulness and an almost feminine delicacy which only Botticelli has. This may be an idealized head, a pictorial daydream into which Botticelli projected something of himself. Botticelli's heads often show a prominent chin, high cheeks, and wavy hair in heavy clusters; hands are long, fingers, bony and thick at the joint (Fig. 145). Botticelli's reputation was based on an earlier version of the *Adoration of the Magi* (Uffizi), because it contained portraits of the Medici in the figures of the Magi. His *Allegory of Spring* is one of his most original inventions, in which Spring scatters roses and the Graces strike languid poses as Mercury chases away the mist. Venus, Goddess of Love, in a bower of rose trees, welcomes the coming of Spring. Related in subject is the *Birth of Venus* (Fig. 146), inspired by a poem by Poliziano. The figure of Venus with her heavy tresses floating in the wind is one of the memorable creations of the Renaissance (Fig. 150).

Domenico Ghirlandaio (1449–1494) was the interpreter of the local Florentine scene in its interiors, its furnishings and costumes. He worked in fresco and also painted altarpieces. One of his best-known frescoes is the *Birth of St. John,* among those he painted for the church of Santa Maria Novella. A young woman of the Tornabuoni family, who commissioned the frescoes, stands with two attendants in the focus of attention. Among his panel paintings are some excellent portraits, including the *Giovanna degli Albizzi* (1488).

Benozzo Gozzoli (1420–1498) painted the frescoes of the *Journey of the Magi* in 1469 for the private chapel of Cosimo de' Medici (Medici-Riccardi Palace), for which Fra Filippo Lippi had painted his *Madonna Adoring the Child* (Fig. 144). On three walls of the chapel the splendid cavalcade making its way over a mountainous road is a decoration in the manner of tapestries. The gorgeous pageant has retained its color and gilt.

Filippino Lippi, son of Fra Filippo and Lucrezia Buti and pupil of his father and Botticelli, completed Masaccio's frescoes. He continued in the fifteenth-century tradition on frescoes and altarpieces at a time when Leonardo was active. Piero di Cosimo (1462–1521), a contemporary of Raphael's, represents the transition to the High Renaissance style. He was influenced by Leonardo, and became a master in horizontal panels, as in the *Death of Procris* (London), a painting for a chest (*cassone*). He is distinguished by his landscapes, in which the vaporous distance has an oriental effect; he approaches Botticelli in originality.

Italian Painting of the High Renaissance. Leonardo da Vinci (1452–1519) was born in the village of Vinci, his real name being Leonardo. He was primarily an engineer and a scientist. He made original discoveries in many fields, but above all he thought it important to collect knowledge. He painted little, and was always dissatisfied with his achievements, yet his paintings represent the culmination of the scientific and the sentimental tendencies. He used the pyramidal form of composition, developed the greatest subtlety in modeling, and became the most brilliant draftsman of the Renaissance. Leonardo used both hands for painting, but his drawings and manuscripts were done with his left.

In his oil painting entitled *Madonna of the Rocks* (*c.* 1482), the sixteenth-century (cinquecento) style of the High Renaissance is foreshadowed in the manner by which hard edges are softened in what is called *sfumato* (dissolved). The fantastic grotto landscape has the minute detail of the studies of a geologist or botanist and is more in the fifteenth-century (quattrocento) style. Age has darkened the colors; originally the flowers were brighter. According to Leonardo, "chiaroscuro united to foreshortening constitutes the greatest achievement of painting," and "children should be expressed by softness and plump roundness and dimpling" (*Treatise on Painting*). The Madonna's outstretched hand accentuates the third dimension, and the well-modeled figures are placed within space. The expressive features, delicate and serious, yet smiling,[10] are Leonardo's most personal creations (Fig. 151). Another version in London is believed by some scholars to be the original, but there is no unanimity of opinion.

The Last Supper, painted in tempera on the plaster walls of the refectory of Santa Maria della Grazie (Milan), was finished in 1498, after eleven years of work. Today only the composition can be appreciated (Fig. 147), as the painting began to deteriorate early: even in Vasari's day it was in ruins. Leonardo selected as his subject the moment when Christ said, "One of you shall betray me," developing the theme from a psychological point of view. The quiet expression of Christ reflects his inner poise. As little is known about the disciples, Leonardo had to invent a character for each one. Peter, demanding an explanation, leans toward John, who sits on the right of Christ clutching a knife. Thomas, on the left of Christ, lifts a finger as if to emphasize one idea: "Who can it be?" James throws himself back in amazement. Philip, pointing to himself, seems to say, "It is not I," and Judas, with a bag of money, pulls back, upsetting the salt cellar. Andrew, hotheaded, lifts both hands indignantly, "I will not have it, it is not I." James, brother of Christ, calms Andrew. Matthew (at end) rises to listen, and John, nearest to Christ, is overwhelmed with sorrow. Leonardo here follows his own advice in the *Treatise:* "The expression of the face must be varied according to the emotional state of the person." "All limbs and attitudes must correspond to the expression of the emotion of the faces" (Osvald Sirèn). *The Last Supper* was Leonardo's supreme masterpiece; it won him his place among the great artists, and became a landmark in painting. His *Mona Lisa,* with her animated brown eyes, eyebrows plucked according to the fashion of her day, and her sweet smile, enjoys great popularity, in spite of the darkgreen tonality accumulated over the years. She is seated on a terrace against a mountainous landscape in a diffused illumination; Leonardo said: "Paint a portrait in bad weather at the fall of evening." The portrait was probably painted between 1503 and 1506, and Leonardo took it with him to France, when he was invited there by Francis I. Vasari says the unfinished portrait represented the third wife of Francesco del Giocondo, patrician of Florence (according to Raymond Stites, she is Isabella d'Este, wife of the Duke of Mantua). Whatever her identity, she has been rendered immortal in one of the great portraits of the world (Fig. 152).

Toward 1485 the High Renaissance style became apparent. Perugino's *Crucifixion* (National Gallery of Art) shows the style the young Raphael took over. The parklike landscape, where figures stand motionless with clasped hands under a calm blue sky, has the atmosphere of a pleasant summer day; the suggestion of suffering goes no further than custom required.

Raphael's short but brilliant life (1483–1520) falls into three periods. During the Umbrian-Perugino period (1483–1504), when he was an apprentice to Perugino, early Raphael paintings were hardly different from those of Perugino. During his transitional Florentine period (1504–1508), he formulated a style after having copied the great works of Masaccio and Leonardo. *St. George and the Dragon,* the *Madonna del Granduca,* and the *Madonna of the Chair,* like most of his Madonnas, large altarpieces, and portraits, are from the Florentine period. His mature period (1509–1520) in Rome included his frescoes, later altarpieces, the *Sistine Madonna,* portraits of Julius and Leo X, designs for tapestries and the *Transfiguration,* his last painting, which was finished by Giulio Romano. Raphael's work was praised by his immediate followers, and Nicolas Poussin and the French classicists acknowledged him during the seventeenth century. He was practically deified during the eighteenth century, admired during the nineteenth, and criticized during the twentieth. Raphael's drawing was based on a study of models, but his saints and madonnas are idealized types. His style was that of Perugino, enriched and perfected; his talent was to absorb influences from several artists—Leonardo, Donatello, Fra Bartolommeo, Michelangelo—and to unite these influences in a style that appeared original.

His international reputation is based on the frescoes in the *Stanza della Segnatura* of the Vatican, entitled: (1) *Disputation* (2) *School of Athens* (3) *Parnassus* (4) *Prudence, Force,* and *Moderation.* They contain no deep-seated philosophical concepts and there is little individual characterization. The interest is rather in the postures of the figures and in the way the figures are interlocked through gestures. The mood in Raphael's *Saint George and the Dragon* (National Gallery of Art) is reposeful, hardly what one might expect in a life and death battle. Rhythmic lines link up the composition in a graceful manner. The rolling Umbrian landscape, with its clear atmosphere and beautiful vistas onto towers and hills, shows nature arranged, improved, and idealized like Greek sculpture during the Classic period. The small *Cowper Madonna* (National Gallery of Art), is calm and serene. The dark cloth merges with the dark earth, and out of this dark tonality rise the light tints, the figures against a clear sky. A thin gauzelike veil encircling arm and shoulders emphasizes the solidity of the figures, and the action of the child, momentarily halted, is opposed to the relaxed posture of the mother. Mother and Child are emotionally united, their minds fixed on the future, the Passion. A meditative, serious spirit and a sweet, subdued melancholy underlie the peaceful scene. This relaxation is but a foil against which Raphael suggests an inner tension that must have been readily felt in Raphael's own day, when thoughts of religion were uppermost in the minds of men. In Raphael's *Sistine Madonna* the Queen of Heaven descends from the clouds as the curtains are drawn back (Fig. 148). Though a heavenly vision, she appears simple and unaffected; this unassuming quality is perhaps the secret of her appeal. The Christ Child's serious expression seems to reveal .is divinity, as his unchildlike gaze is contrasted with *putti* below. The Virgin, slightly embarrassed at presenting a divine Child, remains floating above the clouds. St. Barbara sinks into the clouds with eyes modestly removed from the Virgin. Pope Sixtus II, from whom the painting takes its name, points, as if to recommend mankind to the Queen of Heaven. Coming at the end of a long development of this motif, it seems to represent the ultimate solution, representing for Christian art what the Zeus by Phidias had meant to antiquity.

Raphael's skill as a space composer is well illustrated in his *Galatea* (Fig. 149), a fresco in the Villa Farnesina. Figures are combined into groups, shapes are adjusted to fill spaces, and heads in profile and three-quarter views gaze up or down for the sake of contrasting effects. In spite of wind-blown drapery, fluttering hair, and a brawny fish-tailed triton embracing a Nereid, this is a matter-of-fact presentation. The human figure is given an aloof, unemotional, and sculpturesque treatment. Raphael deals with mythology in the grand manner, and his decorative style forms the basis for a later development by Rubens and Poussin.

After the death of Raphael (1520), the full bloom and joyousness of the Renaissance turned to sober thoughtfulness under the influence of the Counter Reformation. The sixteenth century was dominated by a few outstanding artistic personalities, which include Raphael, Michelangelo, Titian, Tintoretto, and Correggio, though the style was founded on that of Leonardo.

Michelangelo Buonarotti (1475–1564) was twenty-three years younger than Leonardo, and, like Leonardo, left some of his greatest works unfinished. Michelangelo was primarily a sculptor; he painted only incidentally, and yet produced the ceiling of the Sistine Chapel. Unlike Leonardo, who was universal in his interests, Michelangelo concentrated on the human figure. He lived when art had mastered all means of expression and used these means for the illustration of great themes in religion. Directing himself toward the sublime and superhuman, he expressed his own emotions through art. He also created a style of his own, which laid the foundation for the Baroque. He lived most of his life in Florence, but spent the last thirty years in Rome. In his *Holy Family* for Agnolo Doni (1504–1506), a circular painting (*tondo*) in oil, he illustrates a complicated motion of handing the child back over the shoulder of the mother to Joseph. Much action is concentrated in a limited space, which, in its plastic richness, was perhaps aimed to surpass Leonardo's *St. Anne* cartoon. Nude figures in the background were placed there for no reason of story, but because Michelangelo took a delight in the human figure.

The *Sistine Chapel ceiling* (1504–1508), commissioned by Pope Julius II and carried through by Michelangelo under protest, created a sensation when the chapel was consecrated. A painted architecture (Ill. 113) divides the surface of the

Ill. 113 Michelangelo: Sistine ceiling, section, Vatican, Rome.
After Michelangelo, Langewiesche (1911)

barrel vault into panels with nude figures. They illustrate the *Creation*, the *Fall of Man*, and the *Story of Noah*. The vast assemblage of over 340 figures of heroic stature represents a gigantic task, even of physical endurance. Lying on his back on top of a scaffolding looking up toward the ceiling, Michelangelo himself had to press a paper cartoon against the wet plaster so the outlines of the drawing could be pricked through the paper to produce guide lines for the brush. In the *Temptation* and *Expulsion* (Fig. 153), Eve, in an easy reclining pose, receives the apple from the serpent with apparent indifference, whereas Adam reaches out eagerly, thereby assuming a fair share of the guilt. In the expulsion scene Eve crouches in the shadow of Adam. A grand sweep of line is suggested by the continuity of arms, as Adam wards off the angel. In the *Creation* scene, the Lord, rushing toward the languid Adam, passes on to him the spark of life. The energetic hand of the Lord contrasts with the limp hand of Adam, awaiting the life-giving touch. A mighty gesture of arms suggests the Separation of Land and Sea. The Lord, a heroic figure, goes through the act of creation without effort; a thrust of the arm brings forth sun and moon and darkness is held back, opening the sky to light. Five sibyls, classical counterparts to the Hebrew prophets, include three for the continents, Europe (Delphic), Africa (Libyan), and Asia (Persica), one for Italy (Cumea) and one for Greece (Erythraea). In each one an emotional element is brought out; an active force from within stirs the figure to action. Michelangelo probably had himself in mind when he painted Jeremiah, sitting listless, bowed down by sorrow. On the end wall of the chapel Michelangelo later painted the *Last Judgment* (1534–41). Christ, far from sitting in calm judgment, appears agitated with a gesture of condemnation as the Virgin shrinkingly approaches him to intercede for mankind. Patriarchs, prophets, sibyls, apostles, and martyrs crowd around Christ in fear and trembling, and present their instruments of martyrdom as claims for mercy. Michelangelo, perhaps projecting his own sense of guilt, sees doom, terror, and despair on the day of judgment. His theme is "Howl ye; for the day of the Lord is at hand; it shall come as a destruction from the Almighty" (Isaiah 13:6). A reddish glow in the lower right corner denotes the fires of hell. Salvation receives less attention than fear of punishment.

Among the Florentine painters of the High Renaissance, Andrea del Sarto (1486–1531) deserves special mention.[11] Called the "perfect painter" by the Florentines, he maintained a high level of quality, though he produced no work rivaling that of his great contemporaries. He was a fresco painter and produced altarpieces like the *Madonna of the Harpies,* an extremely competent and satisfying work that has retained its popularity.

Titian (*c.* 1477–1576) was the leading master of the Venetian School and one of the greatest painters of all time. During his long life he was enormously productive; nearly 300 canvases have been attributed to him. In his youth he painted like his master Giorgione, but gradually he developed his own style. Titian was the most evenly developed of Venetian painters; realism and idealism, form and color, a lyric as well as a dramatic expression fused in his style. He dealt with every type of subject known to his age—mythology, literature, and religion all contributed to the subjects of his paintings—though at times the idea behind the picture has been lost, as in his *Sacred and Profane Love,* painted in the mood of Giorgione.

In *Bacchus and Ariadne* (National Gallery, London), the color, though somewhat darkened by age, was not equaled till Rubens. In an unsymmetrical composition, the *Rape of Europa* (Gardner Museum, Boston), the weight of the bull on one side is balanced by the cupids in the opposite corner. In this pictorial mode, the distant shore is suggested, but not rendered to emphasize depth by exact value relations. In the *Worship of Venus* or *Garden of Love* (Prado), based on a poem by Philostratus, a swarm of romping blue-winged cupids collecting apples in baskets furnished models for all later paintings of children in landscape settings. Titian painted *Venus with a Mirror* (reproduced on the front cover) in late maturity. In this he depends more on light and shade and less on brilliance of color. Venus is seated on a couch before a mirror, a classical marble come to life, luminous, in the midst of half-tones and shadows. A string of gleaming pearls resting lightly on her blonde hair curves into light and falls back into shadow. A large earring suspended against translucent shadow catches the full light. How convincingly the hand, with its outspread fingers and its bluish and pinkish tints, is detached from the body. Not photographically realistic, it is unique; only Titian could have painted it (Fig. 154). A chain bracelet clings to the wrist, then slips away to hang vertically. The light and shadow are not due to any consistent, realistic illumination. Titian's style was removed by a century from that later mode that studied the effect of real daylight. It was not his purpose to place an object in space with scientific accuracy; he introduced only as much reality into his painting as he cared to absorb into a general decorative scheme. Linear rhythm, counting so much in Botticelli, is of secondary interest here. Titian's style is broad, almost as ample as fresco, yet his brush strokes vary. The fluffiness of hair is suggested without each hair being painted separately. We are made to feel the softness of flesh, the stiffness of brocade, the bulk of the fur-lined mantle by the handling of the pigment. This "Venetian pictorial mode" influenced the painting of the seventeenth and eighteenth centuries. Rubens, Van Dyck, Velázquez and Watteau carried on the tradition of Titian, each modifying the Venetian mode to his own lik-

ing. In Titian's technique, modeling is completed in the monochromatic underpainting, a grayish color that is not unlike
a black-and-white version of the finished painting. The color
is then added in superimposed layers of oil color, applied
thinly and transparently over the underpainting. These so-
called glazes allow the modeling to show through the film of
color.

In Titian's *Young Woman at Her Toilette* (National Gallery of Art), the dark-complexioned companion and the
mirror form a background for the woman's lighter tints. A
fullness of form stresses completeness of relaxation. Gazing
blandly into the mirror, she lifts her golden tresses in a
graceful, measured movement that emphasizes the com-
posure and calm of the scene. In this painting, as in the
Flora (Uffizi), we feel the artist in love with life; such paintings are affirmations of joys. In his *Assumption of the Virgin*
(Fig. 155), the event is made to seem plausible and is
presented as an occasion for joy on the part of the disciples
left behind. This is Mary's hour of triumph, as a cloud of
angels lift her heavenward. All participants are of heroic
stature, and the Virgin is enveloped in massive drapery
which gives her the weighty grandeur required for the
occasion.

Titian's younger contemporary, Jacope Robusti known as
Tintoretto, succeeded him as the leader of the Venetian
School. Tintoretto's aim was to combine the color of Titian
with the drawing of Michelangelo, but his audacious style did
not always meet with his contemporaries' approval. In the
Presentation of the Virgin in the Temple, an incident in the
life of the Virgin is developed into a dramatic event. The little girl appears before the high priest at the top of a magnifi-
cently carved staircase (Fig. 156). To emphasize depth, a
figure in the lower foreground points toward the Virgin, another figure reclines, occupying three steps to suggest exten-
sion in depth. Some of his masterpieces are in the Ducal
Palace and in the Scuola di San Rocco in Venice. In a
painting, perhaps done at the very end of his life, *Christ at
the Sea of Galilee,* the water looks as if it were part of
a vast sea. There is hardly anything to equal it in painting until the nineteenth century. The sea is plowed up into
sharp ridges as clouds move in the distance. Flashes of
light fringe the tops of the waves and accent the leaves. The
illumination is scattered and figures, no longer isolated, have
become a part of the landscape. The figure of Christ beside
the water exists in volume. Though the feeling for reality
seems emphatic, if we examine carefully, we note this is an
artificial storm, inconsistent in detail but powerful in its general impression (National Gallery of Art).

The greatest decorative painter of the Venetian School of the sixteenth century was Paolo Veronese (1528–1588), born in Verona. His art is distinguished by a heightened emphasis on decoration, on fine costumes and magnificent architecture; splendid settings are more important than in Titian or Tintoretto. Pageantry, which disappeared before the concentration of the High Renaissance, returned with all the gains that painting had made since the days of Botticelli. A Veronese has a silvery, cool light in place of Titian's warm glow. The paintings for which he is best known are huge canvases containing many figures, often representing festivals in great marble halls, as in the *Feast in the House of Levi*. A small but very fine canvas, the *Finding of Moses* (Fig. 157), shows that Veronese did not succumb to the influence of the Counter Reformation, but carried the worldly spirit of the Renaissance late into the sixteenth century. The scene of Pharaoh's daughter finding the child Moses is presented like a climax in a play. Every motif is executed with a studied elegance, the kneeling maid presenting the child, Pharaoh's daughter startled, moving back, the supporting ladies pointing to the child as to a miracle. The illumination is decorative; a fringe of light sets off a figure or a shadow brings out an arm or a head.

Correggio (1494–1534) of Parma in North Italy carried Mantegna's illusionism further by painting domes as if they did not exist (Parma Cathedral). Celestial figures are seated on clouds surrounded by angels. Michelangelo labored over human giants in solemn and cosmic grandeur, whereas Correggio tossed off goddesses and angels in a spirit of play. As a late-comer, Correggio profited from the accumulated knowledge of the past. His *Marriage of St. Catherine* (Louvre), in its delicate tenderness, foreshadows the eighteenth century. In his *Holy Night* the mystery of Fra Filippi Lippi and Leonardo is given an extravagant and more obvious interpretation (Fig. 158). A magic, but very real, light emanates from the Christ Child, and every device is used to force the point. Correggio interpreted his topics in the spirit of gaiety; his colors are light, his brush work swift, his manner elegant. What has worried his critics is the fact that he no longer identified himself with his subjects. He reached beyond the Renaissance, and his true followers came in the Baroque and Rococo painters of the seventeenth and eighteenth centuries.

Mannerism in Painting. Michelangelo (d. 1564) and Titian were the outstanding artists of the century. The remaining sixteenth-century painting has been classified under such labels as Mannerism; Academicism, or Eclecticism; and Naturalism. Dates no longer indicate styles, as different styles were in vogue at the same time. Mannerists like Correggio followed Leonardo, and El Greco followed Tintoretto, a Mannerist in his own right. Others in this category were Bronzino, Pontormo, Vasari, II Rosso, Giulio Romano and Parmegianino; these painters were more than imitators. The founding in Bologna of an academy (1585) by Lodovico Carracci (1555–1619) with his cousins Annibale and Agostino brought the idea of the art school and the term Academicism into being. This Bolognese School was eclectic; it selected from all the masters and used plaster casts, medals, drawings, books, and engravings as teaching material; the study of nature was also included. The Venetian School and Correggio were held up as models; Guido Reni (1575–1642) and Domenichino (1581–1641) were late adherents. The naturalism of Michelangelo da Caravaggio (c. 1565–1609) introduced a trend opposed to Raphael in his choice of models, taken from the streets, and in his harsh contrast of white light against near-black shadows.

In the seventeenth century, painting in all countries again took on a spontaneous character; the term Baroque is a convenient common denominator for work done in this period.

Renaissance Sculpture in Italy. The classical influence was less in sculpture than in architecture, and Renaissance sculpture was often more vital than the Roman examples which inspired it. As in painting, a vigorous naturalism developed, as well as tendencies to idealize or to emphasize a devotional element. Brunelleschi, Donatello, and Pollaiuolo represent the natural trend; Ghiberti, the Della Robbias and Desiderio da Settignano the devotional-sentimental. Verrocchio combined both, and Michelangelo established the style of the High Renaissance. Sculpture was largely a Florentine movement, except for Jacopo della Quercia, who was Sienese. The cathedral of Florence, which had been in the process of construction for a century, still required sculptural decoration, and the same was true of the Baptistery. The sculptors who developed in connection with these buildings, Brunelleschi, Ghiberti, Donatello, and others, contributed much to the formation of the style.

In a competition with Brunelleschi, Ghiberti won the commission to design what became his first bronze doors for the Baptistery in Florence. In a second pair of doors, Ghiberti developed a pictorial style for bronze in ten large panels, using small figures in the round on the front planes, a graceful Gothic line, and elaborate perspective with one plane merging into another (Fig. 159). Ghiberti worked on the Baptistery doors for over twenty-five years. Michelangelo praised them, saying that they were worthy of being used for the "gates of Paradise."

A terra-cotta relief of *Madonna and Child* (National Gallery of Art), attributed to Ghiberti or to Jacopo della Quercia, reflects the transition from Gothic to Renaissance. The tilt of the Virgin's head, the pronounced curve in the backward lean, and the sloping shoulders are still in the manner of Gothic art. Sculpture attained freedom in the modeling of the figure before painting. The study of the figure was based on observation rather than on a scientific knowledge of muscles and bones. Much attention was paid to drapery; cloth was soaked in plaster to give it stiffness and draped over a wooden figure to give the sculptor something to work from.

Jacopo della Quercia (c. 1375–1438) of Siena developed a style anticipating Michelangelo. One of a series of reliefs from the portal of San Petronio, the *Creation of Eve*, shows his powerful figure compositions using massive breadth contrasted with linear rhythms (Fig. 160). The *Tomb of Ilaria del Carretto* (Lucca Cathedral), traditionally attributed to Jacopo, shows a recumbent figure on a sarcophagus with *putti* and garlands in high relief. The pleated drapery folds provide a lively contrast to the tranquillity of the figure and the massive breadth of the base.

Donatello (c. 1385–1466), a pupil of Ghiberti and the outstanding sculptor of the fifteenth-century Florentine School, was the first great sculptor of modern art. He excelled in all phases of sculpture, in reliefs and in monumental sculpture, in wood, terra cotta, stone, and bronze. He overcame the Gothic traditions and established a more robust manner, based on individual character. Most of his works were executed for the Church, the guilds or the communal government. Donatello's realistic tendency appeared in such early stone statues as the emaciated *St. John the Baptist* (Bargello), who is represented singing and tottering as he returns from the desert. The bronze statue of *David* was perhaps the first freestanding nude statue since antiquity. The features are calm, but the lean and lanky proportions are quite unclassic. His colored and gilt *Annunciation* (Fig. 161) rivals Ghiberti for graceful elegance. The details are adapted from the Classical. To have something to show the pilgrims at Padua during the jubilee year of 1450, Donatello made a marble and bronze high altar. He also produced for Padua the first equestrian bronze statue on a large scale since ancient times, his *Gattamelata* (9 feet high), an Italian word meaning "honeyed cat" (like our expression "sly dog"). The small rider, represented as a Roman general, was a monument to the Venetian general Erasmo da Narni. Donatello's remuneration for this work was 1650 gold ducats, equal to more than $10,500 (1911). Two bronze pulpits with reliefs of figures modeled with dramatic energy were finished and installed in the Church of San Lorenzo (Florence) after his death. An early statue of *David* for the Martelli family, now in the National Gallery of Art, is perhaps the most important example of Renaissance sculpture in the United States.

Antonio Rossellino (1427–1478) was the designer of the vertical wall tomb for the humanist *Leonardo Bruni* in Santa Croce. A marble sarcophagus supports a bier with the recumbent figure of the deceased. The effect depends on the well-proportioned niche and a wealth of beautifully carved architectural detail and figures in relief.

One of the best-known of Donatello's pupils was Desiderio da Settignano, of whom Vasari says, "He was one of the fortunate few who, without labor, achieved loveliness." Less versatile than Donatello, the delicacy and charm in his specialty, youthful figures, are unsurpassed. He worked only in marble. Desiderio was particularly successful with portraits of young women and children, as in the portrait of *Marietta Strozzi,* which exists in three versions, one of which is at the National Gallery of Art (Fig. 162). Marietta was a young heiress who was considered unduly emancipated: "She lived where she liked and did what she would." In Desiderio's relief of the *Young Christ with Saint John* (National Gallery of Art), the relief is hardly over a quarter of an inch deep, which gives to the head of Christ a vaporous, apparitionlike quality.

Mino da Fiesole (1430?–1484) is known for his exquisite craftsmanship and delicate finish. He worked directly in marble without sketches or models. His portrait busts are his best works, but he is hardly on a level with the leading sculptors. Benedetto da Maiano (1442–1497), chief pupil of Rossellino's, amplified his master's form; his style led to the High Renaissance.

Antonio Pollaiuolo (1432–1498) and Andrea del Verrocchio (1435–1488) were both painters and sculptors. Both worked in bronze and excelled in expressing energy and in bringing out detail. Verrocchio's bronze statue of *David* (Bargello) represents him as a wiry youth, more energetic than Donatello's. Verrocchio's bronze equestrian statue (Ill. 114) of the condottiere *Bartolommeo Colleoni* suggests a man of compelling force. Equally remarkable is the careful rendering of details in the armor and trappings. Verrocchio also communicated something of this grim determination in his terra-cotta bust of *Lorenzo de' Medici*. Force, intelligence, and a penetrating gaze suggest a living personality (Fig. 163).

To produce a sculpture less expensive than marble or

Ill. 114 Verrocchio: Bartolommeo Colleoni, Venice. *After Lübke*

bronze, yet permanent, Luca della Robbia introduced a glaze over the pigment on terra cotta, which protected the color from moisture. The Della Robbia family continued in this craft for three generations, headed by Luca, his nephew Andrea, and Andrea's son, Giovanni. Much of this work is in relief and was designed to be placed in a building, over a door or against a wall. The colors are blue for backgrounds and opaque white glaze for the figure; details are sometimes picked out in other colors. Luca's art is the least archaeological, the least mannered, and the most human.

Michelangelo's statue of *Moses* (Ill. 116) in San Pietro in Vincoli (Rome) is from an unfinished tomb for Pope Julius II. This seated marble statue represents Moses angered when he found his followers about to worship the golden calf. Suppressed aggression is revealed by the knitted brow; pain, in the expression of the eyes; contempt, in the thrust-out lower lip. In the Biblical account, Moses gives vent to his anger and destroys the tablets. Michelangelo has him tightly clutch the tablets, which had almost slipped from his grasp. The moment of the most intense excitement has passed. We may imagine that the left hand, caught in the drapery, had gripped his beard a moment before, but now, relenting, has slipped back. The original intention of rising is still indicated by the feet drawn back. The arm in full front view contrasts with the arm holding the tablets, the thin garment with the heavy cloak draped over his knees.[12] The horns on his forehead are due to a mistranslation of the Hebrew text, which refers to rays of divine inspiration rather than horns.

Michelangelo's activity may be divided into five periods. The *Pietà* (St. Peter's, Rome) and the *David* (Academy, Florence) were the important works of the first period (1475–1505). The Sistine Ceiling occupied much of the second period (1505–1512); the unfinished tomb for Pope Julius II, of which the *Moses* remains as the most important part, took up the third period (1513–1521); the Medici tombs, the fourth (1523–1534); and work on the dome of St. Peter's, his fifth (1534–1564).

Michelangelo's contemporaries did not understand the idealized Medici figures; they complained that Giuliano and Lorenzo de' Medici did not resemble the dukes. Michelangelo, who had no interest in portraiture, replied that in a thousand years no one would remember what the dukes looked like. The feminine figure of Night and the masculine figure of Day were placed on Giuliano's sarcophagus (Fig. 164); Giuliano was frank and forthright, like night and day. Lorenzo, on whom great hopes had been placed to advance Italian political unity, succumbed to mental illness and died early. He was represented by Michelangelo with bowed head and features cast in shadow. On Lorenzo's sarcophagus the figures of Twilight and Dawn, the uncertain hours, symbolize his uncertain, gloomy disposition. However theology and philosophy may be involved in the Medici monuments, and in his Sistine Chapel paintings, Michelangelo's own emotional life holds the key that should give a more complete understanding of them.

Mannerism in sculpture is represented by Jacopo Sansovino, a Florentine artist who settled in Venice, Benvenuto Cellini (1500–1572), Giovanni da Bologna (1524–1608), and Adriaen de Vries, one of Giovanni da Bologna's pupils. Benvenuto Cellini made his reputation as a goldsmith. The *Salt*

Cellar of Francis I, cast, chased, and enameled, is his only
authenticated work of this nature (Fig. 165). The place for the
salt is boat-shaped, the pepper box is in the form of a Roman
triumphal arch. Statues of Neptune, the God of the Sea, and
Tellus, Goddess of the Earth, are seated facing each other
to symbolize salt and pepper as the gifts of sea and earth.
Cellini's best-known bronze is the statue of *Perseus* (Florence), holding the decapitated head of Medusa. With an
abundance of detail, especially in the ornate base, the
Perseus is technically accomplished, though the subject is
repellent.

A Flemish artist, Jean de Boulogne, translated to Giovanni
da Bologna after he had become a naturalized Italian,
was the last great sculptor of the Italian Renaissance.
His bronze *Mercury* poised in flight on one foot is a highly
perfected figure, elegant in proportions, and skillful in balance. *The Rape of the Sabine Women* (Loggia dei Lanzi,
Florence) was planned for variations of posture and for three
types of nudes, to afford changing aspects of forms which
gracefully glide into one another as the group is viewed
from different positions. The figures are intertwined to follow
a spiral line, the contrasting types adding to the interest of
the group.

Adriaen de Vries followed Giovanni da Bologna in style.
In a bronze group of *Virtue and Vice*, idealized classic figures
assume elegant poses; in another period the same subject
might have been staged as a strenuous battle between good
and evil. Feminine form is given a masculine touch, as men
had long served as models in the study of the human figure.

*Painting in France, Spain, the Netherlands and Germany,
1400–1600: France.* During the fifteenth century, when
France was still divided politically, local centers of painting
developed, as at Avignon (p. 203), Dijon, Moulins (Burgundy), Bourges, and Tours. The Netherlandish influence
was strong in such triptychs as *The Burning Bush* by Nicholas Froment (d. 1482). The Master of Moulins in the *Virgin
in Glory* (Moulins Cathedral) combines Netherlandish types
with the breadth of the Italian style. The most distinguished
of painters who worked for the courts of Charles VII and
Louis XI was Jean Fouquet (1415–1477 or 88) of Tours;
Fouquet was primarily a painter of miniatures. In a panel of
a diptych of *Étienne Chevalier* kneeling with folded hands
beside St. Stephen (Berlin), little remains of the Netherlandish style. The right panel represented *Agnes Sorel*, mistress of Charles VII (Antwerp). The Christ Child and angels
seem like additions to atone for the worldly spirit of this
court-art style with no pretense of devotion. Fouquet's por-

trait of *Charles VII* (d. 1465) depicts with sober, unprepossessing realism the king who drove the English out of France.

The School of Fontainebleau. Before the development of advanced means of communication between countries, the Renaissance was introduced to France through ambassadors, bishops, cardinals, merchants, and artists who went to Italy and brought back Italian paintings. Invasions of French kings into Italy also contributed to the spread of Italian art to France. Between 1495 and 1559, four French kings, Charles VIII, Louis XII, Francis I, and Henry II, made raids into Italy under one pretext or another. These wars were comparatively mild; at times the French kings were even well received, and the contrast between medieval France and civilized Italy impressed the French.

Francis I brought Andrea del Sarto, Benvenuto Cellini, and Leonardo da Vinci to France (Amboise). Rosso (1531) and Primaticcio (1532) were settled in his hunting palace at Fontainebleau, where they painted interiors and contributed to the application of Renaissance details to the decorative arts. Primaticcio's elongated forms influenced Germain Pilon and Jean Goujon.

During the reign of Francis I (1515–1547), a vogue started for portraiture, chalk drawings and small paintings of which many have survived (Musée Condé, Chantilly). Jean Clouet, a Fleming, was the chief master of this school. The portrait of *Francis I* (Louvre), attributed to Jean Clouet, has sharp features, elaborate costume and pale flesh tints. Jean's son, François Clouet (*c.* 1510–1572), court painter to Francis I and II and Charles IX, painted *Diane de Poitiers* (?) in a crowded interior seated in her bath beneath a red satin curtain. The drawing is meticulous and sculpturesque, the smooth surface like enamel (Fig. 166); Flemish and Italian influences have merged in a new style. A favorite of the French School is the portrait bust, attributed to François Clouet, of *Queen Elizabeth of Austria*, wife of Charles IX (Louvre). Its delicate flesh tints contrast with a rich pattern of exquisitely rendered costume detail; textures are expressed without a trace of brush work. His full-length portrait of *Charles IX* (Vienna) is essentially an elaborate decoration; though it is inscribed 1563, it was probably painted in 1569 when Charles was nineteen. Corneille de Lyons painted small portraits on wood against blue-and-green backgrounds in a smooth technique. The same type of portrait was produced on enamel by Leonard Limousin. Essentially this portrait style was international and not basically different from Holbein's.

Spain. Unlike Italy and the Netherlands, Spain had no middle class; Church and court were the chief patrons. Her great sixteenth-century artist was El Greco, meaning "the Greek." He was a Cretan by birth (*c.* 1537) and called himself Domenico Theotocopuli, the Spanish equivalent of his Greek name. At the age of twenty-three, he left Crete for

Ill. 115 Strozzi Palace, Florence. *After Roger Smith*

Italy, where he studied with Titian and was influenced by Tintoretto. Around 1572 he settled in Toledo, Spain. El Greco elongated his figures as Parmigianino had done, but differed from the Italian Mannerists in his nervous energetic style full of movement and originality. He introduced tall disjointed figures with impossible heads and color dissonances, chiefly white, ivory, black, vermilion, yellow ocher, and rose madder. Even during his lifetime there was much controversy about his art, but fellow artists and successors such as Velázquez held him in high regard. In the *Virgin with Saint Inés and Saint Tecla* (Fig. 167), the drapery is arranged in jagged folds, and in the color we can see a kinship with Tintoretto. Surfaces hang together; we no longer feel the parts as elements of a geometric pattern, and each figure merges in the total impression. The hands of Saint Tecla continue into the palm leaf she holds, the edge of the Virgin's mantle is taken up by the Child's leg. The head of the Virgin is in shadow, and the heads of the Christ Child and both angels are in the light. The icy blue of Saint Tecla contrasts with the warm orange of the cloak of Saint Inés. Hands are large and heads, small, often arranged in contrasting diagonals. El Greco's style has been called "flamelike"; one's eye seems to glide along lines that undulate from side to side and from shape to shape. Such fusion of color, form, and movement was new in painting. In Botticelli, movement was around contours; where figures meet, the linear rhythm was slowed up. Bellini's *Feast of the Gods* seems static in comparison to El Greco.

The Netherlands. The Italian influence in the Netherlandish sixteenth-century painting produced such painters as

Jan Gossaert (known as Mabuse), Barent van Orley, Pieter Pourbus the Elder, Antonio Moro, Paul Bril, and others. They were able and elegant followers of the Italian formula, but made no basic contributions of their own. The most original painters between the late fifteenth and the early seventeenth centuries were Hieronymus Bosch and Pieter Brueghel the Elder.

Hieronymus Bosch, c. 1450–1511. Bosch, misunderstood for centuries, now stands revealed as one of the great masters of the Reformation. Leonardo expressed himself through a purely rational pursuit of knowledge and seemingly applied this to his art;

Ill. 116 Michelangelo: Moses, Rome.
After Lübke

Bosch, with equal penetration, used an emotional, folklore approach as a disguise to express his own religious convictions, the "Adamite gospel of primally pure, divine nature" (Wilhem Fränger). His use of symbolism was not arbitrary personal imagining of "gruesome pictures of spooks and horrid phantoms of Hell" (Carel van Mander), and his "incoherent imagery," as Fränger has demonstrated, was well founded on mythology and folklore. As revealed by psychoanalytically oriented study, his choice of symbols in many cases is valid today. Until specific Biblical and literary references were discovered and related to these seemingly

fantastic inventions of Bosch's, the background of this
Adamite sect was misunderstood and many wrong interpretations made. Only in certain devotional paintings done for
the initiated did Bosch use this involved symbolism; others
of his paintings were more easily intelligible. The triptychs
with concealed meanings are in Madrid (Prado): *The Millennium* (or *The Garden of Earthly Delights*), *The Temptation of St. Anthony* and the *Hay-Wain*.

In *The Millennium* (Fig. 168) the central panel was not
meant as a warning against a life devoted to sinful lust, but
was intended to describe "the beauty and purity of original human nature as it was created by God in his own
image" (K. Burdach, as quoted by Wilhelm Fränger). This
panel illustrates the joys of Paradise as it was in the time of
Adam, before original sin came into the world. According
to a psychoanalytical interpretation, all culture requires a
sense of guilt; before the year 1000 A.D., Christianity had
created thousands of saints, demanded by its superego to
expiate its own transgressions. Hell, in the right wing of the
Millennium triptych, was reserved for the members of the
old Church. Bosch seems to have belonged to this sect of
the elect. The fountain in the Creation panel is based on the
exact wording of the Latin Vulgate Bible, *fons,* which later
was translated more freely as "vapor." The crystal tubes, glass
globe, and phials of the fountain of life symbolize a pro-
creation "clear and transparent as the play of light on water"
(Fränger). Details that seem incomprehensible to us had a
specific meaning to those initiated in the creed that anticipated the Reformation and was critical of the clergy. Wilhelm
Fränger devoted an entire book to his well-documented
theory that in Bosch's religious paintings of his own convictions his seemingly extravagant imagination is thought-
controlled. In the *Death of the Miser* (National Gallery of
Art), Bosch deals intelligibly with a topic of the *ars moriendi*
type known from woodcuts of the period. Bosch shows full
command of the traditions of Flemish realism and his ability
to express emotions through distortion and caricature in such
subjects as *The Prodigal Son* (Rotterdam), *The Crowning
of Thorns* (Prado), and *The Carrying of the Cross* (Ghent).

Pieter Brueghel the Elder, b. before 1530–1569. Brueghel
was the first among the great Northern painters to paint
easel pictures for private use. He chose his subjects and dealt
with them in his own way, like a modern artist. He made
Biblical subjects thoroughly real; *The Massacre of the Innocents* (Vienna) takes place in a Flemish village with snow on
the ground. Brueghel preferred subjects which called for
masses of people (*Open-Air Wedding Dance,* Detroit); he

created new types such as allegories, animal, still-life, and marine subjects, and genre pictures dealing with manners and customs (*Proverbs*, Berlin). Brueghel was a satirist; like Erasmus of Rotterdam and Rabelais, he was contemptuous of the world, which he believed was the work of the devil. An excellent draftsman, he used a flat style with little modeling and linear perspective. His technique suggests a water-color manner painted on canvas in the oil technique of Van Eyck. He did not use models, but painted from memory.

Ill. 117 Pollaiuolo: Battle of the Nudes, detail. *National Gallery of Art, Rosenwald Collection*

In the *Triumph of Death* (Prado), the power of death, cruel and inexorable, is symbolized by many skeletons in a wide and bare landscape; the story is told by separate incidents. Groups of skeletons war on humanity with arrows, scythes, millstones, nets, forks, swords, and gallows; the human beings are from all classes, including a king and cardinal. In the *Parable of the Blind* (Naples), on a gray, misty morning six grotesque figures, haggard and helpless, stagger across the fields in uncertain movements: "If the blind lead the blind, both shall fall into the ditch" (Matthew 15:14). Brueghel may have had in mind as the blind one of the wandering preachers coming from the lowest and most ignorant classes, who gathered followers and formed sects. Brueghel, a believer, had no sympathy for such persons who were, he thought, misleading the crowds. *Winter* (Vienna) is one of his paintings of the months, of which twelve were originally planned. It shows hunters in a landscape with snow and has a fine atmospheric effect. Brueghel was the founder of the Netherlandish winter scene tradition continued in the seventeenth century. *Summer* (Metropolitan Museum of Art) illustrates a harvest scene when, during the rest period, the peasants eat and nap under the hot midday sun (Fig. 169).

Brueghel had been virtually forgotten for centuries until interest in him revived in our own day. Brueghel, like Bosch, was Dutch, and shows Bosch's influence in the symbolism of some of his religious subjects. Brueghel left many drawings, which were reproduced by engravings for popular distribution. Over half his paintings are in a broad format; fourteen are in Vienna and perhaps half a dozen in museums in the United States.

Germany. Albrecht Dürer (1471–1528) of Nuremberg was a painter-poet, profound and powerful. Traditionally accepted as the greatest German artist, he is in a class with Leonardo and Michelangelo. He copied Mantegna, studied nature, and was influenced by the Venetian School. In his art Dürer showed a grandeur of conception and a richness of feeling affected by medieval fantastic elements. He had imagination, originality, and a love for craftsmanship. Dürer was an excellent draftsman, and developed the woodcut and engraving on copper. As a portrait painter, he painted his friends in the spirit of the miniaturists—every wrinkle, hair, and vein are shown. He paints as if using a pen. In the marvelous portrait of *Hieronymus Holzschuher,* the eyes reflect the window opposite the sitter (Fig. 170). He seeks to express character through detail, and succeeds in catching much of the spirit of his sitter. He is the pioneer of genre painters with his drawings from popular life; studies of animals, flowers, and plants were not taken up again until a hundred years later. Dürer's landscapes also were in advance of his time. Through his books he created a scientific basis for art, as Leonardo had done in Italy. Through Italian influence, the life-size figures, the nude, and composition, instead of juxtaposition of detail, came into German art. Italian artists associated with merchants, princes, and high dignitaries of Church and state; German artists were in a class with saddlers, glazers, and bookbinders. There were no courts and no connoisseurs in Germany to support art, and commissions were modest compared to those of the Medici. The best painters owed their development to themselves rather than to their country.

Dürer was sober and factual, hardly the most emotional

of the German artists of this period. But in the woodcuts of
his *Apocalypse* (Fig. 171) there is tension and struggle, nerv-
ousness and restlessness. Dürer never again achieved lines so
charged with energy. *The Apocalypse* was an instance of an
artist designing and publishing his own book. The story of
the Revelation was illustrated in fourteen woodcuts with the
text on the back. A breadth of manner differentiates woodcuts from engravings; the woodcut line is thick and bold.
Woodcuts are related to pen drawings, as the artist draws
directly on the block. After he has finished, a skilled craftsman cuts and chisels the background away, leaving the pen-
drawn lines.

His engraving *Melencolia* (Fig. 172) represents a winged
figure seated in the foreground, supporting her head on her
hand in a thoughtful, almost brooding fashion; in the other
hand she holds a compass in a listless, absent-minded way.
A closed book is in her lap, her hair hangs in disorderly
strands, she gazes into the distance. Tools are on the floor in
disorder, a bat holds a scroll inscribed *Melencolia I*. Melancholy, one of the four temperaments, implied a person given
to speculation and apathy. Though the instruments for
science and labor are at hand, no action takes place. A great
deal may be read into this print, and it also reflects Dürer's
grief on the death of his mother, which is hinted at in the
magic square (upper right-hand corner).

The engraving of *St. Jerome in His Study* represents the
scholarly saint—the translator of the Bible into Latin—the
saint who loves the quiet of his own study. Light pours in,
reflecting round leaded panes on the reveal of the windows,
and bringing out the grain of the heavy ceiling beams. Shadows are transparent and light, opaque, as in nature. An expression of textures makes cushions seem soft and glass,
hard. The mood is one of peaceful contemplation.

The charm of Dürer's engravings, as in his *Knight,
Death and the Devil*, is partly due to the fact that the medium is so clearly expressed; one feels tool and materials,
burin and metal. What is admired in this print is the precision with which the plate is finished, as shown in the delicate modeling of the horse, the trappings, the ground, with a
lizard on the right and in the opposite corner a skull, at
which the horse of Death sniffs. The Knight, undaunted by
Death and the Devil, is a symbol of the devout Christian
for whom life is a crusade against fear and temptation.

Hans Holbein the Younger (1497–1543) of Augsburg was
on a level with the greatest painters, but was given little
opportunity to show his talents in historical and religious
painting. He lived much of his life in England and ten years

in Basle; he left Augsburg early and, in his art, was an internationalist. Holbein was different from Dürer; he was more objective, and excelled in portraiture. His colors are thin and rich, no brush work is visible; he is clear and precise in the handling of oil and crayons. His drawings were engraved by others on metal and wood, as in his famous series of 41 small plates, *The Dance of Death.* Each one is about 2 inches square, but is remarkable for breadth combined with expressive detail. The plague of 1348 had struck Europe in succeeding epidemics, all but depopulating some districts. Holbein's *Dance of Death* was one of many representations in art, that for centuries dealt with the uncertainty of life following the Black Death.

Ill. 118 Holbein: Dance of Death: The Peddler. *After Brandt (1923)*

His interpretation was inventive, and at times less sinister and touched with satire: as in the expression of misery on the *Peddler* who discovered the skeleton tugging at his sleeve (Ill. 118). His work includes many drawings of individuals of the court of Henry VIII, who took him into service at 30 pounds a year and payment for all works done. Holbein was put in charge of pageants in honor of the coronation of Anne Boleyn; he painted Jane Seymour (two portraits, Vienna and Woburn Abbey), and went to Milan to paint Christina of Denmark, Duchess of Milan. His greatest portrait, that of *Joseph Hubert Morett* (Dresden), was formerly attributed to Leonardo. In the portrait of *Erasmus,* we feel the sensitive, intellectual spirit of the scholar. In the portrait of *George Gisze,* he paints the merchant in his office, emphasizing textures in the many details (Fig. 173). *The Madonna of the Burgomaster Meyer* (Darmstadt), painted for the Burgomaster Jacob Meyer of Basle for his family chapel, is broad and massive in figure and background. Domestic intimacy is combined with a monumental character in the motif of the Virgin affording protection under her mantle.

Matthias Grünewald (*c.* 1480–1530) is the representative of

German painting of a third manner, a soft colorful style. Emotional and realistic, Grünewald suggests space through color and light and shade, as well as through the expressive gestures of his figures. The twentieth century tends to place Grünewald above Dürer; certainly he is the most original of the German painters. The *Isenheim altar*, larger than the Ghent altarpiece, with three pairs of shutters, is painted in oil on wood (*c.* 1510–1520). The altarpiece (now at Colmar) represents chiefly the Nativity and the Crucifixion. The inner panel shows the *Nativity* with a joyful choir of angels playing musical instruments and the Virgin and Child with a flood of colored light shining down upon them. This festive decoration combines the ceremonial impression with simple domestic details such as the washtub and cradle. One inner shutter shows the *Annunciation*, the other the immaterial Christ resurrected as an "astral body." In the *Crucifixion* (Fig. 174), Christ, larger in scale, is terrible and repulsive. The intensely realistic heavy corpse weighs down the cross; fingers cramp and legs twist. St. John in a carmine-red garment points to Christ. The natural is exaggerated, the emotion and grief are carried to an unbearable extreme. The spirit of the age was mournful and terrifying; "dances of death" were painted as a protest against the love of life, luxury, and ease of the Late Gothic. The Passion of Christ was Grüne-wald's special theme; he painted the Crucifixion four times; one of these is in the National Gallery of Art. Grünewald's contemporaries did not judge his art aesthetically, but experienced it emotionally. His capacity to express the extremes of grief and joy is well illustrated in his chalk drawings, as in his *Weeping Angel* (Berlin). The soft chalk, through an accurate definition of the shapes of the lights and darks, gives a vivid impression of distorted features. Of all representations of Madonna and Child outside of Italy, the one Grünewald painted for the small village of Stuppach is perhaps the most favored. With all its German flavor, this painting has much that recalls Leonardo, and for subtlety of expression Grünewald is his equal.

Several movements existed side by side in German painting around 1500: (1) the more general one, linked with the Italian Renaissance, leaned on Raphael and Classic art; (2) the other romantic trend was represented by Grünewald. He belonged to the Reformation, which introduced a conflict between faith and knowledge, creating a state of unrest. This was also the period of the peasant wars against the aristocracy, a revolt in the economic sphere paralleling that in religion.

An appreciation of landscape appeared in the so-called Danube style of western Bavaria and Austria. Albrecht Altdorfer (b. before 1480–1538) and Wolf Huber discovered the beauty in nature. A romantic intimacy characterized Altdorfer's religious settings, as in the *Birth of Christ* (Vienna), placed in a winter landscape at night. In a well-known woodcut entitled *The Holy Family at a Fountain,* Mary has seated the Christ Child on the rim of a huge fountain placed under a Gothic vault. In a painted *Birth of the Virgin,* the event is placed in the choir of a cathedral, the scene includes a cradle and a stately bed. Child angels in the air circle between the piers and beneath the vaults in a dance of jubilation. Altdorfer's most important work represents Alexander's victory over Darius (Munich) and is an extraordinary performance of imagination and skill (Fig. 176). We look down as from a hill upon a sunset landscape with lakes, towns, and distant hills rendered with atmospheric effect and convincing spaciousness (dated 1529). On a wide plain the two opposing armies of massed infantry and cavalry, in full armor, are locked in battle. Thousands of men are included on a wood panel (about 15 by 10 feet); those in the foreground are rendered in considerable detail. Individually the figures are quite free in action, but the postures of the horses are toylike. Strategy rather than the horror of battle is emphasized; the fallen and wounded disappear in the total effect.

Lucas Cranach the Elder (1472–1553), painter and engraver, is stylistically related to the Danube School. He is particularly successful in uniting figures with landscape. In the *Rest on the Flight into Egypt* (Fig. 175), child angels of various ages surround the seated Virgin as attendants and playmates. Cranach was a friend of Luther's and court painter to Frederick the Wise of Saxony. The quality of the works ascribed to him varies because the many assistants in his large shop participated in works that bear his signature. His *Portrait of a Saxon Lady* is a competent example of the international portrait of the period, with special emphasis on a linear ornamental style. It is also a source of information on Renaissance jewelry (Fig. 178).

Renaissance Architecture: Italy. The chief Florentine architects were Filippo Brunelleschi, Leone Battista Alberti, the humanist, and Michelozzo, who began as a bronzeworker. Brunelleschi (1379–1446) designed the dome of the cathedral of Florence on an octagonal base, with ribs and an inner and outer shell (Fig. 104). The dome, placed on a high drum, dominates the skyline of Florence. It was built for external effect, a characteristic of Renaissance architecture, and was the largest dome built since the Pantheon. Thick walls (15 feet), a steep (elliptical) dome, and chains of timber and iron were used to resist the thrust; purists have criticized this use of chains in stonemasonry. Despite these objections, the dome is handsome and an excellent piece of engineering. Brunelleschi also designed the monumental *Pitti Palace* and the graceful *Foundling's Hospital (Opedale degl' Innocenti)*. One of his most refined works is the *Pazzi Chapel* (attached to the Gothic church of Santa Croce), with its finely proportioned façade in the Renaissance style and its interior dome on pendentives. The Early Renaissance used both the Roman basilica type plan and the central Greek cross plan in its churches. Brunelleschi's church of *San Lorenzo* in Florence is unvaulted and uses Corinthian columns supporting round arches for the nave arcade. Alberti's church of *Sant' Andrea* at Mantua has barrel vaults on a Latin cross plan and a dome on pendentives. Inspired by Roman vaults, it has great breadth and repose. A porch in front of the façade was suggested by the Roman triumphal arch, and the use of the colossal order foreshadowed the Baroque.

Michelozzo (1396–1472) became the special architect of the Medici. The *Medici-Riccardi Palace,* which he originally designed for the Medici, was built around an interior court; the exterior, bare and forbidding, is more medieval than Renaissance. Fearing the jealousy of his enemies, Cosimo de' Medici had rejected a more elaborate design submitted by Brunelleschi. The stories on the exterior of the *Medici-Riccardi Palace* diminish in height and the rustication of the stones decreases with each story to avoid monotony. The crowning cornice is one-tenth the height of the building. The *Strozzi Palace* (Ill. 115) by il Cronaca (Simone Pollaiuolo) is another Florentine example. Boldness as well as grace, delicacy, and an emphasis on detail are characteristic of Early Renaissance architecture.

The chief architects of the Italian High Renaissance in Rome were Bramante, Raphael, Baldassare Peruzzi, Sangallo the Younger, and Michelangelo. Architecture expressed through its medium the same balance and repose found in painting. The façade of the *Cancelleria Palace* (Bramante) is undisturbed by strong indentation, but there is variety in space division. Each opening is an individual unit, and a sharp definition of surfaces produces contrasts. As in painting, there are no transitions and modeling is flat and shallow. In the *Cancelleria* and *Farnese* (Sangallo) *Palaces,* beauty depends on a repetition of similar areas, fundamental rectangles are repeated, and diagonals kept parallel. This type of design used in classical art reappeared in the Renaissance. The courtyard in travertine of the *Farnese Palace* was inspired by the Colosseum in the use of the Doric, Ionic, and Corinthian orders. The expression is vigorous compared to the *Cancelleria;* the arches are elliptical to increase the sense of mass and weight. Michelangelo redesigned the three palace façade of the *Palaces of the Senators* and the *Conservatori* and the *Capitoline Museum,* and placed the equestrian statue of *Marcus Aurelius* in the center of the *Piazza del Campidoglio.* In each façade a single colossal order was used to include two stories. The colossal order became part of the architectural repertoire, and found many imitators. The *Medici Library* and the *Medici Chapel* adjoining San Lorenzo in Florence were designed by Michelangelo. In the latter, coupled, recessed columns suggest the free and ornamental use of the orders as used in the Baroque period.

The church of *St. Peter's* in Rome (begun 1506) had its origin in Pope Julius II's ambition to create the most magnificent monument to the glory of the Papacy and the Christian religion (Fig. 177). A competition was won by Bramante, and the old basilica of *St. Peter's* was torn down to make room for the new church. Michelangelo eventually took over the construction of the dome, which was made the dominant element of the design. The cupola rests on double columns which terminate the ribs; the thrust is resisted by chains placed within the masonry walls. The drum springs from a solid base and smaller cupolas are placed in the corners for transition. The dome is made in two shells; the inner shell is hemispherical, the exterior, pointed. In this dome Michelangelo set a standard for every dome thereafter, from *St. Paul's* in London to the *State Capitol* in Madison, Wisconsin. *St. Peter's* is the largest church ever constructed, with an area of 18,000 square yards (*Milan Cathedral,* 10,-000; *St. Paul's,* 9,350; *Hagia Sophia,* 8,150; *Cologne,* 7,400). The diameter of the dome (about 137 feet) is smaller than that of the *Pantheon* (about 142 feet), but the nave is higher than that of Amiens, and there are 29 altars and about 148 columns. The nave is a huge barrel vault and the dome on pendentives is illuminated by windows in the drum. Through a lack of scale, the dimensions are not felt; the main pilasters are 94 feet high, the capitals 9 feet wide and 10 feet high. Carlo Maderna lengthened the nave (begun 1605) and added the façade, which obstructs the view of the dome from the east for a quarter of a mile. The spacious *Piazza San Pietro* with its fourfold colonnade by Giovanni Bernini, its fountains by Maderna, and its Egyptian obelisk forms an impressive approach. To the right of St. Peter's is the *Vatican Palace,* the residence of the Pope and a separate state within the city of Rome. Planned by Bramante but not completed by him, the exterior of the palace is monotonous; the interior is largely given over to offices and galleries housing the many art treasures of the Vatican collection.

Venice also contributed to the Renaissance in the interiors

of the *Ducal Palace* and the façades of the court. Façades of
palaces on the Grand Canal were treated with superimposed
columns and balconies, as in the *Vendramine Palace*. Various
members of the Lombardo family, as well as Michele San-
micheli (Palazzo Grimani), were the architects. Perhaps the
finest Venetian Renaissance monument was created by
Jacopo Sansovino in the *Library of St. Mark's*. The fusion
of architectural form with sculpture in relief, the calculated
proportions, and richness of detail aroused the enthusiasm
of architects down to the twentieth century.

Andrea Palladio (1518–1580) was the most influential architect of the Late Renaissance. The drawings in his published works were the models for architects everywhere. Palladio used a combination of a major order, an arch, and a
smaller order in the arcades added to a medieval hall known
as *The Basilica* in Vicenza. This motif became known as the
"Palladian motif." His design for the *Villa del Capra (Ro-
tonda)* at Vicenza, a square domed building with a pedimented
portico added like part of a classical temple to each side
of the square, was widely imitated in all countries. Another
well-known architect, Giacomo da Vignola, measured fragments of Roman architecture and published the classical orders as a system of proportions.

Renaissance Architecture and Sculpture Outside of Italy.
The Gothic was eventually supplanted by the Renaissance
style in France, Spain, Germany, the Netherlands, and England. Renaissance forms were introduced through Italian architects who built Italian buildings in these countries. During
the Early Renaissance, Lombardy, being closest to the
northern countries, had a preponderant influence. The medallions and candelabra motifs from the *Certosa* of Pavia
were adapted. Portable objects such as Italian furniture,
intarsia, prints, and book illustrations brought the Italian
Renaissance style to the attention of the northern countries
and influenced decoration. Another influence came through
stonemasons, who copied details from engravings of portals,
columns, and entablatures; hence the main change in the
northern Renaissance was one of ornamental detail. Italian
architecture was based on masonry, cut stone and rustication; the northern countries used wood and half timber, so
that Italian forms were often unsuited to local materials.
Façades of city houses were decorated with pilasters, the
steep Gothic roofs remained, and gables in step form were
decorated with obelisks.

France. The role played by the Medici as patrons of art
was taken over in France by the kings. Francis I (Early
Renaissance) and Henry II (High Renaissance) gave their
names to the sixteenth-century styles in architecture and

Fig. 200 Vervoort the Elder: Pulpit, Antwerp Cathedral. *Copyright A.C.I. Bruxelles*

Fig. 201 Hobbema: View on a High Road. *National Gallery of Art, Mellon Collection, 1937*

Fig. 202 Ruisdael: The Jewish Cemetery. *Courtesy Detroit Institute of Arts*

Fig. 203 Vermeer: Artist in His Studio. *Courtesy Kunsthistorisches Museum, Vienna*

Fig. 204   Hals: Witch of Haarlem (*Malle Bobbe*). *Berlin Museum. Photograph, National Gallery of Art*

Fig. 205   Rembrandt: The Mill. *National Gallery of Art, Widener Collection*

Fig. 206   Rembrandt: Night Watch. *Copyright Rijksmuseum, Amsterdam*

Fig. 207   Rembrandt: Self-Portrait. *National Gallery of Art, Mellon Collection, 1937*

Fig. 208 Hogarth: Marriage à la Mode, plate I, The Marriage Contract, engraving. *National Gallery of Art, Rosenwald Collection*

Fig. 209 Rowlandson: Grog on Board. *National Gallery of Art, Rosenwald Collection*

Fig. 210 Blake: Adam and Eve with Archangel Raphael in Paradise, illustration, Milton's *Paradise Lost. Boston Museum of Fine Arts*

Fig. 211 Reynolds: Lady Caroline Howard. *National Gallery of Art, Mellon Collection*

Fig. 212 Gainsborough: Blue Boy. *Courtesy Henry E. Huntington Library and Art Gallery, San Marino, California*

Fig. 213 Lenôtre: Versailles gardens. *Courtesy Pan American World Airways*

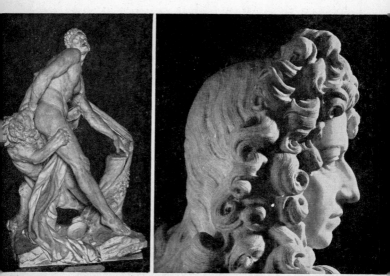

Fig. 214 Puget: Milo of Croton, Louvre. *Giraudon*

Fig. 215 Coysevox: Duc de Chaulnes. *National Gallery of Art, Kress Collection*

Fig. 216 Falconet: Madame de Pompadour as Venus with the Doves, detail. *National Gallery of Art, Kress Collection*

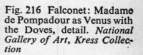

Fig. 217 Poussin: Triumph of Neptune and Amphitrite. *Courtesy Philadelphia Museum of Art*

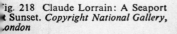

Fig. 218 Claude Lorrain: A Seaport at Sunset. *Copyright National Gallery, London*

Fig. 219 Louis Le Nain: A French Interior. *National Gallery of Art, Kress Collection*

Fig. 220 Watteau: Le Mezzetin. *Metropolitan Museum of Art, Munsey Fund, 1934*

Fig. 221 Boucher: Venus Consoling Love. *National Gallery of Art, Chester Dale Collection, (gift)*

Fig. 222 Chardin: Soap Bubbles. *National Gallery of Art, gift of Mrs. John W. Simpson, 1942*

Fig. 223 Caffieri (style of) corner piece, lacquered wood. *National Gallery of Art, Widener Collection, 1942*

Fig. 224 David: The Sabine Women, Louvre. *Archives Photographiques*

Fig. 225 Ingres: The Apotheosis of Homer, Louvre. *Archives Photographiques*

Fig. 226 Géricault: Raft of the Medusa, Louvre. *Archives Photographiques*

Fig. 227 Delacroix: Greece Expiring on the Ruins of Missolonghi, Museum of Bordeaux. *Photograph, National Gallery of Art*

Fig. 228 Constable: The Cornfield. *Copyright National Gallery, London*

Fig. 229 Millet: The Gleaners, Louvre. *Archives Photographiques*

decoration. The court of Francis I cultivated the arts, and in architecture created a series of splendid châteaux and palaces. These begin with a wing added by Francis I to the *châteaux at Blois*. On the south façade toward the court, the mullioned windows, the elaborate cornice and balustrade, and the steep roof with gargoyles and dormers are in the Gothic spirit. The exterior spiral staircase is a rich combination of Renaissance and Gothic carved ornament and complex stone cutting. In the *château of Chambord* (Fig. 179) the roof is the most striking feature, a forest of dormers, chimney stacks and stone cupolas placed over staircases. Though Chambord has been condemned as "a pleasing failure," we feel less inclined today to pass an artistic judgment on such a prodigious effort of the past. It seems shocking to us that this vast structure was used only for a few days each year by a pleasure-loving court as a hunting lodge. The *palace of Fontainebleau*, enlarged by Francis I and by later kings, became one of the landmarks of the French Renaissance. Il Rosso and Francesco Primaticcio worked on the interiors, an example of which is the *Gallery of Francis I*. A coffered walnut ceiling is combined with paneled walls enriched with fresco paintings and stucco decorations. Il Rosso may have been the first to combine painted decoration and sculptured relief of figures, masks, urns, shells, and festoons on the same wall. Francis I had at least eight châteaux erected, his building activity culminating in the southwest façade of the *Old Louvre*. Within his lifetime the Gothic was transformed into the mature High Renaissance style. Architecture became a matter of disposing orders over a façade, and the emphasis was on unity and proportion.

The influence of the Roman School of Bramante is represented by the Italian architect Sebastiano Serlio, a pupil of Peruzzi's in charge of Fontainebleau, and by Primaticcio, pupil of a disciple of Raphael's. The first French architects were Pierre Lescot, Philibert de l'Orme, Jacques Androuet Du Cerceau, Jean Bullant, and the sculptor Jean Goujon.

The *Louvre* (Fig. 180) is the largest palace in the world (about 49 acres) and the chief architectural monument of the French Renaissance and Classic periods. Originally designed as a royal palace, it is now used as a museum. The *palace of the Tuileries* was added later, but was destroyed by the French Commune (1871). The total development of the Louvre embraced over three centuries (1547–1878). An old Gothic château was replaced when Lescot began work on the southwest wing of the *Louvre*. Fine craftsmanship and excellent taste made the *Lescot Wing* a work of distinction.

Jean Goujon was the most celebrated French sculptor of the sixteenth century. His important carving was architectural.

He strove for effects through elongated forms and drapery arranged in pleats and swirls. His *Diana on a Stag* is graceful and decorative, like the Italian painters of the Fontainebleau School. For the *Fountain of the Innocents*, constructed for the triumphal entry of Henry II into Paris (June 26, 1549), Goujon carved five nymphs with clinging drapery (Fig. 181).

The *Tomb of Louis XII and Anne of Brittany* (Fig. 182) was carved from Carrara marble and erected by Francis I at the Abbey of St. Denis, the royal mortuary, to the memory of his predecessor. This type of tomb was called "house of death"; the nude figures of the deceased were carved on the sarcophagus and placed under an arcaded structure framed with pilasters and carved with arabesque reliefs. Above this structure, the king and queen, as they appeared in life, kneel in front of *prie-dieus*, symbolizing their resurrection. The recumbent figure on the lower platform of these sculptured monuments developed out of the custom of laying out the body on the bier in funeral ceremonies.

Spain. The Classical period (1556–1650) of the Spanish Renaissance was dominated by the sculptor Alonso Berruguete and the architect Juan de Herrera. Berruguete, a pupil of Michelangelo, Bramante, and Raphael, created numerous marble wall tombs for the interiors of cathedrals. The Plateresque (Fig. 102) was the most attractive but not the only Spanish Renaissance style. The *Escorial* (1559–1584) near Madrid, begun by Juan de Bautista and carried on by Herrera, is a domed church in a great complex of austere courts and buildings of yellowish-gray granite. More monastery than palace, the *Escorial* expresses the ascetic taste of Philip II. The Italian sculptor Leone Leoni furnished the church with elaborate bronze groups of the families of Charles V and of Philip II.

England. The dearth of painting and sculpture in England prior to Hogarth is due to the systematic destruction begun by Henry VIII (1509–1547) and completed under the Commonwealth (1649–1660). Remembering the persecution under the Inquisition and in England under Queen Mary, Protestants decapitated statues and slashed paintings as gestures of revenge, symbolically striking at those who had tortured their ancestors. Nevertheless, England has preserved a rich heritage of manor houses, of which many today are being used for educational and institutional purposes. The Early Renaissance includes the Elizabethan (1558–1603) and Jacobean periods (1603–1625), the latter named after James I. As in France, Gothic and Renaissance motifs were combined. Each house formed a unit with its gardens, terraces, fountains, and hedges. Less ostentatious than the French château and more informal than the Italian palace, the English mansion expressed a mode of living different from that of Continental Europe. Among the well-known Elizabethan mansions are *Haddon Hall, Hardwick Hall, Kirby Hall,* and *Longleat House.* The long gallery with its low stucco ceiling, ornamental mantelpiece, and paneled or tapestried walls is the most characteristic feature of the manor house. Windows were large and H- and E-shaped plans opened up courts for light and air. John Shute and John Thorpe were the architects responsible for many of the designs.

The Netherlands and Germany. The combination of brick with stone and emphasis on dwelling houses and guild halls rather than palaces gave the Belgian and Dutch towns a character of their own. Gothic buildings received Renaissance additions, and in Holland churches were converted to Protestant use. The use of stepped gables, as in the houses on the *Grand Place* in Bruges and on the court façade of the *Musée Plantin,* is typical. The *Antwerp Town Hall* (c. 1565) is one of the outstanding examples of the Renaissance style in Belgium; the *Leyden Town Hall* (1579) suggests a Moorish influence in Holland.

Germany was divided into small kingdoms and principalities, each with its own capital. No unified style resulted as it did in France, as a centralized government was lacking. Netherlandish, Italian, and French influences were felt in those regions adjacent to these countries. Municipal architecture in city halls was more characteristic than churches or palaces. A more native German Renaissance style developed during the sixteenth century in Nuremberg, in Strasbourg, and in Stuttgart. Heidelberg Castle was once the most ambitious Renaissance castle in Germany. Destroyed during the wars of Louis XIV, it is a romantic and much beloved ruin. The more recent wars have also destroyed some of Europe's important architectural monuments.

Decorative Art. The stained glass of the Gothic period receded in favor of fresco decoration and wall paneling, but tapestries continued to be produced in the Netherlands and France. Furniture followed the Renaissance style, though few new types were developed. Chests and tables became more sumptuous. The carved and inlaid chairs were heavy and formal and architectural in structure; they were not yet designed for comfort and had to be used with cushions. Costumes for men as well as women received a degree of attention that is in striking contrast to the sober fashions of today. Even men spent large sums on dress and felt their dignity demanded what seems ostentatious to us. In addition, much heavy jewelry was worn, such as the chains and pendants that often appear in Renaissance portraits (Fig. 178). Rock crystal, the hardest of stones, was ground into vases, cups, and crosses, engraved and later carved like sculpture. The Saracchi workshop of Milan had an international reputation with the courts of several countries (Fig. 183). In ceramics, majolica in the shape of plates, vases, jars, drugpots, and ewers was painted in a variety of styles and covered with tin-enamel. Italy, Spain, and France developed their own varieties. Italian potteries—such as those of Faenza, Urbino, Gubbio, Deruta, Castel Durante, and Siena—became known for the styles of individual decorators. In ceramics, France developed its Saint-Porchair and Palissy wares and enamel painted copperware, painted in tones of gray with figure decorations, which was produced by Pierre Reymond and others at Limoges. Though glass had been known since antiquity, it was still not common. Iron received its most distinguished expression in elaborately embossed helmets and parade armor made by well-known armorers of Milan and worn on state occasions. In addition to Cellini, there were many other goldsmiths, such as Jamnitzer of Nuremberg and Altenstetter, who was court goldsmith to Emperor Rudolph II. Inspired by a study of antiquities, the Italian Renaissance developed a specialty in medals and plaquettes modeled in relief and cast in bronze by the cire-perdue process (Fig. 184). Perhaps the most distinguished collection of medals, plaquettes, and small bronzes, formerly the Dreyfus (Paris), now the Kress Collection, is at the National Gallery of Art.

Conclusion. In Western art, the Renaissance appears as the period during which painting and sculpture, subordinate during the Gothic period, came into their own, and the personality of the individual artist, formerly submerged, developed for art unprecedented depth and variety.

Sculpture was enriched beyond the stage of development of Greek art through an insistence on what differentiated one individual from another rather than on an emphasis on elements of a common humanity. Since the loss of ancient painting had been complete, the Renaissance created painting for Western art, defined its problems and produced masterpieces which have remained unchallenged.

The Italian Renaissance laid a foundation for architectural ornamentation that remained valid until the advent of modernism in our own period. Art assumed an importance in cultural life to an extent that has not been equaled since. In the expansion of Italian art to other countries, France produced the most attractive adaptation of the Italian style, while Spain and Germany produced the only painters who stand comparison with the great artists of Italy.

CHAPTER X

Baroque and Rococo Art:

1600 - 1800

Cultural Background. In the Catholic countries, a revitalized Church used art to glorify religion, even though the pre-eminence of the Church as a patron of the arts declined. Art, once the handmaiden of religion, now increasingly served kings, princes, and members of the aristocracy. Absolute rulers flourished during the rise of nationalism, until they were driven out by wars of liberation and revolution in the Netherlands (1648), in the North American colonies (1776), and in France (1789). In the Spanish and Portuguese colonies of Middle and South America, church and state united to create overseas empires. In this conquest, Western Art, through the Spanish and French Baroque, was extended to Latin America and French Canada.

Art broadened its appeal outside of church and court through such painters as Goya, Hogarth, and Rembrandt. In Protestant countries, as in Holland, England, and parts of Germany, the painting of religious subjects ceased entirely. Landscape, heretofore used as a setting for religious topics, was developed for its own sake, and portraiture, which expressed a stately formality during the Renaissance, reflected the individual personality during the Baroque.

During the nineteenth century, the Baroque was looked upon as a period of artistic decadence; Baroque meant theatricality, and its virtuosity was thought to conceal a lack of content. As much of Baroque art was intended to glorify an absolute ruler, it found no favor with the democratic spirit of a new era. But such moralizing against Baroque culture overlooked the vitality of Baroque art. Men had become aware of the size of the world and the telescope had revealed the cosmos beyond. The foundations of

science were extended; mathematics, the purest of the
sciences, invented and developed differential calculus, and
music, the most immaterial of the arts, produced such
composers as Bach, Handel, and Gluck. Architecture developed into city planning, the first since antiquity. Baroque
painting and sculpture reflected the concept of an expanded
universe, as medieval art had sought the salvation of the soul.

Characteristics of the Baroque Style. The term Baroque
applies to the seventeenth century; the Rococo, a more delicate version of the style, is usually preferred for the eighteenth century.[13] In distinguishing characteristics common to
styles in architecture, sculpture and painting, Heinrich Wölfflin differentiated between painterly (*malerisch*) and plastic
(*plastisch*). The Renaissance style was classified as plastic
(sculpturesque), the Baroque as painterly (pictorial). The
plastic character of Renaissance art defined form through
contours and solids that appeal to our tactile sense, as in a
Raphael Madonna. In contrast, the painterly character of
Baroque art softened contours in light and shade, appealing
to our visual sense, as in a Rembrandt painting. Baroque
painting stressed space and used light and color to
"dissolve" form. Sculpture and architecture depended for
effect on the use of light and shade. Contours were irregular
and the total effect, be it of a sculptural group or of a building, was indented rather than compact and solid. In painting,
the "mode of relief" was set aside in favor of the "Venetian
pictorial mode" or the "mode of full visual effect." Baroque
architecture aimed at dramatic effects and Baroque sculpture
portrayed emotional intensity or imitated the startling effects
of nature. The skills of reproducing realistic effects in all
media were developed to an unprecedented degree.

The Baroque was able to fuse three elements inherited
from the past. From the Gothic, Baroque art took over a
striving to express the supernatural and an interest in closely
observed detail in nature, and from the Renaissance, the
Baroque continued the use of Classic forms in architecture.

The Baroque in Italy: Architecture and Sculpture. The
Baroque found its characteristic expression in Italy, Michelangelo having supplied the first trend in that direction (see
p. 246). Maderna's *Façade of Saint Peter's* (Fig. 185) demonstrated a search for surprises through variations. Adjacent
bays differed in the use of triangular and curved pediments
and in the contrast of recessions and projections. Balustrades,
statues, and sculptured groups above the attic softened the
skyline and provided the irregularities the Baroque was so
fond of.

Baroque exteriors developed variety by introducing curves

into the plan. The entrance portion of the central-plan domed church of *Sant' Agnese* (Rome) was recessed through incurving corners and flanked by towers treated like open pavilions. The orders were used in engaged columns, in pilasters enclosing arches, and in pediments enriched with carving and statues (Ill. 119). Variety was obtained through novel combinations, as in the façade of the church of *San Carlo alle Quatro Fontane*. The main entablature of the ground floor curved in over the side bays and out over the center. A huge cartouche crowned the façade between the curved sections of the crowning entablature (Ill. 120). Both churches are by the great Baroque architect Francesco Borromini. One of the most effective of Baroque churches, *Santa Maria della Salute*,

Ill. 119 Church of S. Agnese, façade, Rome

Ill. 120 Church of S. Carlo alle Quattro Fontane, Rome

designed by Baldassare Longhena in Venice, was given a
dramatic location at the head of the Grand Canal. It is eight-
sided, has a central dome buttressed by great scrolls carrying statues, and there is a second dome over the choir. The
exterior furnishes a variety of views, partly due to its prom-

inent location and partly to its complex design, which produces ever-changing perspectives.

The most versatile of Baroque artists was Lorenzo Bernini (1598–1680). In architecture he introduced such novel features as the *Scala Regia* stairs adjoining St. Peter's in which the side walls are not parallel, but converge toward a vanishing point. In the same way, the straight sections of Bernini's *colonnade* adjoining the façade of St. Peter's converge toward the oval-shaped piazza. The Baroque spared no effort to mingle what was real with what was only apparent. In Bernini's bronze canopy over the altar in St. Peter's, the columns twist and bronze consoles, connected by incurving bronze hangings, converge over the center; thus the baldachino was designed of contrasting elements. Placed under the dome of St. Peter's and against a restless and distracting architectural background, only the compelling force of dark bronze could hold its own (Fig. 186). Bernini's most renowned religious work and one of the typical expressions of the Baroque is the altarpiece within a niche representing *The Ecstasy of Saint Teresa* (Fig. 187). A smiling angel holds an arrow pointed at the swooning saint, who is limp and defenseless; a supernatural experience is made so concrete that heavenly bliss is hardly distinguishable from earthly love. The dramatic postures, the drapery broken into torrents of pleats and ridges, marble clouds, and gilt rays are pictorial to a high degree. A colored lighting, reflecting on the group from a concealed source above, adds to the effect. On either side of the niche, members of the family of the donor, carved in relief as if seated in the box of a theater, look down upon the heavenly spectacle. One of the most extraordinary portrait busts of any period is Bernini's bronze *bust of Louis XIV* of France (Fig. 188). Louis XIV represented the height of absolutism in the monarchial system of seventeenth-century Europe, and the bust was intended to give the most elaborate expression to the glorified head of the state. Bernini invented the motif of blown drapery to magnify the impression of grandeur. The false curls are like waves of the ocean, the drapery seems to be slashed by a storm; it is as if only the elements of nature could provide a setting worthy of so colossal a person. Rulers had to be serene like gods, and so the face is calm, like the quiet center of a raging whirlpool.

Academic and Baroque Painting. The Academic followers of the Carracci School—Albani, Domenichino, and Guido Reni—were formerly greatly esteemed, but have lost favor today. The exception is Guido Reni's *Aurora;* its obvious attractions win this painting a following in all periods. What Bernini was to sculpture, Pietro da Cortona (b. 1596) represented in painting; he shared with Bernini a talent for decoration. He was also an architect, and is known for his mural decorations of the Barberini Palace in Rome and the Pitti Palace in Florence. Ceilings were painted as if open to the sky, framed by a simulated architecture with figures enthroned on clouds or surging through space. In the painted sky, the coat of arms of the Barberini family is borne upward, supported, and encircled by mythological figures. For skill, imagination, and a sense of overpowering drive, Cortona's style was completely successful. His style was carried a step further by Andrea dal Pozzo (1642–1709) in the ceiling fresco of Sant' Ignazio (1685) in Rome. In this case, the real architecture of the church is seemingly extended to the open sky through painted columns and arches. From a single station point in the center of the nave, the illusion is complete; the simulated architecture of the ceiling unites with the real architecture into one overwhelming effect (Fig. 189).

Caravaggio (p. 230), named after his place of birth, lived a short but stormy life, during which he created a new artistic style. His influence on European painting was considerable, extending to such artists as Ribera, Velázquez, and Murillo in Spain, to Rubens in Flanders and Elsheimer in Germany, and through Elsheimer, to Rembrandt in Holland. His early manner, represented by a painting of *Bacchus* (Uffizi), was cool in color, porcelainlike in surface, and flat in a precise delineation of areas. Figure and still-life were painted with an objectivity typical of nineteenth-century impressionism. Man was considered as part of the universe, but visually no more significant than the bowl of fruit and the goblet of wine included in this *Bacchus*. In Caravaggio's middle period, as in *The Death of the Virgin* (Fig. 190), illumination was provided for dark interiors by a shaft of light from above. Even in religious paintings, Caravaggio used crowded groups of plainly dressed rough models, selected from everyday life, a kind of realism offensive to the ruling Mannerist painters of the day. The emphasis on expressions of grief was in the taste of the period, but the "bare feet and bloated figure of the Mother of Our Lord" were considered shocking, and this painting was banished from the church (Nikolaus Pevsner). In his *Seven Works of Charity* (Naples), the dark tonality is characterized by night scenes with torch illumination. Figures that are in the path of the light stand out sharply, but most of the action is enveloped in shadow. Caravaggio's illumination of sharply defined contrasts of spots of light and areas of darkness was developed by Rembrandt into a transparency of shadow of greater subtlety.

Caravaggio was a quarrelsome, hot-tempered person who

was in constant trouble with the police due to his aggressive acts, in one case, murder.[14] His talents and good connections, aided by frequent changes of residence, helped to keep him out of prison. Caravaggio's revolution in painting constituted an attack against the established Mannerist School. This attack through the weapons of art against a rival school of painting might have represented an artistic sublimation of his antisocial aggression.

Alessandro Magnasco (1677–1749) was a transitional painter who linked the seventeenth century with the eighteenth. Magnasco's paintings of seascapes represent the agitated forces of nature. In his *Baptism of Christ* (National Gallery of Art), his impressionistic style differed from the scientific impressionism of the nineteenth century by being subjective. The artist was guided only in a general way by natural appearances.

Giambattista Piranesi's most famous etchings, his *Prison Scenes* (*carceri*), are highly imaginative; such prisons never existed except in the mind of the artist, though Roman ruins were suggested in the large interiors and the massive masonry. All plates of the set of fourteen give a sense of tremendous scale, dwarfing the figures, which ascend vast staircases or look down from dizzy heights. Light streams in from above, as it might penetrate into underground vaults.

Venetian Painting. The greatest painter of the eighteenth century in Italy was the Venetian, Giovanni Battista Tiepolo (1695–1770). An inspired decorator, he took over painting where Veronese and the seventeenth-century Roman Baroque painters left off. He covered whole interiors with architectural decorations, including life-sized figures that seem to extend space in all directions (Fig. 191). Tiepolo had complete command of the most astounding problems of foreshortening; his style had gusto and strength without being weighty. Tiepolo introduced a new element in painting—luminosity—and by adding touches of pure red and blue, he made his decorations count as effects of color. In such paintings on canvas as his *Madonna and the Goldfinch* (National Gallery of Art), Tiepolo represented the climax of Italian Madonna painting. Without Raphael and Titian and the seventeenth-century painters of light, this painting would have been impossible, and yet there was no direct imitation, but rather a fusion in which these earlier ideas have merged.

The best representative of the architectural view picture (*vedute*) was Antonio Canale, called Canaletto. He was a contemporary of Tiepolo's and specialized in painting city views, virtually portraits of cities; Venice was a favorite subject. In his *View of the Ducal Palace* (Fig. 106), the eye enters

the picture across a shadow in the foreground. The Library
of St. Mark's (p. 247) beyond the palace and the domed
church of Santa Maria della Salute (p. 255) in the left distance
are shown in contrasts of light and shade. Illumination is
used to keep the regularity of architectural forms from becoming monotonous. The effect also depends on painstaking
draftsmanship and convincing perspective; the color is conventional. Francesco Guardi represented the same subjects
in a light, transparent technique. He painted by hops and
skips, with little dots of color for people and lines that skim
the surface in quick flashes. Pietro Longhi was a specialist
in interiors who painted the diversions of Venetian society
at home or at concerts or balls. The small paintings like
The Simulated Faint (National Gallery of Art) continued the
genre tendency of the Dutch seventeenth-century school on
a more genteel level.

The Baroque in Germany. The Baroque and Rococo styles
were imported from Italy into Germany and Austria and
resulted in some exceedingly fine architecture. The numerous
absolute rulers of German principalities during the period
from 1690 to 1770 aspired to palaces in imitation of Versailles; Zwinger Palace (now destroyed) at Dresden by
Mätthaus Pöppelmann and the Würzburg and Bruchsal palaces by Balthasar Neumann are examples. Fischer von Erlach
and Hildebrandt were the chief Baroque architects of Austria.

The Catholic Church carried through monumental building projects in connection with monastic establishments, with
a religious devotion reminiscent of the Middle Ages. The
order of the Jesuits was particularly active, and the Jesuit
churches in Rome, the Gesù and Sant' Ignazio, furnished the
models for other countries. The monastic church of *Melk*
(Jacob Prandtauer, architect) dominated the landscape from
a cliff above the Danube. Its festive interior of gray marble
with gilt ornamentation replaced the largely white background of Italian naves. Balconies between massive Corinthian pilasters in green and gilt suggested the box of an opera.
Grandeur in the use of the colossal order and the dome on
pendentives was softened by delicacy of detail in sculpture
and carving. An effective exterior is the façade of the
church of the Fourteen Saints (Balthasar Neumann, architect). Classic motifs like pilasters and pediments were used in
an original attempt to reproduce the verticality of the Gothic.

Andreas Schlüter created perhaps the best-known Baroque
bronze in the equestrian statue of the *Great Elector* (Berlin).
It incorporated various influences, including the Roman
from the Marcus Aurelius statue. The painted wood sculpture
of Bavaria and Austria in church altars is undeniably charm-

ing. The figures of the Virgin, Mary Magdalene, the saints, angels, and representations of the Christ Child are attractive, as if the artists had taken pains to search for beautiful models. Their expressive features register grief, tearful sorrow, or radiant joy. The spread of a hand, the gesture of an arm, and the posture of the figure are lively and graceful. Franz Ignaz Günther (1725–1775), court sculptor, had a large shop in Munich. His *Pietà* and *Annunciation* (1764) at Weyarn in Upper Bavaria represent the Bavarian Rococo at its best. The group of the *Guardian Angel* shows the Archangel Raphael leading young Tobias by the hand. The contrast of the haughty angel and the overawed but trusting youngster is unique in sculpture (Fig. 192).

The Baroque in Spain. Velázquez (1599–1660), a native Spaniard, was made court painter to King Philip IV at the age of twenty-four. Velázquez, the opposite of El Greco, was an objective painter who adhered closely to realistic visual appearances. Much of Velázquez's work consisted of portraiture of persons who were unattractive or even deformed, such as members of the degenerate royal family and the dwarfs and imbeciles kept for the amusement of the court. Through his technique of carefully rendered surface textures, he introduced an element of refinement, and to that extent made them more acceptable. But, in addition, refinement is more or less synonymous with aristocracy. Velázquez may have placed such an emphasis on aristocracy because of an attachment to his mother, who was of an aristocratic lineage and whose name he adopted. From a psychoanalytical point of view, it might be said that by cultivating refinement in painting, he demonstrated subconsciously an attachment to his mother. His life work centered around the portraits of court persons and of Philip IV. *The Maids of Honor* (*Las Meninas*) represents the young princess and the two ladies-in-waiting, who are so well painted that they have given the painting its name (Fig. 193). Velázquez himself stands at the left, painting the portraits of the king and queen, though they do not show in the picture except as reflected in the mirror. This painting served as an inspiration to the later French Impressionists. The head of *Pope Innocent X* with his piercing eyes and tight lips suggests the crafty and ruthless character of the man (Fig. 194). Through marvelous dexterity, Velázquez has painted an exact equivalent of life. A vivid fusion of form with light and color makes one feel the flesh and bony structure in the arched forehead and flat temples, in the cheeks that recede into shadow, and in the ear, large and rough in texture, that tilts forward into the light. The shiny nose has the slickness of onion skin, and

the cap, the feel of thick cloth. This canvas appears to be
a closely observed study which preceded the final portrait;
it has the reddish color of the Pope's complexion, whereas
the final portrait in Rome (Doria Palace) gives him a more
agreeable flesh color. In a mythological subject, the *Forge
of Vulcan* (Prado), figures were painted for the sake of textures, not as approximations of classical statues in the Italian
manner. *The Surrender at Breda* records a victory of the
Spaniards over the Dutch, and includes portraits of persons
who actually participated in the ceremony. In *The Weavers,*
which shows the workers in a tapestry factory, illumination
is the chief interest. This painting and *The Maids of Honor,*
both done at the end of Velázquez's career, represent him
at his best.

José Ribera (1588–1652) was born in Spain, but spent
most of his life in Naples, which then belonged to Spain. He
painted martyrs and ascetics and scenes of cruelty and suffering. He was the leader of the naturalists of the Caravaggio dark "cellar illumination" (*tenebroso*). Francisco de
Zurbarán (1598–1664) of Seville painted religious subjects in
a hard, matter-of-fact style. He too shared with Caravaggio
strong contrasts of light and dark. He did not study in Italy,
but acquired his artistic training by copying the masterpieces
in the Royal Collection in Madrid. The Spanish painter who
enjoyed the greatest popularity through the Victorian era
was Bartolomé Murillo (1618–1682) of Seville. He began as a
painter of devotional pictures for export to America, and became best known for his religious paintings like his large
canvas of *The Immaculate Conception* showing the Virgin in
a blue mantle, soaring upward amidst clouds and angels.
Full of sentiment, these altarpieces were painted in silvery
or golden tones and bathed in a soft, vaporous atmosphere.
The youngest of the Spanish painters was Francisco de Goya
y Lucientes (1746–1828). Goya was a romantic figure, an
adventurer, hunter, courtier, bullfighter, and something of
a Don Juan. After an illness toward the end of his life, he
became almost deaf, and it is interesting to note that some
of his best paintings were done after this experience. Goya,
like Velázquez, aimed to give a total impression in his paintings, as if the scenes were being observed from a distance.
Using a flat posterlike style, Goya expresses all the horrors
of the Napoleonic invasion of Spain; his painting of the
Shooting of the Madrid Patriots (May 21, 1808) is a gruesome and striking statement against war. Slate blue, white,
and red are used with dramatic effect. His *La Maja Desnuda*
in the tradition of Giorgione and anticipating Manet's
Olympe, is painted in silvery grays and delicate shadows,

soft and atmospheric, with little suggestion of depth (Fig. 195). Goya was an outstanding etcher and lithographer; his series of etchings later entitled *Miseries of War* rank as one of the most forceful indictments against war in modern art.

The age of Philip IV (1621–1668), the Golden Age of Spanish art and literature represented in painting by Veláz-quez, had its parallel in sculpture. Juan Martínez Montañés (*c.* 1570–1649) was the greatest sculptor of Seville. In his wood-carved statue of the *Virgin of the Immaculate Conception* in the cathedral of Seville (Fig. 196), the natural-istic figure assumes a monumental character through a vo-luminous mantle elaborated by a mass of folds. As in Murillo's paintings, the Virgin on a crescent is supported by winged angels emerging from clouds. Like all religious wood carvings of Spain, this statue was painted to add a lifelike quality, as Spanish taste demanded an illusion of reality, particularly in the color of hair and flesh.

Flemish Painting in the Seventeenth Century: Rubens and Van Dyck. Rubens was the last of the great masters to base his art on the human figure. His warm color was inspired by Titian, his expression of force by Michelangelo, and his clouds, flying drapery, and cool colors derived from Vero-nese. His style became the dominant influence in the seven-teenth-century Flemish painting. Broad and expansive, it re-flected his own generous and swaggering personality; vitality was its essence, as aristocratic refinement was the keynote of the art of Velázquez. Though Rubens had many assistants in his large studio, a "mass production" process was used only when he had large orders for serial decorations, like those for Marie de Médicis' Luxembourg Palace (Louvre). For most of his sketches and single paintings, it is claimed, Rubens used no collaborators (Leo van Puyvelde). Rubens spent little time on preliminary sketches unless either he or his client happened to be very exacting; his exuberant vitality at times includes an element of coarseness. In his *Castor and Pollux Seizing the Daughters of Leucippus,* two horses, four figures, and a cupid seem to slide into positions that pro-duce effective contrasts and repetition of lines and masses (Fig. 197). If one explores the canvas, the many attractions reveal themselves; the transparency of shadows, the pearly texture of the skin, and the silky luster of blond hair. Can-vases like *A Festival in a Garden* (Prado) recall Titian. His *Flemish Kermesse* (carnival) at the Louvre, representing the eating, drinking, dancing, and lovemaking of the villagers, shows his wide range of interests. The portrait of his sister-in-law Susanna Fourment called *The Felt Hat* (Fig. 198) represents her as seen by reflected sunlight. The wistful, half-suppressed smile, the cool shimmering flesh tone, and the dash and sweep with which the costume, hat, and background are painted are all admirable. In *The Battle of the Amazons* (Munich), Rubens solves problems of a complex intertwining of figures. His *Descent from the Cross* (Antwerp Cathedral) shows the influence of Volterra's "Descent" in Rome in a vivified, closely packed composition. In a landscape, nature is represented in her most extravagant mood, with a thunderstorm and a rainbow. A shipwreck incident is included, giving the painting its name, *Shipwreck of Aeneas* (Berlin).

Whereas Rubens did not start his career until he was fourteen, Van Dyck at the age of ten was already inscribed in the Guild of Saint Luke and, when he was eighteen, had established a reputation in his own name. Rubens took this precocious painter into his studio without the least jealousy! Van Dyck's style represented an elegant and refined development of the more robust art of Rubens. His activity was divided among Antwerp, Genoa, and London. Van Dyck was technically as skillful as Rubens; his paintings are cooler in tonality, his portraits, more sensitive and intellectual than Rubens', except Rubens at his best. Van Dyck is well represented at the National Gallery of Art; the Italian period in such outstanding portraits as *Marchesa Elena Grimaldi,* the London period by *Queen Henrietta Marie with Her Dwarf* (Fig. 199). In the latter painting, we have the English setting in a park with a background of marble columns and heavy curtains, the silky glitter of costume, the pale complexion, and the languid, aristocratic hands.

Among the astonishing sculptural creations of the eighteenth century are the wood-carved pulpits in Belgian churches—a pictorial realism and a lack of restraint scandalizes "people of good taste" (Paul Fierens). Condemned as monstrous and decadent, these pulpits are not religious in the ascetic medieval sense, but close to the spirit of Rubens; they took their cue from Baroque altarpieces. They were not painted; contrasting grains and textures were substituted for pigments. These wood carvings were not intended for the timid, but for devout believers, who would have the heavens descend to earth. Their conception of a heaven was one of an earth overflowing with good things, with fruits and flowers, with saints and angels, and with a Virgin, resplendent, robust, and youthful. Michel Vervoort's pulpit (Fig. 200) in Antwerp Cathedral (1713) includes double rustic staircases, a tree complete with trunk, branches, and leaves, a cock, a peacock, an eagle, a turkey, and a parrot.

Cupids in flight busy themselves with the draped tentlike top. Verbruggen's (1655–1725) *Expulsion* pulpit in Brussels is an explosive burst of opulence and invention, but it is coherent, nevertheless.

The Dutch School of Painting. Certain social changes aided in the development of Dutch paintings. In the Middle Ages, the countryside had not been safe, as highway robbers lay in wait for travelers. In the sixteenth century, the sovereigns put an end to such dangers and a comfortable life in country houses became possible. There were something like two thousand painters and many dealers and middlemen, as smaller canvases for domestic use in small rooms were in demand. Specialization of subject matter began, as individual requirements of the patron had to be satisfied. Painted landscapes recalling the outdoors made life more pleasant during the long winter months. Landscape, interiors, and still life are contributions of the Dutch School. If Italy may be said to have created the grammar of painting, Holland increased its vocabulary.

Dutch paintings were painstakingly realistic. Local color was used, though in a narrow range; subdued greens for foliage and muddy browns for earth and shadows predominate. In a typical landscape by Meindert Hobbema entitled *View on a High Road* (Fig. 201), trees are rendered almost microscopically, as if the painter had attempted to include as many leaves, twigs, and limbs as the canvas could accommodate. The movement of the clouds and the silhouetting of dark trees against a light sky are standard devices.

Jacob van Ruisdael (1628–1682) interpreted landscapes in so poetic a manner that Goethe wrote an article entitled "Ruisdael as a Poet." His atmospheric, moody landscapes are without human figures. In *The Jewish Cemetery* (Fig. 202), Ruisdael painted abandoned tombs, a dead tree, a ruin in the background, a stormy sky, and a brook tearing through the uprooted land, a scene of desolation imbued with melancholy.

Jan Vermeer (1632–1675) of Delft was one of the three greatest painters of the Dutch School. In the Dutch rooms with their high ceilings and shuttered windows, illumination could be controlled and studied at leisure. Under such conditions, Vermeer produced the full visual effect of daylight. Often his costumes introduce a color harmony of blue, yellow, and gray, as in the *Young Woman with a String of Pearls* (Berlin) and *The Woman Weighing Gold* (National Gallery of Art). Vermeer's interiors make one aware of each foot of depth; in clarity and convincing truthfulness, they have never been surpassed. In the *Girl with a Red Hat* (National Gallery of Art), there is a lingering suggestion of still life; the immobile features, the smooth surface, and the carefully spotted high lights give this portrait the permanence of inanimate objects. His painting of *A Little Street in Delft* (Amsterdam) is an exact visual reproduction of brick walls; they show the influence of the atmosphere, but nevertheless there is a feeling of solidity. The most spectacular of all of Vermeer's interiors is the *Artist in His Studio*. A model is posed in the cool light of the window in the far end of the room. The sense of depth is extraordinary. Textures suggest the feel and weight of the materials, and the colors are grayed, emphasizing the color harmony (Fig. 203).

Gerard Terborch represented the same type of elegant Dutch room which Vermeer painted. Several figures, often a couple, seem to engage in quiet conversation. In the picture entitled *The Suitor's Visit* (National Gallery of Art), a man in dark costume bows himself into the presence of a waiting lady. Terborch's paintings, like drawing-room plays, take place in the front of the house; for the rest of the house, we turn to Pieter de Hooch. In his painting *The Bedroom* (Berlin), the mother is making the bed; a little girl who opens the door is greeted with a smile. Light streams in through a leaded-glass window, shines on the tile floor, and plays across walls and ceiling. Through an open door, we see a second room into which the morning sun pours in from the back yard. Here we have the spirit of cosy domesticity even where the room is empty, as if the house had a life of its own. Frans Hals (1580/81–1666) had a gift for seizing upon an accidental pose that is spontaneous and expressive of the person he paints (Fig. 204), whereas Vermeer painted his lady as if she were a piece of chinaware. Compared to Vermeer's color, the color of Hals is almost monochromatic. By limiting his palette, using mainly black and white, he could work fast and thus make the most of his sitter's presence. The head is modeled by means of carefully rendered half-tones with crisp touches of light tints placed to define the features. The spontaneous brush work of Hals inspired Manet and Sargent, and Hals became the much-copied master of the impressionistic portrait and figure painters of the latter nineteenth century. His love for gaiety is well known, and many of his paintings reflect his mirth and optimism.

Among the specialists were such painters as Aert van der Neer, who painted landscapes in moonlight, Paul Potter, who created what are virtually portraits of cattle, as in his famous *Bull* (The Hague), Albert Cuyp, who painted cattle grazing. Willem van de Velde (the Younger) did pictures of misty seas, as in his *Cannonshot* (Amsterdam), and Adriaen van Ostade and Adriaen Brouwer painted peasants. Rembrandt's chief pupil, Gerard Dou from Leyden, painted night scenes with candle illuminations. Jan Steen is known for representations of boisterous family festivities, which often tell a story as well; Kalf for decanters and bowls of fruit with partly peeled lemons; Jan van Huysum, for fruits and flowers. Certain subjects became the specialties of the towns of Holland; in Leyden, a university town, the specialty was books and musical instruments, beer and pipes; in Haarlem, still lifes of food and drink; and in Utrecht, fruits and flowers and paintings of poultry and dead game. The last of the native Dutch School painters was Adriaen van der Werff (d. 1722), who painted Biblical subjects with a smooth enamel-like surface that found many imitators.

Rembrandt (1606–1669) was the greatest painter and etcher of the northern countries and one of the masters of world art. Between 500 and 600 paintings have been attributed to him. Unlike Raphael, he owed little to outside influences; disregarding fashion, he painted what interested him; a variety of subjects, Biblical and mythological, and portraits, landscapes, and animals. A combination of homely realism and subtle spirituality is unique in his work. Rembrandt interpreted the Biblical subjects from a human point of view, which did not always correspond to the traditional interpretation. Judas, the most despised of Biblical characters, was painted by Rembrandt kneeling in anguish, returning the thirty pieces of silver (London, private collection). Rembrandt's concern for man and his emotions is illustrated in his etchings, as in the *Return of the Prodigal Son* (Ill. 121). The scene is pictured at the moment when father and son are reunited. The benign father stoops with deep compassion over the emaciated body of his son; a servant, sensing excitement, opens the shutter, and the kitchen boy in his tall hat leans forward, afraid of missing a word of what is taking place. All this is in pure etching, without the use of drypoint. *Christ Healing the Sick,* known as the "Hundred-Guilder Print," and *The Three Trees* are among his great masterpieces of etching.

As the son of a miller, Rembrandt must have been all over his father's mill and seen shafts of light break into its dim interior. His childhood experience is perhaps illustrated for us in the atmospheric painting *The Mill* (National Gallery of Art), in which the light is concentrated, as on a portrait (Fig. 205). His early experience with lighting effects was further reinforced by the paintings of night scenes by Gerard van Honthorst, who had been inspired by Caravaggio. Rem-

Ill. 121 Rembrandt: Return of the Prodigal Son, *National Gallery of Art, Rosenwald Collection*

brandt's chief interest in painting was the treatment of light. A drawing in a few bold and free strokes suggests that the figure is flooded with light. His illumination did not suggest any natural or artificial source, but, as has been said, became a way of making atmosphere visible.

At the age of twenty-six, he painted his *Anatomy Lesson* (The Hague) for the guild room of the Amsterdam surgeons. The unity of this group of portraits is psychological, as all are animated by a singleness of purpose. His largest and perhaps best-known painting is of the members of the shooting company of Captain Banning Cocq (Fig. 206). The various layers of darkened varnish gave the canvas an appearance of night, hence the mistaken name *Night Watch*.[15] In this painting Rembrandt developed a complex interplay of advancing and receding figures and motifs, like halberds and rifles, that aid in the suggestion of depth of space. Some illumination is natural, but there are also brilliant areas that glow with no apparent source of light. Elements of realism are combined with imaginative additions, as in the costumes that Rembrandt introduced for purely artistic reasons. The painting was not well received. It contained not only the members of the company, but others introduced by the painter for reasons of his own; a portraitlike character was largely absent. The adverse reaction of his contemporaries marked a turning point in Rembrandt's popularity; thereafter his commissions declined. The canvas was later reduced in height and width when transferred to a new location. The Greek story of *Philemon and Baucis* is painted as if Zeus and Mercury had come to visit the humble hut of Dutch peasants. The light from the torch falling upon old beams leaves pockets of darkness in corners and recesses. In Rembrandt's *Self-Portrait* of his late period, the source of light is nearly straight overhead, so that eyebrows and nose cast dark shadows. The farther eye is more shaded than the nearer eye; both are remarkable for clarity and depth (Fig. 207). *Joseph Accused by Potiphar's Wife* (Genesis 39:17-18) tells the story of Potiphar's wife, who, angered by Joseph's resistance to her advances, falsely accused Joseph to her husband. With a complete grasp of the dramatic intensity of the scene, Rembrandt made the woman the dominant figure in the composition. Her discomfort and guilt are expressed in her movement away from the touch of her husband's hand; if Potiphar knew the truth, she would have reason to fear his wrath. Potiphar leans forward; Joseph, merely an incident in this play of emotions, awaits his fate with helpless resignation. Rembrandt modulates his brush work to fit the object represented. Within the pattern of broad surfaces there are places of greater refinement, as in the hands of the nearer figures and the more precisely rendered jewelry. The soft atmospheric effects, with brilliant light grading off through half-tones to dark, create a most varied feast for the eye (National Gallery of Art).

Art in England after the Renaissance: Painting. A national style appeared in England in portrait painting in the second half of the eighteenth century. Van Dyck had created the fashionable portrait, Sir Peter Lely of Holland continued Van Dyck's style from 1641 to 1680, and Sir Godfrey Kneller, a German who settled in London, carried on in the Lely manner. Three foreigners, a Fleming, a Dutchman, and a German, laid the foundation for a native school, of which

William Hogarth (1697–1764) was the oldest and most aggressively English. He was the first to achieve for English painting a position of international importance as the representative of a new middle-class culture, interested in contemporary life. Hogarth fulminated against vice, which he criticized in *The Harlot's Progress* and *Marriage à la Mode* (1745). In the latter series of six paintings, reproduced as engravings, Hogarth rejected the immorality of an aristocratic society. The Lord barters his pedigree against a lucrative marriage for his good-for-nothing son (Fig. 208). Having wasted his fortune and ruined his life, he points to his family tree, which goes back to William the Conqueror, to justify the price he expects to receive from the wealth of his future daughter-in-law's family. The painting is filled with a wealth of revealing detail, such as two dogs chained together, symbolizing the unhappy marriage ahead. Hogarth was an excellent painter, as well as a social satirist, as shown by his *Shrimp Girl,* which Whistler declared to be the best portrait ever painted by an Englishman; it is in the tradition of Frans Hals.

Thomas Rowlandson (1756–1827) carried Hogarth's satire further with his keenly observed caricatures of every level of human society. The happenings in drawing room and parsonage, in tavern and prison were all depicted with drastic humor and lusty vigor. His forceful line, drawn with a reed pen, contrasted with the delicate, flat water-color washes, heightened with reds and blues. In a print entitled *Grog on Board* (Fig. 209), facial expressions and exchanged glances convey vividly the emotional involvement of each character. With all the breezy action, the composition is carefully planned; the darks form a frame for the white area, giving emphasis to the sprawling figure of the captured female.

William Blake (1757–1827), illustrator and engraver of the Bible, Dante, Milton, and Shakespeare, was a mystic and a poet besides. He combined printing with engraving, using a novel method of his own invention *(Songs of Innocence)*. For almost thirty years he received substantial support from his farsighted and appreciative patron, Thomas Butts, who purchased his works. Though Blake lived in a dream world of his own, his inspiration came from specific lines in literature. Three lines from *Macbeth* which begin "And pity, like a naked new-born babe . . ." (Act I, Scene 7) sufficed to conjure up two horses with closed eyes sweeping through the air, one rider dangling a babe in mid-air above the mother, who lies outstretched on the ground. In *The Wise and Foolish Virgins*, the wise virgins stand strong in the glow from their lighted lamps, in contrast to the foolish virgins, who writhe in darkness on the other side. *Adam and Eve with Archangel Raphael in Paradise* (Fig. 210) represents the garden as a wondrous bit of fairyland in which nature grows scrolls and lilies and the trees form chairs for the first man and woman. Blake's figures are drawn according to a formula which he developed for types often repeated and imbued with a child-like innocence, recalling Bosch in Fränger's interpretation (p. 238). What was superhuman vigor in Michelangelo became soft in Blake; success and failure are not far apart. Blake at his best, however, has a rare beauty and fresh originality.

The leader of the traditional British portrait school in the second half of the eighteenth century was Sir Joshua Reynolds (1723–1792). During three years in Italy, Reynolds studied the paintings of the Venetian School. He returned in 1752 to London, where he eventually became court painter to George III and first president of the Royal Academy. For his students, he wrote his famous *Fifteen Discourses on Art.* Reynolds was a prolific painter; in 1755, 120 persons sat for portraits; in 1758, he painted 150 portraits. Reynolds was the typical eclectic; he looked to Titian, Tintoretto, and Rembrandt for inspiration. The portrait of *Lady Cornwall* shows the warm, dark tonality of Rembrandt. A good example of his technique is the portrait of a child, *Lady Caroline Howard* (Fig. 211), in which the head is painted with vigor and spontaneity. His great rival, Thomas Gainsborough (1727–1788), worked more instinctively, was perhaps more original, and also painted landscapes. His portrait style, modeled on Van Dyck's, is distinctive; his figures are frail and show a soft and silky texture. Many of his paintings are in the United States. The famous *Blue Boy,* a portrait of young Mr. Butall, was formerly at Grosvenor House and is now in the Huntington Collection at San Marino, California (Fig. 212). According to the story, Gainsborough made blue the dominant color to refute Reynolds's teaching that three-quarters of the colors in a painting had to be warm tones. George Romney (1734–1802), another rival of Reynolds', did not achieve quite so exalted a position, though his yearly income as a portrait painter was also considerable. His portrait of *Lady Broughton* has less depth than a Reynolds and is more precisely drawn than a Gainsborough. Its linear pattern indicates the trend toward classicism. A portrait of *Mrs. Davenport,* with its facile brush work, looks like the ancestor of the popular magazine cover of our own day.

Architecture. Before painting arrived at a native style, architecture rather than sculpture was the leading art in England. Inigo Jones (1573–1652) and Sir Christopher Wren

(1632–1723) were the leading architects. Before Jones, the procedure was for a surveyor to prepare plans and elevations. The surveyors left the details to the craftsmen, who worked them out as the building progressed. Jones was an innovator in that he designed the whole building, including ornamental details. He introduced the Palladian style to England with the *Queen's House* in Greenwich and the *Banqueting Hall* of the Whitehall Royal Palace. By adopting the more severe classic style of Antonio da Sangallo and Bramante, England escaped the Italian Baroque of Borromini and Cortona. By the time Wren had developed design in the Renaissance manner, carvers like Grinling Gibbons had been trained to carry out the details. Wren was a professor of astronomy at Oxford before he gradually acquired a knowledge of architecture. The two-story façade of *St. Paul's* (London), a mask for buttresses, is well proportioned and faultlessly designed. The wood and lead dome is effective, but does not correspond to the interior. Many of the city churches rebuilt after the London fire (1666) were Wren's designs, like St. Mary le Bow and St. Brides, Fleet Street. They have stone spires over 100 feet high; *St. Martin's Ludgate* is one of the simplest and best. American Colonial churches derive from the Wren tradition.

The Baroque Period in France. The Age of Louis XIV represented the culmination of French art. The newly created Academy of Painting and Sculpture became the ruling body, replacing the guilds, which had been independent up to this time. The direction of the development of art was centralized in the persons of Colbert, Lebrun, and Poussin. Only members of the Academy could exhibit in the Salon; state representatives judged competitions, selected artists, and decreed royal pensions for state artists. Artists were housed in the Louvre and sent abroad to study, and foreign artists were imported. The French Academy was a school created in Rome to establish principles of good taste and to place "firm ideals" before the young generation of artists. Charles Lebrun, first painter to Louis XIV, lived at Fontainebleau with the king, who spent much time in the artist's studio.

Economic Background. As art seemed to create high values out of comparatively inexpensive raw materials, art was thought to add wealth to the country. Articles of luxury and expensive festivals seemed to the ruling aristocracy not only pleasant, but a help in supporting a sound national economy by keeping the money in the country. However, too much energy had been diverted into the construction of palaces and away from improving the standard of living of the peasants, merchants, and mechanics who produced the

Fig. 230 Böcklin: Isle of the Dead. *Courtesy Museum der bildenden Künste, Leipzig*

Fig. 231 Renoir: Three Bathers. *The Cleveland Museum of Art, J. H. Wade Collection*

Fig. 232 Monet: Madame Monet Under the Willows. *National Gallery of Art, Chester Dale Collection*

Fig. 233 Seurat: Sunday Afternoon on the Grande Jatte, detail. *Courtesy of the Art Institute of Chicago, Helen Birch Bartlett Memorial Collection*

Fig. 234 Cézanne: Still Life. *National Gallery of Art, Chester Dale Collection*

Fig. 235 Van Gogh: La Mousmé. *National Gallery of Art, Chester Dale Collection*

Fig. 236 Gauguin: Self-Portrait. *National Gallery of Art, Chester Dale Collection*

Fig. 237 Braque: Still Life: Le Jour. *National Gallery of Art, Chester Dale Collection*

Fig. 238 Degas: The Ballet Girl Fixing Her Slipper. *National Gallery of Art, Harris Whittemore Collection (loan)*

Fig. 239 Toulouse-Lautrec: Alfr Le Guigne. *National Gallery of A Chester Dale Collection*

Fig. 240 Kandinsky: 255, No. 26 *Couriesy Solomon R. Guggenhei Museum*

Fig. 241 Picasso: Guernica. *Collection of the Museum of Modern Art*

Fig. 242 Rodin: Morning. *National Gallery of Art, gift of Mrs. John W. Simpson, 1942*

Fig. 244 Maillol: Desire, plaster relief. *Collection of the Museum of Modern Art*

Fig. 243 Moore: Family Group, bronze. *Collection of the Museum of Modern Art, A. Conger Goodyear Fund*

Fig. 245 Stuart: Portrait of Mrs. Yates. *National Gallery of Art, Mellon Collection*

Fig. 246 Whistler: Arrangement in Gray and Black, Louvre. *Photograph, courtesy Museum of Modern Art*

Fig. 247 Quidor: The Return of Rip Van Winkle. *National Gallery of Art, Mellon Collection, 1942*

Fig. 248 Davis: Summer Landscape, 1930. *Collection of the Museum of Modern Art*

Fig. 249 Homer: Eight Bells. *Courtesy Addison Gallery of American Art, Phillips Academy, Andover, Mass.*

Fig. 250 Benton: Arts of the South, 1932. *Courtesy Art Museum of the New Britain Institute*

Fig. 251 Shahn: Sacco and Vanzetti. *Collection of the Museum of Modern Art, gift of Mrs. John D. Rockefeller, Jr.*

Fig. 252 Time-Life Building, Rockefeller Center. Harrison and Abramovitz, Architects. *Courtesy Rockefeller Center, Inc.*

Fig. 253 St. Louis Terminal Building-Lambert St. Airport. Hellmuth, Yamasaki and Leinweber, Architects. *Photograph, courtesy Eastman Kodak Company*

Fig. 254 Steuben Glass, Inc. and Marie Laurencin: Glass Urn. *Courtesy Steuben Glass, Inc.*

Fig. 255 Klee: Around the Fish, 1926. *Collection of the Museum of Modern Art*

Fig. 256 Amino: Jungle, mahogany. *Collection of the Whitney Museum of American Art*

Fig. 257 A model for Simon Guggenheim Museum, New York. Frank Lloyd Wright, Architect. *Courtesy Laurence Vail Coleman*, Museum Building, *1950*

necessities. The spending of vast sums on extravagant art projects contributed to the economic unbalance which ended in the French Revolution.

Architecture and Sculpture. Claude Perrault's design for the *East Façade of the Louvre,* with its fine repose, elegant detail, and fluted columns contrasting against plain walls, had a strong influence on French architecture. The *Apollo Gallery* of the Louvre, now used for exhibiting works of art, was designed by Lebrun and named after Louis XIV, the "Sun King," as Apollo was the Sun God. Piers and architraves support a cornice and a barrel vault; five main panels on the ceilings have paintings by Lebrun. Though the style of the Italian Baroque was modified to conform to French taste, this gallery is most ornate, a blaze of gilt and ivory, with blue accents.

The Palace at Versailles, the residence of Louis XIV and the seat of government, was designed for a court of 10,000 persons. The garden façade, its total length over 1700 feet, has 375 windows. During the French Revolution, the original furniture was sold and the pictures were placed in the Louvre; in the nineteenth century, Louis Philippe made Versailles over into a museum (1833–1837). The palace's *Hall of Mirrors* (1680–1684), decorated by Lebrun, was executed largely in white marble panels, green marble Corinthian pilasters and gilt bronze capitals. The barrel-vaulted ceiling was decorated with paintings. The gardens by André Lenôtre are on a vaster scale than the Italian gardens, and are united architecturally to the palace (Fig. 213). Terraces form transitions from palace to the garden, diagonal vista lines converge on points of interest, there are fountains and a canal nearly a mile long, used for pleasure boats. Court etiquette prescribed wigs and high-heeled shoes and an elaborate ceremonial for state occasions; the classic dramas of Racine and Corneille were declaimed in stately fashion. The garden reflected the artificiality of the period; hedges formed walls and halls of green for outdoor theatrical performances and trees were cut into shapes of cubes, cones, and spheres. Lenôtre remodeled the gardens of Fontainebleau, Tuileries, Vaux, and designed Saint-Cloud. His pupils and imitators laid out gardens in England, Germany, Portugal, Russia, and elsewhere. Pierre L'Enfant's plan for Washington, D. C., owes something to Versailles.

The Tomb of Richelieu (1694), probably designed by Lebrun, represents Richelieu on a raised pedestal-like couch as he sinks, dying, into the arms of Religion, while at his feet the figure of Science crouches in grief. Technically the execution is superior, but the billowy draperies of the Italian

Baroque are avoided. Pierre Puget (1620–1694) of Marseilles, originally a ship-carver, developed the Italian Baroque in an original way. Puget is technically on a par with Bernini. His fame rests on his *Milo of Croton*, ordered by Colbert for Versailles (Fig. 214). Milo, caught in the cleft of a tree trunk, is being attacked by a lion. His expression of pain parallels that of Laocoön, and the muscles and veins are treated realistically. Puget chose his subjects for the possibility of strong emotion. His half-figures of Atlas supporting the balcony on the façade of the Hotel de Ville at Toulon groan under the load they bear.

A naturalistic trend in the sculpture of the period of Louis XIV appeared in portrait busts. In the bust of the *Duc de Chaulnes* (Fig. 215) by Antoine Coysevox (1640–1720), much of the effect depends on the textures of the marble, slightly rough in the wig and smoothly polished in the features. The intense luminosity of the marble with its subtle variations is emphasized in the contrasting textures. Like other sculptors of his period, Coysevox collaborated on large tombs. His nephews and pupils Nicolas and Guillaume (the elder) Coustou carried the same style into the period of Louis XV. Guillaume carved the *Prancing Horses* which stand at the entrance to the Champs Elysées.

Jean Baptiste Pigalle and Étienne M. Falconet represent Rococo sculpture from 1720 to 1760 when the style was at its height. Such works by Pigalle as the tombs of d'Harcourt (Notre Dame, Paris) and the Comte de Saxe (St. Thomas, Strasbourg) represent this sepulchral sculpture as melodrama carved in marble. The Comte de Saxe, fully erect, boldly steps toward his open sarcophagus; in the d'Harcourt monument, the corpse tries to rise out of his coffin while his wife stands by with clasped hands. Technically these monuments are extraordinarily accomplished. Nevertheless, the resources of art hardly compensate for the extravagant adulation portrayed, so offensive to the dignity of man. Falconet illustrates the versatility of the Baroque sculptors. He carved such lovely statuettes as the *Bathing Girl* (Louvre), the group of Madame de Pompadour as *Venus with the Doves* (Fig. 216), and the bronze statue of *Peter the Great* at Leningrad. He also furnished models for the manufacture of Sèvres porcelain for small decorative pieces. Clodion (1738–1814), from the end of the period, interpreted the daintiness and playfulness of the Rococo at its best, as in the *Nymph and Satyr* at the Metropolitan Museum. He and his brother produced terracotta statuettes, commercially, for candelabra, vases, and clocks, but also worked in plaster, porcelain, and marble.

The greatest of all French sculptors of this period was Jean Antoine Houdon (1741–1828). Though he approached the Rococo manner of Falconet and Clodion and the Neo-Classic style of his own period, he also owed much inspiration to nature. His bronze *Diana* (Louvre), which exists in several replicas, and his marble bust of *Diana* fuse the Classic with the natural without entirely eliminating a Rococo contribution. His portrait statues and busts, such as of *Voltaire* seated (Paris) and several Americans of the Revolutionary period, belong among the best produced in any period. His bust of *George Washington* (Mount Vernon), modeled from life, is particularly prized.

Painting. The greatest French painters of the period of Louis XIV were Nicolas Poussin (1594–1665) and Claude Lorrain (1600–1682). Both spent some time in Italy. Poussin combined landscape with figures, though the figures in the foreground received the major attention. In Claude's landscapes, figures were subordinated; land, and more often sea and sky, constitute the essential parts of the picture. The Baroque period emphasized panoramic aspects of nature to suggest that landscape was part of the universe. Poussin's *Triumph of Neptune and Amphitrite* (Fig. 217) is a painting of figures and sea like Botticelli's *Birth of Venus* (Fig. 146) and Raphael's *Galatea* (Fig. 149). Unlike these earlier painters, Poussin created an effect of rich complexity by enveloping his figures in light and atmosphere. Amphitrite, in the center beneath a cloud of angels and billowing drapery, contrasts with the dark dolphins. Major figures look toward her, and every gesture and every motif is related to the total composition. In spite of shadow and space, there is no merging of shapes as in Rubens; basically this is an elaborated drawing, with motifs suggested by Raphael. Poussin's public was interested in figures and subject, as in his *Shepherds of Arcady* (Louvre). The theme, death is inevitable, throws a shadow of gloom over the three shepherds. The intellectual point of view, the classic influence in the relieflike composition, the sculpturesque figures, and the shepherdess, recalling a motif from the *Aldobrandini Marriage*, are characteristic of Poussin.

Claude Lorrain was the first great painter to devote himself exclusively to landscape. He was a painter of light, space, water, and air. A great spaciousness extends toward the horizon; the rays of the setting sun skim the waves and cast long shadows on the shore in the foreground. The architecture is arranged like stage props on the sides, leaving the empty center for the yellow sun. The creation of such a flood of light seemed like a miracle to Claude's contemporaries (Fig. 218).

A third trend in seventeenth-century French painting is represented by the peasant subjects of the Le Nain brothers, Antoine, Louis, and Mathieu, who did not sign themselves separately. Only Mathieu, who outlived his brothers, became a portrait painter. Their peasants (Fig. 219, attributed to Louis) are sober and well-defined portrait groups showing the family in their own humble environment. In their cool and competent objectivity, they are different from the Flemish or the Italian School.

French eighteenth-century painting began with an extraordinary painter Jean Antoine Watteau (1684–1721), who set the style which became characteristic of the Rococo period. Watteau came to Paris from Valenciennes, which had been Flemish and had only recently been incorporated into France. There Watteau saw Rubens; later in Paris he studied Rubens's paintings. Watteau's drawings are in a class by themselves; his oil paintings are directly based on his sketches. Watteau's paintings are small; he did not have the physical strength to deal with the tremendous projects handled by Rubens. He is known chiefly as a *peintre des fêtes galantes,* a painter of imaginary open-air festivals, with ladies and cavaliers dressed in silk and satin walking and resting on the lawns against a background of feathery trees. His success was so striking that he set a fashion. The festivities he had only imagined then actually took place in imitation of his paintings—support for Oscar Wilde's contention that life imitates art. Another field from which Watteau selected his subjects was the theater. His painting *Le Mezzetin* (Fig. 220) shows pearly color in the striped costume and feathery trees in the foliage background. The suggested lightness of spirit is typical of Rococo art.

François Boucher's (1703–1770) subjects have been called frivolous and superficial, but his freshness and delicacy in painting and his talent for interior decoration are undeniable. He was a favorite of the French court and of Madame de Pompadour, and his delicately tinted nudities of Venus and Cupid, floating in a welter of crinkly satins and soft-hued vegetation, belong to his world as much as Madonnas and saints belong to the Middle Ages. Love of nature was one of the affectations of the period, and Boucher's shepherds and shepherdesses are triumphs of artificiality. Boucher's technique, with all its ivorylike smoothness, shows variation in his brush work to express different textures, as in the fluffy feathers of the doves (Fig. 221). Jean Honoré Fragonard

(1732–1806) represented the same subjects with equal success. He also painted for Madame du Barry and is well known for the decorative panels he did for her, now in the Frick Collection (New York).

Jean Baptiste Chardin (1699–1779) painted still life and interior subjects from the lower middle class. He developed his own technique, in which he aimed for broad masses and paid as much attention to design as to color. Often a subject was painted several times, so that subsequent versions show a matured, simplified interpretation. Chardin's paintings of orderly everyday existence were just as French as the boudoir paintings of the court. In his *Soap Bubbles* there is something genteel and distinguished which makes it different from Dutch paintings (Fig. 222). The large surfaces in neutral tones are enlivened here and there by warm touches of sunshine and bits of foliage. In a subtle way they relate the scene to a wider world beyond. With Chardin, we begin to sense the closeness of the eighteenth century to our own period.

Decorative Arts. The changes in the style from Louis XIV (Baroque), to Louis XV (Rococo), and to Louis XVI (Neo-Classic) are most apparent in the decorative arts, which include interiors. Baroque architecture virtually transferred the designs of the façade to the interior, where the same orders were repeated. With few exceptions, the Rococo expressed itself on interiors only. Pilasters and cornices disappeared in favor of a free merging of wall and ceiling in curvilinear scrolled motifs in plaster or wood, painted and gilt. Plant and floral designs fused with curves, shells, garlands, sprays, and tendrils in a fanciful but orderly manner. Walls were divided into panels which often contained mirrors, paintings, or tapestries framed to harmonize with the wall decoration.

The characteristic piece of furniture of the Louis XIV style, perfected by Charles André Boulle, was the tall cabinet of ebony; it was inlaid with brass and tortoise shell, giving an effect of somber splendor. Wood marquetry at times replaced tortoise shell. In the time of Louis XV, the gravity in etiquette and in decoration gave way to lightness. In one type of furniture, black lacquer covered the structural base as a thin layer, eloborated with bronze mounts called ormolu. Chinese porcelain vases for mantel ornaments over the fireplace and Chinese motifs in ornamentation became popular (Fig. 223). Under Louis XVI and Marie Antoinette, the Classic manner returned; straight lines again replaced curves. This later phase produced magnificent furniture in which colored lacquer and porcelain plaques were added to marquetry and ormolu.

Conclusion. The two centuries between the end of the Renaissance and the French Revolution marked a culmination for sculpture and painting. The classical heritage, developed by the Renaissance, achieved its most vital expression. In sculpture, the possibilities of the medium were extended to the utmost; in architecture, the classical orders were enriched through the use of curves and a striving for effect of light and shade. Painting further developed its style and in subject matter added new categories. In the largest projects painting, like architecture and sculpture, engaged many assistants under the direction of a master. Paris superseded Rome as the art capital of Europe, and under royal patronage France made the arts a function of the state. The major arts, still united, aimed to glorify the client as much as to set a memorial to the artist. Bernini and Rubens reflected the past brought to new heights. Velázquez and Vermeer were their equals, but included in their styles elements that pointed to the future. The century that witnessed the greatest control of art under a monarchy in France, in Holland produced Rembrandt, one of the most individual artists of any period.

CHAPTER XI

Modern Art in Europe:

1800 - 1950

Cultural Background. The French Revolution had a profound influence on the minds of men everywhere. A new emphasis was placed on individuality, though the force of traditions in customs and in art subsided only gradually. The freeing of men's minds was accompanied by the industrial revolution. Trains, transatlantic liners, airplanes, the camera, and more recently radio and television put an end to isolation and made possible the one world of today. These changes of environment were reflected in art, which lacked unity until the style finally matured in the twentieth century. Heretofore there had been but a single style for each period; now there were several styles, concurrent and also one superseding the other. Art was approached from the point of view of improvement, though what appeared to contemporaries as progress seems in retrospect more like a succession of changes.

Formerly artist and craftsman had occupied a position of security in society. Art during the Baroque period had tended to become a luxury product, but it was produced by artists under contract. After the aristocracy lost power, artists had to depend on a new public and a free market to sell what they had produced to please themselves. With the disappearance of a single accepted style, artists divided into hostile factions and the bond of a common understanding which formerly had linked artist to patron also disappeared. Eventually this led to an estrangement between art and public and the misunderstood artist, despising a seemingly uncultured public, raised the cry, "art for art's sake" (*L'art pour l'art*). The conservative, or academic artist fared better economically than the radical who pursued new ideals of his own choosing.

In the wake of the French Revolution science and technology developed their modern status, the crafts declined, and the machine age led to a deterioration of taste. A reaction, which prepared the way for the industrial art of today, started in England around 1890 under William Morris. During the nineteenth century only painting preserved a vigor of its own; sculpture participated incidentally, but architecture was oriented toward the past. Photography tended to replace painted portraits and colored reproductions, oil paintings, and yet there are probably as many artists in the Western world today as existed in any previous period, in proportion to population as well as in absolute number. There are several reasons for the continued prestige enjoyed by art; a new category of amateur artists contribute to public interest in art, professional artistic skills are used in industry, and art is also looked upon as a source of national pride. New agencies to serve art came into existence: art schools, art critics, art historians, art museums, and art reproductions. These agencies contributed to a greater knowledge of the art heritage of mankind than any previous age possessed. A broadening influence of art for the enrichment of life is a unique aspect of our culture.

General Survey: Architecture. Architecture remained conservative during the nineteenth century and arrived at a style of its own only during our own period. The progressive aspects of nineteenth-century culture led to new types of buildings, railway stations, factories, commercial, administrative and office buildings, apartment blocks, theaters, and airports. Out of the use of new materials, such as steel, concrete, glass, and aluminum, a new functional style emerged in the early part of the twentieth century. Structure and decoration had lost contact with each other during the nineteenth century, as the exterior was conceived as an ornamental covering not necessarily expressive of either materials or function. Historical motifs were looked upon as a vocabulary for the able designer who exploited the riches of past styles: Egyptian, Greek, Roman, even Aztec and Japanese, and all medieval, Renaissance and Baroque styles of the various countries. Even the historically minded nineteenth century had its architectural triumphs. Paris was replanned to become the most beautiful metropolis of Europe, its spectacular opera house forming a climax to the French Renaissance style. This search for a style continued until the pioneers of the modern movement in England, Holland, Belgium, Germany, and the United States took over and functionalism came into its own during the twentieth century.

Painting. The succession of historical styles in architecture had its parallel in painting's search for subjects. This began with a return to classical antiquity, the taste for which had begun in the mid eighteenth century with the rediscovery of Herculaneum and Pompeii and Winkelmann's *History of the Art of Antiquity*. The period style of Louis XVI had already concentrated on this new fashion. After Napoleon's rise to power, Neo-Classicism found its chief promoters in David and Ingres. Thomas Couture dealt with ancient history (*The Romans of the Decadence*) and Jean Louis Meissonier dramatized Napoleon (*1814, Napoleon in Russia*) and his pupil Edouard Détaille, the Franco-Prussian War (*The Dream*). Religion found a fashionable interpreter in Adolphe William Bouguereau (disliked by modernists), as in his sweet and sentimental *The Virgin as Consoler*. Bouguereau and Alexandre Cabanel both painted a *Birth of Venus*, one vertical and one horizontal, fusing all preceding styles, including those of Boucher and David.

The second half of the nineteenth century turned away from a literary type of subject matter and sought a closer attachment to nature. The peasant was idealized by Jean François Millet and landscape by Jean Baptiste Camille Corot. Gustave Courbet, the realist, sought by his paintings to shock his generation into accepting his idea that the beauty of art and the realities of life should be one. Edouard Manet and the Impressionists represented the figure as part of the natural environment in the still-life manner of Velázquez and Vermeer. Claude Monet and Camille Pissarro went a step further by eliminating the human element and by painting the landscape as reflecting surfaces. Edgar Degas concentrated on the figure in motion, and Auguste Renoir specialized in women and children suffused in light and color.

Paul Cézanne represented a turning point; the last vestige of Renoir's loveliness of natural appearances disappeared and a formalizing impersonal geometric trend set in. Vincent van Gogh added brilliant color and technique, a personal contribution derived from the unconscious drives of his neurotic personality. Georges Seurat, Paul Gauguin, Toulouse-Lautrec, and also Henri Matisse emphasized the larger pattern that gave their canvases a decorative quality. The geometric basis of Cézanne became the dominant note of Cubism, as in Georges Braque, Fernand Léger, and in one phase of Pablo Picasso's works. Natural appearances were subordinated by the Expressionists who rearranged the visual facts. All resemblances to recognizable objects vanished in Kandinsky, who constructed his paintings out of color and complex effects of voids, transparencies and solid forms. Never before had an art so completely transformed itself as painting and sculpture during this period. Hesitatingly and slowly the trends built up, developed, and expanded with an inexorable logic that seemed to transcend the individual who took each succeeding step.

Neo-Classicism. Paris became the center, and Jacques Louis David (1748–1825) and Jean Auguste Dominique Ingres (1780–1867) the representatives, of Neo-Classicism. That Greek art was originally painted was unknown; white plaster casts served as study material and Winckelmann's happy phrase of "the noble simplicity and quiet grandeur" of classic sculpture became the magic formula. Argument and debate about the aims of art assumed an almost religious fervor, perhaps made possible by the waning of the authority of religion following the French Revolution. Painting, according to the Classicists, should have the qualities of sculpture, severe beauty of line and firm modeling. Light and color were looked upon as nonessential fluctuations, whereas form was eternal. The self-imposed limits of Classicism excluded self-expression, as artistic merit was believed to be inherent in the ideal subject. What was perfect and heroic was considered worthy of great art, what was common, painful and ugly in subjects or people was rejected. Qualities that appealed to the mind—clearness, harmony, proportion and serenity—were thought to be the supreme qualities of art. David, a student of Vien's, painted excellent portraits, but he did not think of portraits as great art. His painting of *The Sabine Women* (Fig. 224) illustrates his style. The Sabine women, having been taken by the Romans in warfare, attempt to stop the battle between their husbands and fathers and brothers by exposing the children; casualties of battle were minimized in the painting, which is like a stage scene, the actors frozen in their poses. The painting's lack of integration, rather than its unreality, is disturbing. The attraction is in the archaeological detail, in profiles, fully modeled statuesque forms, and restrained expressions, at most showing wrinkled brows and parted lips. David could not sell his painting, but it proved to be popular, as he charged admission to see it and earned 72,000 francs. His famous pupil Ingres was commissioned by the State to paint *The Apotheosis of Homer* (Fig. 225). Like David, Ingres was a fine draftsman, and his emphasis on drawing became a tradition in French painting. Homer, seated on a pedestal, is being crowned by Victory. Draped, seated figures at the base personify the *Iliad* and the *Odyssey*. Apollo on Homer's right takes Raphael by the hand; on the opposite side Pindar holds up his lyre, Phidias presents his mallet, and Alexander the Great, a casket said to contain the works of Homer. Ingres infused his figures with more life than David would have approved of, as in the spontaneous pose in the portrait of his friend *Bertin* (Louvre, 1832).

Romanticism. The Romantic movement was contemporary with Classicism and lasted in France from the fall of Napoleon (1815) to the Franco-Prussian War (1870). Théodore Géricault (1791–1824), Eugène Delacroix (1799–1863), Honoré Daumier (1808–1879), and Jean François Millet (1814–1875), of a later trend toward realism, were the chief representatives in France. Emotion and color, despised by the Classic painters, became the new objectives. Subjects were still selected with care and an heroic element was stressed, often based on the Romantic poets, and Shakespeare, Tasso, Goethe, or Dante. Dramatic action was preferred to absolute beauty; the mysterious, the fantastic and morbid, and pathos and tragedy became acceptable. Painting out-of-doors began and brush work and effects of light and shade replaced line and sculpturesque modeling. The battle of the Classicists and Romanticists centered around the Academy and the Salon Exhibitions. The revolution of the Romanticists was set off by Géricault's *Raft of the Medusa* (Fig. 226) at the Salon of 1819. This represented a scene that had actually occurred. Survivors of the shipwreck are grouped in various stages of exhaustion; bodies dead or dying are about to slide off into the turbulent sea. To study the effects of exposure, Géricault had visited hospitals. He had the carpenter from the *Medusa* construct a model of the ship's raft for use in his studio. The picture, proclaiming the freedom of the artist, set itself in opposition to Classicism and aroused a storm of abuse. Géricault's stand against authority in painting may also have expressed his own rebellion against his father, against whose wishes he had secretly studied painting. After Géricault's death at thirty-three, Romanticism was taken over by his friend, Delacroix, a gifted musician and author of the *Journal,* a notable contribution to art criticism. Delacroix revered the masters of the past; his struggle was against the stifling influence of the Academy. His style represented a fusion of the art of Rubens, Titian, and Tintoretto, with an emphasis on objective reality and glowing color. Delacroix, son of a revolutionist, sympathized with the struggle of the Greeks for independence. The brave defense of Missolonghi, an incident in this war, Delacroix personified by a figure amidst ruins pleading with outstretched arms for sympathy (Fig. 227). An ominously dark background brings out the figure in native costume illuminated from above.

Daumier (1808–1879) took advantage of the new lithographic process introduced from Germany and became the most formidable caricaturist of the century. Daumier sati-

rized social classes rather than individuals, ridiculing the
follies of government and the hypocrisies of lawyers and
courts. Growing up in Paris, he observed life at close quarters
as a messenger to a lawyer and clerk to a bookseller. Self-
taught, his style developed from a pictorial manner into an
impressionistic, linear, and dramatic style. Later in life
Daumier devoted himself to painting. The breadth and
power of his satire owe much to his ability to convey character through facial expression and gesture (Ill. 122), but his
cartoons, fantastic exaggerations, seem dated today.

– Voilà le ministère public qui vous dit des choses très désagréables...... tâchez-donc
de pleurer au moins d'un œil......ça fait toujours bien!.......

Ill. 122 Daumier: Les Gens de Justice. *National Gallery of Art,
Harris Whittemore Collection (loan)*

Theodore Rousseau was the founder of the Barbizon School
of landscape painting. The masters of this School, Diaz,
Daubigny, and Dupré, sketched outdoors, but finished their
canvases in the studio. Corot became the best-known painter
of this school, and Millet identified himself with the same
trend toward the native scene. A heavy, warm tonality related Millet's style to the past, but Corot developed a gray-

green, diffused atmospheric color that gives his painting a
soft, misty appearance which became popular with American
collectors. Millet painted the peasant as the heroic tiller of
the soil. His broad, massive figures are placed outdoors, exposed to light and atmosphere. *The Gleaners* (Fig. 229)
who gather in the last bit of grain, and *The Angelus* (Louvre),
peasants stopping work for a prayer at the sound of the
church bells, are among his best-known works.

Painting Outside of France. John Constable (1776–1837),
who concentrated on the native English landscape, became the
founder of modern landscape painting before the appearance
of the Barbizon School. He exhibited in Paris in 1824, and
French painters admitted their debt to Constable. His dark
tonality was reminiscent of Hobbema. Through large brush
marks, he fused ground, foliage, and sky into a unit. His
Cornfield (Fig. 228) is a carefully composed picture that combines the heritage of the old masters with a new appreciation
of atmospheric effects. Joseph Turner (1775–1851) made
light, space and atmosphere his subject matter. Ruskin placed
Turner, as the master of diffused light, on a level with Michelangelo, master of form. In Turner's late work exhibited
in 1844, *Rain, Steam and Speed,* solidity of form is lost in a
colored mist that obscures the sun. Turner worked indoors
freely from his own imagination, but he derived his visions
from nature. He anticipated the impressionists without shar-
ing their objective approach.

In the second half of the nineteenth century, England also
produced Dante Gabriel Rossetti and Sir Edward Burne-
Jones, members of the Pre-Raphaelite group that revolted
against the conventional style of their day. Their subjects
were legendary, mystical, and poetical, and at times religious.
Such works as the *Golden Stairs* by Burne-Jones long retained
popularity and became well known through reproductions.

Germany too had its Classic and Romantic painters. Among
the latter, Philip Otto Runge and Caspar David Friedrich
produced a peculiarly German variety of Romanticism. Such
painters as Spitzweg, Schwind, and Richter stressed a poetic
approach in subjects from folklore and German life. The
German Romantic painters were not innovators in the manner of the French, and their leading art schools of Munich
and Düsseldorf, as attractions for foreign students, never
rivaled Paris, where Germany also sent her young artists.
An exception to this dependence on Paris was the German-
Swiss painter Arnold Böcklin (1827–1901). He was not only
a Romantic painter but also a poet who filled his colorful
land and seascapes with Nereids, centaurs, and tritons of convincing vitality. His *Isle of the Dead* (Fig. 230) was a poetic
invention of his imagination. The overwhelming influence of

French art resulted in a neglect of the artists of the nineteenth century in Spain, Belgium, Holland, Scandinavia, Poland and Russia. Mariano Fortuny y Carbó, Joaquín Sorolla y Bastida, and Ignacio Ziloaga of Spain, Edvard Munch of Norway, Anders L. Zorn of Sweden, and Giovanni Segantini of Italy became known outside their own countries. What happened in art during the nineteenth century in the Slavic countries hardly penetrated beyond their own frontiers. We therefore return to the France of the second half of the nineteenth century.

Realism. In nineteenth-century French painting, realism is associated with Gustave Courbet (1819–1877), the son of a peasant. Courbet had no use for "art for art's sake," but desired "to make a living art." Painting should deal only with visual objects and tangible things. Ribera, Zurbarán, and Velázquez in their studies of the life of the people bear an affinity to Courbet's work. Courbet still continued the dark colors of the old masters. *Stone Breakers* (Dresden) and *Burial at Ornans* (Louvre) represent simple people in unidealized attitudes, undesirable subjects for painting from the Academy point of view. At the World's Fair Exhibition in Paris in 1855, the jury rejected two of Courbet's canvases. In defiance, Courbet erected at his expense his own "Pavillon du Realism" close to the Exhibition building in which he exhibited fifty of his paintings, including the two rejected ones. This gesture did not increase Courbet's popularity, though it took on historical significance.

Impressionism. A lighter tonality and a tendency toward a flat surface, away from the sculpturesque modeling of the Classicists, characterized the leading painters of the period 1855 to 1886. The near view that emphasized form was replaced by the distant view of objects seen out-of-doors under the influence of light and atmosphere. The Japanese wood block print that selected sections from nature contributed to the formation of Impressionism. Outlines were replaced by opposing patches of light and dark and fewer objects were represented in a large scale. The huge canvases which the Classicists took years to complete were now replaced by smaller studies of motifs which the painter repeated until he had achieved the effect he desired. Impressionism was a step away from the realism of Courbet; it meant selection from nature and a sketchy improvisation rather than imitation. This trend toward time-saving simplicity has continued to the present day.

Though studies became numerous, the more finished canvases specifically painted for the Salon were still being done. Edouard Manet's (1837–1887) *Déjeuner sur l'Herbe* (Louvre)

was a new version of Giorgione's *Concert*, but its modern
style and contemporary setting invoked a storm of criticism.
In his *Olympe* (Louvre) showing a nude on a couch receiving
a bouquet of flowers from a Negro maid, the appeal was
based on subtle variations of color and design. The public
did not react to its artistry, claiming that the figure was too
nude and her expression, stupid. Manet covered a wide range
of subjects: portraits, still lifes, landscapes, interiors, horse
races, and boating scenes. There was no single focus, and
figures were related to suggest momentary groups.

Auguste Renoir (1841–1919) retained something of a preciousness of surface, the pinks and ivories which he had absorbed in his youth as a decorator of porcelain. To retain
form, not to dissipate it, was his aim. Renoir was essentially
a figure painter, and by subordinating head and face, his
paintings appear wholly unintellectual, as in his *Three Bathers*
(1897), here in bluish flesh tint heightened with pinks. (Fig.
231). His light and airy canvases, nudes reflecting a warm
glow mingled with pearly iridescence in the shadow, clearly
denote his joy of life—a modern Boucher. This unproblem-
atic and charming art of Renoir enjoys uncontested popularity.

Edgar Degas (1834–1917), the draftsman of the Impressionists, preferred pastel. He used photography as an aid in
studying the figure in motion and he made numerous studies
of the same motif. His dancers, as in *The Ballet Girl Fixing
Her Slipper* (Fig. 238), and his race course scenes, are studies
of movement. The general trend toward realism is demonstrated in Degas's treatment of both the ballet dancers and
the laundresses as working people. Though he was fascinated
by the glamor of the theater, many of his studies show the
dancers in awkward postures emphasizing the strenuous training required of them.

For Claude Monet (1840–1926), the Impressionist landscape painter, the objects that reflected the light were less important than the quality of the light itself. In order that the
light be recorded on canvas correctly, he painted series of
the same object under different light, as in his haystacks,
water lilies or in his twenty canvases of Rouen Cathedral.
In *Madame Monet Under the Willows* (1880), the figure is
blurred, the meadow is a loose texture of green, spotted with
transparent shadows and warm reflected sunlight. Brush
strokes and pigment squeezed onto the canvas directly from
the tube combine into a light fabric (Fig. 232).

Impressionism deprived form of its substance, so that
painting came closest to the ethereal quality of music. Courbet in painting is a parallel to Zola in literature, and Monet

finds his equivalent in the music of Debussy. Monet called his paintings "impressions," as he felt that they were not pictures as pictures were then understood, and yet they were more than studies.

Post-Impressionism. Paul Cézanne (1839–1906) exhibited with the Impressionists and was considered one of the group. It appeared later that he had started a new trend in painting which aimed at form. A well-known admonition of Cézanne's, that forms in nature could be seen as cylinders, spheres, and cones, was perhaps taken literally by the Cubists. His expression "to make of Impressionism something lasting like the art of the museums" became almost a dogma. Cézanne was an eccentric and frustrated man, fiercely determined to achieve goals that seemed constantly to be evading him. He was dedicated more to the activity of painting than to the completion of canvases to be exhibited and sold. He often failed to bring home his studies, which his wife collected where he had left them. As he had a small allowance from his father, he did not have to depend on his painting for a living. His *Still Life* (1890–1894), painted with rocklike solidity, is typical, and one of his finest creations in its balance and repose (Fig. 234). Resemblances to cloth, lemons, and pears are general. Cézanne admired and copied old masters, but he wanted to start painting all over again, so that he might owe nothing to others. He was fearful that he might paint like someone before him and was anxious to create his own style wholly out of his own effort. This unintelligent approach to art suggests a deep-seated emotional conflict.

In Vincent van Gogh (1853–1890), as was repeatedly the case in modern painting, the artist's style was affected by the artist's personality. Emotionally, Van Gogh never grew up; he remained a child tied to his brother, Theo. There is something childlike about his painting in its bigness and simplicity and lack of interior detail. By daubing on paint in heavy strokes, as in his *La Mousmé* (Fig. 235), Van Gogh carried into art the same fierce desire to "go the limit" which earlier in life he had shown as a preacher among the Belgian miners. What made Van Gogh significant was this intense emotionalism; it determined his subjects and his brilliant color, and made his technique forceful and direct. Van Gogh gave to painting a new strength which retained the freshness of Impressionism without its frailty. His artistic style achieved great intensity, his choice of subjects, though linked to influences from Courbet and others, also suggests a trend that seems to have had its driving force in his own inner conflicts. Van Gogh shot himself after leaving a mental institution.[16]

Paul Gauguin (1848–1903), friend of Van Gogh, was another of the Post-Impressionist painters. In his *Self-Portrait* (1889), the head without body protrudes from a background of yellow, symbol of envy, and red, symbol of love (Fig. 236). He gazes disdainfully upon a blossom out of which a serpent, symbol of evil, coils between his fingers, as saintliness, a halo, hovers above. This early portrait, a posterlike decoration, is said to have been painted as a satire on himself as the Messiah of a new art. What troubled the artist—if his painting is a confession—may go back to an earlier period in his life. Any psychological interpretation must remain conjectural, due to our limited understanding of the artist and the emotional experiences he went through.

Gauguin is best known for his South Sea subjects painted in Tahiti. He used the island landscape and brown-skinned Polynesian people as subjects, injecting native sentiment. His slow-moving, languid rhythms in glowing color seemed exotic when shown in the capitals of Europe. Born in Paris of a Peruvian Creole mother, Gauguin spent some time in his early youth in Peru. At the age of thirty-two, he gave up a successful business career in exchange for a precarious life as a self-exiled, starving artist. His flight to his oceanic paradise has been viewed as a rejection of decadent Europe in exchange for a healthy life among the primitives. It is more likely that Gauguin's strange action was determined by personal motivations rather than merely a dislike for civilization.

Neo-Impressionism. This was a short-lived experiment based on the science of optics of Chevreuil. Small spots of pure colors were placed mosaiclike on the canvas on the theory that complementary colors at a proper distance fuse in the retina of the eye. Its purpose was increased luminosity. Georges Seurat (1859–1891), the chief painter of this divisionistic method (pointillism), produced some fine paintings. This was due to the fact that he was an excellent designer rather than a result of his scientific experiments with light, as is shown in his *Sunday Afternoon on the Grande Jatte* (Fig. 233), painted between 1883 and 1886.

Toulouse-Lautrec (1864–1901) was a great illustrator and creator of the modern poster of the late nineteenth century. He sought out the cafés, bars (Fig. 239), and dance halls; the *fin de siècle* night life of Paris lives again in his paintings and pastels, executed with breadth and vigor.

Abstract Traditions. A trend toward abstract art had its origin in Cézanne and Seurat on the one hand and in Gauguin and Van Gogh on the other. The Cézanne influence led to an intellectual geometric style illustrated in Cubism.

Van Gogh's and Gauguin's free and emotional style led to Expressionism, and more recently to Surrealism. Though these two tendencies also intermingled, they appeared in Piet Mondrian in a severely geometric style of rectangles, squares, and lines, and in Joan Miró in curves and shapes that suggest an organic origin. In sculpture, the two trends were represented by the rectilinear style of Pevsner Gabo and the soft, bulging style of Árp. Young painters who had come to maturity during the first decade of the twentieth century followed one trend or another and became pioneers themselves.

Pablo Picasso (b. 1881 in Spain) was brought up in an intellectually stimulating atmosphere. His father, a professor at the Barcelona Academy of Fine Arts, had early encouraged his son in drawing. Before his twentieth birthday he had won prizes and was painting in the styles of Renoir and Lautrec. In exploring the possibilities of expanding painting, Picasso passed through various stages before 1937; he produced the *Guernica* mural (Museum of Modern Art) in 1937, probably his best known single work.

Cubism. In the years before the First World War, Picasso and Braque became founders of Cubism. A painting by Cézanne (*Town of Gardanne*, 1885–86) and one by Picasso (*The Poet*, 1911) suggest how Cézanne's style developed into Picasso's Cubism. An early painting (1907) by Picasso (*Les Demoiselles d'Avignon*) shows the influence of African wood sculpture. Cubism went through several stages, from a deeply indented, modeled form to a flat linear pattern and boldly decorative manner (*Three Musicians*, 1921). Neither Picasso nor Braque nor Gris entirely eliminated all resemblances to objects. Picasso rejected interpretations "as nonsense or pure literature and theory." According to Picasso, "Cubism is painting that deals primarily with forms, and drawing, design and color are understood and practiced as in all other schools." After some experience with Cubistic paintings, like the one by Braque, *Still Life, Le Jour* (Fig. 237), one reacts spontaneously and with pleasure, but one should not expect to appreciate Cubism at first glance.[17]

Guernica. On April 28, 1937, German bombers destroyed the Basque town of Guernica. Two days later, Picasso began work on his mural *Guernica*. The painting is intellectual; its emotional element, expressed through design and symbols, expands and deepens the theme. Figures cry out in agony, the arm of a statue holds a broken sword, lilies sprout from graves, and poppies, from a field of battle. A lamp is swept in from the outside to cast light on destruction, as the bull, symbol of aggression, looks on unperturbed. The

horse, stabbed, shrieks out in pain; Pegasus, once pet of the
Muses, is slit and slashed paper-thin. If this curled paper
suggests anything, it is newsprint, the morning paper cut
in anger to fantastic bits. How often the world's misery is
served to us in that fashion; tragedies read about seem as
unreal as these painted shapes. Perhaps this is a message of
bitter irony at man's limited comprehension, his lack of compassion, his self-protecting isolation against the meaning of
Guernica. This is an empty, cruel world lacking humanity
and subject to destruction; black, white and gray colors
convey the feeling of mourning (Fig. 241).

Non-Objective Painting. By 1923 Wassily Kandinsky
(1866–1944), a Russian, had eliminated all semblances to
natural objects. His paintings bear no title today; one is
identified as 255 (Fig. 240). Its fresh green background ar-
rests attention, but even the black-and-white reproduction is
exciting with its large scale, its clearly stated contrast of
foreground and distance, and its different shapes and kinds
of lines. Associations may be dimly suggested, but bear no
obvious comparison with nature; the painting has weight, a
bottom and a top. Kandinsky founded a new group in
1911 called *"Der Blaue Reiter"* (The Blue Horseman), and
was joined by Paul Klee, a Swiss, and Franz Marc, a German. Some of Klee's drawings or water colors bear a resemblance to children's drawings. They are small in scale and
have little substance. His oil painting *Around the Fish* (Fig.
255) appeals by its invention and variety of shapes and its
precision of technique. Its calculated space relationships
seem free, and yet any change would disturb the balance.

Expressionism. This was essentially a German phase,
emotional rather than intellectual. The group was organized
under the name "The Bridge" (*Die Brücke*) in Dresden in
1905, and included Erich Heckel, Karl Schmidt-Rottluff,
Emil Nolde, Ernst Barlach, Ernst L. Kirchner and Max Pech-
stein. The woodcut of Nolde's *The Prophet* (Ill. 123) suggests
a dynamic spirit oriented away from reality. Of gigantic
stature was Käthe Kollwitz, the most moving graphic
artist of modern Germany. As wife of a physician who lived
in a working-class section of Berlin, she was in close touch
with the poor, before and after the First World War. In
lithographs, woodcuts, and etchings, she poured out her
sympathy with the grief and desperation of the suffering
people in moving documents. *The Parents* lament the loss of
their son in war (Ill. 125) and children with starved faces
look to their mother for bread. George Grosz (1893–1859) in
a drawing entitled *Cannibal in Modern Dress* (Ill. 124) shows
us a well-nourished Nazi profiteer amidst bones and skulls
against an industrial background. The most devastatingly

satirical artist of his era, he castigated unmercifully the
evils left in Germany in the wake of the First World War.
Max Beckmann's triptych of the *Departure* (1932–35),
smuggled out of Germany, dealt with another nightmare
of Nazi tyranny. The quiet triumph of the central panel, with
its blue water and light sky, compensates for the oppressive
side panels. The crowned figure raises his hand in farewell,

as the hooded one
lowers his arm to
symbolize the ty-
rant's downfall; the
sentimental men
gaze back, but the
woman, child in
arm, courageously
looks ahead.

*Matisse and the
"Fauves."* As the
German Expression-
ists were organizing,
Paris was featuring
Henri Matisse,
André Derain,
Georges Rouault,
and Maurice de
Vlaminck at the
"Salon d'Automne"
(1905). They be-
came known as *Les
Fauves* (wild beasts)
due to their "wild"
color and uncouth

Ill. 123 Nolde: The Prophet. *National
Gallery of Art, Rosenwald Collection*

vigor. This was il-
lustrated in the work of their leader, Henri Matisse, whose
Woman with the Hat shocked everybody. Matisse (1869–
1954) had studied law in Paris before his father finally
permitted him to study under Bouguereau, who said
that his pupil would never learn to draw. His second
teacher, the liberal Gustave Moreau, gave him intelligent
encouragement. The sensuous appeal of the *Odalisque with
Raised Arms* (1920, reproduced on the back cover), is typical
of Matisse, to whom painting meant relaxation. Matisse emphasized color, design, and pattern, often introduced as textiles, in ever-varying combinations; volume, depth, and space
were often minimized. Many of his paintings are flat decorations, with vibrant color and breadth of pattern (*Egyptian
Curtain*); others show bold, curvilinear rhythms (*Lady in
Blue*), or at times massive compactness and spatial re-

lations (*Odalisque with a Tambourine*). Matisse's drawings have freshness and ease. The small textile pattern is calculated to emphasize the larger areas of the figure, which stands out in contrast. They are among the exhilarating creations of modern art.[18]

Ill. 124 Grosz: Cannibal in Modern Dress. *Courtesy of the artist*

Various Trends: Cubistic, Futuristic, Primitive, Fantastic. Artists of varying styles received international attention. Delaunay (b. 1885) derived his style from Cézanne. His *Eiffel Tower* (1910) is an inspired abstraction, precise, but imbued with an explosive drive. Léger's *Le Grand Déjeuner* in the Cubistic manner is a mechanization of the figure rather than a humanization of the machine. Futurism began in Italy with a literary manifesto proclaiming motion as its subject matter. Theory and painting did not agree, but Gino Severini, Umberto Boccioni, and others produced attractive paintings in an abstract or Cubistic manner. The mass effect of Marcel Duchamp's (b. 1887) *Nude Descending a Staircase* conformed to a downward rhythmical swing. Shown in the 1913 Armory Show in New York, this painting amused or infuriated the world with its abstracted figures, stacked like sections of plywood. Henri Rousseau (1844–1910) was a self-trained folk or amateur painter, a "Sunday" painter; on weekdays he was a customs official (*dou-*

Ill. 125 Kollwitz: The Parents, War Ill. *Courtesy Kleemann Galleries, New York*

anier). His primeval forests with wild beasts, sleeping beauties, and tapestrylike foliage backgrounds are universal favorites. The Italian Amedeo Modigliani (1884–1920) developed a linear style of elongated figures, flat or modeled in light tints, orange, black, blue, and green. Long verticals or diagonals set against undulating curves contribute to his distinctive style. Giorgio di Chirico (b. 1888) was born in Greece of Italian parents and studied in Munich, where he was influenced by Böcklin. In his *Nostalgia of the Infinite,* the high sky is partly obstructed by a massive tower, and the lonely, sunlit middle ground is separated from the foreground by a deep shadow. A flood of light on the side of the tower suggests a vastness beyond, but a high wall cuts us off from its source. The title expresses what the painting conveys, nostalgia, a longing mingled with pain. In *The Village and I* (1911) the Russian Marc Chagall (b. 1887) combines reminiscences from his native village, the street, a milking scene superimposed on a cow's head, a profile head —all in vivid pink, green, gray, and white. Yves Tanguy's landscapes, filled with unreal creatures, have an other-worldly fascination. Whether glimpsed from the depths of the ocean or from another planet, the subject matter is unfamiliar but not irrational, and the style violates no principle of accepted aesthetics. His titles, such as *Four O'clock in Summer, Hope* or *Mamma, Papa Is Wounded* add to the mood of strangeness. Joan Miró (b. 1893) is playful and childlike in the *Circus* (1934) and precise and intellectual in *Maternity* (1924); his paintings call for no psychological interpretations.

Dada and Surrealism. Dada was started in a cabaret in Zurich (1916) by outraged, disillusioned poets and painters during the First World War. Wholly negative, Dada produced nonsense for its own sake rather than works of art. Surrealism grew out of Dada and continued its antirational character, but formulated a program by André Breton, a Dadaist poet of Paris (1924). Cubists had included bits of newspaper as parts of their designs to demonstrate that art did not depend on brush and pigment; the Surrealists used comparable objects because they were absurd, and also painted "ready-made" objects, such as manufactured articles.

Salvador Dali, the painter of "applied Surrealism," returned to literary sources. Ideas from psychoanalytic literature were illustrated, such as open drawers projecting out of female figures. Well-known neurotic symbols, flabby as "bent time" watches, suggest an association with Einstein's "bent light-curved space" concept. An academic technique and the novelty of fantastic inventions made Dali popular. Surrealistic painting appears self-conscious, though Surrealists claimed to explore the unconscious through "dreams and hallucinations." The contribution from the unconscious is comparable to Neo-Classic subjects in David or Romantic subjects in Delacroix. There was no Surrealism before Freud and psychoanalysis became known. Surrealist tendencies were discovered in the art of the past where they probably did not exist, as in Bosch. On the other hand, the unconscious has played a part in artistic creation, and at times has made itself felt in the work of the artist, but not as deliberately as in the professional Surrealists of our own day.

Max Ernst (b. 1891), a self-trained German artist and student of philosophy, was a natural Surrealist. In his early youth he made rubbings from the wood grain of a mahogany plank and studied leaves for their network of veins. He discovered patterns in natural materials, just as Leonardo had. Another approach was to study the illustrations in commercial catalogues of scientific implements and materials from mineralogy and anthropology. By drawing backgrounds on the printed page suggesting sky or horizon, Ernst united irreconcilable objects, such as parts of machinery standing in a desert. From such studies, he created his paintings and influenced the Surrealists.

Sculpture. Neo-Classicism produced the Italian sculptor Antonio Canova, the Dane Bertel Thorvaldsen, the Englishman John Flaxman, and others in Germany and Austria. This was followed in all countries by numerous statues of generals and poets done in a style influenced by realism. Antoine Louis Barye produced some fine animal sculpture, and Jean Baptiste Carpeaux's decorations of the Louvre were related to the Baroque. Impressionism in sculpture found its interpreter in Auguste Rodin (1840–1917). By leaving parts of the unfinished block from which his figures emerged, the contrast of the rough marble with the sensitive modeling of flesh and bone gave his work a living quality (Fig. 242). Aristide Maillol (b. 1861) emphasized repose and massiveness of form. In his plaster relief *Desire* (Fig. 244), solidity is close to archaic Greek sculpture without its stylization. The Belgian sculptor Constantin Meunier (b. 1831) specialized in figures of miners and found inspiration in the hardened muscles of the body used to physical toil. Like Millet, he brought out the dignity of labor. In the Yugoslav Ivan Meštrović (b. 1883), the archaic Greek art again became a potent influence. Post-Impressionism in sculpture was represented by the Rumanian Constantin Brancusi and the Russian Aleksandr Porfirievich Archipenko; a Cubistic treatment and sculptural bulk replaced naturalistic modeling. Henry Moore (b. 1898) has expanded our sympathy for abstract form derived from nature. He expresses himself in several directions: one of organic growth with a preference for the horizontal, another of geometric forms in simple contours; both may be combined. The human element is often more felt than seen. In his *Family Group* (Fig. 243), the relationship of child to parents is sensitively portrayed. The Swedish sculptor Carl Milles (b. 1875), often using bronze, created an individual style on a monumental scale. His fountains (*Orpheus Fountain,* Stockholm) are grandly conceived, impressive works. Germany produced a great sculptor in Wilhelm Lehmbruck. His *Standing Youth* and *Kneeling Woman* represent a highly individual style of linear rhythm combined with a spiritual quality. Designed for side view, this latter figure suggests a delicate resignation, perhaps derived from a deeply felt Gothic inspiration; however, Lehmbruck is not in the least historical.

Modern Architecture. A break with the revival style of the nineteenth century came with "*Art nouveau*" or "*Jugendstill*" around 1900, following the English pioneers under William Morris. The style, based on curves suggesting plants and flowers, did not last long enough to leave many monuments. The early trends toward modern architecture were represented by an American, Frank Lloyd Wright; the leaders of twentieth-century architecture in Europe, Walter Gropius, Le Corbusier, and Mies van der Rohe, came later. Between 1919 and 1933 machine-age design in all the arts was integrated in Dessau, Germany, in the so-called Bauhaus School. Gropius designed the school buildings and became the founder and first director. Comparable trends were pursued in France by the architect Le Corbusier (b. 1888 in Switzerland), who was also a painter, sculptor, and city planner. All arts found a unified expression based on structural logic and new materials, out of which developed a new aesthetic. The style became international and produced outstanding monuments in many countries.

Conclusion. With the development of the industrial era based on science and technology, the artist lost ground. There were fewer great artists, though more people participated in art. Architecture, sculpture, and painting lost touch with one another; painting became the stronghold of art, architecture moved closer to engineering, and sculpture receded as a major art.

The professional painter, dedicated to advancing the tradition of the past, still commanded prestige, but at the expense of his economic security. Amateur painters adhered to no single approach—their style varied according to ability or environment. The commercial artist, a new type, virtually took over professional painting, serving advertising devoted to the distribution of goods. The industrial designer replaced the craftsman of an earlier period and often possessed the skill of craftsman, sculptor, painter, and designer.

In the span of a century and a half, the prestige of the painter and sculptor declined; the architect, serving practical ends, maintained his station in life. By mid-twentieth century, a unified style in architecture began to give the metropolis and its environs a semblance of order. Technological changes had produced a severely functional style, but a basic desire for beauty exercised a modifying influence; to restrain ugliness and make the world more beautiful continued to be a powerful motive.

CHAPTER XII

Art in the United States:

1700 - 1958

Introduction. American art began in the seventeenth century as European art transplanted to the Western Hemisphere. Here in the British colonies and in New York, then held by the Dutch, painting developed as a provincial style of the homelands. The altered living conditions of pioneer settlements were reflected in art from the beginning. After the founding of the republic, indigenous trends appeared, and before the middle of the nineteenth century, a native development, aided by the teachings of Europe, had taken root. By the end of the century, American painting had achieved a character of its own and American-born painters like James Whistler and John Sargent had acquired a reputation in Europe. American painting kept in touch with European trends up to the period of Impressionism and through the subsequent developments until 1913 (New York Armory Show).

The Colonial Style. The British settlers of Jamestown and Plymouth had little interest in art, even before they came to this country. To the serious Calvinist, art was suspect, as it brought with it the danger of idolatry. Portraiture appeared early because artists had no other outlet for their talents and the colonists, as the founders of a new state, were anxious to be remembered by posterity. Artists were called limners or face painters, and an emphasis on the head characterizes even the best of early American painters. In New York as many as half a dozen painters were limning the burghers of the region. Gustavus Hesselius came from Sweden to Maryland and Virginia, John Smibert and Pelham from England to Massachusetts, and the visiting painters taught others. Early colonial painting, before Copley, was portraiture transplanted from Europe; it formed a bond, slight as it was, between the English, Dutch, Swedes, French, and Germans. Religious art had almost died out in England and it played only a minor role in the colonies.

John Singleton Copley (1738–1815) was the most important colonial painter, but he eventually settled in London. Growing up in the artistically limited environment of early Boston, Copley developed a solidity of style without Reynolds's elegance, but with an emphasis on design and an expression of the personality of his sitters. A painstaking realism in the head was fused with freer brush work in the costume, a technique which Copley had learned from English portraiture. The portraits of *Nathaniel Hurd* (Cleveland Museum) and *Mrs. Sylvanus Bourne* (Metropolitan Museum of Art) are among Copley's best.

Benjamin West, a Pennsylvania Quaker, succeeded Reynolds as president of the Royal Academy in London, the first American to be so honored. The painting *Penn's Treaty with the Indians* (1772), now in Independence Hall, is well composed in the Neo-Classic manner, but setting and costume disguise the sources of inspiration. Here, as in his *Death of Wolfe,* he introduced contemporary costumes rather than the classical dress then prescribed for historical subjects. In West's studio in London, American artists, among them Charles Willson Peale and Gilbert Stuart, received encouragement and training. Stuart (1755–1828) was the best face painter of the period; his style is illustrated in the *Portrait of Mrs. Yates* (Fig. 245). His most famous American portraits were the Athenaeum portraits of *George and Martha Washington,* which he purposely left unfinished, so that he would not be tempted to sell them. Stuart painted Washington from life only three times, but from these models came from 111 (Park) to 175 (Eisen) replicas. Charles Willson Peale of Philadelphia, ranking below only Copley and Stuart, acquired a reputation for his portraits of Washington; he was also a coachmaker, watchmaker, and silversmith. He excavated the first mastodon skeleton and founded the first scientific museum. John Trumbull (1756–1843), diplomat and son of the governor of Connecticut, was the historical painter of the Revolution, as illustrated in the well-known painting *The Declaration of Independence* (Yale Gallery of Fine Arts, and the Capitol in Washington, D.C.).

The National Period. Samuel F. B. Morse (1791–1872), though a pupil of West's, was influenced by French Classicism in his portrait of the *Marquis de Lafayette.* Not content with painting alone, he helped to organize the National Academy of Design and invented the telegraph.

Between 1812 and the Civil War profound social changes took place. Instead of painting ancestral portraits, artists and laymen became conscious of American life. The artists who succeeded the portrait painters grew up in a society that was less cultured than that of Copley and Stuart. Chester Harding (b. 1792), a Massachusetts farm boy, had been a pioneer woodsman, soldier, drummer, saloonkeeper, chairmaker, and peddler before he took up painting. The native literature of Cooper and Bryant is paralleled in painting by the trend toward local subject material. *Raffling for the Goose* is a typical work by William Mount (b. 1807), who began as a house painter. John Neagle painted *A View of the Schuylkill River* that was surprisingly competent considering his few months' training from a coach painter. Asher B. Durand, John Frederick Kensett, and Thomas Cole of the Hudson River School painted the rural landscape of the Catskills in a hard, precise style, emphasizing detail. Frederick Church pictured nature in all its splendor with spectacular panoramic effects (*Falls of Niagara*). He claimed that a picture should be more than a transcript of everyday nature; the subject itself should be noble. Albert Bierstadt (b. 1830), who had studied at Düsseldorf and Rome, painted *The Rocky Mountains* from sketches in the studio; though he was successful in his own day, his reputation was short-lived. More enduring success came to his contemporary George Inness (1825–1894). Inness broke away from Durand's linear style, and his large canvas *Peace and Plenty* (Metropolitan Museum of Art), representing the Connecticut Valley, has a serene grandeur that stands comparison with the best landscape painting of any period. Nature here is sunny and spacious; other landscapes of his, influenced by Corot, are more atmospheric. An impressionistic technique characterized the paintings of Homer Martin (*Harp of the Winds*, 1887) and Childe Hassam (*Church at Old Lyme*, 1905).

James Abbott McNeill Whistler (1834–1903), after two years of art study in Paris, settled in London, where he became an international celebrity. He learned from Velázquez and from Japanese prints, and developed a flat, decorative style. In his landscape motifs Whistler preferred a twilight illumination, and eventually achieved a refined style of gray harmonies. His early canvas, *The Woman in White* (National Gallery of Art), is painted in broad areas and light values. He labeled his paintings symphonies, or arrangements, in order to emphasize his interest in the decorative aspect of painting. His well-known portrait of his mother (*c.* 1871), entitled *Arrangement in Gray and Black* (Fig. 246), has long been appreciated as a classic example of a sensitively related space and color harmony. It is hard to believe that this painting remained unsold for twenty years, finally being purchased by the French Government for $800. When brought to the United States for exhibition in 1932, it was insured for $500,-

000. Whistler was also a prolific etcher, according to Pennel, better (!) than Rembrandt.

Mary Cassatt (1845–1926) was born in Pittsburgh, studied in Philadelphia, and lived in Paris, where she became a member of the Impressionist group. She specialized in young mothers and children painted in high key, and also produced fine prints.

John Singer Sargent (1856–1925), born in Florence of well-to-do American parents, acquired an excellent training at Carolus-Duran's studio in Paris. He made London his European headquarters, after his *Portrait of Madame Gautreau* had been criticized in Paris as too décolleté. Perhaps under the influence of Velázquez, Sargent painted *The Four Daughters of Edward Darley Boit* (1882) placed informally in a room of their own home. Admired by his own generation for his brilliant technique, the trend today is to dismiss Sargent as having no more than surface attraction.

An objective kind of realism became the characteristically American style during the nineteenth century. James Audubon, of French birth, set out to be a frontier merchant; instead, after training under David, he became a student and painter of American birds. With truly inspired endurance and energy, he sought out the birds in the wilderness, drew them in full-size water colors, had his originals engraved, and wrote the scientific text. His 435 plates with 1065 illustrations, published in four volumes as *The Birds of America,* had an unequaled success (1827–1830).

Thomas Eakins (1844–1916) studied in Paris under Gerôme. He returned to Philadelphia as a teacher at the Academy, where he emphasized anatomy and drawing from the living figure. Whether showing the clinic of *Dr. Gross* (1875), the boxing ring (*Between Rounds*), or the river (*Max Schmidt in a Single Scull*), Eakins placed each object accurately in space to suggest depth. His artistry compensates for the drabness of his world.

Romanticism, when applied to American painting, implies a sense of unity with nature close to that of such German Romantic painters as Friedrich and includes such painters as Washington Allston (*Moonlit Landscape*), Thomas Cole (*The Voyage of Life*), and Asher B. Durand (*Kindred Spirits*). John Quidor (1801-1881), an artisan painter of banners and fire-engine panels, painted *The Return of Rip van Winkle* (1829), an interpretation of the famous story from Washington Irving's *Sketch Book* (1818). Rip, after a twenty-year sleep, wakes up, unkempt and ragged, to find himself in a strange world, surrounded by a staring crowd caricatured through grotesque expressions (Fig. 247). Whether or not Quidor had Albert Pinkham Ryder (1847–1917) as a pupil is uncertain, ~~but~~ both have been called Romantic. Ryder's Romanticism seems to have grown out of his personal experience; he was largely self-taught. His eyes were always weak and he worked from memory of observed impressions collected on his walks at night. Ryder is best known for such moonlit seascapes as *Toilers of the Sea* or *Moonlit Cove.* His *The Race Track,* showing a skeleton on horseback, was painted in memory of a friend who committed suicide after losing his life savings on a horse race.

George C. Bingham, Eastman Johnson, Winslow Homer, Thomas Eakins, and William M. Harnett represent realistic trends. As a boy living on the Missouri frontier, Bingham (1811–1879) copied engravings. Chester Harding, who had received little training himself, started Bingham painting during a visit. After a few months of study at the Pennsylvania Academy in Philadelphia and several years of portrait painting in Washington, Bingham returned to Missouri to paint (1845) *The Fur Trader Descending the Missouri* (Metropolitan Museum of Art) with its mirrorlike surface of the water, its humid, misty background, and the sharply outlined canoe. Bingham was active in politics, and his *Verdict of the People* (c. 1855) is a lively Election Day scene. Eastman Johnson (1824–1906) painted the sentimental *Old Kentucky Home* (1859). His later paintings are less superficially staged and more objective, such as *Shucking Corn* (1864) in Toledo. Whistler and Sargent became well known in Europe, but Winslow Homer (1836–1910) was perhaps the most revered painter in his own country. Born in Boston, Homer began as an illustrator and made drawings for *Harper's Weekly* while with the Union armies during the Civil War. His oil painting *Prisoners from the Front* (Metropolitan Museum of Art) made him famous. Settled at Prout's Neck on the Maine coast, he developed the theme of man's contest with wind and weather on the coast and on board ship. In his *Eight Bells* (Fig. 249), we are made to feel the weight and mass of the heaving sea and the moist clouds, and also the stamina of the men. Homer became equally outstanding as a water colorist, using the medium to suggest solid form while retaining its transparency and fluidity. William Harnett (1848–1892) was an engraver of silver in Philadelphia before he took up painting still life as a career. Toward the end of his life, after having studied the seventeenth-century Dutch masters, he applied textures and luminosity to his paintings in his *trompe l'oeil* style in such subjects as *After the Hunt* (San Francisco, California Palace of the Legion of Honor Collection).

Modern Trends. Painting during the first half of the twentieth century was marked by another succession of styles, each one in the nature of a revolt of short duration.

The "Group of Eight." Though Whistler, Sargent, Homer, and Eakins were still living in 1900, a younger generation of painters carried their tradition of realism further. A slashing brush stroke and a lust for life characterized the first decade of the century. Robert Henri, working in the Hals-Velázquez-Manet tradition of realism, was the leader of "The Eight": William Glackens, George B. Luks, John Sloan, Everett Shinn, Arthur B. Davies, Maurice B. Prendergast and Ernest Lawson. This twentieth-century revolution of the so-called "Ash Can School" brought to art subjects from slums and saloons, poolrooms and theaters, factories and workshops. In literature, Jack London and Frank Norris paralleled this movement. Sloan painted New York and the waterfront in a broad, vigorous style. His strength lay in his spontaneous interpretations of what he had seen and experienced, as in *The Wake of the Ferry*. Glackens's style was closer to Renoir and Manet. Jerome Myers dealt sympathetically with motifs from the slums of New York. George Bellows introduced a note of excitement in his paintings and lithographs of prize fights and of Hudson River scenes. In his painting *The White Horse*, the sun breaking through light clouds over the distant hills gives nature a touch of magic splendor upon which even horse and dog gaze in wonder (Worcester Museum).

Stieglitz, Marin, Demuth, O'Keeffe, Sheeler, Hopper and Burchfield. American painters who studied in Paris from 1900 on felt the impact of the Fauves and of Cubism. Among them were Bernard Karfiol, Charles Demuth, Charles Sheeler, and Marsden Hartley. Alfred Stieglitz in his Photosecession Gallery "291" introduced Matisse to America and sponsored the advanced French and American painters of his day. In his own right, Stieglitz became the dean of photography as an art. The Armory Show of 1913 stirred up the public and stimulated American collectors to purchase French paintings, but did not bring on any lasting American School of Fauves or Cubists. The decade of the twenties was one of ferment. New collections dedicated to twentieth-century art were founded, and dealers who arranged one-man exhibitions also contributed toward a broadening of taste in contemporary painting. New York skyscrapers and the Maine coast inspired John Marin's water colors. Marin was an individualist, at times strong and sensitive in his work. He speaks of "buildings large and small, seen as great forces at work, pushing, pulling, sideways, downward, upward. . . ." Perhaps his water color *Lower Manhattan* (1920) illustrates these forces. This often-produced work, to paraphrase Grant Wood, "seems to be carried by a knowledge of the feelings that inspired the artist." Demuth's water-color

style is one of flowing washes enframed within a crisp linear
pattern in subjects from architecture (*My Egypt*, 1925) or the
old vaudeville stage. His fine craftsmanship offers no ob-
stacle to appreciation. Edward Hopper's style is also simplified, but his treatment of urban motifs reiterates, in the
abandoned street on a *Sunday Morning*, in a glimpse into a
theater lobby in *New York Movie*, the loneliness of the big
city. Hopper's injection of feeling into commonplace sites
takes on an increased emotional tone in Charles E. Burchfield's water colors of the American small town. The term
"immaculate" well describes the magnificent flowers, the
sharply profiled skulls or the simple architectural motifs of
Georgia O'Keeffe. Her style is severe and precise in contours,
velvety in expansive forms that curve and flow to achieve a
luxuriant perfectionism. Charles Sheeler turned an industrial
site of tracks, silos, cranes, and ducts into a carefully integrated pattern, smooth and almost geometric. The subjects
are American; they exist in a cleansed and rarefied atmosphere, stripped of human attributes.

American Scene Painters. During the thirties the native
element received emphasis in the work of Thomas Hart Benton
of Missouri, Grant Wood of Iowa, and John S. Curry of
Kansas. Benton developed a vigorous, agitated style; a wealth
of remembered detail is worked into a grand, well-ordered
turbulence. Photographic accuracy, lush textures, romance,
humor, and symbolism all appear in his murals and lithographs. Pictorial devices are used unobtrusively to bring together six different subjects combined in one mural *Arts of
the South* (Fig. 250): Salvation and Ecstasy (Holy Rollers),
Negro Singing, Craps, Feeding the Baby, Mule Driving, and
The Sabbath Call. Grant Wood evolved a simplified style composed of rural Midwestern motifs. He enlivened his softly
modeled hills and patterned fields with signs of human activity, as in *Stone City*. His romantic *Midnight Ride of Paul
Revere* shows a lovely moonlit landscape that is immediately
captivating; his *American Gothic* (The Art Institute of Chicago) established his reputation and his acid *Daughters of the
Revolution* is frankly satirical. Wood said modestly that this
painting is "carried by its subject matter." John Curry made
his reputation with *Baptism in Kansas; The Tornado* is perhaps
his best-known work. He deals with native material in a forceful illustrative style (*The Line Storm*).

Federal Art Projects. In the depression of the thirties the
Federal Government organized relief projects for unemployed
artists. Public buildings were decorated with murals, paintings, and prints, works of sculpture were produced, and
local art centers established. Holger Cahill, who had discovered American folk art, directed the state projects which

resulted in the 17,500 water-color renderings of *The Index of American Design*, now in the National Gallery of Art. Through exhibitions and publications, this unique collection has served to make American crafts and folk arts known in this country and abroad.

Social Realism. Toward the late twenties and in the thirties, the Soyer brothers represented with sympathy the life of the poor, Reginald Marsh, the miserable lodging houses of New York's Bowery or bathers piled up on the beaches of Coney Island. William Gropper struck a sharp note of protest (Ill. 126) which made the Henri realists seem mild. Aaron Bohrod described the desecration of the landscape made ugly by the clutter of junked cars. Ben Shahn (b. 1898) developed an individual style in which realism has human significance. *Sacco and Vanzetti* (Fig. 251), seated and chained together, look out at the world perplexed, unbelieving, a muted protest insistent in its emotional impact. In a drawing *Girl Jumping Rope* (1943), the gaunt contours, a silent reminder of hunger, also count as linear rhythms; the ungainly child playing is expressive; a sweet, intense sadness arouses our compassion. Shahn's artistry is reticent but compelling. Jack Levine's (b. 1915) social realism depends on grotesque distortions of people, rich men at banquets, miserable characters from the underworld playing cards.

Ill. 126 Gropper: Under the "El," drawing.

Abstraction. The severely intellectual Cubism of Europe became something else in the American environment, as in Max Weber's interpretations (*Chinese Restaurant*, 1915). The specific and concrete were also present in Joseph Stella, as in his *Brooklyn Bridge* (1917), and Man Ray created abstractions using water color and air brush (*Aerograph*, 1919). Abstract painters like Macdonald-Wright and Morgan Russell temporarily aimed to purify their art of anecdote and illustra-

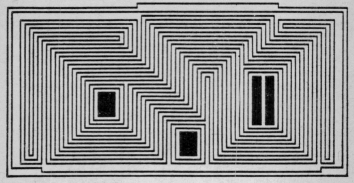

Ill. 127 Albers: Sanctuary. *Courtesy National Gallery of Art, Rosenwald Collection*

tion, paralleling color and painting with music (Synchromism). In *Summer Landscape* (1930) Stuart Davis used suggestions from Cubism, so that the natural landscape was translated into flat colors and sharply outlined shapes (Fig. 248). The total impression is cheerful, the natural and the abstract enhancing each other. The abstract style gained followers from 1930–1950; the artists of the Bauhaus faculty came to this country, and the Solomon R. Guggenheim Museum was founded (1937) for non-objective painting. Abstract painting, in its intellectual phase, developed mechanical and geometric effects and, in its expressionistic-emotional approach, tended to organic and other sources of inspiration. Abstract painting and sculpture approach each other and, when reproduced in a book, a painting may look like sculpture or vice versa. The pure geometric style has produced fine works in the paintings of George L. K. Morris and Carl Holty and in the sculpture of John Ferren, Jose de Rivera, Richard Lippold and Theodore Roszak. Alexander S. Calder's constructions in wood, steel, and lead or in sheet aluminum are exciting creations, beautiful, and revolutionary only to the extent that shapes have been abstracted from any content. Lippold's brass and copper wire structures (*Primordial Figure,* 1947) have purity and ethereal delicacy; Seymour Lipton's nickel-silver sheet metal *Germinal* (1953) has a massive quality as well. Leo Amino's *Jungle* (Fig. 256) is 56 inches high, a construction of mahogany of interrelated shapes, solids, and hollows, subtle and freely invented. A design by Josef Albers, *Sanctuary* (Ill. 127), is a rigid pattern of repeating horizontals and verticals that create an illusion of light and dark by virtue of a change in the weight of line.

A pupil of Albers's, Sue Fuller, uses plastic string for a linear maze strung within an open frame. Curves result from tangents and, through the use of colored threads, optical color mixtures occur; background as well as reflected light make for additional variations.

Contemporary Painting. The most potent influences today are "the order of Mondrian, the monster of Picasso, and the maze of Jackson Pollock"[19] (1912–1956), chief rep-

Ill. 128 Pollock: Echo, 1951. *Collection of Mr. and Mrs. Ben Heller, New York. Photograph, courtesy Sidney Janis Gallery, New York*

resentative of the Abstract Expressionists. Standing on a large canvas, Pollock would drop, squirt, or splash paint freely in a version of the traditional free brush stroke technique elaborated to include accidental shapes. The resulting freshness produced an attractive vitality; the action of the hand transferred to a surface is reactivated in shapes and splashes. The sweeps originate in the lower left-hand corner, rise, rebound,

drop, and rise again in a turmoil of movement (Ill. 128). The
planned total pattern must not interfere with the spontaneous details. A splashy abandon in an inkblot type of pattern is set off effectively against a more restrained background in Pollock's *Number 12, 1952.* Art that makes composition its subject sets aside man's reaction to the realities
of his immediate environment. And yet, Abstract Expressionism, as in Jackson Pollock's *Autumn Rhythms* (Metropolitan
Museum of Art), has a cosmic breadth suggesting the grandeur
of the universe. Infinite variety borders on chaos, but retains
an inner consistency. No longer hand painted, the swinging
arm of the moving figure has left its traces behind.

Professional Primitivism. Just as there are advanced painters who reject the academic traditions of the past, so there
are retarded, or "primitive," painters. These painters have an
urge to paint, but feel no compulsion to absorb the traditions
through art-school study. Though they lack skill in drawing
from nature and the human figure, their objectives are realistic. John Kane (1860–1932), a carpenter and housepainter of
Pittsburgh, painted landscapes. Morris Hirshfield (1872–
1946) is represented in the Museum of Modern Art by a
painting entitled *Tiger,* a beautiful ornamentalized stuffed
beast with a fierce expression. Horace Pippin (1888–1946) became a painter after a war injury had incapacitated him for
manual labor. A well-known primitive painter is Grandma
Moses of Eagle Bridge, New York.

Graphic Art. Prints in every medium are closely associated
with painting and sculpture and follow similar trends. Commercial advertising using mechanical aids such as the camera,
air brush, and reproduction machines (Auto-graph and
Camera Lucikon) represent that branch of modern art that
supports artists the way engraving, before its photomechani-
cal development, often gave the nineteenth-century artist his
start. A type of humor, based on the frustrations and futility
of modern living, has become associated with artists of the
New Yorker magazine (founded 1925) such as Helen Hokin-
son (1893–1949), James Thurber, Charles Addams, Peter
Arno, Robert Day, Whitney Darrow, Jr., Richard Decker, and
George Price. In the newspapers, the comic strip developed
its own artists, the editorial pages, its political cartoonists.
Ranking above others is Herblock, who has become a national
institution through his cartoons in *The Washington Post and
Times Herald,* a keeper of the public conscience. Though
Herblock is comparable to Daumier, he has a style of his
own (Ill. 129). On occasion, the weekly magazines produce
artistically significant designs in black and white. A triumph
was scored by the New York *Nation* (November 4, 1944)
when Al Hirschfeld turned the gleeful grin of F.D.R. into

a symbol of the flag accompanied by the sign for victory
(Ill. 130).

Sculpture, Architecture, and Industrial Art. John Rogers
(1829–1904) was a popular sculptor who gave first consideration to the telling of a sentimental story rather than to the
nude figure, then considered the basis of sculpture. Of the
87 groups (approximately) which he patented and advertised,
100,000 copies in red plaster were sold. *Checkers Up at the
Farm* is one of his best works. Academic sculptures up to
the Centennial Exhibition of 1876 followed the Neo-Classic
tradition. After that a French influence gave sculpture a new

Ill. 129 Herblock: Cartoon "Look Lady—You Don't See Me
Worrying." *Courtesy* Washington Post and Times Herald, *the
artist and Hall Syndicate*

direction. Augustus Saint-Gaudens (1848–1907) was the outstanding sculptor of the century. His *Adams Monument*
(Washington, D.C.) showing a seated mourning woman is
impressive; the *Standing Figure of Lincoln* (Chicago) is one
of his well-known works. Lorado Taft (1860–1936), influenced by Rodin, designed monumental groups, including few
or many figures with a symbolic meaning. A more varied de-

velopment of sculpture came with the twentieth century, as has been previously discussed (p. 306).

The colonial period has left us a rich heritage of distinguished work in domestic architecture as well as in such public buildings as *Independence Hall* in Philadelphia. The Neo-Classic period produced the *Capitol* in Washington, D.C., a monumental design that does justice to the aspirations of the several architects who evolved the building as it stands today (1959). American architecture during the nineteenth century paralleled Europe in adopting one historical style after another. Many of the vigorous and even original buildings in downtown Philadelphia and New York were demolished before they had received sympathetic consideration. This included even such modern buildings as Frank Lloyd

Ill. 130 Al Hirschfeld: First in War, First in Peace! drawing. *Courtesy* The Nation *(New York) and the artist*

Wright's *Midway Garden* (Chicago), built in 1914 and demolished in 1923. However absurd the application of the classic orders to a steel frame, eclecticism of the first quarter of the twentieth century produced buildings designed in exquisite taste. Post-World War I architecture revolted against the unattractive nineteenth-century industrial architecture and large-scale housing projects as well as against the classic orders. In the early 1890's Louis Sullivan created the modern skyscraper of steel construction. In the *Guaranty Building* in Buffalo, height was emphasized and the terra-cotta exterior was decorated with a delicate ornamentation of Sullivan's own creation. Nevertheless, the historic trend persisted and affected skyscraper design as late as 1911 in Cass Gilbert's Gothic *Woolworth Building* (New York). This trend culminated in the distinguished work of the firm of McKim, Meade and White in such New York buildings as the *Morgan Library*, the *Gorham Building*, and the *Pennsylvania Railroad Station* (1906–10) and in Washington, Henry Bacon's *Lincoln Memorial* (1914–21). The success of this "American Renaissance" delayed the introduction of Modernism. With the work of Henry H. Richardson, Louis Sullivan, and Frank Lloyd Wright, American architecture achieved independence. After World War I, a more simplified expression appeared in such buildings as the New York *Barclay-Vesey Telephone Building* (McKensie, Voorhees and Gmelin, 1923–26). *Rocke-*

feller Center, an architectural monument unique in Western art (Ill. 131), brought this development to a monumental climax (begun 1931). The horizontal strip and all-glass type of design, so typical of today's architecture, produced the *Museum of Modern Art* (Philip L. Goodwin, 1939), Eliel Saarinen (d. 1950) designed the *General Motors Technical Center* (1951–55) near Detroit, and Wright, *The Price Tower,* Bartlesville, Oklahoma (1955). A recent example of this development is Rockefeller Center's *Time-Life Building* (Fig. 252), designed by Harrison and Abramovitz. The massive tower is accented by cleanly defined exterior columns which frame a wall pattern of glass in windows and spandrels. The vertical grid appearance of the base structure harmonizes with the tower façade. Equally contemporary, but of a

different type, is the *St. Louis Terminal Building — Lambert Street Airport* (Hellmuth, Yamasaki and Leinweber, 1953–55). Reinforced concrete shells 4½ inches thick span the interior like a flat barrel vault, 412 feet long, with unprecedented lightness and elegance. What the Pantheon started and Hagia Sophia continued, here finds a d r a m a t i c solution made p o s s i b l e by modern materials and method (Fig. 253).

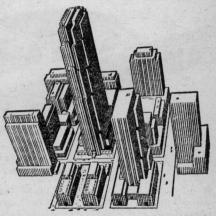

Ill. 131 Rockefeller Center, New York City. Architects: Reinhard and Hofmeister; Corbett, Harrison and Mac-Murray; and Hood and Fouilhoux. *Courtesy Public Relations Department, Rockefeller Center, Inc.*

Flexibility in "open plans," which avoid a boxed-in appearance, and the contrast of bearing members and screen members are basic to contemporary architecture, which Mies van der Rohe helped to prepare. The most important contribution to the architecture of the twentieth century came from Frank Lloyd Wright (1869–1959). Ridiculed at first after he had designed the *Larkin Building* (1903), *Unity Temple* (1908), and the *Imperial Hotel* in Tokyo (1916), he was appreciated more in Europe than in the United States. Wright has advanced architecture in every field, in planning, engineering and ornamentation. What distinguishes Wright is his imaginative

solution of each building in an original way: precast ornamental concrete block, used externally *(Millard House)*, hollow and flowerlike reinforced concrete columns *(Johnson Wax
Company Building)*, or a house projected on cantilevers across
a waterfall with holes left in porch roofs for existing trees
to grow through *(Kaufmann House)*. This latter is a supreme
example of Wright's genius for relating the building to the
environment. The design for the *Guggenheim Museum* in
New York, based on a spiral, shows that Wright, after
more than sixty years of architectural design, was still a
revolutionary (Fig. 257).

In the industrial arts, the automobile, like household appliances, reflects modern trends; in the best examples, line,
form and color are well integrated (Ill. 132). Modern crafts

Ill. 132 Fairlane 500 Town Victoria, 1957 Model. *Courtesy Ford
Motor Company*

continue in connection with industry, well-known designers
furnishing the decoration, as in Marie Laurencin's Steuben
Glass Urn (Fig. 254).

Conclusion. The conquest of a continent and the industrial
revolution delayed art in America, but did not prevent its
appearance. There were artists in all periods through the
short history of the country. Often the folk arts developed
before the historical arts based on the academic traditions
of Europe could take hold. After the last frontier had disappeared, art developed in the United States on a par with
Europe, and, by the middle of the twentieth century, Europe
was becoming increasingly aware of American art. In the
cultural exchange between nations, there are indications today that in art the United States may be turning from a position of receiving to one of giving.

NOTES

1. Dating follows Herbert Kühn.
2. For a different interpretation with less stress placed on technical origins, *see* Wilhelm Worringer, *Egyptian Art* (1927). For a psychoanalytical interpretation of Amenhotep IV, *see* Karl Abraham, *Clinical Papers and Essays on Psychoanalysis*, Basic Books, Inc., 1955, pp. 262 ff.
3. The dating follows W. S. Smith, *Ancient Egypt as Represented in the Boston Museum of Fine Arts*, 1946.
4. Period and dates follow Henri Frankfort (1955).
5. Periods are quoted by centuries in round figures; in every case they should be read prefixed with *about*.
6. The American pavilion at the Brussels Fair (1958), designed by Edward Stone, spanned 340 feet.
7. For a psychoanalytical study, *see* Richard Sterba (Vienna), "Zur Analyse der Gothik," *Imago*, Vol. X, 1924, p. 361, and Erwin O. Christensen, "Unconscious Motivations in Gothic Art," *Journal of Clinical Psychopathology*, Vol. VI, Nos. 3 and 4, Jan.–April, 1945, pp. 581–600. Medical Journal Press, Monticello, New York.
8. This portrait at the National Gallery of Art, formerly attributed to Pisanello, Dr. Fern Shapley has given to Pol Limbourg; *see* Shapley, F. R., and Shapley, J., *Comparisons in Art, A Companion to the National Gallery of Art*, New York, Phaidon, 1957, p. 55.
9. For a psychoanalytical discussion of the symbolism of the bird, *see* Jacques Schnier. *The Symbolic Bird in Medieval and Renaissance Art*, 1953, pp. 304 ff.
10. For a psychoanalytical interpretation of Leonardo, the reader should consult Sigmund Freud, Gesammelte Schriften, Vol. IX, *Eine Kindheitserinnerung des Leonardo da Vinci*, Leipzig and Vienna, 1910 and 1914. For a discussion, *see* Erwin O. Christensen, "Freud on Leonardo da Vinci," *The Psychoanalytic Review*, Vol. 31, No. 2, April, 1944.
11. For a psychoanalytical interpretation *see* Erwin O. Christensen, "Basic Determinants in the Art of Andrea del Sarto," *The Psychoanalytic Review*, Vol. 29, No. 3, July, 1942.
12. This interpretation is based on or made by Freud (published anonymously), also in *Collected Papers*, tr. by Joan Riviere, p. 239; "The Moses of Michelangelo," *Imago*, Vol. III, 1914, p. 15.
13. The term *baroque* is believed to derive from a Portuguese word meaning an irregular pearl. Rococo derives from *rocaille*, grottowork, the term the French applied to the Louis XV style.
14. Such extremes of personality among artists as the saintly Fra Angelico and the aggressive Caravaggio suggest that psychologically the artist does not represent a unique type of person. Today Caravaggio would be considered a criminal, and would be in prison or in a mental institution.
15. Schmidt-Degener, as quoted by Weisbach, *Rembrandt*, 1926, p. 341, has suggested that the painting represents an historic event. In 1639, Queen Maria de' Medici visited Amsterdam; the painting represented the company getting ready to participate in the official reception. The little girl in the painting holding a goblet was to welcome the Queen.
16. For a psychological study, *see* A. J. Westerman-Holstijn, "Die Psychologische Entwicklung Vincent Van Goghs," *Imago*, Vol. X, 1924, p. 389.
17. The reader should study the following reproductions: *Cubism and Abstract Art*, Museum of Modern Art, 1936, Figs. 29, 30, 74, 76, 79, 89 (reproduced in black and white). *Picasso to Surrealism*, Skira, 1950, Figs. 62, 65, 74, 75, 77 (reproduced in color).
18. The reader should study the color reproductions and drawings in *Four French Moderns: Matisse, Picasso, Bonnard, Braque*, text by Cassou, Braun & Cie., Paris.
19. Quoted by Ben Shahn, "The World of the American Artist," *The New Republic*, July 7, 1958, p. 12.

SELECTED BIBLIOGRAPHY

Books with color plates are marked with an asterisk (*)

General

*Cairns, Huntington, and Walker, John. *Masterpieces of Painting from the National Gallery of Art.* New York: Random House, 1944.

*————. *Great Paintings from the National Gallery of Art.* New York: Macmillan, 1952.

Fletcher, Sir Banister. *A History of Architecture on the Comparative Method.* New York: Scribner, 1954; London: Batsford, 1956.

Friedländer, Max J. *On Art and Connoisseurship.* London: Cassirer, 1942.

Gombrich, E. H. *The Story of Art.* New York: Phaidon, 1950.

Hauser, Arnold. *The Social History of Art.* 2 vols. New York: Knopf, 1951.

Hildebrand, Adolf. *The Problem of Form in Painting and Sculpture.* New York: Stechert, 1907.

Hind, A. M. *History of Engraving and Etching.* Boston: Houghton Mifflin, 1923.

Kris, Ernst. *Psychoanalytic Explorations in Art.* New York: International Universities Press, 1952.

La Farge, Harry (ed.). *Lost Treasures of Europe.* New York: Pantheon, 1946.

Michel, André. *Histoire de l'art depuis les premiers temps chrétiens jusqu'à nos jours.* 8 vols. Paris: Colin, 1905.

Ogden, C. K., Richards, I. A., and Wood, J. E. H. *The Foundations of Aesthetics.* London: Allen and Unwin, 1922.

Pope, Arthur. *The Language of Drawing and Painting.* Cambridge: Harvard, 1949.

Sewall, J. I. *A History of Western Art.* New York: Holt, 1953.

Seymour, Charles. *Masterpieces of Sculpture from the National Gallery of Art.* New York: Coward-McCann, 1949.

Shapley, Fern Rusk and Shapley, John. *Comparisons in Art, A Companion to the National Gallery of Art.* New York, Phaidon, 1957.

Stites, Raymond S. *The Arts and Man.* New York: Whittlesey House, 1940.

*Venturi, Lionello. *Italian Painting from Caravaggio to Modigliani.* Geneva: Skira, 1952.

Waterhouse, Ellis K. *Painting in Britain, 1530-1790.* Baltimore: Penguin, 1953.

Woermann, Karl. *Geschichte der Kunst aller Zeiten und Völker.* Leipzig: Bibliographisches Institut, 1922.

Wölfflin, Heinrich. *Principles of Art History.* New York: Holt, 1932.

1. Prehistoric Art in Europe

Breuil, Abbe H., and Windels, Fernand. *Four Hundred Centuries of Cave Art.* Montignac: Dordogne, 1952.

Hoernes, M. and Menghin, O. *Urgeschichte der Bildenden Kunst in Europa.* Vienna: Schroll, 1925.

Kühn, Herbert. *Die Felsbilder Europas.* Zürich-Vienna, 1952.

2. Egyptian Art

Lhote, André. *Les chefs d'oeuvre de la Peinture Egyptienne.* Paris: Hachette, 1955.

Murray, Margaret Alice. *Egyptian Sculpture.* New York: Scribner, 1930.

Ranke, Hermann. *The Art of Ancient Egypt: Architecture, Sculpture, Painting, Applied Art.* Vienna: Phaidon, 1936.

Schäfer, Heinrich. *Von ägyptischer Kunst.* Leipzig: Hinrichs, 1932.

3. Near Eastern Art

Bossert, Helmuth T. *The Art of Ancient Crete.* London: Zwemmer, 1937.

Frankfort, Henri. *The Art and Architecture of the Ancient Orient.* Baltimore: Penguin, 1955.

4. Greek Art

Buschor, Ernst. *Greek Vase Painting.* New York: Dutton, n.d.

Furtwängler, A., and Ulrichs, H. L. *Denkmäler Griechischer und Romischer Skulptur.* Munich: Bruckmann, 1911.

Lawrence, Arnold Walter. *Greek Architecture.* Baltimore: Penguin, 1957.

Richter, Gisela M. A. *The Sculptures and Sculptors of the Greeks.* New Haven: Yale, 1950.

Seltman, Charles T. *Approach to Greek Art.* London: Studio, 1948.

Swindler, Mary H. *Ancient Painting.* New Haven: Yale, 1929.

5. Etruscan and Roman Art

Goldscheider, Ludwig. *Roman Portraits.* New York: Oxford, 1940.

*Maiuri, Amedeo. *Roman Painting.* Geneva: Skira, 1953.

*Pallottino, Massimo. *Etruscan Painting.* Geneva: Skira, 1952.

Scherer, Margaret R. *Marvels of Ancient Rome.* New York: Phaidon, 1955.

Strong, Eugénie. *Art in Ancient Rome.* 2 vols. New York: Scribner, 1928.

6. Early Christian and Byzantine Art

Bunt, Cyril G. E. *A History of Russian Art.* London: Studio, 1946.

Dalton, Ormonde Maddock. *East Christian Art.* Oxford: Clarendon Press, 1925.

Demus, Otto. *Byzantine Mosaic Decoration.* London: Trubner, 1948.

Diehl, Charles. *Manuel d'art byzantin.* Paris: Pickard, 1925-26.

————: *Byzantium: Greatness and Decline.* Rutgers University Press, 1957.
*Grabar, André. *Byzantine Painting.* Geneva: Skira, 1952.
Lowrie, Walter. *Art in the Early Church.* New York: Pantheon, 1947.

7. Early Medieval and Romanesque Art

Hinks, Roger. *Carolingian Art.* London: Sedgwick and Jackson, 1935.
Kendrick, T. D. *Anglo-Saxon Art to* A.D. *900.* London: Methuen, 1938.
Kitzinger, Ernst. *Early Medieval Art.* London: British Museum, 1940.
*Metz, Peter. *The Golden Gospels of Echternach.* New York: Praeger, 1957.
Stenton, Sir Frank. *The Bayeux Tapestry.* New York: Phaidon, 1956.
Swarzenski, Hanns. *Monuments of Romanesque Art: The Art of Church Treasures in Northwestern Europe.* Chicago University Press, 1953.

8. Gothic Art

Colombier, Pierre de. *Les Chantiers des Cathédrales.* Paris: Picard, 1953.
*Dupont, Jacques, and Gnudi, Cesare. *Gothic Painting.* Geneva: Skira, 1954.
Simson, Otto von. *The Gothic Cathedral.* New York: Pantheon, 1956.
Worringer, Wilhelm. *Form in Gothic.* London: Alec Tiranti, 1927.

9. Renaissance Art

Berenson, Bernard. *The Italian Painters of the Renaissance.* New York: Phaidon, 1952.
Bode, Wilhelm von. *Florentine Sculptors of the Renaissance.* New York: Scribner, 1909.
Burckhardt, Jacob. *The Civilization of the Renaissance in Italy.* New York: Harper, 1929.
Fischel, Oskar. *Raphael.* 2 vols. London: Paul, 1949.
Fränger, Wilhelm. *The Millennium of Hieronymus Bosch.* London: Faber, 1952.
Friedländer, Max J. *Die Altniederländische Malerei.* 14 vols. Berlin: Cassirer, 1924.
Goldscheider, Ludwig. *The Sculptures of Michelangelo.* New York: Oxford, 1940.
Grossmann, F. *Brueghel, the Paintings.* London: Phaidon, 1955.
Panofsky, Erwin. *Albrecht Dürer.* 2 vols. Princeton University Press, 1943.
Pevsner, Nikolaus, and Meier, Michael. *Grünewald.* New York: Abrams, 1958.
Sirèn, Osvald. *Leonardo da Vinci.* New Haven: Yale, 1916.
Tietze, Hans. *Titian Paintings and Drawings.* Vienna: Phaidon, 1937.
Walker, John. *Bellini and Titian at Ferrara.* London: Phaidon, 1956.

Wölfflin, Heinrich. *The Art of the Italian Renaissance.* New York: Putnam, 1913.

10. Baroque and Rococo Art

Bergström, Ingvar. *Dutch Still-Life Painting in the Seventeenth Century.* London: Faber, 1956.
Bredius, Abraham. *Rembrandt Hermanszoon van Rijn. The Paintings of Rembrandt.* 2 vols. Oxford: Allen, 1942.
*Faniel, Stéphane (ed.). *Le XVIIIᵉ Siècle.* Paris: Hachette, 1956.
Friedlaender, Walter F. *Caravaggio Studies.* Princeton University Press, 1955.
Goldscheider, Ludwig. *El Greco.* London: Allen and Unwin, 1938.
Mander, Carel van. *Dutch and Flemish Painters.* New York: McFarlene, 1936.
Puyvelde, Leo van. *Rubens.* Paris: Elsevier, 1952.
Trapier, Elizabeth Du Gué. *Velazquez.* New York: Hispanic Society of America, 1948.
Voss, Hermann. *Die Malerei des Barock in Rom.* Berlin: Propyläen, 1924.
Wittkower, Rudolf. *Gian Lorenzo Bernini. The Sculptor of the Roman Baroque.* London: Phaidon, 1955.

11. Nineteenth-Century Art in Europe

Barr, Alfred H. *Masters of Modern Art.* New York: Museum of Modern Art, 1954.
*Raynal, Maurice. *Matisse, Munch, Rouault.* Geneva: Skira, 1950.
Rewald, John. *The History of Impressionism.* New York: Museum of Modern Art, 1946.
Vollard, Ambrose. *Paul Cézanne.* New York: Brown, 1923.
Wilenski, Reginald H. *The Meaning of Modern Sculpture.* Philadelphia: Stokes, 1933.
Zervos, Christian. *Pablo Picasso.* 7 vols. Paris: Cahiers d'art, 1932-57.

12. Art in the United States

Baur, John I. H. *Revolution and Tradition in Modern American Art.* Cambridge: Harvard, 1951.
Davidson, Marshall. *Life in America.* 2 vols. Boston: Houghton Mifflin, 1951.
*Eliot, Alexander, and Walker, John. *Three Hundred Years of American Painting.* New York: Time, Inc., 1957.
Larkin, Oliver W. *Art and Life in America.* New York: Rinehart, 1949.
Morrison, Hugh Sinclair. *Early American Architecture—from the First Colonial Settlement to the National Period.* New York: Oxford, 1952.
Richardson, Edgar Preston. *The Way of Western Art.* Cambridge: Harvard, 1939.

INDEX